D1829310

Claiming Brazil

Pitt Latin American Series

Catherine M. Conaghan, Editor

Claiming Brazil

Performances of Citizenship in the Centenary of Independence

Gregg Bockett

University of Pittsburgh Press

Published by the University of Pittsburgh Press, Pittsburgh, Pa., 15260
Copyright © 2022, University of Pittsburgh Press
All rights reserved
Manufactured in the United States of America
Printed on acid-free paper
10 9 8 7 6 5 4 3 2 1

Library of Congress Cataloging-in-Publication Data

Names: Bocketti, Gregg, author.
Title: Claiming Brazil : performances of citizenship in the centenary of independence / Gregg Bocketti.
Other titles: Performances of citizenship in the centenary of independence
Description: Pittsburgh : University of Pittsburgh Press, [2022] | Series: Pitt Latin American series | Includes bibliographical references and index.
Identifiers: LCCN 2022029989 | ISBN 9780822947219 (cloth) | ISBN 9780822988939 (ebook)
Subjects: LCSH: Brazil--Civilization--20th century. | Brazil--History--Declaration of Independence, 1822--Centennial celebrations, etc. | Exposição Internacional do Centenário da Independência (1922 : Rio de Janiero) | National characteristics, Brazilian. | Collective memory--Brazil.
Classification: LCC F2510 .B594 2022 | DDC 981--dc23/eng/20220629
LC record available at https://lccn.loc.gov/2022029989

Cover art: “South American Brotherhood,” *A Careta*, 7 October 1922. Courtesy of Charles E. Young Research Library, University of California, Los Angeles.
Cover design: Melissa Dias-Mandoly

Contents

Acknowledgments

This book is much different from the one I set out to write. If, as I hope, it is more interesting and meaningful, this is in great part because many people have offered me their help, advice, and patience as I found the story I ended up telling. I am grateful to have the opportunity to thank some of them here.

The members of the Transylvania University community have always offered me their encouragement, listening to me talk about the project, asking insightful questions, and providing concrete support for the work. My students have taken an interest in the work and, more important, over and over have inspired me with their sense of curiosity and wonder. Melissa McEuen, Frank Russell, and Ken Slepyan have been mentors and partners and have made the History program a true home. Katie Banks has provided invaluable advice and logistical support, and she designed the beautiful map that illustrates the book. Michael Cairo and Jeremy Paden have helped me work out my ideas about the subjects of the book, and Brian Arganbright, Simonetta Cochis, and Ellen Cox have provided their assistance on thorny language questions. Phil Walker has once again proved incredibly resourceful in bringing the world to the campus through interlibrary loan. And the school trustees and administration have provided concrete support for the work, especially through the William R. Kenan Jr. Fund for Faculty and Student Enrichment.

Of course, most of the research and thinking that resulted in this book took place in Brazil. Among the many who helped me navigate archives, libraries, and several cities that were new to me, I am especially grateful to Fabiano Pries Devide and Sancler Nascimento Silva, and Sérgio Mendes and Éloa Carvalho, for their friendship and guidance. I am afraid I often made myself a nuisance at the libraries and archives where I conducted much of the research for the book, but library and archive staff were consistently patient with me, and I am grateful for their knowledge and help. I owe special thanks to the staff at the National Library, the National Archive, the Instituto Histórico e Geográfico do Rio Grande do Norte, and the Museu da Comunicação Hipólito José da Costa.

I owe thanks to many fellow historians and other scholars of Brazil and of Latin America for their advice and their interest in the work. I do not have nearly enough space here to thank every one of them individually, but I would be remiss if I did not name a few of the most important, especially Molly Ball, Richard Conway, Christopher Dunn, and James Woodard. Thank you all. My ideas about the book came together during the excellent workshop on Brazilian regionalism organized by Courtney Campbell and Glen Goodman at the University of Birmingham in 2018, and I am grateful to both of them for providing that space and for sharing their insights on conducting research in Recife and Porto Alegre, respectively. Among the other participants in the workshop who helped guide the project were Durval Muniz de Albuquerque Júnior and Hendrik Kraay; Hendrik has been unfailing in his generosity and encouragement over the years, and I continue to be grateful for his guidance.

Finishing the book during the global pandemic meant confronting particular and peculiar challenges, and Joshua Shanholtzer has been an excellent guide at the University of Pittsburgh Press. I am grateful to Josh, to series editor Catherine Conaghan, to the anonymous readers of the manuscript, and to the rest of the staff at the press for their interest in the project and their assistance in its completion. Not least of the challenges presented by the pandemic has been collecting the images to illustrate the book, and I have received extraordinary assistance in this regard from a number of people, including Andrea Felder at the New York Public Library, Molly Haigh at the University of California, Los Angeles, Thaiane do Nascimento Koppe at the Instituto Moreira Salles, Diana Ramos at the National Library of Brazil, and Nathacha Regazzini at the Fundação Oswaldo Cruz. I owe special thanks to Beverly Burns, who helped me gain access to the remarkable archive organized by the late Benjamin Burns, as well as McFarland and Company for permission to reproduce an image originally published in *The Flying Firsts of Walter Hinton*; and to Ruth Levy, who responded to my request for advice about images related to Brazil's centenary exposition with frankly stunning generosity and priceless assistance.

As always, my family has been my unflagging wellspring of love and encouragement. I am so grateful to my parents, Philip and Angela, and my brothers, Jon and Brian, and their families for their unfailing and unconditional support. I am also grateful to Kathryn Metzger and David Brown for welcoming me into their family and, especially, for letting me write most of the book at their place in Oklahoma.

Finally, I am exceedingly fortunate to have had two amazing readers in Elizabeth Manley and Randi Ewing. They helped me realize and articulate my arguments, identify all of the many places where I was imprecise or repetitive, and think through everything from how to open the book to chapter titles and image selection. The book is far better than it would have been without their interest and insights.

Randi has been my constant throughout—in adventures and misadventures, in apartments that always seemed to be next to construction sites, in minibuses after canceled flights, in statuary parks and under the world's biggest cashew tree—in Buenos Aires and throughout Brazil. Her intelligence, sense of humor, and encouragement have been everything to me, and I have wanted to do the work because I was doing it alongside her.

Claiming Brazil

Introduction

In 1921, Catholic activists revived an old idea for the erection of a monument depicting Jesus Christ on one of the iconic peaks of Rio de Janeiro, then Brazil's capital. Though the monument was not completed until 1931, in 1921 and 1922 the ground was prepared and the key arguments for the project were won. The monument to Christ the Redeemer has come to define the skyline of the "marvelous city," but it was not clear one hundred years ago that advocates would have their way. The proposal required the permission of the republican authorities who governed the city and controlled the Corcovado *morro* where planners hoped to erect the monument, and the Catholic Church had suffered a conflicted relationship with the republic since it had replaced the imperial monarchy in 1889, its architects having adopted a neutral stance on religious matters that many Catholics read as anticlerical. Advocates acknowledged the challenge, and so alongside their argument that the monument would announce to the world that Brazilians were a people dedicated to the faith they also argued that its erection was a necessary political act.

Advocates like the historian Afonso Celso said that 1922 was the exact right time to undertake the project because it was Brazil's centenary year, the hundredth year since the Portuguese prince Pedro had declared independence on 7 September 1822. They argued that in celebrating the country's centenary it was essential to rededicate it to God, and in their

As festas eucharisticas do Centenario

O que a Egreja vae fazer

As virtudes christãs não poderiam deixar tambem de ser celebradas no anno do Centenario da Independencia, porque, catholica como é a Terra de Santa Cruz, a maioria de seus filhos, em todos os regimens, desde o descobrimento até hoje recebem as mesmas influencias espirituaes, que não podem impunemente ser desligadas da historia dos nossos progressos e civilisação. E' a religião, seja este ou aquelle o credo, trate-se desta ou daquella seita, que orienta afinal o individuo em sua vida particular e publica, sendo portanto cousa facil de perceber-se, independentemente da ausencia de qualquer crença, os reflexos poderosos que os altares exercem sobre os grandes phenomenos nacionaes. Demais os factos todos os dias estão a demonstrar no nosso paiz a influencia da Egreja, porque, máo grado os principios constitucionaes que a separam do Estado, é uma só a fé que congrega a maioria immensa do nosso povo. Nem precisamos, para accentuar a verdade, invocar os exemplos diarios em que o governo, directa ou indirectamente, participa das crenças catholicas, da religião dos nossos soldados e marinheiros, ou lembrar cerimonias de affirmação especial de fé, como as que recentemente foram celebradas com a benção das espadas.

Mas, mesmo que não existissem essas razões, não poderia passar esquecida entre as festas do Centenario a do Congresso Eucharistico que se vae reunir nesta cidade de S. Sebastião do Rio de Janeiro a 28 de Setembro proximo, sob os auspicios do Cardeal Arcoverde, e se deve encerrar a 1.º de Outubro deste mesmo anno festivo, que é tambem eucharistico, porquanto fica em seu curso exposto dia e noite, em varias egrejas, á adoração do povo, o Santissimo Sacramento.

Não é demais portanto que se esclareça ser o Congresso Eucharistico uma lembrança a um tempo religiosa e patriotica, porque é uma homenagem a Jesus Sacramentado e uma solemnidade da historia nacional, banhada dos sentimentos da religião de Christo. E' um Congresso esse que se estende a todo o Brasil porque o seu exito está ligado as benção de todo o clero e aos actos de adoração de todo o povo, visando

Do valor das theses que costumam ser debatidas nessas assembléas originaes de religião christã, bem se póde ter uma segura idéa quando se consultam seus preciosos annaes. Ainda em 1906, no de Turnay, entre os mais attrahentes assumptos, houve a conferencia do Conego Collin, da Cathedral de Metz, que brilhou no seguinte thema: « A Eucharistia e os trabalhos economicos ». O padre Godefroid Kurth, professor da Universidade de Liège, no Congresso de Bruxellas, em 1898, tratou como um estheta verdadeiro da Eucharistia e da Arte Christã; e Horacio Marucchi, sem duvida a maior auctoridade moderna da archeologia, no Congresso Eucharistico de Roma, em 1905, fez esplendecer sua erudição e sua fé com a seguinte thése: « A Eucharistia e as Catacumbas ».

Podemos ainda citar, para melhor comprehensão do alcance social das festas eucharisticas do Centenario aquella thése que o Padre Delaporte, poéta corôado pela Academia Franceza, defendeu em 1884 no Congresso de Reims, tratando da Eucharistia e da vida nacional da França.

Foi nesse mesmo congresso que Lemius, superior dos capellães de Montmartre, proferiu um bellissimo discurso de profunda analyse, fallando dos designios do Sagrado Coração de Jesus sobre a França. Não será preciso citar ainda a these de um vice-almirante francez, de Cuverville, exposta com muita impressão no Congresso Eucharistico de Angers, em 1900, versando sobre o Christo e a vocação da França.

E' como se vê uma obea de recordação nacional e de attestado de crenças religiosas o que se faz nos Congressos Eucharisticos, como esse que vamos realisar nos dias 28, 29 e 30 de Setembro, e de cujo programma, constarão, entre outros, os seguintes actos: uma precissão solemnissima pelas principaes ruas da cidade, tendo á frente, com a imagem de Christo, um enorme ostensorio, ou melhor, custodia; a communhão geral das creanças do Rio e a communhão geral dos homens; missa campal, com o canto da Gloria e Crédo, em canto-chão, pelo povo e por fim, se os bispos approvarem, a

I.1. Original design for the monument of Christ the Redeemer, *A Exposição de 1922*, August 1922. Courtesy of the New York Public Library.

public comments they often reminded their fellow citizens of the country's original Western name as the land of the True Cross (Vera Cruz). Just as important, they insisted, the monument would symbolize and encourage a sense of community among all Brazilians; all were joined in the family of the faithful. It was clear, they said, that the nation was wracked by the challenges of modernity and divided against itself, and that the republican state had not, could not, provide Brazilians with the sense of national communion that would bring them together despite their differences. Only the Catholic faith could give them the means to confront these challenges and resolve their differences. The image of Christ the Redeemer on the tallest peak of the capital city would serve as a call to tradition and remind them of their common heritage at a key moment in their history.

In the event, and despite the objections of some, the plan did win the approval of many residents of the capital and the permission of national and city authorities. Advocates staged a ceremony to dedicate the monument site in early October 1922, claiming Corcovado for the faith, keynote speaker Raphael Pinto calling it one of the most important "integrative forces of Brazil."[1] This was part of their attempt—along with a Eucharistic congress and enormous outdoor masses and processions—to make the centenary of national independence a Catholic celebration. However, as the project's advocates acknowledged when they discussed the challenges and divisions Brazil faced in 1922, theirs was not the only view of what Brazil was and ought to be. Indeed, the project for the Redeemer monument itself displayed the volatility that seemed to define Brazilian life during the period, for its original, naturalistic design reinforced the traditionalist message its advocates asserted, but the completed and familiar version put on display the rising influence of modern artistic styles in Brazil. Nor were Catholic activists the only people who saw the centenary as a deeply meaningful occasion. They were joined by many, many others, including not only Brazilians but also immigrants and even foreigners, all of whom used the centenary of independence to assert their views about the nation, and, as with the Redeemer monument, to attempt to install their claims on Brazil in an enduring way.

Few years in Brazilian history have been as eventful as 1922. Artur Bernardes won the presidency in March, another victory for the "coffee with milk" coalition that had dominated Brazilian politics since the foundation of the republic in 1889, rooted in the economic power of São Paulo and Bernardes's own Minas Gerais. But the costs were high. The electoral campaign revealed the fractures in the republic order, as regional oligarchs turned against one another and civilian-military relations foundered on allegations of the new president's disrespect for the armed forces, and the political crisis deepened as the year went on. In July, soldiers stationed at the Forte de Copacabana in Rio de Janeiro rose against the government, while local power struggles in Pernambuco and Rio Grande do Sul turned violent, the first conflict leading to the occupation of Recife by federal forces in August and the second seeding the so-called Gaúcho Revolution of 1923. Among other measures, the national government reacted to these events by declaring a state of siege, first in Rio de Janeiro and then throughout the country. Meanwhile, outside the narrow confines of the institutional arrangements of the republic, activists launched their own campaigns against the political status quo, including the Partido Comunista do Brasil (founded in March) and the Federação Brasileira pelo Progresso Feminino (a product of the first Conferência pelo Progresso Feminino, held in August). Finally, 1922 saw several events of great social and cultural import, including the Semana de Arte Moderna, the literary, musical, and plastic arts festival that took place in São Paulo in early February. The week became the year's best-known event, though in the moment contemporaries showed much greater interest in an event that took place in October, the South American football championship, won by the Brazilian *seleção*.

Every nation has its defining dates, from Britain's 1688 to China's 1949, from the United States' 1776 to Mexico's 1910. Like France's 1789—perhaps the most evocative and well known of these touchstones—such chronological metonyms help tell the stories of nations. They can be used to legitimize particular interpretations of a nation's past and to communicate the purported values of its people, establishing the parameters of belonging and exclusion.[2] Brazil too has had its essential moments, such as 1888 (the year of the abolition of slavery) and 1964 and 1985 (the beginning and end dates of dictatorial rule by the military), but none carries the import and resonance evoked by 1922. This has to do with the significance of the year's events in themselves, and also with the way they suggest larger, long-running developments. Thus, the controversies surrounding Bernardes's election were matters of urgent import in 1922, and they also distilled the kinds of tensions that characterized the republican order, including divisions within the country's governing classes. Similarly, while the Copacabana revolt failed, it helped launch the *tenentista* campaign of junior military officers against the national state and, along with regionalist conflicts and the formation of new leftist and women's rights groups, it demonstrated just how many Brazilians felt left out of the political system and helped bring about its collapse at the end of the decade. The victory in the Campeonato Sul-Americano de Futebol was only the second in what has become the seleção's extraordinary number of international triumphs, and it was massively important at the time, not least because, despite what we might assume, football was still controversial in 1922, enough that Congressman Carlos Garcia proposed a legal ban on international matches due to controversies that beset the tournament.[3] And the Semana de Arte Moderna was not only a weeklong festival; it also announced an enormously influential movement that would transform Brazilian arts and letters and brought the attention of contemporaries to artists who until then were not widely known, such as Victor Brecheret and Guilherme de Almeida.

It is little surprise, then, that historians have afforded these events close attention, especially in order to understand the larger developments to which they were linked—the breakdown of the republican order, the tenentista movement, the campaign for women's suffrage and civil rights, the career of Brazilian football, and the character of modernism.[4] However, they have done comparatively little to scrutinize the particular circumstances of 1922 that had prompted many of the year's most important events and help explain why contemporaries saw it as a pivotal, foundational period. That is, it was in great part the marking of the centenary of independence that gave shape and significance to the events, debates, and conflicts of national life, in September and throughout the year.

Brazilians organized massive celebrations to mark the centenary, the largest and most elaborate of which was a world's fair–style exhibition, the Exposição Internacional do Centenário da Independência, which opened in Rio de Janeiro on independence day. The exhibition was an enormous undertaking, involving the renovation of the capital's downtown and including displays of products from every Brazilian state and territory and more than a dozen countries. And there were many other events in the capital and throughout the country, each one seeming as meaningful to its participants as did the ceremony to break ground for the Redeemer monument to its planners. Beginning in January of the centenary year and running well into the next (the exposition closed its gates only on 24 July 1923), Brazilians dedicated their attention, time, and resources to celebrating the centenary and arguing over what it meant—for each individual citizen and resident, for the national community as a whole, and for its place in the world. Beyond the fair, they organized parades, erected monuments, and opened new museums. Scholars and other groups gathered to share knowledge about the past and their plans for the present and future, with historians, linguists, educators, and industry and business figures joining Catholics in organizing their own conferences, releasing special publications, and offering lectures in public and private settings. Poets, writers, musicians, and painters presented new works designed to interpret Brazilian life and contribute to public conversations about the nation at the centenary. And Brazilians staged athletic performances of patriotism and nationality, including through the participation of the seleção in the South American football championship and in other special "centennial" sporting events.

Like the other remarkable events of 1922, the celebrations and performances of the centenary were important in their own time and they were seminal in shaping Brazilian life in the ensuing years and decades. On one hand, the scale and reach of centenary efforts—from the massive exhibition, which welcomed more than three million paying visitors, to the pioneering long-distance flights undertaken by aviators as a way to honor the occasion and link Brazil to locations as far away as Lisbon and New York—marked them as matters of great import throughout Brazil and beyond its borders, before 1922 began and into 1923. On the other hand, like the plan to erect the Reedemer monument, the centenary moment reverberated long after the celebrations were over, for the events of the centenary distilled the weightiest matters of Brazilian life, from the proper structure of modern government and the challenges of uneven development to the essence of *brasilidade* and the claims that Brazilians, immigrants, and foreigners made on the nation.

The continuing power of 1922 also owed a great deal to the ways in which the celebrations of the centenary functioned as rites that marked the year as special. That is, they worked to make the centenary a "time out of time," as Roy A. Rappaport has described the experience of ritual, breaking from the mundane, stoking strong emotions, and focusing minds.[5] When Brazilians attended outdoor masses to give thanks for independence; when they marched in parades and attended ceremonies dedicating new monuments; when they toured the exhibition campus, an arresting space of eclectic architectural styles and brilliant electric light; and when they filled the stadium of the Fluminense Football Club to help the seleção win the South American championship, they celebrated the centenary, but they did more than celebrate. As a set of rituals, the celebrations of the centenary called Brazilians to step out of the quotidian and concentrate their attentions on ideas and issues that many of them rarely considered, making the centenary an experience and a performance of what it meant to be Brazilian and what Brazil had been and should be. Thus, the celebrations of the centenary were short-lived events but they were not transitory; they afforded Brazilians special opportunities to display their values and their beliefs and extraordinary venues for practicing politics and shaping the substance of citizenship.[6]

Joining with Latin Americanist and other historians, scholars of Brazil have taken an interest in the ways that civic rituals helped define the nation, and a few have examined facets of the centenary story as well.[7] Hendrik Kraay has done essential work in this regard, showing how Brazilians in the nineteenth century used the celebration of holidays to define the character and boundaries of regional and national identities and to negotiate the parameters of political power in the imperial state and early republic.[8] The architects of the republic were especially attuned to the utility of civic rituals in legitimizing the new regime, abolishing imperial holidays like the celebration of the emperor's birthday and designing a new calendar of "holidays that the Republic calls us to celebrate," as Lúcia Lippi Oliveira describes the effort.[9] Scholars of Brazil have also demonstrated how eager the nation builders of the nineteenth and twentieth centuries were to participate in international exhibitions, and the ways they sought to use these events to broadcast to domestic and foreign audiences their own distinctive ideas about Brazil.[10]

I.2. Brazil in 1922, designed by Katie Banks, based on original produced for the centenary celebrations by the Club de Engenharia. Note the inset image of the São Pedro and São Paulo archipelago, top right. Courtesy of the Acervo da Fundação Biblioteca Nacional—Brasil.

The centenary exhibition was Brazilians' most ambitious initiative in this regard, and scholars have paid it particular attention. Ruth Levy and James E. Wadsworth, among others, have demonstrated that its organizers aimed at making it a display of Brazilian modernity and cosmopolitanism, a proof that the nation was ready to take its place among the first rank of nations.[11] In her pioneering work on the centenary, Marly da Silva Motta shows how elite powerbrokers in Rio de Janeiro and São Paulo attempted to use the centenary to legitimize their own claims to power, another episode in their seemingly endless struggle for hegemony in the republican era.[12] She also emphasizes that the celebrations of the centenary extended beyond the grounds of the fair and beyond the capital city, but scholars have only begun to examine how the centenary unfolded in Brazil at large.[13]

This book builds on the important work undertaken by these scholars, offering analysis of debates among Brazil's intellectual and political leaders and of the largest centenary events, including the exhibition, the football championship, and the inauguration of major new monuments and museums, such as the Monumento à Independência in São Paulo and the Museu Histórico Nacional in Rio de Janeiro. It also offers a wider perspective on Brazilians' experience of the centenary, because all manner of Brazilians—as well as immigrants and other foreigners resident in and visiting Brazil—celebrated the occasion, argued about its meaning, and performed their own understandings of identity and citizenship. The largest and most important "official" events of the centenary took place in the national capital and in São Paulo, the seat of the country's most economically dynamic and developed region, but Brazilians all over the country celebrated the occasion, so studying the breadth of that experience is essential to our understanding of the centenary. Thus, while it is not possible to know how the centenary unfolded in every village, town, and city in the enormous country, the book looks beyond Rio de Janeiro and São Paulo and the southeastern region, examining Brazilians' celebrations in the South, in particular in Rio Grande do Sul, and in the North and Northeast, focusing especially on Pernambuco.

Furthermore, it was not only in events organized by national and state governments that the centenary was celebrated, nor was it only elite actors who organized and interpreted them. As Kraay points out, in order to understand the political and cultural significance of civic rituals it is important to examine what happens beyond officially sanctioned and organized celebrations, for such events are opportunities for state actors as well as common citizens to make assertions about and shape the practices of citizenship and the substance of identity.[14] Thus, the book examines official events and those planned by major regional and national institutions, such as historical societies and chambers of commerce, as well as unofficial and "popular" ones. For example, it examines the remarkable "raids" of the centenary, in which aviators, fishermen, and athletes undertook long-distance journeys to reach the national capital as a means of celebrating the occasion, and the efforts made by immigrant groups throughout the country to participate in their own ways, from private parties to the erection of monuments.[15]

This more ample view demonstrates the extent to which the rituals of the centenary matched the hopes of organizers and powerful actors to broadcast the notion that Brazil was advancing rapidly toward its destiny as a modern, unified nation on the Western model, and to use the occasion to guide Brazilians toward the practices they believed would bring about this happy result. The centerpiece of this project was the centenary exposition, which brought together products and exhibitors from every state and region of the country and a handful of friendly nations in a carefully curated display of Brazil's advancements, economic potential, and global standing, the audience at once foreign and domestic. The organization of a number of other "national" and multinational events, including sports competitions, industry meetings, and cultural festivals amplified the exhibition's messages. And civic rituals that took place throughout the country—including parades by state and national military forces, the erection of centenary monuments, and formal ceremonies in which every school child swore allegiance to the nation—drew in the many millions of Brazilians who did not visit the exposition or attend congresses or football matches, and involved them in the articulation of the centenary's meaning as it was defined by elite organizers.

However, the adoption of a broader view of the centenary also demonstrates the complexities and the limits of this centenary project. Powerful figures in Rio de Janeiro and São Paulo were never as sure about the meaning of the centenary as suggested by their most confident assertions about the exhibition and other events, and they carved out space in their commemorations for inquiry and debate about the character of Brazil, its past, and its future. They were joined in their arguments by many others, including political leaders in other cities and states who used the centenary to make claims on regional and national power. Just as important, beyond the circles of the politically powerful and well connected, millions of men and women from all walks of Brazilian life met the centenary according to their own lights and drew from it their own lessons, whether by attending official events or organizing their own, and even by announcing their refusal to celebrate it. As they engaged in the rituals of the centenary, they confronted the challenges and enacted the tensions that defined Brazilian life in the early twentieth century, between modernity and tradition, over race and ethnicity, and between nation and region. The book thus shows that the centenary did as much to deepen the divisions of the national community as it did to unify it under the guidance of its purported elites.

Because the centenary involved both the marking of historical events and a celebration of the maturing nation, it called forth a consideration of the relationship between tradition and modernity. To a great extent, Brazilians celebrated the centenary in ways exemplifying the modernizing project that had led to the foundation of the republic and animated efforts to remake the country in the previous three decades through such means as ambitious public health campaigns, major infrastructure initiatives, the reorientation of the nation's diplomacy, and even a renovation of its pastimes.[16] The cosmopolitan and technocratic character of that project was most clearly displayed in the centenary exhibition, which organizers based closely on the world's fair model designed to promote the worldview and interests of the dominant classes of the developed nations.[17] But amid the seemingly headlong pursuit of modernity the republic also saw the persistent "force of tradition," in José Murilo de Carvalho's words, both because of elite commitments to maintaining social hierarchies and popular resistance to their "improvement."[18] The centenary experience showed as much, and also illustrated the growing interest among many Brazilians in thinking anew about the prerepublican order and the traditions that the fathers of the republic had seemed to abandon. There were indications of that interest in the years preceding 1922, such as the prominent place afforded Portugal in official celebrations of the centenary of the opening of Brazilian ports to international trade in 1908, and the 1920 reversal of the republican banishment of the members of the imperial family. The celebrations of 1922 served as a platform for Brazilians who wanted to share more generous assessments of traditions they hoped to reinvent for the modern day, so the centenary featured jarring examples of the clash between dreams of the future and nostalgia for an imagined past as well as illustrations of the possibility that the tension between modernity and tradition could be productive, as seen in the neocolonial architecture that characterized much of the exhibition campus.

In inviting consideration of Portugal's influence in the making of Brazil, growing interest in the colonial period also contributed to ongoing debates about race and national origin, and these debates too played out in centenary events. The encouragement of the migration of millions of Portuguese, Germans, Japanese, and Italians in the late empire and early republic was rooted in elites' anxiety over the supply of labor the country required for its economic development and their belief that the lessons of European science showed that Brazil must be "whitened" if it were to flourish in the modern world. However, few Brazilians had ever accepted the most severe interpretations of Eurocentric racial doctrines, and by the 1920s there was increasing willingness in some quarters to reject those doctrines altogether, along with rising confidence about how state power might be used to create a stronger Brazilian woman and man and lead them toward a bright future.[19] Of course, this was no racially democratic outlook, but it did mean that at the time of the centenary many truisms about issues of race and national origin, widely held among the well-to-do and well educated, were being questioned, if not discarded. Official centenary events put that conflicted perspective on display, for example, in the exhibition's Museu da Criança and the first Congresso Brasileiro de Protecção à Infância, and many conversations and debates inspired by the centenary echoed the tension between pessimism and confidence. Thus, the centenary saw efforts to revalorize the role of Portugal in the making of Brazil *and* evidence of Lusophobia, celebrations of the contributions of European immigrant laborers *and* assertions that the mixed-race *caboclo* was the quintessential Brazilian who would build a great nation.[20] In other words, the centenary was in great part a display of Brazilians' concerns about race and national origin and how they might be expected to shape the country's future.

When Brazilians pondered these issues—of race and nation and *raça*, the term they used to refer to either and both, eliding the distinction—they often thought and spoke of the country's regions. The settlement of immigrants primarily in the states of the South and Southeast made geographic differences seem racial and "national" as much as climatic or economic, and thus reinforced the long-standing regional identities that distinguished Brazilians from one another. Those identities were crucial to the function of the country in the preceding decades, not least in the structure of the nation's government. The federalist principle on which the republic was built satisfied the demands of the Paulistas and Mineiros who presided over the country's most economically dynamic regions for more thorough control over their own affairs. It also bred resentment in places like the Northeast, where the decline of traditionally important industries and persistent drought conditions left local elites demanding the assistance of the national government, and it encouraged separatist sentiments in Rio Grande do Sul.[21] These were powerful ideas, helping Brazilians in different parts of the country articulate ever-more precise notions about their distinctive places in the nation and informing political arrangements and decisions, thus making it difficult to pursue the kinds of great national projects championed by many early twentieth-century Brazilians.[22] Brazilians put all these issues on display during the centenary celebrations: in the centennial fair, which organized Brazilian products according to the states from which they came; in sporting events, which pitted state teams against one another; and in Brazilians' disagreement on which set of events should be commemorated in the celebration of independence, each region narrating its own history. The centenary thus displayed regional differences and, in displaying them, exacerbated them.

Finally, the book draws attention to the rising tensions between older and younger Brazilians. While it is difficult to discern precise and consistent lines of demarcation according to age cohorts, it is at least clear that the centenary served as a platform for younger Brazilians—especially those who had come of age and been born after the foundation of the republic—to announce their deep dissatisfaction with the character of Brazilian society, culture, and government. A few contemporaries noticed this shift, including, for example, the lawyer and future jurist Pontes de Miranda, who turned thirty in 1922 and published the first part of a series of articles on "the new generation" in Rio de Janeiro's *O Jornal* in July of that year. He wrote of its "historic mission" to remake

Brazil, which he called "gigantic but ill." This required knowing Brazil as it really was, rather than as wealthy and powerful—and older—Brazilians preferred to imagine it, and Miranda noted that his generation was ready to undertake that work, for it "declares loudly, very loudly, what it does not know and what it wants to learn"; unlike its forebears, "it listens to Brazil."[23]

As Miranda continued the series in August, he paired biting critiques of older generations with comments about the matters that most concerned his cohort, including immigration and regionalism, and, especially, the character of the Brazilian political order. The next month, the highly influential *Revista do Brasil* republished the original piece, and one of its young directors, the historian Brenno Ferraz do Amaral, connected Miranda's argument directly to the year's great occasion in the magazine's centenary editorial. Ferraz called Miranda's words "justified, quite justified," and labeled these young Brazilians "the Centenary generation." Like Miranda, who called them "an army . . . which will find its generals," Ferraz left no doubt of the disappointments or the ambitions of the new generation. These Brazilians would, he said, work a "revolution in our ideas and our customs" and would ultimately tear down and reconstruct society and the political system, "the indolent moral order that has ruled us for one hundred years."[24]

The festivities of 1922 provided this "Centenary generation" the platform to begin their work, and, as the book shows, other young Brazilians used the celebrations to advance arguments similar to those made by Miranda and Ferraz. They spoke not of accomplishments but of failures, not of independence but of the nation's false sovereignty, and they promised to accept the responsibility for change, for making Brazil a true community and a great nation in its second century. For the most part, during commemorative events these generational distinctions were suggested rather than made explicit, but they do seem to have informed many Brazilians' experience of the centenary.[25] They ran through the events of commemoration and celebration and civic ritual, and they joined with Brazilians' arguments about modernity and tradition, over race and raça, and about regional differences to make the centenary as much an expression of fracture and doubt as it was a display of unity and confidence.

In order to demonstrate the variety of Brazilians' experiences of the centenary and the ways those experiences exemplified and heightened the tensions of Brazilian society, the book provides a multifaceted analysis of the rituals and debates of 1922. It covers events in the national capital and a handful of other regions; it examines the experiences of "official" organizers commissioned by the national government as well as those of private citizens, immigrants, and visitors to Brazil; and it analyzes conversations about the centenary and a number of the ritual events these people staged to mark and celebrate it. Chapter 1 explains how and why a handful of fishermen, aviators, cyclists, and pedestrians undertook long journeys aimed at the national capital as a way of participating in the centenary celebrations. It explains that these "raids" demonstrated much about what the raiders and the wider public believed it meant to think about Brazil, what it meant to be Brazilian, and who belonged to the nation and who did not in the 1910s and 1920s. It focuses on two groups, fishermen called *jangadeiros* (after their simple sailing rafts, called *jangadas*) from the Northeast and two groups of aviators, a pair of Portuguese naval officers who completed the first air crossing of the South Atlantic and a group of American and Brazilian flyers who completed the first flight from New York City to Rio de Janeiro. Each of these raids took many weeks, affording contemporaries the opportunity to read deep meaning in the journeys.

The chapter tells the stories of the raiders and explains why the raid phenomenon struck a chord throughout Brazil, drawing from a wide variety of contemporaneous sources from many places and expressing many different points of view. These include general-audience newspapers and magazines published in Rio de Janeiro, the raiders' destination and home to publications that were distributed nationally. They also include periodicals produced in the places from which the raiders departed and called home and many of the locations through which they passed during their journeys; specialized periodicals such as the *Revista Maritima Brazileira*, which devoted special attention to the fishermen; and extraordinary publications, such as a glossy volume prepared in Lisbon to honor the Portuguese aviators' accomplishment.[26] These sources demonstrate how contemporaries used the raids to think about the meaning of the centenary and about the ways that time, race, and region defined the nation as it marked the great date. They also indicate the way in which the tensions that defined the centenary were complicated by issues of class and gender, as only one raider of the centenary was a woman and there were clear social distinctions between aristocratic aviators and working-class fishermen. Surveying the raiders' experiences as well as reactions from various places in Brazil, the chapter therefore reveals the challenges Brazilians faced as they sought to use the centenary to perform their views about nationality and citizenship, identity and belonging.

Chapter 2 focuses on the work of the national government and its partners in planning and executing "official" events, focusing especially on the centenary exhibition and sporting events organized especially for the occasion, including Brazil's first national football championship, the first "Latin American" Olympic games, and the South American football championship. Drawing from many of the same periodical publications as chapter 1 does, as well as the enormous archive of documentation produced by the national government's specially established centenary commission (the Comissão Executiva da Comemoração do Centenário da Independência), the chapter demonstrates the great lengths to which government officials and their partners went in their attempts to use these events to display the image of Brazil as a modern, unified, optimistic nation, and that in some ways the historical record demonstrates their success. However, it argues that these events also amplified differences among Brazilians, making the fair and centenary sports sites of fracture and regionalist resentment rather than venues of national community.

The chapter begins with an examination of organizers' plans for these events as well as an introduction to the function of international fairs during the period and Brazil's prior experience with them. It then explains the successes and many difficulties organizers of the fair faced in executing their plans, which included enthusiastic cooperation in São Paulo, difficulties in less-well-developed places like Rio Grande do Norte, and outright resistance in Pernambuco and Rio Grande do Sul. The final section of the chapter focuses on centenary sporting events, which were among the most successful official events of the celebrations and yet suffered from difficulties similar to those confronted by the fair. The chapter shows that there were several reasons for these problems, including mismanagement by administrators and disagreements among political figures. The principal reason that officials were unable to make the centenary what they hoped it could be, though, was that regional differences and regionalist sentiment compromised their efforts. The official events of the centenary thus exhibited not unity but difference and even discord; they displayed Brazil as a nation of parts.

In some ways, Brazilians' centenary celebrations focused on the country's present and future, displaying its products and economic potential and providing venues to debate issues of citizenship and belonging. But the centenary also meant engagement with the past, and chapter 3 examines how Brazilians in different places and situated in distinct social and political positions used the country's history to consider what it should mean to be Brazilian as it began its second hundred years of independent life. It shows that in this period there was very little in the way of agreement among Brazilians about the history of independence or national history in a general sense. The centenary brought their disagreements out into the open, even as "official" history offered a synthetic and homogenizing narrative that aimed to bring Brazilians together.

The chapter introduces academic historiography and discusses the plethora of new works by professional scholars produced for the centenary. Its focus, however, is on the public performance of memory, as seen in discussions of history in the popular media and in public events, for example, in the carefully managed inauguration of new monuments and museums. Thus, it is informed by close attention to works produced both by scholars and academic organizations, such as the Instituto Histórico e Geográfico Brasileiro and its state-based siblings, and by newspapers and magazines aimed at general audiences, which afforded extraordinary attention to historical subjects and intensive coverage of public events focused on the performance of historical memory.

The chapter shows that the people of every region made claims on Brazil's past—and thereby on its present and future—by referencing their own region's history, and specifically its role in independence. It shows how actors in Rio de Janeiro attempted to rehabilitate the empire—and political order—by focusing on the role of independent Brazil's first leader, the emperor Pedro I, and how those in São Paulo focused on the state's own role in Pedro's story, as well as São Paulo's reputation as the home of colonial-era pioneers, to assert its dominance in the national community. Elsewhere, residents of Pernambuco and Rio Grande do Sul reminded one another and their fellow Brazilians not only of their forebears' contributions to independence but also of the ways that independence and localist identities coincided and had threatened national union in the past, the implication clear to contemporaries that regionalism could also threaten the union in the present. Finally, the chapter includes an extended examination of the role played in these debates by the institutional Catholic Church, which did much more than help organize the effort to erect a monument to Christ the Redeemer in Rio de Janeiro. The church was active in celebrations of the centenary throughout the country, and in some regions it took the lead in organizing them, always tying its claims on the nation's present and future to the church's role in the Brazilian past, a call to tradition against the secularizing claims of modernity.

Chapter 4 focuses on immigrants and foreign residents of Brazil, who were particularly important to the centenary experience, both as participants in their own right and as objects of Brazilian interest. It draws from the same broad variety of sources as the rest of the book, as well as periodicals and other materials produced by foreigners and immigrants themselves, such as the newspapers of São Paulo's Italian community and the magazines of Portuguese mutual aid and commercial groups. It shows how many foreigners resident in Brazil sought to use the centenary celebrations to claim belonging in Brazil and to shape their relationship with one another and with Brazilians, as well as how Brazilians used the celebrations to test immigrants' commitments to the nation and seek to marginalize those whom they did not see as future citizens.

As immigrant communities came together to perform the roles expected of them, the centenary reinforced their identities as members of distinct, discrete communities. Centenary rituals also strengthened the legitimacy of traditional social hierarchies, as well-to-do immigrants used the celebrations to reinforce their claims as leaders of those communities, which was a relief to authorities faced with the social discord they often associated with working-class immigrants. The chapter emphasizes the ways that regional circumstances affected the immigrant experience of the centenary, as the Germans of Rio Grande do Sul faced very different circumstances and reactions than did the Portuguese of Rio de Janeiro or the Italians of São Paulo. The centenary became a test of loyalties, as immigrants navigated the tensions between their allegiances to their mother countries and their hopes of making claims on Brazil in venues including the centenary exhibition, the visits of prominent diplomats from home, and initiatives to erect centenary monuments. In the end, just as it was for Brazilians, for immigrants the centenary was an experience of discord as much as of community, which fueled division where statesmen and events organizers had hoped to build unity.

The Epilogue draws together the threads of the episodes recounted in the book and discusses the legacies of the centenary, focusing on the fissures it revealed—and indeed helped to widen—which traced tensions between modernity and tradition, over race and ethnicity, between nation and region, and among older and younger Brazilians. It notes how these tensions defined the rest of the 1920s, including in the emergence of the Regionalist movement in Pernambuco, in the proliferation of critiques of the First Republic, which contributed to its collapse, and in ongoing debates over immigrant ethnicity and citizenship. It also offers a consideration of how they defined the regime of Getúlio Vargas, the Rio Grande do Sul politician who seized power in 1930 and built a nationalist, authoritarian system that reshaped many aspects of Brazilian life. Among other projects, the Vargas government sought to destroy regionalism and renovate the political system through centralized authority, to "restructure" hierarchy in order to confront the ways that modernity threatened Brazil's traditional social order, and to nationalize immigrant communities and others deemed outsiders.[27] That is, it sought to meet and resolve the most prevalent challenges the rituals of the centenary revealed and the particular tensions they exacerbated, underscoring how examination of the centenary can help us understand the dynamics and character of Brazil in the years since 1922.

As the book narrates the ways that the people of Brazil marked the centenary, through raids, major official events, performances of memory, and displays of immigrant identity, it thus shows how the centenary helped define Brazil as the country began its second century of independent life. It emphasizes the ways in which the centenary functioned as a set of rituals, affording contemporaries opportunities to display their values and to practice politics. Centenary events were rites of identity in which participants performed their understandings of the meaning of Brazil and of citizenship. They were also political events in which the people of Brazil negotiated the shape and character of power and the boundaries of belonging and exclusion. They defined the national community according to the preferences of the powerful, well-connected figures who organized the exhibition and other major events of the centenary's official celebrations. However, despite the hopes and work of these figures, the more prevalent effect of the centenary rituals was to promote fracture and difference, so that the centenary served as much to divide the people of Brazil from one another as to bring them together, and it exacerbated the crisis of Brazilian society that wrecked the status quo and transformed the country in the years after the last of the raiders departed for home, the bunting came down, and the gates of the exhibition closed.

Chapter 1

Fishermen and Aviators

Time, Race, and Region in the Raids of the Centenary

Over four million people visited the Exposição Internacional do Centenário da Independência, which opened to the public on independence day and closed on 24 July 1923, well after the planned closing date of 31 March.[1] However, as chapter 2 shows, while some argued that the exposition was a success (and, of course, there was more than one way to measure its performance), the more widespread opinion was that attendance fell short of expectations, especially given that many visitors preferred the Parque de Diversões (amusement park) to the supposedly more edifying industrial and educational pavilions. As Marly Silva da Motta points out, this led critics to ask uncomfortable questions not only about organizational inadequacies but even about the patriotism of Brazilian citizens.[2]

Rather than the fair, many contemporaries were sure that the most successful and important event organized to celebrate the centenary was an endeavor undertaken by foreigners before the centenary date arrived, a journey across the South Atlantic by two Portuguese aviators, Sacadura Cabral and Gago Coutinho. As was the case with the fair, there were reasons to doubt the success of the flight from Lisbon to Rio de Janeiro, the first such journey across the South Atlantic. Like all long-distance flights in the early twentieth century, the journey required multiple stops for fuel and mechanical repairs; the aviators needed seventy-nine days

1.1. "By Seas Sailed Never Before," *A Careta*, 15 April 1922. In the caption, "Brazil" salutes Sacadura Cabral and Gago Coutinho: "Hail to the intrepid Portuguese aviators, whose *raid*, inspired by our ancient brotherhood, pierces the insignificant clouds of local nativism." The cartoonist has included a drawing of the Brazilian aviation pioneer Santos Dumont in the distance. Courtesy Charles E. Young Research Library, University of California, Los Angeles.

to complete sixty-two hours of flying time, but this was not only because of planned stops. It was also because they crashed and had to be rescued by naval vessels on two occasions. The aviators lost both their original hydroplane and a replacement, and each crash caused significant delays as the aviators awaited the Portuguese government's delivery of new aircraft. Cabral and Coutinho arrived in Rio de Janeiro only on 17 June 1922, long after their originally planned arrival date.

A few critics claimed that these complications and accidents amounted to failure, as the nativist periodical *Gil Blas* asserted in its coverage of the flight, calling it a "disaster" and its celebration a Portuguese plot against Brazilian nationalism.[3] But the vast majority of commentators celebrated it as a great accomplishment of ingenuity and technology, and many depicted the aviators' difficulties not as failures but as proofs of their bravery, their resilience, and their embodiment of Portugal's alleged genius for discovery and exploration. The popular motto attached to the flight, in Brazil and in Portugal, took Luís de Camões's description of the discoverers of the age of sail as pioneers of "mares nunca dantes navegados" (seas sailed never before) and exchanged seas for air (*mares* for *ares*), making Cabral and Coutinho the inheritors of the tradition of Bartolomeu Dias, Vasco da Gama, and, of course, Pedro Alvares Cabral. The flight seems to have been the single most-discussed story in the Brazilian press between April and June 1922, as broadsheet newspapers and all manner of other periodicals published detailed descriptions of the aviators' progress and challenges, introductions to the technology they employed, essays on the journey's political, cultural, and "racial" meaning, and enormous coverage of the seaplane's touchdown at each Brazilian port, including interviews, speeches, and extraordinary photographic coverage of the receptions afforded them all along the coast.

Moreover, press coverage suggests that the writers' reactions and enthusiasm were matched by the reading and larger publics. It shows tens of thousands of residents crowding the docks in the port cities on the route to Rio de Janeiro to welcome the aviators as they arrived, and tens of thousands accompanying them on obligatory parades through city streets to accommodations set aside by local organizing committees. These events were made possible in part because local governments established arrival dates as city holidays and because local committees planned well in advance to greet the aviators, making sure to have the finances and organization in place to provide lyrical welcoming speeches, music, and pageantry, and to ensure the participation of leading citizens and groups, from Boy Scout troops to chambers of commerce. However long it lasted, the aviators' stay in the cities was full of activity, and they attended so many receptions and parties and made so many visits that Rio de Janeiro's leading humor magazine, *Careta*, depicted them as Christlike figures whose airplanes became a cross to bear and Brazilians' celebrations as their Calvary.[4] Much of this outpouring of esteem came from Portuguese residents of Brazil's coastal cities, as Portuguese diplomats and the other leading figures of the immigrant community helped organize and pay for the events to welcome the aviators, and Portuguese writers and speakers provided some of the most laudatory of the commentary on the flight. But Portuguese residents were a minority of those who celebrated Cabral and Coutinho; much to the annoyance of *Gil Blas*, what it called the "mindlessness of the crowd" led the Brazilian public to see the flight as an extraordinary success and to join in a mania of celebration the magazine deemed unpatriotic and unmerited.[5]

Cabral and Coutinho touched a deep chord in Brazilians and other residents of Brazil in 1922, and theirs was not the only "raid" on the centenary, the English term borrowed by Portuguese speakers to describe not only a violent attack but any long-distance expedition that demands resilience and endurance.[6] In fact, many others conducted raids aimed

1.2. "The Great International *Flame* and the Modern Moths," *A Careta*, 16 September 1922. Note the depiction of the Brazilian Republic as a demure, young white woman. Courtesy Charles E. Young Research Library, University of California, Los Angeles.

at Rio de Janeiro as a way of celebrating the centenary, some traveling by air, some over land, and some by sea. The centenary saw another unprecedented long-distance flight, from New York to Rio de Janeiro, undertaken by a crew led by the American Walter Hinton and the Brazilian Euclides Pinto Martins and underwritten by the *New York World* newspaper. Other long-distance flights to the Brazilian capital included journeys from Santiago, Chile, and Buenos Aires, Argentina, and Anésia Pinheiro Machado completed the first flight by a woman from São Paulo to Rio de Janeiro. Closer to the ground, Wanderlino Nogueira and Alipio Costa conducted a "walking" raid that began in Salvador, and the brothers Settimo and Attilio Sozzi cycled from the state of Rio Grande do Sul. And over fifty fishermen traveled there from various points on the coast, in canoes and aboard jangadas, the simple fishing rafts of the Northeast.

There were so many of these journeys that in September *Careta* depicted raiding airplanes as swarming moths buzzing the capital and its fair, but for the most part every raider enjoyed an excited reception, if not always as effusive as that reserved for Cabral and Coutinho.[7] Indeed, such was their number and the attention they received that the raid became a central feature of the centenary—a lexicon of the themes and tensions that characterized the commemorations and helped contemporaries articulate the meanings they read in the centenary and in Brazil itself as it marked the great date. They used the raids to discuss the relationship the country ought to cultivate between celebrating the past and anticipating the future; to think about the character of the Brazilian people and define who ought to be Brazilian and who should not; and to look for ways to resolve what seemed to be intractable tensions among the regions of the country in order to make Brazil a unified national community.

First, the raids helped Brazilians think about time and the tension many believed the nation to be facing, between the attractions of modernity and the call to tradition. On one hand, contemporaries were excited about the aviators' demonstration of the possibilities of modern technology, as they seemed to collapse time and space aboard their Fairey and Curtiss aircraft and to show that Brazil would take its place among modern nations. On the other, many said Cabral and Coutinho reminded Brazilians of the importance of tradition, a view even more prevalent in the response to the fishermen travelers, who were the only raiders to have won acclaim comparable to that afforded the Portuguese aviators. These jangadeiros (as the fishermen were collectively described, regardless of their type of craft) attracted an enormous amount of attention in the local and national press, they were celebrated in numerous festivities at home and in the capital, where they visited Epitácio Pessoa at the presidential palace, and they were awarded cash prizes for their accomplishments by the national government. All this was not *in spite of* the way fishermen conducted their raids, but *because* they did so aboard jangadas, an antique technology of lashed-together logs and a single fixed sail. While their raids seemed to challenge the dominant note of official centenary events, with their celebrations of modern industry and electric light, many read the jangadeiros' accomplishments as proof of the strength and resourcefulness to be found if the people of the centenary could rediscover Brazil's "true" but often neglected traditions. The raids thus seemed to offer a means of working out how Brazilians should balance their eagerness for the future with the value of the past.

Closely related to this was the sense that all the raiders provided a lesson in nation-building and reckoning with the country's racial constitution. Cabral and Coutinho reminded many Brazilians of the accomplishments of the adventurers of the fifteenth and sixteenth centuries and they were also understood specifically as embodying the so-called racial strengths of the Portuguese people and, more important for Brazilians, people of Portuguese descent. Similarly, many admirers depicted the jangadeiros as demonstrating the inherent but hidden potential of the Brazilian people, especially the people of color who populated the fishing communities the jangadeiros called home. In other words, the raids helped give the people of the centenary confidence in the future of the Brazilian raça, a confidence that seemed especially necessary during a time of both the Lusophobia articulated by *Gil Blas* and its allies and eugenicist thought, which suggested that because many Brazilians were people of Portuguese or African or indigenous descent the country might be doomed to backwardness. Indeed, the health and constitution of the Brazilian "race" was one of the major concerns of the organizers of the official commemorations of the centenary, especially in the activities attached to the international exhibition. The raids helped Brazilians engage with these matters, as they thought about the meaning of the Portuguese aviators and especially the jangadeiros, but they also saw lessons about race in considering the other raiders, for example, when contemporaries said Walter Hinton displayed qualities inherent in Anglo-American people and Euclides Martins was the embodiment of the prototypical Latin.

Finally, contemporaries valued the raids for the way they acquainted Brazilians more fully with the geography of their country and its regions. They understood the raids as promoting awareness of the country's geography in the plain sense that they advertised the locations of cities and towns all along the coast, introducing Brazilians to the existence of places that they might have been unaware of, such as the São Pedro and São Paulo and the Fernando de Noronha island groups, where the Portuguese aviators had stopped before they reached the mainland.[8] Brazilians were not introduced to their whole country by the raiders, whose travels tended to track closely along the coast and ended in Rio de Janeiro. Still, for many commentators this was one of the most important contributions of the raids, their lessons in geography and region reminding Brazilians of the importance of the country's regions beyond the South and Southeast, whose enormous cultural influence, political hegemony, and economic power were ratified by the exhibition and many of the other official events planned for the centenary. The raids reminded Brazilians what they did *not* know, that, in the words of the Rio de Janeiro–based columnist Benjamin Costallat, "Brazil is more than Avenida Central." Instead, Costallat and other admirers said, they reminded Brazilians of the "real" Brazil to be found in fishing villages and small towns and on ranches and farms, that had gone neglected for far too long but must be noticed and their potential realized if Brazil were to meet its great destiny.[9] Such comments were especially common when admirers discussed the jangadeiros and their seeming resilience, their arguments often echoing Euclides da Cunha's famous reminder to a previous generation of city dwellers not to forget their compatriots, that "the sertanejo, or man of the backlands, is above all else a strong individual."[10]

Brazilians thus used the raids to think and talk about the big questions posed by the centenary—questions of time, race, and region—and to consider how they might address those questions in order to make the centenary more than a commemoration and a celebration. They used the raids to try to make the centenary into a space of substance and construction, a way of knowing the country and its people better and learning to use that knowledge to build the national community. The questions of the centenary were often knitted together, so that discussion of the seeming tensions between tradition and modernity often also meant consideration of the cultural and racial constitution of the nation. Similarly, contemporaries' ideas about questions of geography were linked to exploration of the distinctive traditions of each of Brazil's regions. And, as commentators' frequent allusions to Cunha's "strong" backlander in their admiring remarks about the jangadeiros showed, their discussion of region was also a way of discussing racial matters. Indeed, Brazilians' views of race have often been rooted in and mapped closely on their perspectives on the country's regions. As Hendrik Kraay and Barbara Weinstein point out, they have found civic rituals particularly useful in working out their views on the exact relationships between race, national origin, and region.[11]

Such connections allowed for insinuation and elision, but could also make it difficult to generate intelligible conversations about weighty matters, hence the complaint voiced by many Brazilians during the centenary year that they and their compatriots did not know their own people and their own land, and thus could not build its future. The raids of 1922 were exciting and romantic, but, as this chapter shows, they became a touchstone of the centenary because they were understood to be much more. They also seemed extraordinarily useful in their capacity to make the big questions of the centenary more legible and responses to them easier to articulate, for they provided contemporaries seemingly simple stories of resilience, endurance, and strength of character that Brazilians could imbue with deep meaning—whatever meaning they might prefer.

Official and Popular Commemorations, and the Raid Phenomenon

As Kraay points out in his work on civic rituals in nineteenth-century Brazil, in order to understand the political and cultural significance of such events it is important to examine what happens beyond official celebrations. Civic rituals like Brazil's centenary celebrations are opportunities for a state to organize its priorities, perform its power, and attempt to shape the people it purports to represent. They are also opportunities for citizens and other residents to make their own statements about their relationship to the state and nation, sometimes corresponding to official assertions, sometimes contradicting or announcing alternatives to them.

The raids undertaken by aviators, fishermen, and others in 1922 provide a lens through which to examine this more popular understanding of the meaning of the centenary. Though official Brazil did associate itself with the raids in various ways, especially in receiving the raiders and claiming them, they were not organized by the official administrators appointed by the national government. Commentators often depicted the raids as impromptu adventures undertaken by men and women inspired by patriotism. This was not quite the case. Many of the raids were in fact supported by official actors, which was especially obvious in the Lisbon–Rio de Janeiro raid. Sacadura Cabral and Gago Coutinho were officers in the Portuguese navy, and their raid was in many ways an initiative of the Portuguese state, which was intent on using the Brazilian centenary to cultivate stronger Luso-Brazilian relations.[12] Thus, the Portuguese military provided the aviators not one but three hydroplanes, the second and third having to be delivered to the aviators in the Fernando de Noronha archipelago.[13] The Portuguese navy also tracked their progress via vessels patrolling the Atlantic, a decision that proved prescient when the aviators needed to be rescued after their first crash.[14] On the mainland, Portuguese consuls and the Portuguese ambassador helped organize the aviators' stays in each Brazilian location where they touched down and in their visits after the completion of the raid, a role the American diplomatic corps in Brazil also played during the raid conducted by Walter Hinton and Euclides Pinto Martins later on, even though their raid was financed by an American newspaper.

Other raiders also benefited from official assistance of various types. Many of the jangadeiros were members of government-supported fishing cooperatives, which helped organize preparations for the raids and provide financial assistance for the families of the raiders during their time away.[15] Mayors and governors of their cities and states helped oversee festivities as they launched their raids, and receptions when they returned; a Brazilian naval vessel accompanied many of them down the coast, providing telegraph updates about their progress and calling on coastal communities to be ready to offer any assistance the raiders might need. The governors of the states through which the Sozzi brothers cycled ordered government employees to provide needed mechanical repairs; authorities in towns visited by Italian and Brazilian raiders who completed a unique raid that descended by river from São Paulo to Asunción in Paraguay offered repairs and other assistance; and those who walked enjoyed government-sponsored hospitality as they traveled from various points to Rio de Janeiro.[16]

Still, it is true that the raids were not planned by the official body organized by the national government in 1920 to oversee the centenary events, the Comissão Executiva do Centenário da Independência do Brasil, which focused on promoting events in the capital centered on the international exposition. Nor were they planned by committees established by state and local governments; they were not "official" events. According to the federal senator Antônio Azeredo, almost all the commemorations of the centenary were "official" ones, and "only two or three can be considered popular." Among these were the raids, and Azeredo felt it was important to celebrate them, for example, by including the fishermen among those given cash rewards by the national government for services and accomplishments related to the centenary.[17]

Beyond this distinction between "official" and "popular" celebrations, the raids were met with enormous public attention, and many of the raiders encountered rapturous receptions during their journeys. The excitement with which residents of Recife, Pernambuco, met the Hinton–Martins raid gives a sense of the raids' popularity. The raid met many difficulties, so that a journey the aviators had expected to complete in a little over a month took almost six. All of Recife's papers followed the aviators' progress assiduously, from the announcement of the plan to the departure from New York in mid-August and the journey down the east coast of the United States and into the Caribbean, which is where the raiders faced their first serious difficulties, beginning with a crash landing and loss of their hydroplane off the coast of Cuba. It was two weeks before they were off again, and it was not until late November that the aviators arrived in South America, mainly due to a monthlong delay in Trinidad because of a damaged propeller. It was December when they arrived in Brazil, and February 1923, not early September 1922, when they completed the raid in Rio de Janeiro.

Combined with all the energy residents expended in welcoming the Portuguese raiders who visited the city earlier in the year, the delays led some commentators in Recife to worry that the local population would lose interest in the endeavor before the American and Brazilian aviators arrived. The *Jornal do Recife* complained about what it saw as "criminal indifference" among public authorities, and the *Diario de Pernambuco*'s A. Fernandes said, even before the aviators arrived, "Our imagination has been exhausted and our rhetoric spent." In an essay in which he encouraged his fellow citizens to spare the aviators the exhausting number of events to which the Portuguese had been subjected, he offered the visitors a more prosaic "strong and cordial handshake."[18] But the many delays allowed the press to provide readers with in-depth introductions to the raiders, who included Hinton and Martins as well as a reporter from the *World*, a cinematographer, and a mechanic. Martins, who was the only Brazilian in the group, was a subject of particular interest, and Recifenses had the opportunity to get to know him quite well even before the raiding party arrived. They learned that, although he was born in Ceará and at the time of the raid was living in the United States, he had grown up in Recife and his family still lived there in the Boa Vista neighborhood.[19] Moreover, during a monthlong delay in Natal due to mechanical difficulties and Hinton's need to recover from dysentery, Martins took a car to Recife to gather supplies and visit his family, during which time he sat for long interviews with local reporters. By the time the aviators finally arrived, the reading public, at least, was familiar with Martins and his version of the story of the raid, a well-practiced assertion of patriotism and alleged humility.[20]

The aviators attempted to make it to Recife on 28 December, and the city did in fact muster plenty of excitement, despite Fernandes's own exhaustion. Thousands of residents crowded the docks to watch the landing and congratulate them, while some took to small watercraft in hopes of getting close to the hydroplane, and bands prepared welcoming numbers.[21] But they were disappointed, another in a long list of mechanical problems delaying the attempt to the next day, when the pattern repeated. The *Jornal do Recife* described "a moment of true delirium" when the crowd received news that the aviators had left Parahyba (now João Pessoa) for Recife. It was "an overwhelming joy, which spread chaotically among the incalculable multitude that filled the area set aside for the 'splashdown.'"[22] Again, though, the aviators had to abandon the attempt to make it to Recife, and made an emergency landing shortly after takeoff.

It was not until late January that the aviators tried again, but many in Recife maintained or rediscovered their excitement. According to the *Jornal do Recife*, "the regrettable setbacks that have made it so difficult to pursue the remarkable aerial feat have in no way robbed it of its importance or the enthusiasm of the people, who recognize the unshakeable will and invincible moral resolve of the daring adventurers."[23] On 22 January the aviators tried again, and the paper was proved right. It reported that "the human current grew more and more, sometimes making vehicle traffic impossible," an "incalculable" number of people awaiting them in the summer sun through morning and into late afternoon, making for "a painful sacrifice" that went unrewarded, another engine problem delaying the raid once again.[24]

Finally, on 26 January the aviators finally made it to Recife, and the novelty still had not worn off. Although the latest attempt was not announced to the public in advance, once notice was posted residents responded quickly. The *Jornal* stated that it took less than thirty minutes for admirers to fill the docks and their surroundings, and by the time of the coordinated announcement that the airplane had been sighted, which came via a twenty-one-gun salute and the ringing of church bells from neighboring Olinda and throughout Recife, "the people's joy grew into delirium." The paper described the city's response as a "sensational, dreamlike, and colossal demonstration that yesterday shook the Pernambucano soul, in an extraordinary outpouring of the most intense joy." Celebrations began with welcoming speeches at the docks and then a cortege that carried the heroes to a more formal welcome at the packed Theatro do Parque, led by city leaders and the American consul Charles Cameron. The parade was so large and boisterous that the horses pulling the heroes' carriage balked at moving down the streets, leading excited people to remove the traces and pull the carriage themselves. As the parade carried the raiders, people crowded around to applaud and cheer and throw flowers from the windows of buildings along the route.[25] And these were only the first events of the celebrations. Some were small and limited the participation of the mass of residents, such as another event the first night at the Theatro do Parque, masses of thanksgiving, and visits to local institutions, while others gave the public the opportunity to claim the event as their own. Chief among these was a "patriotic parade" the evening of 27 January organized by the welcoming committee to include as many citizens and residents as would like to participate. Led by public authorities and leading citizens and residents, who claimed precedence in the order of march, members of the city police and state guard and their marching bands, hundreds of students and scouts carrying flags, banners, and lanterns, and members of the press participated at the invitation of organizers, and these were accompanied by what the *Jornal* said was "a countless multitude" of excited admirers.[26]

Because of all the delays they faced before their arrival in Recife, the raiders remained in the city for less time than locals had hoped, but there was still time for a sports jamboree in their honor, which included a football match between the Torre and Sport clubs; a dance at the Country Club; and a hugely well-attended farewell at the docks on 30 January, as the raid continued on to Maceió. The rest of the raid was considerably more efficient, so few communities had the chance to provide the kind of proof given by the residents of Recife of Brazilians' interest in the raid phenomenon, the aborted flights from Paraíba to Pernambuco suggesting a more than ephemeral interest in these feats of long-distance travel. But the aviators found popular enthusiasm wherever they landed, even given all the difficulties and delays. Like A. Fernandes, *Careta* suggested that some excitement for Hinton, Martins, and their group had indeed diminished in the almost six months of their journey, during which time many of the centenary's major events had taken place, including numerous other raids, depicting Martins in one cartoon as having been forgotten by the public authorities who had so feted the Portuguese aviators and the jangadeiros in particular.[27] But many others in Rio de Janeiro did remain interested, such as the members of the Tenentes do Diabo, Democraticos, and Fenianos clubs, each of which honored the aviators in their Carnival parades that year.[28]

It was in such ways that the people of Brazil fulfilled the hopes of Hinton and Martins, of Cabral and Coutinho, and of the many other raiders of the centenary, making their raids and the raid phenomenon a central part of their civic rituals in 1922. The raids were especially important because they demonstrated what Brazilians beyond official circles valued and what they believed was worth celebrating as the country commemorated its independence. The raids decentralized the experience of the centenary, as their organization, pursuit, and reception extended the celebrations beyond the capital city, beyond the grounds of the exhibition, the academic and medical congresses, and other "official" venues, allowing contemporaries exciting opportunities to make the centenary their own. While there was no one reason for their enthusiasm, it is clear that what they found most meaningful in the raids—and in the centenary—was the opportunity they afforded for contemplation of the competing claims of modernity and tradition; of the questions Brazilians faced as they thought about matters of race and nation and belonging; and of the tensions they perceived between building the national community and the claims of its distinctive, often competing regions.

Modernity × Tradition

The most apparent reason for Brazilians' interest in the centenary raids, and for the mania for raids that characterized much of the Western world in the early twentieth century, was their display of technological progress and their announcement of the modern. Of course, this quality was most obvious in air raids, and Brazilian press coverage was full of the technical details of the vessels used by the raiders and exacting measurements of raiders' speed, distance, bearing, and time. For example, readers of the *Diario de Pernambuco* learned that Cabral and Coutinho began their raid in a Fairey aircraft that could make land or sea landings and was outfitted with a 360-horsepower, 12-cylinder Rolls Royce Eagle engine. It had a fuel capacity of 104 liters of gasoline, on which it could travel 1,052 kilometers, carrying a maximum weight of 725 kilograms at 180 kilometers per hour. It could cover 5,790 meters in six minutes.[29] Readers of the *Jornal do Recife* learned that Martins had planned the raid from New York "with precision," using a variety of instruments and resources, including "a parallel frame for measuring the direction of the winds, a compass, a barometer, the Bowditch navigation guide, prismatic binoculars, etc."[30] And readers of Belém's *Folha do Norte* learned that Hinton and Martins's Curtiss flying boat touched down in the bay at "precisely 3:12" on 2 December 1922.[31]

The few Brazilian pilots and small but growing number of Brazilians familiar with automobiles might take an interest in these details, but it seems the more important thing was to highlight that raiders were using the most advanced technologies and bringing them to Brazil.[32] That this was the case is suggested by commentators' persistent reminders that the aviators were not sportsmen and that their raids were not sporting events; rather, the aviators were to be understood as explorers and experts, and the raids as scientific endeavors. By the 1920s, modern sports had achieved a prominent position in Brazil, team sports like football and activities understood to be "sporting" ones, including aviation, accepted by many as playing crucial roles in making Brazilians better soldiers, better workers, and better citizens.[33] But there were still doubts about sports during the period, as expressed, for example, in the pedagogue Carlos Sussekind de Mendonça's 1921 book *O Sport está deseducando a mocidade brasileira* (Sport is miseducating Brazilian youth) and in a bill to prohibit international football matches in Brazil, sponsored in Congress by Carlos Garcia after the South American football championship hosted in Rio de Janeiro as part of the centenary celebrations was marred by controversy.[34] More apposite was the critique that aviation, and to a lesser extent, automobile driving, was a "sport" for wealthy dilettantes, a pastime and an amusement, but in general of little practical value.[35]

Commentators made a point of telling their readers and listeners that these concerns were not relevant to the raids of the centenary. The raid from Lisbon was not a "speed test" or a horse race, not "a sporting adventure."[36] It was not "a 'performance' by dilettante 'sportmen.'"[37] It was not "an excursion" or "a rehearsal" or "a sporting event."[38] Instead it was an accomplishment of technology and expertise, "science" the magic word admirers used to announce the seriousness and importance of the raid and the raiders. It was "a great and scientific test of aviation," "a scientific demonstration," and "a great scientific experiment."[39] Most commentators agreed that the aviators were heroes, but theirs was not a foolhardy or headstrong heroism; rather it was undergirded by their training and what the capital's *O Jornal* called "impressive mastery."[40] To illustrate the point, admirers infallibly pointed to two inventions made by Gago Coutinho, which he used to navigate the raid: a device to measure wind speed and direction and a naval sextant adapted to flight.[41] The two Portuguese "scientists," according to *Fon Fon*, had exhibited courage and daring, but also calm and "technical ability" that allowed them to make "valuable studies" of the atmospheric conditions in the South Atlantic. They had thereby made "precious and invaluable observations" on which future aviators would rely.[42] In the more florid language of Natal's *A República*, the aviators were "eagles of science" and "condors of human ingenuity," who were "tearing open larger horizons and wider spaces" for other aviators and the entire human race.[43]

Usually a little less effusive, commentators used the same terms in discussing Hinton, Martins, and their crew, and many other raiders of the centenary. For example, though some doubted the value of the river raid undertaken from São Paulo to Asunción by the Brazilian Alcindo de Castro Monteiro and the Italian Luigi Longobardi, proponents drew attention to the studies of the Paraná and Paraguay Rivers that Longobardi would carry out, which meant the raid was "of great scientific importance."[44] Their hosts invited raiders to discuss their experiences in the pages of newspapers and magazines and in public talks, and encouraged them especially to discuss the technical details of the raids, such as when Martins "offered a scientific explanation of the causes of the winds" that troubled their attempts to fly from Natal to Parahyba.[45] The most popular speakers were Cabral and Coutinho and Hinton and Martins, who gave talks at each stop along the coast and in Rio de Janeiro, as well as during visits, in the aftermath of their journeys to Rio de Janeiro, to other cities that were not on the raids' itinerary. Packed crowds in the cities' municipal theaters, institutes of history and geography, and libraries listened to the aviators discuss the scientific contributions they themselves believed their raids would make. Their message of the value of aviation and the importance of technological progress was carried throughout Brazil, by the press and by other apostles of the modern, such as the Portuguese journalist Simões Coelho, who traveled to parts of northeastern and northern Brazil not visited by the Portuguese aviators to discuss the "scientific lessons of the 'raid.'"[46] And anyone who visited the Portuguese pavilion at the international exposition could inspect the *Santa Cruz*, the last aircraft used by Cabral and Coutinho, which organizers suspended from the building's rafters.

The obsession with the modern and with advanced technology is one reason that the difficulties faced by Cabral and Coutinho and Hinton and Martins did not keep Brazilians from admiring them and celebrating their achievements. As *O Malho* put it, after the many months of waiting, the residents of the capital were still excited to celebrate Hin-

1.3. Jangadeiro raiders from Ceará, *A Exposição de 1922*, November 1922. Courtesy of the New York Public Library.

ton and Martins—and in fact offered "devotion to the heroes which exceeded the most optimistic predictions"—due to their courage and resilience, but also because they demonstrated the possibilities that advanced technology could offer. The important thing in such "tremendous aerial tests," the magazine said, was not the length of time of the journeys, but "to show that they can be completed, despite every difficulty." One day technical improvements would allow faster, uninterrupted flights. In the meantime, Hinton and Martins gave a view to a future in which the world would see "the wonders of rapid transportation between the continents of the Earth."[47] That is, Hinton and Martins exemplifed one of the most important themes of the centenary celebrations, a sense of the possibilities offered by modernity for the world at large and, more important, for Brazil, whose great future could be glimpsed as each airplane came into view.

Raid watchers' fixation on advanced technology and other aspects of the modern is also why it is so important to understand the popularity of what were in many respects the quite unmodern raids of the jangadeiros. While today's jangadeiros have updated the design of their craft in several ways, their forebears in the 1920s were still making the rafts by lashing together boards or logs and installing a simple mast and cloth sail, the entire craft just large enough for two or three fishermen and their handwoven net. Unlike the aviators, the jangadeiro raiders carried few if any navegational instruments or other aids in making the journey to Rio de Janeiro; they knew the waters near their hometowns and ports, in (from north to south), Fortaleza, Ceará; Natal, Rio Grande do Norte; Aracajú, Sergipe; Maceió, Alagoas; Salvador, Bahia; Santos, São Paulo; Paranaguá,

Paraná; and Pelotas, Rio Grande do Sul, but few had ever sailed far from home before the raids in 1922.

In contrast to their coverage of the aviation raids, commentators tended to stress the stripped-down, ancient character of the jangadas (and the other boats and canoes) used by the fishermen conducting raids. They were nothing more than "a few boards," according to *O Jornal do Brasil*.[48] As Jonathas Barreto wrote in introducing the jangada to the uninitiated readers of the *Revista da Semana*, it was not only a "a primitive means of maritime transportation" but one that could be "characterized as the most simple and rudimentary of all marine constructions, used for journeys of short duration."[49] He emphasized that fishermen made the rafts by hand, pointing out that most used logs rather than finished planks, and ratified the notion developed throughout the press that these were simple, fragile crafts—they were "very fragile boats," "very fragile vessels," "very fragile jangadas," and "very fragile boards tied together and set with wooden nails!"[50] To reinforce the point, many publications printed photographs and cartoons of the jangadeiros and their "simple" jangadas.[51] And the first few jangadeiros to arrive in Rio de Janeiro saw their crafts lifted out of the water and placed onto trailers for a parade in the fishermen's honor, allowing residents of the capital a chance to see the jangadas for themselves.[52]

Such a celebration made for a startling contrast to a previous attempt to sail a jangada to a world's fair. In 1903, when a small group of Brazilians announced their intention to sail a jangada to St. Louis for the Louisiana Purchase Exposition, the prominent poet Olavo Bilac campaigned against the idea, fearing that the unmodern jangada would embarrass Brazil on the world stage and calling it "comical" and "futile."[53] Fortunately for Bilac and his sense of decorum, the travelers decided against the attempt despite their months of planning.[54] Nineteen years later, hosting their own international exposition, many Brazilians were still very concerned with foreigners' opinions, but no repetition of Bilac's embarrassment seems to have been registered. Instead, the jangadeiros and other fishermen conducting raids on the centenary celebrations in the capital met with universal acclaim. There were even some who were more impressed by the fishermen than by the aviators who had come from much farther away and aboard the most modern aircraft, specifically because of the contrast in technology.

Writing in Natal's *A República*, J. R. pointed out that while aviators enjoyed all the benefits of "scientific precision," the jangadeiros leaving from his own city and elsewhere along the coast could count only on "the compass that Nature and the Heavens has given them in distant landmarks—trees, hills, and mountains—and the glow of the stars of the

Southern Cross." Though on one hand such comments seem very much to have misrepresented the fishermen's scientific knowledge and to have discounted their long years of training, on the other, admirers used them to make greater claims about the significance of the accomplishment, so that J. R. went on to claim that because of the lack of technology the raid was "a high point among all of the events of the centenary festivities."[55] Similarly, *O Progresso*, a paper in the town of Penedo in Alagoas, specifically rejected the idea that "the greatest event among the accomplishments of the centenary" was the Lisbon–Rio de Janeiro raid. "No!" the editors wrote, if anyone were to ask which was "the most brilliant" accomplishment of that year, they would say that it was the raid on Rio de Janeiro undertaken by the Alagoano fishermen, which was "the true commemoration of the centenary."[56]

Local pride could explain why residents of the towns and cities from which the fishermen set out would be so effusive, but they were not the only ones who made favorable comparisons between jangadeiros and aviators. The eminent statesman Ruy Barbosa said in a widely published valedictory that none of the pilots of the "giants of the infinite" who flew into Brazil in 1922 outmatched the jangadeiros in "audacity" or "skill."[57] The *Jornal do Brasil* pointed out that while many of the aviators who made raids confronted serious problems and required multiple crafts to complete their journeys, the jangadeiros "completed their journeys without incident or accident," and that most arrived "unharmed, their light vessels similarly undamaged—the same ones in which they left their home ports." According to the paper, such a contrast seemed meaningful, and "it makes one think."[58] The president of the republic was even more explicit, telling the jangadeiros during their visit to the Catete Palace: "You, in your confrontation with the fury of the seas, deserve more praise than those who traversed the skies!"[59]

Though few if any contemporaries seem to have remarked upon it, at first glance these reactions appear to have conflicted with the dominant message offered by Epitácio Pessoa and his government in the official celebrations of the centenary, of Brazil's commitment to Western modernity, into which the aviation raids fit comfortably. Within that broader, dominant message, though, were dissonant notes, including not only the raids of the jangadeiros but also, for example, displays of nostalgia for the empire in Rio de Janeiro's newly organized Museu Histórico Nacional. In the centenary Brazilians displayed both their eagerness for modernity and their sense of the importance of tradition and of the uneasy but potentially fruitful tension between insisting on the future and contemplating the past. Most famously, this tension was exhibited in the Semana de Arte Moderna with which a group of innovative artists and intellectuals began the centenary year in São Paulo and in which they exhibited works that drew on Brazil's traditions as well as the most contemporary of styles in the world of Western modernist art. More accessible and more participatory, the raids seemed to exemplify that tension and its possibilities, which goes a long way to explaining Brazilians' excitement about them.

Thus, in considering the Portuguese aviators, commentary on the minutiae of sophisticated engines and navigation inventions was paired with constant references to the past, including all those allusions to the explorers of the sixteenth century. Rather than seeing these ideas as opposed to one another, admirers brought them together in their claims that the raid ratified Brazil's claim to prominence in aviation history and that it proved the indomitable strength of Portugal and of Brazil's Portuguese inheritance. In the first instance, their most obvious reference point was the early twentieth century Brazilian balloonist and pilot Santos Dumont, a worldwide celebrity as an aviation pioneer, who in 1922 also played a prominent role in public events celebrating Cabral and Coutinho.[60] Another was Bartolomeu de Gusmão, the Brazil-born priest who designed a lighter-than-air vessel in the eighteenth century. Though much less well known than Dumont, commentators cited him frequently as they sought to link Portugal and Brazil to one another and to the history of aviation.[61]As the prominent nationalist writer Gustavo Barroso put it, while together the raids of the centenary welcomed Brazilians into "the future's bold embrace," the Lisbon raid also served as a reminder of the power "of tradition, of the raça, of the past."[62]

The reminder was urgent because many seemed to doubt Portugal. They considered it decadent, its glories confined to the past, which suggested that Brazil must abandon its Portuguese traditions if it were to meet the future. The raid helped dispel such notions, Barroso and others said. It offered lessons in technology and engineering, of course, but more important, it proved that the Portuguese still possessed the capacity for great deeds, which could give Brazilians confidence in their cultural and, as the next section shows, "racial" inheritance. As one writer put it, Portugal may have suffered a period of decline and inertia, but the raid showed it had experienced "the rebirth of the phoenix."[63]

In a similar vein, *O Malho* said that the aviators proved false the idea that the "spirit of tenacity" that animated Portugal's sixteenth-century accomplishments had disappeared. It said of Portugal that "the moribund lives and rediscovers its lost strength, because the breed that can produce specimens like these two aviators, who have completed the crossing of the Atlantic, has not gone extinct."[64] Commentators explained that Portugal's "rebirth" began with the founding of its republic in 1910, after which the new government prioritized its relations with Brazil, an effort that included its eagerness to participate fully in Brazil's centenary, through the raid, in the exhibition, and in the visit of President António José de Almeida. Indeed, the fact and idea of the republic helped give shape and significance to the raid. Much of the planning for the receptions of the aviators in Brazil was undertaken by groups like Rio de Janeiro's Gremio Republicano Portuguez, many celebrations paired the republican flag with the Cruz da Malta flag associated with the colonial era, and two of the ships sent to accompany the aviators in the Atlantic were the *República* and the *Cinco de Outubro* (a reference to the republican revolution).

Thus, Sacadura Cabral and Gago Coutinho were at once both ancient adventurers reborn and prophets of a great present and greater future, celebrated for providing reminders of past glories and promises of future accomplishments—for Portugal but also for Brazil. Similarly, the tension between past and future was developed as contemporaries tried to understand the significance of the jangadeiros. The fishermen seemed to recall the past and tradition in their craftsmanship and their trade. They also reminded many Brazilians of an earlier moment when the jangadeiro had been a national hero, in the story of Francisco Nascimento, the jangadeiro called the *Dragão do Mar*, who it is said worked for abolition in late nineteenth-century Ceará by leading his fellow jangadeiros in refusing to transport slaves who were to be sold to the south. Among others, Ruy Barbosa mentioned Nascimento in his remarks congratulating the jangadeiros on their raid, calling their accomplishments "reminders of the legend writ on the past."[65] The official magazine of the exhibition narrated the Nascimento story to introduce readers to the jangadeiros, who, it said, lived mostly ignored by their compatriots, obscure despite their heroic past.[66] The *Revista da Semana* called them "descendants of the jangadeiro Nascimento" and used that assertion to make a broader point: the raids were not only journeys to the capital but assumed "the character of a typically Brazilian manifestation, where the perspectives of the present moment are connected to the glorious traditions of the past, to the accomplishments and the sacrifices of four centuries of civilized existence." In this the jangadeiros served a vital role, reminding the residents of the capital and the more urban Southeast that amid the disclocating frenzy of modern city life other Brazilians "preserve the outlook of yesteryear, the beliefs and the desires of earlier times, conserving within their souls Brazil's genuine soul and within their hearts Brazil's true heart, which only knows how to beat with love for the *patria* and for humanity."[67]

As much as the jangadeiros seemed to remind many Brazilians of the past, though, many commentators also depicted their raids as evidence that Brazil was beginning to realize its enormous potential and embrace its bright future. For example, in the *Revista Maritima Brazileira*, a writer made the case that the jangadeiros' accomplishment pointed to specific advantages the country would enjoy if its leaders could organize its large population of fishermen, which, he said, was both "a powerful nucleus for our maritime defense" and "a weighty element in our economic expansion, building an industry with a great future." Beyond these practical contributions, the jangadeiros' demonstration "of the worth and the high sense of civic duty of its sons" provided "an eloquent confirmation that Brazil will grow and progress," an opinion echoed by many of their admirers.[68] In a rousing speech on the floor of the national congress, the Rio Grande do Norte deputy, Alberto Maranhão, argued that the country would be built by the "courage" of such men as the jangadeiro raiders, who braved the seas without compass or engine but still constituted "one of the great economic forces" of the Northeast. Theirs was a human potential waiting to be unleashed, and so, along with his backing of the proposal to offer a cash reward to the raiders, Maranhão also called for governmental intervention to regulate the fishing industry and to provide coastal communities credit, education, and health care, which, he promised, would make make them into a "grand, immense, indestructible national force."[69] His speech incredibly well received, Maranhão was speaking for many of his compatriots, who saw the future in the modest rafts of the jangadeiros. As the *Revista da Semana* put it, the jangadeiros brought to the capital a hopeful and affirming message, of "a truly unified patria, feeling in every locale the same sentiments and driven by the same lofty ideas, marching together to the glories of a future ever closer."[70] The jangadeiros might not match the technology of the aviators, but like them they were seen to embody the best of the past and the promise of the future; for many of their admirers, therefore, they exemplified the centenary spirit as well as did any statue, display, or address.

Race and the Brazilian People

The potentially productive tension between the traditional and the modern that the Portuguese aviators and the jangadeiros seemed to embody was in many ways an expression of contemporaries' ideas about nation and what they often conflated with the concept of nationality, ideas about race. Although one theme of conversations about the raids was that they helped break down barriers between one country and another, more often commentators used the raids to make sweeping claims about the character of nations and to depict aviators, cyclists, fishermen, and even pedestrians as performing their nationalities and the qualities of their

1.4. Celebration of Walter Hinton and Euclides Pinto Martins, unknown location and date. From the collection of Benjamin J. Burns. Courtesy of Beverly H. Burns and McFarland and Company.

raça. This was the case whether the raider was Brazilian or not. For example, while in its coverage of the New York–Rio de Janeiro raid the *Jornal do Recife* asserted that aviation broke through frontiers and showed that in truth "there is no distinction between races or between nations," it also said that Walter Hinton and Euclides Pinto Martins embodied the characteristics of two very different peoples.[71] Walter Hinton was "a good representative of the inherent qualities of the Anglo-American race," which, the paper said, were its powerful will, matchless energy, and intelligence.

It had more to say, unsurprisingly, about Euclides Pinto Martins. He was "the bold and intemperate Latin, worthy heir of the essential qualities of his race." This "invincible" Latin race had traveled the oceans, discovered new worlds, conquered continents and "barbaric" empires, and founded nations and civilizations. He was also a "worthy exemplar" of the "Brazilian raça," which had penetrated the country's inhospitable backlands, expelled foreign invaders, toppled tyrannies, fought for the republican idea, liberated slaves, discovered flight, and civilized savages. It had done all this because of what the paper said were the "qualities of the Brazilian raça, of patience, perserverance, will, bravery, and unselfishness," which, happily, "are distilled in a brilliant way in the person of its beloved son, Pinto Martins."[72] Gustavo Barroso made similar points, saying Hinton embodied Americans' daring and their progessive outlook, while Martins showed Brazilians' typical patience and civilizing influence, which made their raid the union of two "strengths": "Anglo-Saxon strength that has flowered in Yankee lands and become all daring, and Latin strength, forged by Arabic fatalism under the terrible sun of the Land of Light!"[73]

This perspective helps explain why contemporaries saw the raids as so important, and why it was so crucial that the raiders complete their raids, despite any difficulties they might face—the raids were performances of the strengths and value of entire nations and peoples, and a failure to complete a raid could be read as a failure of the nation and its people. As a writer put it in Natal's *A República* when many in Brazil and Portugal worried that one of the crashes would end the Lisbon raid, Cabral and Coutinho realized they had no choice but to continue. Once begun, the aviators carried the hopes of humanity as well as the pride of their nation and the honor of their raça, and therefore "no longer had the right to turn back."[74] The theme was ubiquitous in discussions of all the raids of the centenary, and was especially apparent in coverage of and comment on the Lisbon raid and the raids of the jangadas. These raids were undertaken by representatives of the peoples who made up what Brazilians saw as the main elements of their nation, the "three races" of the Portuguese, the African, and the indigenous. Admirers used Cabral and Coutinho's triumph to insist that the Portuguese continued to belong in Brazil, while they said the jangadeiros showed that those of "Brazilian" stock would be central to the project of development and greatness. The contribution of the jangadeiros was also a timely one, since the Portuguese had arrived in June and Hinton and Martins did not complete their raid until February 1923. No matter how much the *Jornal do Recife* and others wanted to argue that Martins proved "the critics of the Brazilian people" wrong, his was a tardy arrival, especially from the perspective of the capital and the southern states.[75]

As chapter 4 shows, the Portuguese community in Brazil joined the Portuguese government in committing fully to participation in the centenary, imbuing it with ideological meaning and attempting to use it to make immigrants' place in their new home more secure. Brazilians matched them, using the centenary to debate their Portuguese heritage and what it meant for the modern nation. They argued over Portugal's governance and its contributions and failures during the colonial era, over the clash between the countries at independence and Portuguese figures like Pedro I, over the role of Portuguese immigrants in contemporary Brazil, and the consequences for Brazil of their biological and cultural inheritance. These conversations and arguments took place in many venues, for example, in Portuguese immigrants' plans to build a monument in São Paulo to the seventeenth-century *bandeiras*, which they abandoned after local nationalists objected on the grounds that the *bandeirantes* belonged to Brazil, not Portugal, and replaced with plans to erect a "Monumento à Raça." Of course, São Paulo's now-famous monument to the bandeiras was not completed until 1954 and the monument to the "Raça" was never built, but such initiatives gave nationalists, Lusophiles, and Lusophobes plenty of opportunities to discuss what Brazilians should think of their historic and contemporary relationship with Portugal and the Portuguese. Few were quite as urgent, and none touched as many people and places, however, as did the Lisbon–Rio de Janeiro raid.

A few commentators saw in the raid confirmation of their own negative views of Portugal and the Portuguese presence in Brazil, such as the editors of *Gil Blas*, who doubted whether the raid could be considered successful and depicted its celebration in Brazil as proof of the unhealthy influence Portuguese immigrants held in the country's port cities.[76] Arthur Gaspar Vianna afforded Cabral and Coutinho grudging respect in the magazine, but argued that Brazilians must beware of attempts to use the raid to conflate the Brazilian and Portuguese peoples. He alleged that the raid "was cover for a strike at nationalism," an attempt to replace "brazileirismo" (Brazilianism) with "luso-brazileirismo."[77] Whether this was the intent of the Portuguese government, the aviators, Portuguese immigrants, or Lusophile Brazilians, an emphasis on the Portuguese influence on Brazilian culture and nationality was indeed a theme developed by many admirers, despite Vianna's warnings.

Unsurprisingly, the *Revista da Semana*, run by the Portuguese Carlos Malheiro Dias (himself one of the chief targets of *Gil Blas*'s criticism), did much to promote the idea. Among other contributions, it called the aircraft flown by Coutinho and Cabral "the Hydroplane of the Raça" and published many features about the raid that were produced by the Portuguese journalists assigned to cover it.[78] It also published a number of pieces by Brazilian writers who reinforced the notion. For example, as Marquez de Denis wrote in his column, the aviators embodied the bravery that was "one of the beautiful and manly characteristics of the Raça."[79] He argued that Brazil honored and perpetuated "the intelligence and the virility" of the mother country, and the visit of the aviators was a reminder that the relationship between Brazil and Portugal was indissoluble, regardless of political sovereignties. "Capitão X" went farther, writing that the raid was "the reaffirmation of the worthiness of *our* raça" and calling Brazilians "the youngest branch" of the "Portuguese raça" rather than a distinct nation in its own right.[80] During a period when some Portuguese and Brazilian citizens were promoting a project of confederation or other formal association between their countries, the fact that Capitão X was a Brazilian soldier would have been especially concerning to nativists like Vianna, as would the fact that the "captain" was far from alone in his reading of the raid.[81]

Many Brazilian publications and other Brazilian commentators joined the *Revista* in making the case for the "racial" significance of the raid and the continuing importance of the Portuguese legacy for Brazil in its second century. For example, as *Careta* tried to explain why the raiders had garnered a reception that it characterized as "spontaneous and unanimous" with few recent parallels, it said the celebrations showed how wrong were Lusophobe nativists, Brazilians of "little sense," who saw tension and rivalry between Portuguese and Brazilians "which never existed," and that instead the raid and the local response showed that there were two countries but only one "brotherly emblem." It argued that the Rio de Janeiro public understood that Cabral and Coutinho had accomplished a great feat of aviation, and, just as important, that it wanted to express "its Latin pride, for we all belong to the same Raça that makes its conquests as poets and lovers, and discovers reality through its dreams."[82]

Similarly, *O Malho* said the raid demonstrated "the never-belied worth of the Portuguese people, whose children we are," and this was evidence that the anti-Portuguese sentiment cultivated by the nativists was a "foolish and ridiculous campaign." Instead what Brazilians needed to do was strengthen their relationship with Portugal, "with which we must walk together towards a noble destiny, among the most worthy."[83] In Recife, where the scale of celebrations more than matched those in the capital, most probably because of the number of Portuguese immigrants resident in the city and the fact that the city was the aviators' first stop on the mainland, writers used the raid to remind their compatriots that even as theirs was a distinct nation, it was still the "daughter of Portuguese blood, of Portuguese genius, of the Portuguese soul!" Furthermore, their national character had "as its principal part the Portuguese raça," and, within Brazilians ran the "blood of the same Raça, for within our veins run the cells that carry the bravery, the audacity, and the temerity of the navigational heroes of yesteryear and of today's fearless aviators!"[84]

As this last quotation suggests, the preoccupation of many commentators was to use the raid to highlight the strengths and value of that supposedly shared "race." It was not only Sacadura Cabral and Gago Coutinho who were bold, audacious, and brave—it was the Portuguese people itself and, through the Portuguese, the Brazilian nation. This was urgently important during a period in which eugenic science purported to demonstrate that Brazil's Iberian heritage would condemn the nation to backwardness and inferiority. The raid helped Brazilians combat not only the nativism of *Gil Blas* and other Lusophobes, *O Malho* said, but also those who doubted Brazil's potential because of its racial makeup. Cabral and Coutinho "puts into magnificent relief the marvelous qualities of our raça, doubted by many skeptical souls."[85] The raça was "almost always judged poorly by biased pessimists," but the aviators had shown that Brazilians ought to be optimistic for the future; the allegedly inherent strengths Brazil carried with it as the child of Portugal were resources it would need to become a great nation.[86] Crucially, according to their admirers the jangadeiros provided their own proof of the "marvelous qualities" of the nation, a proof that was if anything even more important than that provided by Cabral and Coutinho, because their provenance, their race, and their class marked them out as exactly the kind of Brazilians over whom racial pessimists most worried.

The centenary celebrations took place during a period when, as scholars like Julyan G. Peard and Nancy Leys Stepan have shown, some Brazilians were beginning to reassess the lessons of Eurocentric eugenics, rejecting strict racial determinism that purported to condemn Brazil and its people to backwardness and underdevelopment.[87] The anxieties of earlier generations persisted, however, showing up, for example, in planners' attempts to use the exposition and other centenary events to educate attendees on the best practices of hygiene, childrearing, and nutrition (see fig. 2.4).[88] As James Wadsworth and Tamera Marko argue, even where organizers attempted to tell a story of progress and modernity, as in the children's museum inaugurated as part of the centenary festivities, their fears about Brazil's poverty, its climate, and, especially "the proliferation of so-called of inferior races" among its population led them to use the celebrations to call for much more aggressive state intervention into child welfare and childrearing.[89]

In public discourse, commentators often distilled this fear and pessimism by referencing Jéca Tatú, Monteiro Lobato's fictional portrayal of provincial and mixed-race Brazilians as uneducated, uncouth, and unhealthy. By 1922 Jéca had become ubiquitous in Brazilian discussions of the nation and its people, often used as a shorthand for Brazilian backwardness and as a warning about Brazil's destiny if it did not modernize. Into an atmosphere at once hopeful and worried came the jangadeiro raiders, however, and some said the jangadeiros were proof against the idea of Jéca Tatú. Others used them and Jéca to tell a different story of Brazil: unspoiled by the affected modernity of the capital and other cities, Jéca Tatú could redeem Brazil and save it from a decadent present and future. The jangadeiros and other embodiments of Jéca could do so because of their allegedly inborn racial strength and an extraordinary resilience produced by their confrontation with Brazil's particular environmental challenges, making the raids a means by which to challenge the assumptions of those who questioned the value and potential of the Brazilian people and the circumstances of Brazil's climate and geography.

Thus, in a poem on the front page of the *Jornal do Brasil* that celebrated the jangadeiros, "the voice of the people" announced Brazil's pride in the fishermen and their strength, bravery, and energy. The narrator said the jangadeiros showed that Brazilians were not as pessimists depicted them and that the idea that "the people are Jéca" was slander. Instead, the jangadeiros proved, "guaranteed, with certainty," Brazilians' greatness and their worth, whatever the naysayers said.[90] The *Correio da Manhã* allowed that some Brazilians might have "congenital defects" associated with Jéca Tatú, but the "incomparable jangadeiros" showed that many who might seem at first glance to fit the image of the Brazilian as "lazy and incapable" had been "severely" misjudged. For these Brazilians, and the nation as a whole, the jangadeiros had rendered a great service, proving that, regardless of appearances and despite stereotypes, "not everything is *jecataturismo*."[91] And the editors of the magazine of the Confederação Geral dos Pescadores do Brasil, which took a leading role in hosting the fishermen in Rio de Janeiro, called those who broadcast the image of Jéca Tatú cowards who vanished when the jangadeiros arrived in the Guanabara Bay and proved theirs was a "false view." The editors saw the raids as confirmation of their view of the strength, courage, and patriotism of Brazil's fishermen and all its working people, and imagined the raiders as delivering a combative message to the country's pessimists, that "Brazil does not have Jecas! What it has are brave and worthy men; in the backlands each man is a field captain, on the shores each one a helmsman, a hero!"[92]

Other commentators accepted the figure of Jéca, but used the jangadeiros to reimagine him. *O Malho* highlighted the jangadeiros' courage and combated the prejudices of urban dandies in a cartoon depicting a jangada flying the Brazilian flag as it sailed on stormy seas, the scene narrated by a coarsely dressed male figure pointing to the boat and addressing readers directly, saying, "Dandies! It's Jeca Tatú there within!" The cartoon was titled "When he wants to . . . ," implying that Jéca and his like possessed the character and capacity for great deeds, perhaps even more so than their well-to-do, sophisticated compatriots, and would produce such deeds when given the opportunity, but on their own terms.[93] Benjamin Costallat wrote that he had been one of those ignorant urbanites, and that the jangadeiros had opened his eyes, showing him that Jéca Tatú was much different than many had assumed. The fishermen proved Jéca was, Costallat wrote, "a hero in the guise of a rogue."

It was time for Cariocas and other urbanites to rethink their prejudices, and for the jangadeiros and others like them to fulfill their rightful roles in making Brazil, and so Costallat called on Jéca to "take off the mask" and "rise up! On your feet!"[94]

For all these commentators and more, Jéca Tatú was a touchstone of their readers' stereotypes and prejudices about Brazilians like the jangadeiros, and an entry point to using the raids of the jangadas to elaborate a more hopeful and confident discussion of citizenship, race, and national character.[95] Some commentators spoke and wrote of the jangadeiros' experience and their intelligence and ingenuity in making the journey to Rio de Janeiro, qualities without which their courage and strength would be admirable, but not useful.[96] Much more often, though, admirers explained the jangadeiros in terms of race and nature. For urban well-to-do commentators, part of the appeal of the jangadeiros was that they seemed untrained and uncultivated, examples of a raw and latent human potential that Brazil possessed and too many doubted. This was the main theme writers and speakers in the capital developed in discussing the jangadeiros, and it was echoed by their counterparts in the regions from which the raiders had come; it was what made their accomplishments not only interesting, but meaningful.

According to *Careta*, the jangadeiros showed what real patriotism looked like, for having neither "pretty words" nor "pompous verses" they risked their lives by making the raids to honor the nation in its centenary. They thereby revealed essential truths about the whole nation, as "today they embody all of the heroism of the Brazilian people." They were, the magazine said, "men of action, full of a new energy, peerless, a robust raça forming; dreaming, it is true, and sentimental, but truly strong, because this same prodigious nature which provides them with reasons to dream gives them creative energy and prepares their souls for heroic efforts." The jangadeiros, these "heroes of the sunlit lands," proved that the Brazilian people was "indomitable and proud," shaped by its environment, and this lesson would endure far beyond 1922.[97] The congressman Maranhão made a similar argument, and spoke of the "instinctive will and inner strength," which he depicted as a natural response to the conditions of their life confronting the sea, and which drove the jangadeiros to undertake the raids.[98]

Numerous commentators discussed and explained the jangadeiros explicitly in racial terms, such as the *Correio da Manhã* writer who referenced the myth of the three races and called them "authentic representatives of our raça, which grew from the forging of the black man, the Indian, and the civilized." This made the jangadeiros "true sons of the Brazilian land."[99] Referencing this "forging," the press in the capital tended to refer to the jangadeiros as "caboclos," using a conveniently vague term often used by early twentieth-century Brazilians to refer to mixed-race people, as well as Indians and even farm laborers. This was the refrain of the *Jornal do Brasil*'s poet, who called the jangadeiro raider a "daring caboclo," a "good caboclo," a "virile caboclo," and a "strong caboclo," among other appreciations; *O Brasil* called the jangadeiros from Rio Grande do Norte "courageous caboclos from the Northeast"; and for the president of the Confederação Geral dos Pescadores, they were "valiant caboclos."[100] In a long essay in *O Imparcial*, Hermes Fontes wrote that he saw deep meaning in the raids and the jangadeiros, saying, "They exemplify something important in today's Brazil." This "something" was a lesson in the inherent value of the Brazilian people, for the jangadeiros were neither sophisticated nor well supported, but were instead "primitives" who faced forbidding nature as well as poverty, ill health, illiteracy, and other challenges. "These bronzed caboclos," Fontes said, must be celebrated upon their arrival in the capital, for theirs was "*the* heroic moment" among all the events of the centenary.[101]

In fact (at least as revealed by contemporaneous photographs), the majority of the jangadeiros who conducted raids on Rio de Janeiro in 1922 seem to have been Afro-Brazilian, and, by Brazilian standards, black men. But many commentators called them "caboclos," following a timeworn tactic used by Brazilian commentators to navigate thorny racial questions and to efface the African influence on Brazil.[102] On one hand, calling the jangadeiros "caboclos" allowed contemporaries to acknowledge that these were not white men, and to allude to a larger, familiar discourse about race and culture in the same way that references to Jéca Tatú did. On the other hand, they used the term to downplay the influence of Afro-Brazilians on the Brazilian raça and elide the consequences this influence would mean for Brazil should the eugenicists and pessimists be correct.

While this was an approach used most often by writers and speakers in the capital, writers, editors, and speakers in the jangadeiros' home states employed the rhetoric of elision as well. For example, the Alagoas correspondent of the *Diario* referred to the jangadeiros as "the worthy and taciturn caboclos of Alagoas," and in his speech celebrating the completion of the Natalenses' raid, the official orator of their fishing cooperative did not mention the caboclo but did assert that the jangadeiros had proved "the value of the mestizo raça."[103] As much as Brazilian commentators wanted to celebrate the jangadeiros and what they seemed to signify for Brazil's present and future, some were also clearly uncomfortable with their racial profile. As with so many questions the centenary celebrations prompted, the appearance of the jangadeiros seems to have left many middle-class and well-to-do Brazilians conflicted, optimistic about their project of building the nation but dubious about some of Brazil's social realities. Many commentators used the image and figure of the caboclo and other rhetorical ploys to avoid confronting that ideological and metaphysical conflict.

Thus, commentators elaborated on their appreciation of the jangadeiros and the alleged racial meaning of their raids by depicting the fishermen as modest, humble, and unassuming. In contrast to the celebrity aviators who completed raids during the year of the centenary, whose accounts of their experiences filled innumerable newspaper columns and drew thousands to theaters, libraries, and halls, over and over again writers and speakers described the jangadeiros as men of few words, "simple" fishermen who did not consider themselves remarkable and who had little to say about their lives or the raids.[104] Some of the jangadeiros seem to have been perfectly willing to discuss their raids in detail and at length, but they were rarely given such opportunities. Some of them appear to have wanted or at least been willing to use the raids to their immediate benefit, but few commentators allowed for the possibility of their agency in this regard. Instead editors and writers, event organizers, and politicians insisted the fishermen were stoic and nigh on silent, and preferred to speak *for* the jangadeiros. Commentators decided that the jangadeiros were "humble" and uninterested in fame, and their deeds heroic but unconscious feats of patriotism and bravery, rather than feats accomplished by well-trained experts of sail and sea. The jangadeiros were thereby made more useful, for it meant the meaning of their raids required the intervention of their more lettered and powerful compatriots, whose leadership was necessary if the Brazilian people were to realize the promise suggested by the fishermen's allegedly instinctive courage. In much the same way that commentators seem to have preferred the jangadeiros to be convenient caboclos rather than complicated, racially worrying Brazilians, admirers preferred to think of the raiders not as actual and individual people but as objects of the hopes and plans of would-be nation builders. So they must be, as *Careta* put it, "anonymous."

Of course, the jangadeiro raiders were not anonymous, and we do know many of their names, for at least a few writers, editors, and speakers made note of them, but it would have been an attentive reader or listener who learned them in 1922.[105] Rather than presenting them as individuals, contemporary writers and speakers simply described them as jangadeiros, fishermen or *raidmen*, occasionally mentioning their regions or native states. Still, those raiders who did not fit the quickly developed public image of the raiders as fishermen from the North and

Northeast, such as those from Rio Grande do Sul and São Paulo, rarely figured in the public conversation about the raids, even in their home states. Writers and speakers referred to them in collective terms and broad generalities, which never governed discussions of the raiders who arrived by airplane, bicycle, or on foot. These other raiders were never "anonymous," but Benjamin Costallat called the jangadeiros "great, nameless heroes." *O Imparcial* told the jangadeiros from Alagoas who arrived in Rio de Janeiro in November, "Your names will be fixed in the greatest pages of History," but the paper did not actually see fit to print those names.[106] About those same Alagoanos, Congressman Costa Rego gave a speech in the Chamber of Deputies calling on the body to acknowledge their raid, but he did not know what to call them. Instead, they were "these brave but anonymous Alagoanos (so anonymous that I still do not know their names)."[107]

Practicalities may help to explain this tendency, insofar as aviators like Cabral, Coutinho, Hinton, and Anésia Pinheiro Machado were already public figures before their raids and the sheer number of fishermen who journeyed to the capital in 1922—over fifty by the end of the centenary year—would have made it difficult for writers and speakers to acknowledge every one in their discussions of the raids. But it also seems to have been a choice made by writers and orators, since beside brave, strong, and resilient, the most common description of the jangadeiros in 1922 was that they were "humble." They were "our humble Brazilian brothers," "humble oarsmen and sailors," "a group of humble and obscure Brazilians," "the most humble people" of the Northeast, "humble and brave defenders of our coasts," "humble men of the sea," and, interestingly, "humble and proud fishermen."[108]

One telling example can be found in a story on the jangadeiros in Rio de Janeiro's *Correio da Manhã*, one of the few to take care to name many of the jangadeiros. The reporter began the piece by quoting Paulo Vianna, the president of the Confederação Geral dos Pescadores in the capital, who often spoke on their behalf at public events and who cautioned against expecting from the fishermen "the well-phrased comment or correct speech."[109] The reporter reinforced Vianna's point by stating that the acknowledged leader of the jangadeiros from Rio Grande do Norte, Benjamin Alves de Mendonça, "speaks in monosyllables." Here Vianna and the *Correio* reporter were echoing a perspective common in the contemporary press, for example in the comment by the *Revista da Semana* that the meaning of the jangadeiros' raids needed to be interpreted by others, because theirs were "silent expressions."[110] But these were odd assertions, since much of the *Correio* story relied on long quotations from Mendonça (called Benjamin by the reporter), who seems to have been more than happy to discuss in detail the jangadeiros' decision to make the raid and their experiences during the journey, as well as his experience in making the same journey in 1899, which suggests he, at least, may have approached the raid with plenty of forethought.[111] But Mendonça's facility in talking about the raid did not fit the narrative that emerged about the jangadeiros any better than did their knowledge and practice in becoming master sailors.

It suited journalists, politicians, and other commentators to think of the jangadeiros as anonymous and humble, intuitively brave and inherently strong, their accomplishment to be explained not by planning, training, or intellect but by the qualities Vianna told the reporter he should seek to learn from them instead of facts, narrative, or eloquence: "courage, patriotism, fraternity, and naïve but brilliant heroism."[112] Thus, Mendonça spoke of the raiders' discussions about what to call the jangadas, which they originally named for Columbus's three ships and might indicate their sense of the ambition of what he called their "odyssey." But the reporter wrote that the names were proof of "the simplicity of the good northern people" because they seemed to him to communicate the fishermen's naïveté about the power of naming to guarantee the raid's success. Mendonça and his companions spoke of their observation of the winds; the careful measurements they made throughout the journey of sea depths using plumb lines and the adjustments they made according to the readings; and the measures they undertook when one of the three jangadas went missing. But the reporter referred to the fishermen as stereotypical examples of "the caboclo of the North," who, in his words, was not a thinker or a planner but a "romantic" who in the face of danger "prefers to sing." And there was plenty of evidence of the fishermen's sense of the attention and esteem they had won by making the raids. The jangadeiros from Sergipe made a special visit to the offices of the *Correio* to tell their story. The Cearenses stated that part of the reason for their raid was to participate in the nautical parade that constituted part of the government's plans for the centenary. And the raiders participated in many public events celebrating their journeys, from the parade down Avenida Rio Branco to festivities at the presidential palace, at the grounds of the exhibition, and upon their return to their hometowns. Still, figures like Vianna and the *Correio* reporter insisted on depicting the raiders as humble, unambitious, and uninterested in attention.

This discourse seems to have been fueled by particular assumptions about class and gender—certainly the difference between the "scientist" aviators and the "humble" jangadeiros seems at least partly a distinction based on social class, and gendered language often inflected discussions of the raiders and their "manly courage."[113] Above all it was shaped by

Brazilians' assumptions and also their anxieties and hopes about how the country's racial constitution affected its past and how it would shape the future. They saw in the raids of the centenary performances of race and nation, and found in them evidence for optimism about the country's "three races" and their capacity to make Brazil the country they hoped it could be. Still, even as admirers claimed the raids filled them with confidence, in their celebrations of the raiders they also demonstrated their continued worry over racial questions, especially in regard to the roles nonwhite people should play in building the national community. They thus made the centenary a venue for a racial reckoning that was tense and conflicted, at once relieved and anxious, hopeful and doubtful. Furthermore, as the *Correio* reporter suggested when he referred to the jangadeiros as typical examples of the "caboclo of the North," Brazilians' thinking about the racial meaning of the raids was also freighted with their worries and assumptions about the country's different and distinctive regions.

Region and Nation

One of the characteristics that distinguished the raid phenomenon from other performances and celebrations of the centenary year was its embodiment of distance and its particular rendering of Brazilian places and regions. As Todd Diacon shows in his work on Cândido Mariano da Silva Rondon and his efforts to bring telegraph communications to the country's interior, many Brazilians in the early twentieth century were deeply concerned with challenges related to the country's size and scale. Diacon argues that the national government viewed as an urgent necessity the "incorporation of faraway lands and people," which he calls "quite possibly [its] primary activity" during the era of the First Republic.[114] The centenary celebrations reflected this concern in various ways, for example, in organizers' provision of venues for Rondon and his commissioners to introduce their work at the exhibition, which itself was organized around showcasing the productive capacities of each state and territory. What the raiders helped do was to give contemporaries evocative and romantic performances of space and distance, drawing attention to what for many Brazilians were little-known and sometimes mysterious regions without actually disturbing the cities of the Southeast from their positions at the center of national life; after all, almost every one of the raids ended in Rio de Janeiro.

References to place were ubiquitous in coverage and conversation surrounding the raids, and the distances traveled by the various raiders were among commentators' favorite subjects. In one of many, many examples, *O Jornal* made sure to tell its readers that the Fernando de Noronha archipelago, which few knew well but which figured prominently in the unfolding of the Cabral–Coutinho raid, was 340 nautical miles, or, the paper pointed out helpfully, more than 630 kilometers, from the even less well-known São Pedro and São Paulo archipelago, while Fernando de Noronha lay 291.5 nautical miles, or 539 kilometers, from Recife, the raiders' first stop on the mainland (see fig. I.2).[115] Similarly, organizers of the parade honoring the jangadeiros in Rio de Janeiro placed placards atop the trucks carrying the sailors and their jangadas; these identified each group's home state and the distance they traveled to arrive in the capital, in both nautical miles and kilometers.[116] Another approach was that of the *Diario de Pernambuco*, which informed readers that Hinton, Martins, and their companions at one point touched down in the Baía Formosa, which it identified as lying off the coast of Rio Grande do Norte, "at approximately 6 degrees and 18 minutes of southern latitude and 8 degrees and 10 minutes of eastern longitude from the Rio de Janeiro meridian. It is formed by the falls of the Curimatahú River a few kilometers from the town of Canguaretama."[117]

These calculations may or may not have meant much to readers and parade watchers beyond the notion that the raiders came from far away. But they also seem to have served a similar purpose to the fetish for technical language writers and speakers demonstrated in their discussion of the airplanes flown by centenary raiders. In the latter case, highly technical descriptions of aircraft matched contemporaries' use of the air raids as part of their discursive and substantive project to promote the country's modernization through advanced technologies like air travel and rapid communications. Similarly, the constant recitation of exacting data about distance and geography was complemented by other, qualitative demonstrations of contemporaries' desire to use the raids and the centenary as a whole to know Brazil and its regions more fully, and, they hoped, to draw those regions closer together in order to build a stronger nation.

Beside narrating the journeys, reciting the distances the raiders traveled, and providing details of the technologies they employed, editors helped readers experience the raids by publishing an extraordinary number of photographs and drawings to accompany their features. Dozens of photographs and other images of the raiders depicted the crafts they flew, rode, and sailed, and the often-gigantic crowds that gathered to celebrate them, as well as maps identifying the routes each group took as they traveled to Rio de Janeiro and every stop along the way and images and descriptions of the places they visited. In the case of the raids made by air, these sometimes included photographs taken by the raiders

1.5. Arrival of the *Sampaio Corrêa II* in Rio de Janeiro, 8 February 1923. From the collection of Benjamin J. Burns. Courtesy of Beverly H. Burns.

themselves, which gave readers rare aerial views of cities and towns along Brazil's coast. Illustrated magazines like *Careta* and *Cigarra* covered the raids in this manner, but so too did broadsheet newspapers. Papers in the cities the raiders visited usually gave over the entire front page on the day after their arrival to large-format photographs of the raiders and their crafts, the crowds awaiting them, and long-distance views of the scene and the city.[118] By 1922 Brazilian newspapers and magazines were becoming increasingly dependent on photographs to fill column space, and the raids were particularly well suited to the approach, because many of the raiders carried cameras with them and because of the novelty of both the technologies aviators used and the views they were able to share with the reading public.

The *Revista da Semana* specialized in publishing pieces like this, as the Portuguese editors of the magazine followed their exhaustive coverage of their compatriots' feat with lesser but still extensive coverage of other raids. For example, "The First Flight from Portugal to Brazil" was a multipart narrative of the Lisbon–Rio de Janeiro raid, each installment offering a detailed description of one leg of the journey and illustrated with descriptions and photographs of each place where Cabral and Coutinho stopped.[119] The magazine paid special attention to Fernando de Noronha, for example, in a short history of Amerigo Vespucci's visit to the archipelago along with photographs and drawings of its impressive coastline and landmarks from the colonial period.[120] Later, it also published a series dedicated to the New York–Rio de Janeiro raid, "Connecting the Three Americas by Air," again with descriptions of the journey and dozens of photographs, including images taken by the aviators themselves, such as one taken by the expedition mechanic from 1,000 meters above Recife.[121] Another kind of novelty came in a series of photographs provided to the magazine by Wanderlino Nogueira, taken during his walk from Salvador to the capital and introducing readers to towns like Rio de Contas, Estiva, Camamú, and Canavieiras (all in Bahia) and Rio Bonito (in the state of Rio de Janeiro).[122]

Through such means admirers asserted that the raids were important in helping Brazilians know their country, and they asserted that the raids' lessons in geography were also moral lessons. For example, in another of the items introducing readers to Fernando de Noronha, Afonso Celso argued that Brazilians' neglect of the archipelago was a national failing. He said they must take advantage of the attention brought to the islands by the Lisbon raid and make sure it was Brazilians rather than foreigners who would realize the potential of the archipelago, "a wasted gem."[123] Another lesson was to be found in the example of Euclides Pinto Martins, who many commentators presented as proof of the strength and particular character of the Latin and of the Brazilian, and who was of special interest to residents of Ceará, Rio Grande do Norte, and Pernambuco, who claimed him as a native son and presented him as embodying their own distinctive qualities.[124]

The idea that the raids provided a moral lesson in the country's geography was most prevalent in coverage and discussion of the jangadeiros. Commentators used the fishermen to highlight what Brazilians did and did not know about their country and to advance the argument that understanding Brazil's regional identities was necessary to any successful project to build the nation. This was, for example, one of the main themes of the well-received speech given by Alberto Maranhão celebrating his fellow Potiguares. Maranhão focused his attention on the fishermen as well as the backlanders of the Northeast and claimed that the realization of their particular forms of "national fortitude" was essential to improving Brazil. He also made sure to name several other examples of "collective bravery" that Brazil's leaders must find ways to engage and enlist, attempting to cater to his colleagues' pride in their own regions:

> When I demand recognition and justice for these two forms of national courage, which are written onto the land of the Northeast—the courage of the backlander and the courage of the fisherman—I also want to join to them the other great forms of courage of the South and the far North and of the interior—of the mountaineer, of the farmer, of the rubber tapper—of the mountains of the central regions—of the Gaúcho of the South—of the miners—of the men of the pampas, and those who triumph over malaria in the ominous green hell where our great future resides. There are innumerable national strengths, and all of them ought to be realized, with care and with justice![125]

Amid commemoration planners' attempts to depict Brazil as a unified whole—through a short-lived plan to abolish state flags and other regional identity markers, for example—Maranhão spoke of a nation of parts. He demanded acknowledgment of the particular strengths and character of Brazil's regions and argued that this was the chief significance of the raids undertaken by the jangadeiros. Conflating the forms of "courage" found in Brazil's regions with the lives and labor of the working classes, he posited that the raids' most important contribution was to remind Brazilians like his congressional colleagues and the inhabitants of the more developed Southeast of the existence of those other regions and the roles their inhabitants must play if Brazil were to achieve its lofty destiny.

Perhaps more interesting, it was not only proud fellow natives and residents of the jangadeiros' home states who made such arguments. Both the editorial writer for *O Jornal* and Benjamin Costallat in the *Jornal do Brasil* said that the jangadeiros reminded residents of the capital to pay closer attention to their country and compatriots. The former said that the raiders' demonstration of strength, bravery, and audacity "was a real surprise to the civilized people who walk our avenues" and that the fishermen were among millions of Brazilians "who work and live forgotten on the coasts, in the interior, and in the backlands," ignored by more cultured Brazilians, who were "more or less well assimilated to the European civilization that we worship."[126] In a similar vein, Costallat admitted, "I do not know the North." He went on to say, "I am like many Brazilians, a stranger in my own land" but "I have the happy certainty that Brazil is not only Avenida Central, land of the dandy, not only the scoundrel asphalt that I walk each day."[127]

Drawing from the same set of devices as their comments on the importance of tradition and the raids' lessons about race, such writers also asserted that the jangadeiros came from the parts of Brazil where the nation would find the resources to build a better country. While cities like Rio de Janeiro were "only the superficial Brazil," according to the *Jornal* writer, there was another Brazil, "larger, stronger, more real, though less sophisticated, because little remembered by the cities and especially by this proud and vain capital." While in the cities "the refinements of civilization improve us or ennervate us," in the backlands, in the forgotten littoral, and in the interior "resides the certainty of a surprising strength, which will one glorious day produce the great Brazil of tomorrow."[128] Costallat also spoke of "the true Brazil," which he associated with the coffee farms of São Paulo, the ranches of Rio Grande do Sul, the forests of the Amazon, and the beaches of the North, from whence the raiders came. Costallat understood the fishermen's lives as determined by the region's particular geography and climate: the beaches where they lived were "infinitely white, infinitely melancholic, where the coconut tree is an aspiration to the beauty of the skies and where man, small, dark, robust, was born face to face with the sea, ready to confront it, ready to take on the eternal challenge, as if to say—'I am here!'" The jangadeiros had proved the worth of such Brazilians and their capacity for helping the nation achieve great ends, and it was up to their compatriots in urban areas to listen to their proclamation and learn from their example.[129]

All these commentators used the raids to work out their understanding of Brazilian reality, mapping onto the country's geography their own interpretations of the nation's strengths and weaknesses. On one hand, by idealizing the periphery they were challenging the dominant discourse of the centenary and of the First Republic as a whole, which was closely associated with the development of cities of the Southeast and South. On the other hand, however, they continued to arrogate to themselves the responsibility for interpreting the meaning of the raids and for directing the nation's destiny. For example, the *Jornal* editorialist insisted that the principal reason for the underdevelopment of the periphery was the ignorance and neglect of the national capital and the cities. And Costallat was sure that his imagined Jéca Tatú, while not the rascal of the stereotype, still "does not know what you are capable of." His imagined jangadeiro raider had no sense of the scale of his accomplishment, "as unaware of your prowess as of your worth."

This was the discourse of the raids of the jangadeiros, at once awed and condescending, understood according to the ideological requirements of writers, politicians, and activists. These figures used the example of the jangadeiros for many purposes, not least to help them articulate their ideas about what the concept of region meant in modern Brazil. At the time of the raids figures like Costallat were still conflating the North and what is now called the Northeast. Alberto Maranhão and others, meanwhile, were already delineating between the two, making a distinction that became important and remains so. Durval Albuquerque shows how the "invention of the Northeast" unfolded, as politicians, intellectuals, and artists worked to define it as a discrete region, the repository of "authentic" Brazilian traditions that had been forgotten in more developed areas. For its advocates, establishing the Northeast as a distinctive region was much more than a semantic exercise, for among other substantive ends it justified the maintenance of its traditional hierarchies and its claims for special treatment on the national political scene, as well as helping to explain and legitimize northeasterners' supposedly typical rebelliousness. The region's "inventors" built on earlier efforts, such as Euclides da Cunha's depiction of the backlander and his allegedly emblematic strength, and the work of regional politicians in the late nineteenth century to lobby the national state for assistance in confronting persistent drought conditions. Still, as Albuquerque shows, much of the most influential work to define the region came in the second half of the 1920s, led by well-known ideologues like Gilberto Freyre and José Lins do Rego.[130]

In 1922 neither the notion of a difference between the North and Northeast, nor the exact boundaries between the two, nor the significance of the designations was a settled matter. But the project of invention was underway, and it seems clear that the centenary celebrations contributed to it. In Pernambuco, for example, local partisans wove together old and new regional identifiers as they marked the anniversary. They drew on both the traditional image of the state as the "Lion of the North" and the symbolic power of the centenary, with its implications of liberty and resistance, to develop a regionalist argument against the decision of the national government to send federal forces to intervene as the state's 1922 gubernatorial succession descended into violence. Meanwhile, Pernambuco's civic leaders also hosted two events explicitly designated as "northeastern" and which competed with centenary events in the national capital: a sports tournament for regional athletes perceived to have been excluded from Rio de Janeiro's "Olympic" games and the Congresso da Lavoura do Nordeste Brasileiro, a conference and agriculture exhibition that opened in January 1923, during the same period in which the national and international exhibitions were running.[131]

The centenary raids also helped develop the idea of the Northeast. The Lisbon and New York raids focused the nation's attention on the region, with each group not only traveling through it but spending much more time there than they had anticipated. Residents claimed Martins and used his participation in the New York raid and memory of the contributions of Bartolomeu de Gusmão to posit the notion that the region was central to the history of aviation. And, because the majority of the fishermen raiders came from the region, many commentators depicted the raids as a northern, and especially a northeastern, accomplishment. Moreover, comments like those by Costallat and the editorial writer for *O Jornal* that defined the jangadeiros as representatives of the "real" Brazil fit neatly into the discourse of the inventors of the Northeast, depicting their region as the one that protected the nation's most distinctive, "authentic" traditions.

This is not to say that there was a direct line from the raids to the arguments of activists like Freyre and Lins do Rego and their many successors. But it is clear that the notion of a distinctive Northeast was being articulated in the years before Freyre's famous 1926 *Manifesto regionalis-*

ta, and that the raids of 1922 helped Brazilian thinkers and writers conceive and articulate some of the challenges and opportunities the idea of the Northeast presented. The centenary served as a liminal space for the working out of Brazilians' ideas about place and region; about the Northeast and the nation as a whole; about Brazil and its peoples and how a gigantic and diverse country should be conceived and could be organized. The raiders of the centenary played an essential role in this regard. They performed and embodied the concepts of region and nation, and gave Brazilians a tangible set of symbols and stories that they used to think about how to make Brazil a nation united, even as regional differences and inequalities remained.

Beyond the symbolic significance contemporaries imbued them with, the raids of the centenary did produce practical and substantive consequences. There were the mapping and other "scientific" contributions the raiders made, such as the lessons that Hinton and Martins learned about how the prevailing winds of the Northeast affected air travel and what Luigi Longobardi purported to have learned in observing the Paraná and Paraguay Rivers.[132] There were the ways that natives of the jangadeiros' home states living in the capital, American expatriates, and, especially, Portuguese immigrants used the raids to knit their communities together and strengthen their ties to home—for example, Portuguese immigrants more than fulfilled what patriots called their "duty" to contribute to a fundraising campaign to purchase a hydroplane and offer it to the Portuguese navy in the name of their heroes.[133] There were the short-term political uses to which contemporaries put the raids, as with Maranhão's use of the jangadeiros' raids to attempt to gain support for his plan for a federal development program aimed at coastal communities.

The raiders also gained practical benefits from their journeys, most obviously in the form of cash prizes from the Brazilian government. The national government awarded such prizes in 1922 and 1923 for various accomplishments related to the centenary celebrations, and most of the raiders received cash awards, including the members of the Lisbon and New York raids, the crews of the jangadas, canoes, and other watercraft who completed the journey to the capital, and the cyclists from Rio Grande do Sul. Senator Antônio Azeredo explained his support for the prize for the fishermen by saying, "It is not a payment, but an incentive for Brazilians' qualities, so well exemplified by the accomplishment of the jangadeiros." Reinforcing the notion that the raiders—and perhaps especially the jangadeiros—were symbolic figures rather than individual citizens, Azeredo argued that this was an award for all Brazilians, only incidentally given to a few dozen specific Brazilian people.[134]

Of course, the raiders were not simply symbolic figures. Walter Hinton parlayed his celebrity in Brazil and the connections he forged there into employment as an aviator with a group conducting a geographic survey of the Amazon basin in 1924 and 1925.[135] Sacadura Cabral and Gago Coutinho both won significant promotions in the Portuguese navy, from captain-lieutenant to frigate captain and from captain of sea and war to vice admiral, respectively, among many other honors awarded them back home.

The jangadeiro raiders from Rio Grande do Norte were also able to capitalize on their newfound celebrity. While they were away from Natal, conflicts erupted over the leadership of their fishing cooperative and the administration of the city port. When dissident members of the cooperative attempted to install the journalist and labor activist (and future Brazilian president) João Café Filho as president in contravention of the organization's constitution, his opponents and the port captain called on the city police, who helped restore control of the group's headquarters to its "legal" directors. Café Filho and his partisans refused to give in, and the situation worsened. The cooperative's school remained closed for over a month due to teachers' fears about safety, and the dispute eventually descended into violence, including a gunfight, and the jailing of dozens. Amid this conflict, the raiders returned and helped confirm the legitimacy of the authorities who had served as their patrons and champions of the raid. They threw their support behind the "legal" directors in their struggle against Café Filho.[136] They also helped reinforce the position of the port captain Appio do Couto, whose involvement in the dispute had attracted criticism but who had done much to assist the raiders and helped lead the celebrations of their accomplishment upon their return. Couto surely welcomed the raiders' statement to the city's leading newspaper regarding the captain, "whom they supported and whose orders they were ready to follow."[137]

Still, while the raiders gained more than cash awards from their journeys, most contemporaries appear to have quickly forgotten their excitement and what had seemed like the urgent significance of the raids. Thus, while the populist Getúlio Vargas felt obliged to fulfill some of the demands made by the jangadeiros who journeyed from Ceará to Rio de Janeiro in 1941, in 1922 the assistance and development proposal advanced by Alberto Maranhão did not materialize. Memory of the air raids lingered somewhat longer, as commemorative volumes, renamed streets, and monuments maintained the reputation of the aviators, especially Cabral and Coutinho. Even there, however, the accelerating development and proliferation of aviation technology meant that within a few years even the most impressive of the air raids of 1922 would seem mundane, and the raid phenomenon as a whole had lost much of its hold on the public imagination by the end of the decade.

What lingered in Brazil was the imagining and reimagining the raids animated and the questions they raised. Some Brazilians said the raids demonstrated the wisdom of their commitment to development and Western modernity, while others insisted they demonstrated the power of Brazil's "authentic" traditions that should not be left behind as the nation met the future. The raids helped Brazilians think about who the Brazilian people were, about their character and capacities, and especially about how race and national origin should affect decisions about belonging, exclusion, and the proper roles of different kinds of people in building the national community. And the raids taught Brazilians about the country and its regions, reminding them of the significance and persistence of regional identity and tensions, even as many attempted to use the centenary to posit a unified and homogeneous nation. The raids did not resolve these tensions or provide definitive answers to these questions. Still, Brazilians and other residents of the country found them enormously compelling, for they used the raids to identify the precise nature of the challenges Brazil faced and found in them evocative language and absorbing stories that helped them think and talk about ways to resolve those challenges. The raids made the centenary more than a time of celebration; they made it a "time out of time" that encouraged the posing of crucial questions and the recognition of the urgent tensions that defined 1922 and the years to come, even if the raids themselves were forgotten.

Chapter 2

A Nation of Parts

The Centenary Exposition and Centenary Sports

One of the reasons commentators read deep meaning into the journeys undertaken by aviators, fishermen, cyclists, and pedestrians was that the travelers helped Brazilians and foreigners learn about the country and its people. As Sacadura Cabral and Gago Coutinho traveled from the São Pedro and São Paulo archipelago to the Fernando de Noronha islands, and from Recife to Rio de Janeiro, Brazilians learned about parts of the country they did not know. Thus, Benjamin Costallat's comment that the jangadeiros from Natal had helped him understand the "North" better, which in his estimation made their journey more than a demonstration of the fishermen's courage and resilience; the raid encouraged him to think about the country beyond the Southeast, beyond its cities and their claims of cosmopolitan modernity.

The sense that the centenary provided an opportunity and an obligation to know Brazil was one of the most prevalent themes of the celebrations of 1922. As Livia Rezende puts it in her analysis of the exhibition, organizers sought to use the fair to offer Brazilians "a series of object-lessons," and "the object to be learned by Brazilians was the nation itself."[1] Chapter 3 demonstrates that this sensibility helped drive more than usual interest in the country's history, as Brazilians explored the independence story and other historical episodes in hopes of understanding the character of their people as well as finding historical evidence to justify their own (often competing) outlooks on the country's present and future. As chapter 4 shows, immigrants and foreign residents sought to do the same, using the centenary to offer Brazilians historical and present-day proofs of their contributions to the country in order to validate their claims of belonging.

Understanding contemporaries' impulse to use the centenary to know the country more fully also goes a long way in explaining the meaning of the centenary's biggest events, including not only the centenary exhibition but also the medical, religious, and other congresses organized to coincide with it and the national and international sporting events planned to celebrate the great date. Of all the many events related to commemoration of the centenary, scholars have afforded these state-sponsored and -supported events the most attention, for good reason. These were the largest events of the centenary, in terms of scale, expense, and duration. Because they were guided by the national government, often in partnership with prominent private actors, local and regional governing bodies, and international organizations, understanding these events gives us a sense of the priorities and attitudes of many of Brazil's most powerful and well-connected figures. Organizers also aimed to involve both Brazilian and foreign audiences and participants, meaning the reach of the experience of the centenary could extend far beyond the national capital, where most of the events were situated. Thus, in the case of the most important of these official events, the centenary exposition opened on 7 September 1922 and closed to the public on 24 July 1923; it was organized by a commission appointed by the country's president but relied on the input and involvement of delegates and local governments representing every state and territory; it included exhibitors from across Brazil and thirteen other nations; and its attendance surpassed four million visitors, and millions more were aware of it through the extraordinary coverage afforded it by newspapers and magazines throughout Brazil and other participating countries.

Like those who oversaw other international fairs and exhibitions, the organizers of the centennial exposition adhered to a familiar script, conceiving of it as a chance to spread knowledge of and stoke interest in Brazil. Unsurprisingly, one of the main themes of this script was that Brazil was a nation unified, ordered, and committed to progress as defined by Western notions of modernity. Scholars such as Livia Rezende, Marly Silva da Motta, and Noah C. Elkin have described the ways in which the exhibition narrated this powerful and optimistic depiction and have demonstrated how it matched the expectations and ambitions of the national government and the cultural and social elite of the First Republic, many of whom saw the centenary as the perfect moment to

2.1. The centenary exposition at night. Photograph by Bippus Rio. Courtesy of the Instituto Moreira Salles.

announce that Brazil had come of age as a modern, cosmopolitan, confident nation.[2]

However, despite the hopes of organizers and their sponsors, the message was ambiguous, complicated, and sometimes conflicted. The official magazine of the exhibition acknowledged the challenge of balancing optimism and worry, knowledge and ignorance:

> What Brazilians need is to know their country better, to know it well, to throw light on all the corners of its territories, to keep their eyes open in all directions. Right here in our own country, there is much to see, much to learn, much to admire, many teachings that can and should be put to profitable use. All that has to be done is to view what goes on in Brazil with the proper attention, with understanding, with interest, with a sincere wish to possess an exact comprehension of our strength and our possibilities, as well as of our deficiencies and our evils.[3]

Organizers seem to have been more interested in advertising the country's strengths and possibilities than its deficiencies and evils, as might be expected, but they do appear to have been willing to make room for inquiry, and not only lessons. Thus, for example, on one hand, organizers were proud to be able to light up the exhibition grounds, inside and out, with the most modern electric light system yet installed in Brazil; they opened the fair with a welcoming speech by the country's president shared via the country's very first radio broadcast; and they offered visitors the opportunity to take short airplane rides over the city, a true novelty for most (see figs. 2.1 and 2.3). On the other hand, even as they hoped the exhibition campus would display a "national" school of architecture and design, they acknowledged the lack of consensus on what that style should be, so they constructed buildings designed by architects working in a variety of styles. Similarly, while they sought to demonstrate the progress of the entire country, and worked to ensure that every state in Brazil exhibited its products at the fair, they also had to acknowledge the country's uneven development and regional differences. The state displays were therefore wildly inconsistent, from the extraordinary breadth and size of the São Paulo section to the much smaller, more modest Rio Grande do Norte area. That is, the exhibition and other official and semi-official events displayed the tensions and complexities that the raids of the aviators and the jangadeiros had seemed to exemplify, and thus challenged the events' capacity to deliver the clear and confident messages organizers hoped to offer their domestic and foreign audiences.

Given that government-appointed administrators controlled these events much more than they could private and foreign activities like the raids, it is interesting that these tensions and complexities should have been put on display; after all, the commission appointed by the national government was able to organize the exhibition on an almost completely blank slate of new ground, in new buildings in downtown Rio de Janeiro. Still, the exhibition they produced did not tell an uncomplicated story of Brazil, but one of national unity and regional difference, of nostalgia mixed with forward-looking optimism, of nationalism and cosmopolitanism. The key to understanding this complexity seems to lie in the absence of a unanimous view on what Brazil was or who Brazilians were, even among event organizers, and, furthermore, as the editors of the exhibition magazine suggested, they came to understand they could not display one cohesive, unified view of the nation as it counted its hundredth year.

Instead, sometimes in purposeful ways and at other times, despite their intentions, the exhibition organizers and other Brazilians involved in planning and participating in centenary commemorations seem to have been as interested in questions as answers, using the centenary and its events to create spaces wherein participants could engage with fundamental challenges, of what Brazil had been, was, and could be, of who Brazilians were and could become, of knowing Brazil. Like Benjamin Costallat, event planners showed that they and many of their compatriots did not know Brazil, but that they believed the centenary and the events celebrating it could and should provide opportunities to begin to learn about it. More than any specific message, that is, they created spaces to bring Brazilians together, so that a country of parts and pieces could begin to become a nation unified. They were able to accomplish much in pursuit of this goal, but they also created spaces that exhibited, and, in some instances, exacerbated Brazilians' arguments about the nation, reinforcing divisions rather than bridging them.

Mapping Brazil at the Centennial Exhibition

In many respects the centenary exhibition was the culmination of generations of effort by civic leaders to use national and international fairs to realize the goal of making Brazil a modern nation on the Western model. The organizers of the great exhibitions, international exhibitions, and world's fairs of the late nineteenth and early twentieth centuries promised their events would provide concrete benefits, for example, in helping producers to reach future customers and potential investors. But Robert W. Rydell, Werner Plum, Paul Greenhalgh, and other scholars have shown that what distinguished these events from earlier efforts to organize trade and industrial fairs was that European and North American innovators made them into venues for the exhibition of their intellectual commitments and cultural values. Fairgoers found displays of agricultural and industrial products, and also artistic exhibitions, educational programs, and popular entertainments, these last two efforts exemplified in the people shows that put non-Western cultures on display for visitors' edification and amusement. The exhibitions were totalizing, universalizing experiences, attempts to bring the world into one place and make it legible amid modernity's dizzying changes and challenges, the experience carefully planned and highly ordered to produce a display of the rightness of capitalist expansion, Western hegemony, and social hierarchy.[4]

In great part because of their ideological character, Brazilians were eager to participate in these events. Jens Andermann has called them "a kind of trans-Atlantic rite of passage during which people and things entered the new, global time-space of capital," and organizers of Brazil's participation in international exhibitions understood them in just this way.[5] They hoped to use the fairs to generate attention for what they saw as the country's limitless economic potential and to prove to Europeans and North Americans that its civic and economic leaders were dedicated to the meaning of modernity as it was defined by the world's most advanced peoples, showing them that Brazil was ready to join in their "civilizing" projects. Brazilians' efforts were complicated, though, by the fact that they faced very different conditions than did their counterparts in the industrial West. Rezende demonstrates that organizers of Brazil's participation in foreign exhibitions acknowledged the country's underdevelopment by mounting displays of "the raw and the manufactured," telling a story that admitted to Brazil's "tropical" reputation but insisted that it could be "de-tropicalized" by foreign capital and industry. And they showed their awareness of Western attitudes toward the peoples of Latin America by presenting a Brazil without people, so that "'Brazilians' themselves were largely absent from the national representations seen abroad, especially those from working and peasant classes, black descendants and indigenous peoples."[6]

Organizers were particularly concerned about the opinions of foreign audiences, especially in the United States, France, and Britain, but they were also interested in how they could use Brazil's participation in these exhibitions to pursue their goals in the domestic context. As Sandra Jatahy Pesavento shows, in this regard organizers hoped to appeal to satisfied and well-to-do Brazilians who did not seem to understand the importance of embracing modernity, and they used the fairs to deliver the good news of capitalist development to economic leaders and policymakers at home, to insist on the urgent need to abolish slavery, to promote immigration, and to encourage the mechanization of agriculture, among other projects.[7] They aimed at such figures through their efforts to prepare for Brazil's participation in international exhibitions, which included not only political work to obtain government support and intensive propaganda campaigns to encourage producers to exhibit their wares but also the organization of preparatory expositions in regional capitals and in Rio de Janeiro. Familiarizing Brazilians with the practice and ideology of exhibition culture, these "national" expositions were carefully curated and closely controlled, helping organizers show their compatriots the nation as they preferred to imagine it and polishing the image before it was exported abroad.[8] Brazilians also demonstrated their sense of the utility of exhibition culture by organizing a number of other events focused on particular industries and subjects, such as the "Exposição Antropológica" of 1882, which made clear their commitment to the principles of Western social science.[9] However, in part because of the challenges of finance and transportation, which were especially urgent for expositions designed to prepare for the major international exhibitions, these events were often limited in scale.

Before 1922, Brazilians' most ambitious fair project was a national exhibition in 1908, which was made international by the inclusion of Portuguese exhibitors who were invited to participate because the nominal reason for the fair was to celebrate the centennial of the opening of Brazilian ports to international trade in 1808. The fair opened in August

2.2. Destruction of the Morro do Castelo. Photograph by Augusto Malta. Courtesy of the Instituto Moreira Salles.

and ran for three months, welcoming over one million paying visitors to pavilions displaying commercial, agricultural, and industrial products, as well as venues for music and theater performances, plastic arts exhibitions, a cinema, and a skating rink. Organizers boasted of the fair's "colossal proportions" and "opulence," especially in comparison with earlier exhibitions that, in their words, had been "mounted in cramped spaces."[10] They oversaw the construction of an entire exhibition campus in Rio de Janeiro's Urca neighborhood, including the kind of specially constructed, ephemeral architecture that characterized international exhibitions hosted in North America and Europe and allowed organizers to join physical space to the display of objects in the attempt to make the exhibition an immersive experience.[11]

The exhibition deepened Brazilians' experience of Western fair culture, its form and substance offering lessons in the republic's commitment to Progress. Moreover, though many of its constructions were designed not to endure, in practical and conceptual ways it had a lasting influence, for it contributed to the ongoing transformation of the city itself. This was a project most commonly associated with the tenure of Francisco Franco Pereira Passos, who served as mayor from 1902 to 1906 and oversaw a variety of interventions, including the renovation of the city's historic center along lines inspired by the modernization of Paris.[12] Passos's successors sustained the effort, not least in the 1908 exposition and, especially, when the city prepared to host the centennial exhibition and the other celebrations of 1922.

Carlos Sampaio was the mayor from 1920 to 1922, during which period he also served as the fair's general superintendent. Sampaio seems to have been less interested than was Passos in attempting to balance the city's historical roots with its doubtlessly cosmopolitan and dazzling future; therefore, even more than his predecessor he embraced the chance to remake the landscape so it accorded more fully with the requirements of transforming the city.[13] Most famously, this meant the complete demolition of the Morro do Castelo, the site where Estácio de Sá refounded the city after its recapture from French forces in 1567; by the twentieth century, it had become emblematic of the city's colonial inheritance, for good and ill. The scheme to demolish the hill opened up new space in the city center for modern construction and infrastructure development. It also provided infill for its expansion at water's edge, where the fairgrounds for the centenary exhibition would be constructed.

On the demolition site Rio de Janeiro's architects and engineers advanced the project to remake the city, and in the ensuing decades the newly claimed space allowed for the widening of streets to facilitate movement and the installation of new and larger buildings for government and cultural entities and commercial interests. In the meantime, Sampaio and his partners focused on the exhibition, which would provide a venue for the celebration of the centenary and the display of a winning image of a nation come of age. Carlos Kessel, Ruth Levy, and other scholars of the city and Brazilian architecture have done enormously valuable work in analyzing the exhibition site and its many constructions.[14] They demonstrate that organizers hoped to use the exhibition to go beyond the display of Brazil's wares and economic potential, seizing the opportunity for the construction of the fairgrounds to explore and define Brazilian identity in terms of architecture and design. Organizers therefore encouraged architects applying for the right to plan the exhibition's buildings to develop and employ a coherent design language that could be identified as authentically Brazilian, which accounts for the prevalence of the neocolonial style of many of the buildings constructed to house the exhibition. However, as Levy points out, organizers also afforded space for buildings that did not employ the neocolonial style. In fact, organizers accepted applications from architects who contributed both neocolonial and other designs in which they used entirely different approaches. That is, while they understood the exhibition—and the centenary as a whole—as an opportunity for the articulation of a clear national narrative, planners also acknowledged that such a narrative had yet to be composed, whether in the language of architecture or any other field.

Like other world's fairs, one of the hallmarks of the centenary exposition was that participating countries used its space and structures to exhibit their aims for the event, contemplating both home and foreign audiences. Organizers of Mexico's participation in the centenary used the fair to broadcast the nationalist perspective of the country's fledgling revolutionary government, erecting a pavilion inspired by the style typical of Hispanic Mexican traditional architecture and offering to Brazil the gift of a monument to the Mexica leader Cuauhtémoc.[15] Similarly, the Italian and Portuguese pavilions were designed according to styles accepted as typical of those countries, the former monumental and classical, the latter inspired by the elements associated with the reign of João V. Elsewhere, United States administrators took a different tack. Hoping to flatter Brazilian opinion, they worked with the North American Chamber of Commerce to erect a monument to Brazilian–American friendship and they oversaw the construction of a pavilion in what they said was a "Brazilian" style, though contemporaries do not seem to have been convinced of their success.[16]

Part of American planners' trouble was that Brazilian architects themselves disagreed on what a "typical" Brazilian construction should be. The architect Armando de Oliveira spoke for many of his contemporaries when he said in 1922, "It is urgent and necessary that we find our own style," one that had emerged as "a consequence of our own climate, our own culture, our own temperament."[17] For Oliveira and many others, including Carlos Sampaio, the answer to the challenge was to be found in the colonial period, in the purportedly unique ways that Portuguese builders adapted European architecture to the Brazilian context.[18] Among other features, they pointed to walls constructed of wood and clay, carved wooden door and window frames, painted ceramic tiles, and interior patios. Advocates said these features of colonial architecture gave Brazilians an authentic design language from which they could articulate a national architecture and thereby contribute to the promotion of a distinctive national identity.

The project of adapting the colonial approach to a style that could meet the requirements of modernity had been underway for some time before 1922, championed by influential figures including Oliveira and Sampaio and also the São Paulo–based Portuguese architect and engineer Ricardo Severo and the novelist and critic Mário de Andrade, who argued that, because of its authentically Brazilian roots and its attention to Brazilian needs and the Brazilian environment, the neocolonial was the most modern architectural style in Brazil, and indeed represented its "vanguard."[19] The centenary offered such advocates a rare opportunity to display the neocolonial style before an especially large audience. Thus, many of the Brazilian pavilions and other structures erected or adapted for the exhibition were neocolonial in style or exhibited neocolonial features; contemporaries categorized something like half of them as neocolonial, including the north-side entrance, the Palácio da Fiação, the Palácio das Grandes Indústrias, the Pavilhão das Pequenas Indústrias, and the Pavilhão de Caça e Pesca (the pavilions for textiles, large- and small-scale industry, and hunting and fishing).

However, colonial architecture was itself varied and inconsistent. For some architects and historians, neocolonial architecture meant finding inspiration in the flourishes and ornate façades of baroque religious constructions often associated with Ouro Preto and the other towns of the mining region developed in the eighteenth century. For others, it meant adapting the clean lines and simpler designs of early settlers, as seen, for example, in northern and northeastern cities such as Recife. Further, there were differences in emphasis and application among architects working in São Paulo and in Rio de Janeiro and between those who understood neocolonial architecture to be a way of recognizing Brazil's links to Portugal and those who saw in it an elucidation of distinctions between the countries that could be traced back hundreds of years. There was no one, coherent notion of neocolonial architecture in 1922, and this was made manifest at the centennial exposition. Thus, while Nestor de Figueiredo and C. S. San Juan designed the Pavilhão das Pequenas Indústrias in the tradition of the Jesuit baroque, with an ornate façade and an emphasis on decorative flourishes, Armando de Oliveira adapted what he understood to be the legacy of Portuguese residential architecture in the Pavilhão de Caça e Pesca, with simple lines and an explicit acknowledgment of geography and environment, seen in its patios and other open spaces, including a terrace opening directly onto the harbor. The Palácio das Grandes Indústrias was not a new construction but a renovation and adaptation of the old Arsenal de Guerra, the Casa do Trem, and the Forte do Calabouço; Archimedes Memória and Francisque Cuchet employed both iterations of the neocolonial in their design for the renovation, for example, by adding a new façade to recall the baroque religious as well as new patios of the type associated with Portuguese private residences.[20]

Surveying these disjunctions and differences and noting the debates architects and other contemporaries engaged in as they observed them, Levy argues that while the neocolonial influence on the exposition is unmistakable, it did not represent a fully realized national style. Instead, she says, the use and discussion of neocolonial architecture in the exposition should be seen as part of an ongoing inquiry, "a search for the essential elements necessary for the formation of something new."[21]

2.3. Visitors to the centenary exposition could take short airplane rides to view the city and the fair campus from a rare vantage point. Note the French-inspired Palácio dos Estados (left) and the neocolonial Pavilhão de Caça e Pesca (right) in the distance. Photograph by Augusto Malta. Courtesy of the Instituto Moreira Salles.

That the search continued in the exposition itself was clear not only in discussion of and disagreement about the character of the neocolonial but also in the fact that the neocolonial was not the only architectural approach employed in the exposition spaces set aside for Brazil's own displays. Beside making use of various iterations of the neocolonial, architects designed buildings according to neoclassical principles, such as the main entrance, the Pavilhão do Distrito Federal, and the Pavilhão de Estatística, and others inspired by the Louis XVI style, such as the Palácio das Festas, the official restaurant, and the Pavilhão da Música. Elsewhere, the design of the exposition's most popular venue, the Parque de Diversões, was inspired by various styles, including the Gothic and the rococo, and its decoration referenced the folklore and diversions of many countries as a nod to the universalist message of the fair. That is, the exposition planners offered space to architects who worked in what had been the dominant approach of republican Brazil, the eclectic revival of some of the most influential traditions of Western design. Although advocates of the neocolonial depicted the presence of buildings exhibiting different architectural styles as a failure of nationalism, it is perhaps more accurate to understand the heterogeneous character of exposition spaces as a demonstration that the centenary was a period of searching and questions. Rather than a confident proclamation of a settled sense of the nation, the centenary exhibition seems to have been a venue in which Brazilians explored the nation and its identities, making the fair more complex and potentially more fruitful than Armando de Oliveira and his partners in the neocolonial movement might have liked to admit.

The exploration continued after the pavilions were erected and the exposition opened. The buildings displaying Brazilian products encouraged visitors to know Brazil through its economic activities, calling on Brazilians to be proud of what their country produced and optimistic about its future, as well as aiming to stoke the interest of investors both foreign and domestic. Organizers also invited visitors to know the country through other means, among the most important of which was found in the Pavilhão de Estatistica. Inside this pavilion, visitors encountered a quantitative rendering of Brazil, with the display of statistics on everything from industrial output to population surveys designed to impress, because of the scale of aggregate data for the large country as well as the sensibility of the modern and the expert that contemporaries tended to grant statistical work; the pavilion symbolized, according to the commissioners, "the science of certainty," which was one of the themes of the exposition.[22] Complementing the pavilion, "Statistics" was one of the sixteen major sections of the exposition (with Agriculture, Commerce, Instruction, Transportation, Fine Art, and so on), and other sections included subsections dedicated to statistical displays; for example, the Indústria Pastoril section included data quantifying milk, butter, and cheese production.

Similarly, as Elkin points out, organizers filled the exposition with maps, "to both physically and metaphorically delineate the nation."[23] Thus, organizers tasked the Club de Engenharia with producing the detailed "Carta Geographica do Centenario" (see fig. I.2), which was exhibited alongside a similar map of Brazil in 1822, and the exposition also included a three-dimensional wooden diorama of South America measuring four meters by three meters and including rivers with running water, working lighthouses, volcanoes casting off red light and smoke, illuminated labels of the capitals and states of Brazil, and other features.[24] Other maps focused on particular subjects, such as the ninety-nine new maps produced by the Ministry of Agriculture to help familiarize visitors with the character and potential of the country's farmland.[25] Elsewhere, a series of maps produced by the São Paulo delegation displayed the state's railways, agriculture, public education, industrial and commercial establishments, and immigrant colonies, each one accompanied by statistical data.[26] Foreign delegations made their own contributions in this regard, as was the case in the British pavilion, where the first floor was dominated by an enormous map of the world set into a water-filled well and including model ships that moved along common trade routes; its designers flattered their Brazilian hosts by lighting the map "in such a manner as to emphasise Brazil and the British Empire," according to the exposition magazine.[27]

The exposition also mapped the nation onto the fairgrounds themselves. In their own way just as ambitious as the destruction of the Morro do Castelo, to remake downtown Rio de Janeiro and create space for the exposition, were the great lengths to which organizers went to ensure that visitors would encounter every part of Brazil. The commission invited all Brazilians to participate in the fair as exhibitors or visitors, but it emphasized geographic distinctions by organizing the national sections of the exposition by region. It reached directly into local communities by appointing representatives for every Brazilian state, the federal district, and the Acre territory. These representatives worked to encourage participation in a variety of ways. They gave interviews and undertook advertising campaigns to spread word of the fair in local newspapers and magazines; they worked with regional governments to help strategize their participation; and they traveled—in some cases widely—to meet with potential exhibitors and local officials. Jayme Castello Branco Coimbra, the representative for Pernambuco, for example, was based in Recife and did much of his work there, but he regularly visited towns along the coast and in the interior throughout 1921 and 1922, sometimes hiring a car and sometimes traveling by train. Travel expenses for trips to places such as Iguarassú, Goyanna, Itambé, Barreiros, Escada, and Palmares were among his largest budget items.[28] To the south, the Rio Grande do Sul representative Júlio Azambuja notified the commissioners that traveling throughout the state was taking up so much of his time that he had felt compelled "to make my children perform work that is not theirs," and he therefore requested funds to hire two or more assistants beyond the one that the commission had already approved; after his second request, the commission agreed to let him hire one more assistant.[29]

The result of this work was an exposition that included the display of products and references to all of Brazil, from north to south and from the densely populated coastal areas to the far west, though, as the next section shows, the contributions from the various states were very different in scale and scope. Organizers also found other ways to introduce the country to visitors, offering space in the Palácio das Festas to politicians, scholars, and others (such as the "walking" raider, Wanderlino Nogueira) who offered lectures on various aspects of Brazil and its people and partnering with others who could help contemporaries know the country.[30] For example, the organizing commission carved out space in the exposition for the participation of the Instituto Oswaldo Cruz, in order that visitors would encounter publications, photography, film, and other displays of the institute's research and campaigns on behalf of public health in Brazil (see fig. 2.4).[31]

Similarly, they promoted the work of Cândido Mariano da Silva Rondon and the commission he led to explore the Brazilian West and link it to the rest of the nation via telegraph. Although by the year of the centenary Rondon's star had begun to dim, the centenary commission sponsored the publication of a series of maps and surveys produced under his guidance, including one thousand copies of a detailed map of the state of Mato Grosso, surveys of the rivers and climate of central Brazil, and maps of the ethnic, botanical, zoological, and geological makeup of the region.[32] The Rondon commission also helped organize a display of indigenous artifacts in a "secção indígena" of the Palácio da Indústria e Comércio and a visit to the exposition by a group of indigenous men from Mato Grosso, Pareci speakers who excited the Carioca public when they staged a public performance of their traditional ball game.[33] As the *Revista da Semana* put it, their participation helped remedy the fact that the official celebrations of the centenary had for the most part "lacked the participation of the Brazilian Indian," a reminder that there were limits to organizers' commitment to the project of knowing Brazil as it was instead of as they wished it might be.[34]

Organizers also encouraged efforts undertaken by other groups to explore and understand the country and knit it together, from special publications and academic congresses to commercial fairs and sporting events. The commission provided financial assistance to many of the groups organizing these events and helped advertise and coordinate them. They varied in size and scope, with some focused tightly on Brazil and others following the exposition by situating Brazil within international communities and conversations. As they informed the commission in their requests for funds, the organizers of each group deemed their request to be of vital significance and in need of urgent attention. However, except in a few cases—such as the sporting events discussed below—these efforts garnered little interest from the broader public. In the case of the many congresses of the centenary, for example, few contemporaries seem to have taken much interest in the Congresso Brasileiro de Carvão, the Congresso Brasileiro de Esperanto, or the Congresso Americano de Expansão Economica e Ensino Commercial, in part because almost two dozen such congresses and conferences were held in Rio de Janeiro alone, dedicated to the natural sciences, commerce and

2.4. Medical and social hygiene exhibition mounted by the Instituto Oswaldo Cruz at the centenary fair. Courtesy of the Fundação Oswaldo Cruz.

industry, transportation, education, and a variety of other subjects. Befitting the reason for the celebration, among the few initiatives of this type that enjoyed more public attention were those dealing with historical memory and national identity. Discussed in detail in chapter 3, these efforts, including the new Museu Histórico Nacional and the Catholic Congresso Eucharistico, made the centenary an arena for debates over Brazil's histories and traditions. They helped ensure that the spirit of inquiry and exploration on display at the centenary exposition extended beyond the fairgrounds; moreover, they ensured that the tensions displayed in the exposition also extended beyond its gates.

Displaying São Paulo, and Also Brazil

As much as its scale and ambition, the spirit of inquiry and exploration that animated much of the centennial exhibition distinguished it from Brazilians' earlier experiences in the arena. Rather than tightly controlled messages and studious attempts to elide the condition—and even existence—of the Brazilian people, the visitor who stepped into the pavilions constructed in 1922 confronted a variety of messages about the character of Brazil and Brazilians. The 1922 effort was more complete than any previous attempt to exhibit Brazil at a national or international fair, and it included the Brazilian people themselves. They were exhibitors at the fair, as the creators of the products displayed in the Brazilian pavilions, the speakers invited to address fairgoers on their experiences, and the members of the crowds that lent significance to major events like the inauguration of pavilions. They were also exhibitors in the official events that took place outside the fair's gates, for example, as the athletes in centenary sporting events and the children who staged patriotic performances and parades. Further, they were exhibited, the subject of the facts and figures shared at the Pavilhão de Estatistica, the newly inaugurated Museu da Criança, and many of the lectures offered at the congresses of the centenary. The display was partial and conflicted, as the comment in the *Revista da Semana* about the lack of indigenous participation suggested. But the fact that the official magazine of the exhibition contributed to the celebration of the jangadeiros with a glowing appreciation of their triumph—complete with photographs of the group from Ceará in their modest garb and aboard their unmodern vessels—gives a sense of the extent of organizers' willingness to acknowledge that Brazil was not only a set of products and resources but a place and a people.[35]

While they allowed and even invited inquiry and variety, the organizers of the exhibition did follow their predecessors in attempting to share a dominant message, the hopeful view of the First Republic's social and political elite, a Western, modern, and rapidly developing nation ready to take its rightful place in the global community. In the inaugural issue of the exposition's official magazine, Padua Rezende spoke of organizers' ambitions, asserting that the exhibition was much more than a commercial fair, for through it Brazilians played a critical role in the reconstruction of the West in the aftermath of the Great War, bringing together friendly nations in the recognition of all that they shared.[36] "All peoples," he said, accepted "the same principles," they were inspired by "the same incentives," they took on "the same progressive initiatives," they experienced "the same anxieties," and they shared "the same idea of perfection." That is, every people aimed "to improve and perfect free and representative government and to ensure the greatest possible productivity of the nation's vital forces," and Brazil's centennial exhibition would provide them the opportunity to encourage one another, learn from one another, and demonstrate how far they had come in realizing these goals. For its part, Rezende said, Brazil would have much to display. The fair would show "the results we have achieved in the spheres of political, social, and economic activity during the last hundred years," and, more than this, it would serve "not only to exhibit the nation's labors, but, specifically, to document our perfect commitment to the general progress of all nations."[37]

Animated by this hopeful perspective, the exhibition commissioners invited the participation of many different countries, appointed delegates to carry the message and organize exhibitors in every state and territory, and made the event a multifaceted one, with commercial and industrial sectors and areas dedicated to the arts and health and hygiene; they also helped organize professional congresses focused on various subjects as well as sports competitions. As they reached out, they found enthusiastic partners who joined them in trying to make the exhibition a display of "the 'promised' Brazil that they hoped to build" and a "civics lesson," as Marly Silva da Motta describes the effort.[38] They also found unlooked-for complications, such as the arrival of the jangadeiros, as well as reticence on the part of their would-be partners and those who had their own visions of what the exhibition should be. These troubles threatened to make the exhibition a display not of unity and progress but of discord and disparity, a problem characterized above all by regional differences and regionalist disputes. In fact, the fair's most eager contributors committed themselves to putting those regional differences on display.

Motta demonstrates that many of São Paulo's leading figures saw the centenary as an important opportunity to advance the argument that their state was Brazil's most dynamic region, and that its model of industrial development and its progressive character represented the only possible future for the nation at large. Concurrent with this argument, advanced by prominent cultural figures such as Monteiro Lobato, Menotti del Picchia, and Oswald de Andrade, was the rejection of Rio de Janeiro, which they depicted as backward and insufficiently nationalistic; as Motta shows, against their understanding of São Paulo as the embodiment of the true nation, they depicted the capital as the decadent "anti-nation."[39] These figures were matched by others in industry and government, and exposition commissioners therefore found enthusiastic partners when they reached out to São Paulo to organize participation in the fair, eager to display their state before the nation and the world. The government of São Paulo was one of a number of state governments that organized its own exposition commission, and much more than most it committed to working with the representatives appointed by the national commission, first João Maurico de Sampaio Vianna and later José Vergueiro Steidel, to encourage participation by residents of the state.

Though in earlier decades São Paulo had not been well represented in Brazil's exhibition displays, the scale and ambition of the state's contribution to the centennial fair outmatched those of any other state, as state organizers sought to use it to depict Paulistas as a modern and progressive people who were the natural leaders of the nation. This project began with their attempts to shape the physical space of the fairgrounds. Paulistas were among the only participants to construct their own pavilions, with the city of Campinas and several São Paulo–based companies, such as the Matarazzo and Antarctica firms, displaying their wares in their own buildings, while the state government constructed a cinema to broadcast films about Paulista life. Meanwhile, Paulistas were among the most numerous of the contributors to each of the venues offered to Brazilian exhibitors, the Pavilhão de Pequenas Industrias, the Palácio das Grandes Industrias, and the Palácio das Expositores Particulares (for private citizens).

Elsewhere, organizers assigned space in the Palácio dos Estados in part based on state contributions to construction costs, and the state made an enormous commitment, claiming six hundred square meters of space for its contribution of 300 contos de réis.[40] But this was not enough, and Sampaio Vianna lobbied administrators in the capital for even more space, arguing that since "the assistance provided by the State was larger than that provided by the other States, the area afforded it should be larger as well."[41] Exposition planners acceded to the request, giving São Paulo almost one hundred square meters more than was originally planned, and also gave the state a prominent position within the palace, though even that does not seem to have satisfied the Paulistas' ambitions.[42] Finally, São Paulo hosted the Exposição Internacional de Gado, the livestock fair organized to run concurrently with the main exposition and in effect to extend the exposition's reach.

In these spaces, Paulistas displayed a variety of coffee products, of course, but also merchandise from dozens of other industries, from textile and prepared foods manufacturing to pastoral activities. Indeed, a visitor to the exposition would have found São Paulo's contributions hard to miss; the state was represented in every one of the exposition's twenty-six product categories and it was the most prominent contributor to the horticulture exposition held in conjunction with the main fair.[43] In the Palácio dos Estados, the state commission provided an overview and a distillation, portraying the state as both extraordinarily productive and thoroughly modern, through maps and statistical renderings of the state's economic and social life and displays of the work of its agricultural and industrial schools and its research institutes, such as the Instituto Butantan.[44] As the exposition's official magazine put it, "São Paulo produces everything which is necessary for the life of a people," and its contribution to the fair demonstrated how it had earned its reputation as "*Leader* of the Federation."[45] Even more flattering was the comment offered by Epitácio Pessoa after his visit to the the state's displays. Articulating exactly what state leaders hoped visitors would learn at the fair and from the commemoration of the centenary more broadly, the president said the exposition confirmed his view that "São Paulo is a nation in itself."[46]

Although none took up more space or made a bigger impression on the exposition, other locales made significant investments and commitments. Among those figuring most prominently were the state of Minas Gerais and the federal capital (which had its own pavilion). In many instances, however, the organizing commission faced difficulties in convincing the governments and citizens of other states of the republic to participate. Less well-developed and populous states did not have the means to contribute much to the financing of the event, nor did they produce the variety of goods of a Minas Gerais or a São Paulo. Writing from Rio Grande do Norte in early 1922, for example, the exposition delegate José Garibaldi Dantas reported that the state government was committed to celebrating the centenary and was interested in the fair, but he also informed the commission that because the state was "small and poor" participation would be difficult; with only four industrial enterprises in the state capital and a few sugar refineries outside it, the most that could be expected was the display of items from the state's salt, cotton, sugar, palm wax, and leather producers, none of which, Dantas said, "offer much variety."[47] In comparison to São Paulo's 300 contos de réis, the government of Rio Grande do Norte contributed 50 contos for the construction of exposition space, and in comparison to São Paulo's almost seven hundred square meters Dantas reported that Rio Grande would need no more than fifty.[48]

Even filling up that space would prove difficult. Along with a few delegates appointed by the state government, Dantas traveled throughout Rio Grande to encourage participation, but, he reported, their effort "did not meet with the success they had hoped for."[49] They found it next to impossible to convince Potiguares to exhibit their products, which Dantas explained was a result of poverty or because they "did not understand the true reach of expositions."[50] Finding little interest in the private sector and denied his request to use commission funds to purchase products himself, he turned to state and local governments to help identify, purchase, and submit representative samples. These bodies did provide some assistance, but it was not much; Dantas said the monies made available by the state government were "negligible," while in many cases the sums approved by municipal governments were "so insignificant that it is embarrassing even to mention them."[51] Undaunted, Dantas and his assistants collected a sufficient number of products to ensure that Rio Grande do Norte would be included in the exposition, if only in the "official" display included in the Palácio dos Estados, but even that level of participation depended on a final contribution from the national commission and Dantas's office, which in the end covered all the transportation costs of the products, first to the state capital and from there to Rio de Janeiro.[52]

Just to the south in the state of Paraíba, the situation confronted by the delegate Joaquim Pessôa Cavalcanti was not much happier, and in some ways seems to have been more difficult. Like José Garibaldi Dantas, Cavalcanti enjoyed substantial support from the state's government and especially its governor, Sólon Barbosa de Lucena, who appointed six delegates to work directly with Cavalcanti to promote the exposition and helped secure 30 contos to support their work. After months of advertising, travel, and direct appeals, Cavalcanti reported that he and his partners were able to organize a contribution including over four hundred exhibitors and over one thousand different products. These included mineral ore samples, leather products, farming tools, cotton textiles, and processed drinks, which they displayed in a brief but well-attended "preparatory exhibition" in the state capital before shipping them to Rio de Janeiro.[53]

However, in Cavalcanti's telling this was an unlikely outcome, because, like their northern neighbors, Paraibanos expressed little interest in the exposition. Cavalcanti said that in their travels he and his assistants "had to face every kind of difficulty: here was indifference, here demoralization; there ill will, disregard, and even hostility." The problem was apparent both among individual producers, who "in general have been withdrawn," and among the municipal authorities that, "with few exceptions, have done nothing at all." Thus, just as in Rio Grande do Norte, Paraíba's participation in the exposition owed to the work of Cavalcanti and his partners appointed by the state government. It was they who did the work of identification, selection, and collection of the state's products, as well as their organization and display in the preparatory exhibition and their final packaging and shipment to the national capital. In some cases they used state funds to purchase items they believed should be displayed at the exposition, because, according to Cavalcanti, owners and manufacturers had "refused to display them." Summing up the situation, the delegate said that the Paraíba contribution came together only through "a constant publicity campaign in every municipality, distributing a great number of prospectuses, publishing announcements, sending out circulars, and above all providing financial assistance to a great number of exhibitors."[54]

Even allowing for a certain amount of exaggeration and résumé building, Dantas and Cavalcanti do seem to have found very little interest in the exposition among the citizens of Rio Grande do Norte and Paraíba. Dantas excused Potiguares' attitude by pointing to the state's relative poverty and its citizens' ignorance of the benefits of participation in industrial exhibitions, rejecting the possibility that they lacked patriotism or an interest in the "the nation's great events," though Cavalcanti appeared less sure of the good will of the Paraibanos as he complained of their indifference and even hostility.[55] It is certain that northeasterners did indeed take an interest in the centenary, which they demonstrated in a variety of ways, from large and well-attended events organized around the centenary date to the enormous enthusiasm many expressed for the exploits of the raiders of the centenary, among whom were, of course, the celebrated jangadeiros from Rio Grande do Norte. They showed less interest in events like the exposition, which obligated Brazilians to accept the priorities and preeminence of their compatriots in the more developed and politically powerful Southeast.

That a localist or regionalist perspective, rather than ignorance or poverty, might explain the purported indifference of Paraibanos and Potiguares, is suggested by the experience of exposition delegates in nearby Pernambuco and faraway Rio Grande do Sul. Neither of these states was impoverished or insensitive to the possible benefits of exhibition events; indeed, in earlier decades leaders and producers in both states had been among the most eager of participants in such events.[56] Still, contemporaries judged the states' participation in the centenary exhibition to be disappointing, even embarrassing. In the final months before the opening of the fair, as one Pernambucano commentator lamented, it was clear that his state "[would] not participate in a respectable manner," while a Gaúcho writer alleged that his state's showing would be less impressive still, comparing Rio Grande do Sul's contribution directly and unfavorably to that of Pernambuco.[57] This outcome was foretold by the experiences endured by the commission's representatives in two states, Jayme Castello Branco Coimbra and Júlio Azambuja, who faced serious difficulties in their work to promote the exhibition, not least because the governments of these two states were troublesome and often truculent partners.

Coimbra reported that his first interactions with Pernambuco's civic leaders in late 1921 were productive. The interim governor, Severino Pinheiro, expressed support for Coimbra's work and helped him make contact with the members of the state commission organized to promote Pernambuco's participation in the event and with other state officials.[58] By the end of the calendar year, however, it had become clear that the work would be difficult, and the first warning signs began to appear in the press. Writing in the *Diario de Pernambuco*, A. Fernandes said that the state must participate in the exhibition, because "no one knows us. No one wants to get to know us." The exhibition was a rare opportunity to call attention to the state and prove to those, like the stereotypical Carioca "snob," that Pernambuco was more than the sugar it produced. According to Fernandes, "it requires only incentive in order to develop."

Unfortunately, little had been accomplished, and he warned of the "disaster" Pernambuco would face if it failed to participate in the event or if "at the last minute we hastily arrange a meager display."[59]

By early 1922 Coimbra was describing the state's participation in the exhibition as "an almost inevitable failure," which he explained as the result of the state government's failure to provide the kind of financial support other states had made available. State officials suggested that they could not do more because of the uncertainties surrounding the withdrawal of Governor José Bezerra from public activity for reasons of ill health and because of a crisis in the state's finances, but the *Jornal do Recife* rejected these as excuses and lies, as stories "to deceive children." Instead, the paper blamed Pinheiro and Bezerra for what it depicted as a lack of foresight and perhaps a lack of patriotism. Later in the year the *Jornal* would decide that the fair was a demonstration of the unseriousness of the Brazilian people and their leaders, but in observing the early difficulties faced by Coimbra it attacked "the sickening and criminal indifference of the government of Pernambuco in regard to the exhibition that will be our worthy celebration of centenary of independence, displaying to the whole world the great progress we can say we have made in a century of national life."[60]

As the weeks and months wore on, Coimbra continued to struggle to convince the state government to provide assistance, and in March 1922 he cabled his superiors at the exhibition commission to suggest that he be relieved of his position, "entirely convinced [of the] uselessness of my efforts."[61] They convinced him to stay on and attempted to support him in his work, in part by corresponding directly with the acting governor with a reminder that the exhibition was a "unique occasion" to promote the state.[62] However, neither the commission nor Coimbra managed to convince Pinheiro and his government to act. Meanwhile, Coimbra also struggled to persuade the private sector to participate; indeed, as late as mid-August 1922—well after the original deadline for inscription—he was still making public appeals to sugar producers to take part in the exhibition.[63] In his final report Coimbra said that despite the unanimous support of the local press and the "patriotism and enterprise" of a few Pernambucanos, the state government remained "deaf and indifferent," exhibiting "an attitude pernicious to its development." He admitted that the state's contribution would be "modest," focused especially on cotton and sugar production, which meant that although Coimbra hoped it would be sufficient "to maintain and even raise our reputation in the seat of the confederation," it would instead correspond to Fernandes's fear that the exhibition would reinforce negative conceptions about Pernambuco.[64]

In the country's far south, the exposition delegate Júlio Azambuja faced a different kind of challenge in working with the government of Rio Grande do Sul. Unlike Severino Pinheiro, Governor Borges de Medeiros took an interest in the exhibition, which he demonstrated in a variety of ways, from appointing a commission to oversee the state's participation to taking a personal interest in the production of films about Rio Grande's economy and infrastructure to be shown at the fair.[65] However, the interest taken by Medeiros and his government did not translate into a successful contribution to the exposition itself, despite the governor's claims to the contrary; for example, the state display included fewer products from fewer exhibitors than "indifferent" Paraíba.[66] One explanation for the poverty of the Gaúcho contribution is that, far from cooperating with Azambuja, Medeiros and the members of the state commission attempted to restrain him from doing the work for which he was appointed.

As Azambuja began making plans to canvas the state in order to promote the exhibition and recruit participants, the president of the state commission informed him that "my personal interaction with the chief executives of the state's municipalities was unnecessary" because Medeiros preferred that the commission interact with local officials. Functionally this suggestion amounted to an assertion that he should do no more than advertise the benefits of the exposition and perhaps collect statistical information about the state economy, leaving the work of organizing the state's contribution to the fair in the hands of the state government and its commission.[67] As Azambuja explained to his superiors in Rio de Janeiro, he felt obligated to accept this situation. He realized that local authorities objected to "the interventionist role" implied by his office, and therefore recommended that it be left to the state commission to interact with local officials and individual exhibitors, to select, collect, and classify products, and to arrange for their display at the exposition in the national capital. As he put it, "with any other approach I would not have been able to remain on good terms with state authorities."[68] For their part, the commissioners in the national capital were happy to allow the state and its commission to take charge of the work, both because they expected the local bodies would produce a successful contribution and because the arrangement would lower the financial commitment of the national commission.[69]

While the state commission took over most of the responsibilities for organizing Rio Grande's participation, Azambuja continued to promote the exposition and the state's place in it, for example, by gathering a number of publications about and maps of the state for submission to the exposition library. As the deadline for contributions approached, however, it became obvious that this arrangement was not working. On several occasions between late 1921 and mid-1922, Azambuja hinted that all was not well, reminding the state commissioners, his superiors in the national commission, and the local press that he was not responsible for the organization of the state's contribution to the exposition, whether in the collection of products, their display in the state capital, or their shipment to Rio de Janeiro.[70] For example, when exhibitors in the town of Bento Gonçalves sent a letter to the *Correio do Povo* blaming him for failing to provide assistance in having their products shipped to Porto Alegre, he issued a statement reminding them that they must turn to their own local and state governments for assistance, and that neither he nor his assistants had "responsibility for the failures" of which they had complained.[71] As in other states, the state commission also abandoned the idea of holding a preview exhibition to display the state's contribution before a local audience, in part because, having run out of time in collecting submissions, it had to ship many products to Rio de Janeiro directly from the towns and cities where they were produced, rather than gathering them in the state capital.[72] It was little surprise, then, that the anti-Medeiros *Correio do Povo* commented unfavorably on Rio Grande's participation in the exhibition, while *A Federação*, produced by Medeiros's own Republican party, had little to say about the event at all.[73]

It does not appear that Gaúcho or Pernambucano producers objected to the idea of the centennial exposition, or that the governments of the two states sought to hinder the organization of their citizens' contributions to the fair.[74] At the same time, they also did not embrace the purported opportunities of the exhibition, which was apparent in the difficulties faced by Coimbra and Azambuja and in the relative poverty of the displays the states did contribute. That the outcome of efforts in Rio Grande do Sul and Pernambuco disappointed both national organizers and some local commentators might be explained by inefficient and ineffective organization or by financial challenges of the sort that Severino Pinheiro said kept his government from contributing more to the effort. But it also does not seem coincidental that in the bitter presidential election of March 1922 the political leaders of both states had supported Nilo Peçanha and the Reação Republicana movement against Artur Bernardes and his backers in São Paulo and Minas Gerais. Bernardes's victory assured the continued domination of national politics by Paulistas and Mineiros, as well as continued frustration and increasing alienation in places like Rio Grande do Sul and Pernambuco. Perhaps even more important, in both states the centenary celebrations themselves took place amid serious political turmoil, and the conflicts drew on deep wells of regionalist identity and resentment.

This is not the place for a detailed accounting of the political conflicts that led to the intervention of federal forces in Pernambuco in 1922 or the so-called revolution of Rio Grande do Sul in 1923. These events had as much to do with intramural politics as they were disputes pitting locals against the national state, as scholars of each episode have demonstrated.[75] However, both instances highlighted the ways in which state-level political disputes during the First Republic were often inflected with regionalist feeling, resentments about the function of the national political system, and disagreements over the meaning and practice of Brazilian identity and citizenship. In both instances partisans used the centenary as a touchstone for articulating their grievances, some using it to articulate their sense of belonging in the national community and casting doubt on their opponents' patriotism, while others used the celebrations to critique local rivals as well as the influence of the national government over state affairs. It is likely that these perspectives and disputes complicated efforts to organize participation in the centenary exposition.

In mid-1922, a new paper appeared in the small town of Santa Maria in Rio Grande do Sul, called *O Separatista*. True to its name, the newspaper's mission was to advocate for the state's secession from Brazil because, according to the publisher and editor, Júlio Raphael de Aragão Bozano, and the paper's other writers, the nominally federative structure of the First Republic was a fiction. The reality, they said in an editorial published on the eve of the centenary, was that Rio Grande do Sul suffered exploitation under "the infamous and disgraceful yoke of S. Paulo and Minas."[76] They complained of Paulistas' and Mineiros' lack of respect for the interests and needs of other regions, and of what they depicted as incessant and unjust demands on Rio Grande to contribute much more than its fair share of taxes to support the national government, as well as many more soldiers than warranted for its defense. Failing secession, Bozano and his partners would be willing to accept a maximalist version of the federal order that allowed Rio Grande almost unfettered liberty of action within the republican system. This position, they often reminded readers, was the fundamental demand and posture of the "Patriarch" of Rio Grande do Sul, the much-loved journalist and politician Júlio de Castilhos, who was also the mentor of then governor Borges de Medeiros.[77]

In itself, neither the appearance of *O Separatista* nor its political platform seems particularly significant. The paper was published in a small town, in a state with a long history of regionalist sentiment, and the voicing of regionalist and even secessionist views was not an uncommon occurrence in Rio Grande or many other places during the period. However, the publication brought to a head ongoing debates about the character of the state and its relationship to the rest of Brazil, and it contributed to the violent breakdown of civic order that came to be called the "revolution" of 1923, which pitted supporters of Borges de Medeiros against those of his challenger for the governorship, Joaquim Francisco de Assis Brasil. More important for the present work, the fact of the centenary was not coincidental but meaningful for the participants in these debates and this struggle; before the first violent episodes in late 1922, it served as a venue for the articulation of grievances and accusations and the first minor skirmishes of the larger conflict, as was suggested by Azambuja's comment about local anxiety regarding "the interventionist role" some Gaúchos read in his appointment and activity.

Reaction to *O Separatista* was immediate and far-ranging. Newspapers throughout Rio Grande do Sul took notice of their new rival, some expressing support and many more objecting to the paper's very existence. This was the position taken by the state capital's most important paper, the *Correio do Povo*, which printed a series of broadsides against separatism and *O Separatista* over the course of the second half of 1922 and into 1923.[78] It also drew attention to the reactions of like-minded Gaúchos, such as the members of the Federação Academica de Porto Alegre, who convened a special meeting to confront the threat the paper seemed to represent and issued a long manifesto attacking its "sad separatist campaign" and insisting on the Brazilian patriotism of the vast majority of Gaúchos that the *Correio* was happy to publish.[79] For its part, the Liga Rio-Grandense Nacionalista called on the authorities to suppress the expression of "such unseemly and harmful ideas" in an extraordinary session convened specifically to condemn Bozano and the paper.[80] The controversy also attracted attention beyond the state's borders, including in the national capital, where the *Revista da Semana* went so far as to say that because Bozano was the child of immigrants he was neither a Brazilian patriot nor a "true Gaúcho."[81]

Part of the reason for the intensity of the reaction to the paper was that many suspected Bozano and his supporters of articulating views that Medeiros shared. Bozano himself said as much, stating in an editorial in September 1922 that the governor "is at heart a separatist."[82] And though some of Bozano's critics rejected the suggestion, the governor's enemies believed his assessment was correct.[83] They argued that *O Separatista* might be a small, local paper, but it was significant because it stated in print what Medeiros believed and what his policies often seemed to promote, which meant that the gubernatorial election of 1922 was about more than political power; according to the Comité Pró-Assis Brasil, the organization formed to advocate for the candidacy of the governor's rival, "it is for the very unity of the Patria or against it that you will be voting."[84] As the conflict between Borgistas and Assisistas unfolded and became violent, such accusations meant that the political disagreements between the sides seemed existential for Rio Grande do Sul and for Brazil.

Related to this, another reason for the furor that met the paper's publication was that Bozano and other separatists sought to undermine the legitimacy of the national state by challenging the principle of military discipline from within the ranks of the Brazilian armed forces. In early July, the editor of São Sebastião do Cahy's *A Evolução* called on Rio Grande's reservists to refuse to comply with the order to participate in the military parades organized for the centenary, and Bozano and others took up his call, with *O Separatista* stating that "the Rio Grandense who takes part in the parade on 7 September rejects Rio Grande's history and celebrates the enslavement of Rio Grande by Brazil."[85] Complicating matters was the fact that, like many active in public life in the First Republic, Bozano was a reservist of the Brazilian army, even as he did not consider himself Brazilian. The regional commander of Brazilian forces reacted by ordering the arrests of Bozano and Eduardo Pacheco de Andrade, another reservist who encouraged his peers to refuse to report and who, for good measure, took the opportunity of his momentary celebrity to accuse the commander of being a traitor to Rio Grande and an anti-Borgista partisan.[86]

Coming as they did in the immediate aftermath of the revolt of soldiers stationed at the Forte de Copacabana in the capital, it is not surprising that the regional commander and his superiors took seriously the separatists' calls to reservists to reject their orders, though it seems likely that only a few did so, and both Bozano and Andrade were released shortly after their arrests. However, this minor episode illustrates the centenary's capacity to distill larger debates and ideas, and it was just one of the ways that the controversies over separatism and regionalism in Rio Grande do Sul in 1922 became connected to the centenary and its celebrations. *O Separatista* used the centenary to attack both the national union and the authority of the central government. Brazilian independence day, according to the paper, was not a time for Rio Grande to celebrate but instead carried the "odious meaning of its passage from the weak and mild oppression" of the colonial system "to the most complete and demeaning subjection" that characterized the new Brazilian state.[87] Moreover, the celebrations the hated government of the federation organized to mark the centenary's passage were predictably narrow and unpopular, "fashionable and aristocratic," in the words of the columnist Antonius, since there was little reason for Gaúchos and many others to express enthusiasm for what the paper called "the first centenary of the political emancipation of S. Paulo and Minas."[88] Bozano and his colleagues were therefore surely happy to report that, at least in Santa Maria, the events of 7 September 1922 were small and poorly attended. According to the paper, in Santa Maria "no one wanted to celebrate independence, which everyone knows is a sham," and so the "event was a disaster." Most residents, it said, looked forward instead to the state's most important holiday, the celebration of the mid-nineteenth-century rebellion by republicans and separatists called the Revolução Farroupilha, two weeks later.[89]

At least in terms of official, public events, celebrations in the state capital do not seem to have been much more ambitious or successful. Medeiros named a commission to organize events in Porto Alegre, which included some of the same figures who oversaw the state's participation in the centenary exposition, such as it was, but this came only a month before the centenary date. Beside the kinds of activities held every year and on almost every holiday, such as football matches, lectures, and a military parade, there were only a few special events. These included the inauguration of a new public library, events to break ground on a new railway and two new educational facilities, and a parade for students enrolled in local schools as well as, tellingly, an "evangelical rite" at the city's most important monument, the monument to Júlio de Castilhos.[90] Moreover, even this limited program relied heavily on private initiatives, such as those undertaken by sports clubs and the Catholic Church, and it was not finalized and announced until 2 September. As "a patriot" wrote in a letter to the *Correio do Povo*, it was embarrassing to open the paper each day to read of the ambitious events planned in other places and by private organizations while wondering what the state government would do to bring the community together. He worried that the centenary would come and go with little proof that Portoalegrenses had marked the date, not even in the form of the dedication of a modest plaque.[91]

Many private groups, from social clubs to political organizations, did organize events celebrating the centenary. It is meaningful that among the most active and ambitious of these were immigrant organizations: Italian, German, and even Polish groups took the opportunity of the centenary to assert their sense of belonging in the country. Many Gaúchos joined them, but even critics of separatists like Júlio Bozano used the centenary to remind their fellow citizens of the shortcomings of the nation and the republican government that ruled it. *Imprensa*, published by the state's press advocacy organization, celebrated the centenary and the most familiar heroes of the independence movement, from Pedro I to José Bonifácio. But it also marked the occasion by reminding readers that the Brazilian people "has no well-founded reasons" to love the republic, and noted the "miserable reality" of the celebrations coming under the state of seige and other measures undertaken by the Epitácio Pessoa government in response to the Copacabana uprising and the other threats that arose in 1922.[92]

This sentiment was especially prevalent among young Gaúchos, a demonstration that the centenary also displayed and helped consolidate generational differences among Brazilians active in civic life. Thus, when the students Gastão Dias and José Pereira Coelho de Souza gave the keynote addresses at centenary celebrations organized by the Gremio dos Estudantes de Agronomia e Veterinaria and the Federação Academica, respectively, they both championed Brazil and rejoiced in its political independence, but the two focused their attentions on Brazil's challenges—its economic dependency, its inequalities, its deficiencies in health and education.[93] It is worth noting that texts of these speeches were printed not in the Borgista *Federação*, but in the *Correio do Povo*, which followed a much more unionist editorial line and took much greater interest in the exposition and the centenary than did its rival. In other words, in Rio Grande do Sul, the separatists of Santa Maria and the proud patriots of Porto Alegre shared in the conviction that neither Brazil nor its republic was what it should be, and they saw that the centenary need not be only a moment of celebration. It was also an opportunity to call for change, perhaps fracture, perhaps renewal, and as much as any pastoral or industrial product, the call was what they used the centenary to display.

In the same month that *O Separatista* debuted in the South, federal forces marched into Recife. Their appearance was the denouement of a long-running conflict between rival political groups, which had resulted in civil unrest and violence, including murder. However, many Pernambucanos understood the occupation to be a clear infringement on state sovereignty, and they found the centenary especially useful as a means of articulating their criticisms of the Pessoa government and the intervention's local supporters. The *Jornal do Recife*, for example, compared Pessoa's plans to celebrate Brazil's having become a "free nation" and an "American" one to his decision to send soldiers to attack freedom and liberty in Pernambuco. He ordered the armed forces, in the paper's words, "to strangle our Constitution" and thereby revived the memory of the "twilight times of our condition as a Portuguese colony, during which captains general and grantees governed our forebears at their own pleasure, free of legal constraint." Pernambucanos would not accept a return to the unfree, colonial past, the *Jornal* said, and would fight "hand to hand" to defend the rights for which their forefathers had educated them.[94]

As chapter 3 demonstrates, Pernambucanos were especially interested in using the centenary to explore the meaning of the Brazilian past, and found historical precedent useful in drawing the connection between the centenary's celebration of liberty and what they said was their own defense of local autonomy. Critics also used the exposition and what they viewed as the outward-facing character of the Pessoa government's approach to the centenary to try to embarrass it. Thus, the Rio de Janeiro–based journalist Mário Rodrigues suggested that if foreign visitors to the exposition were to find out that the national government had used the federal armed forces in Pernambuco to "kill, murder, torture, humiliate, demean, [and] degrade an entire population," those visitors would laugh at the idea of Brazilian independence. "What independence!" they would ask, "in this land of slaves which the avarice of a shameless oligarchy lowers itself to such acts of grief and shame?!"[95] The *Jornal do Recife* said the same. Despite its earlier enthusiasm for the fair, it asserted that because of the intervention, Pessoa's attempt to impress the foreign "elite" would backfire, as instead of a modern country they would see "orgies where the operators of the privileged tribe collect gigantic profits." They would hear "Pernambuco's cry" denouncing Pessoa's crimes and corruption, so that "illuminated by the bursts of light produced by powerful electric works, Brazil will appear to foreign eyes a country shackled by despotism."[96] A little less strident, A. Carneiro Leão offered his regrets about the image the intervention was presenting to foreigners whom Brazilians had invited to see an image of the country's progress; a "beautiful picture" it was, he wrote.[97]

A few months later, José Euclides picked up on these themes as he surveyed the country at the centenary. Writing from Paraíba for the *Jornal do Recife*, he emphasized the regional differences within Brazil to draw broad, national lessons and critique the official events in the capital. He wrote that because of the Northeast's "physical misery" and "moral inertia" Brazil was "a country without the right to commemorate the Centenary of its political emancipation." He rejected the notion that Brazil had accomplished much in its first hundred years of independent life, saying, "We have done nothing and there is everything to do. . . . To this point, we have begun nothing, produced nothing." How, then, could Brazil justify the expenses of the centenary's "parties and orgies"? How could it explain its "festive and ostentatious shows, these dreary and odd displays"? What good was "this exhibition, this public display, this parade of the ossified busts of the founders of the nation," in the face of the country's lack of health, lack of education, and financial dependence? Rather than a celebration, he said, because of Brazil's underdevelopment and dependence the exposition would be "our undoing before foreigners."[98] In other words, Pessoa's foreign audience would understand the centenary events not as proof of Brazil's progress but as evidence of its lack of seriousness.

It is difficult to know how widespread this view was, and how much it affected Pernambucanos' willingness to participate in the centennial exhibition. It was the case, though, that there was little in Recife to mark the centenary itself beyond the ordinary in the way of official public celebrations. Besides the usual military parade and events in schools, the only major initiatives that received government support were a sports competition and a new hospital, each of which tended to reinforce the regional tenor of the centenary in Recife. The former was a regional event, the "Campeonato do Norte," described below, while promoters of the Hospital Centenário aimed to confront common claims, such as those offered by José Euclides, that northeasterners in particular were worryingly unhealthy. A. Fernandes, more optimistic and generous than Euclides, wrote in the *Diario de Pernambuco* that the region's health challenges meant that the hospital was the "the exact right commemoration with which we should mark the occasion of the Centenary in Pernambuco."[99] He went on to point out that besides its practical benefits the hospital would demonstrate to Europeans and people in other developed nations the seriousness of Pernambucanos, and he asserted that he would rather Pernambuco build the hospital than offer any other kind of commemoration of the centenary.[100]

It is worth noting that in January 1923 Recife hosted the Congresso da Lavoura do Nordeste Brasileiro, an event organized by the state's Sociedade Auxiliadora da Agricultura to celebrate its fiftieth anniversary, which included participants from Pernambuco, Alagoas, and Paraíba. It consisted of a conference focused on "local" economic questions and exhibitions of agricultural produce and machinery, demonstrating that Pernambucanos and their neighbors were indeed attuned to the benefits they might gain by such events, even as they had appeared hesitant to participate in the international exhibition that was still running in the national capital. For its part, the state government offered little more than encouragement, which helps explain why the fair was over a month late in opening.[101] Otherwise, state authorities did little, refusing not only funds for the centennial exposition but also monies that had previously been promised to the Instituto Archeologico e Geographico Pernambucano to organize public celebrations in the city and to build a commemorative monument to celebrate the centenary.[102] Instead, celebrations of the centenary were left largely to private actors like the Sociedade Auxiliadora, and these tended to exhibit the parochial concerns of their organizers rather than a broad sense of community, as seen, for example, in the celebrations of Portuguese residents excited about the Lisbon–Rio de

Janeiro raid and the religious events organized by the new archbishop of Olinda and Recife, Miguel de Lima Valverde.

Residents in the capital took note of the conflicts in Rio Grande and Pernambuco, just as residents of those cities had followed news of the revolt in Copacabana earlier in the centenary year. Cariocas read the events in the North and South through the lenses of their own partisan loyalties, with critics of the national government—and especially of Epitácio Pessoa—expressing sympathy for the regionalists, and supporters depicting them as misguided or disloyal. For example, the *Correio da Manhã* savaged Pessoa for his decision to intervene in Recife, calling it proof of the "impudence of a bloodthirsty and dishonest absolutism," but the paper was confident that national opinion and local resistance would triumph over what it depicted as the corruption of the president and his "gangster and arsonist relatives."[103] At the same time, the *Jornal do Brasil* described the intervention as an unfortunate but probably necessary step because of the irresponsibility of local politicians and the tendency of Pernambuco and "a number of states of the North" to indulge regularly in "a fit of nerves which threatens to cause seizures."[104] It did not doubt, though, the "perfect impartiality" of the president and his government, and trusted them to restore order in the region.[105]

Four months later, with the Pernambuco crisis resolved and the Rio Grande dispute just beginning to threaten public order, the Rio de Janeiro press focused on the exhibition and other events in the capital and the Southeast, but it did report on the ways that the centenary was marked in other regions. It tended to strike a celebratory chord and avoid mentioning the disputes of the centenary, and rarely alluded to the restraint residents of Pernambuco and Rio Grande do Sul noticed and complained of. Thus, in short notices *O Brasil* informed readers that the student festival in Porto Alegre was "most brilliant" and that the military parade that annoyed *O Separatista* was "majestic," but the only suggestion it gave of the relative paucity of the official program organized by the official state commission was the comment that "all of the celebrations have been of popular origin."[106] The illustrated magazine *O Malho* afforded readers a similar view through the publication of photographic essays featuring images of celebrations at, for example, a shooting club in Alfredo Chaves in Rio Grande do Sul and a school in Victoria, Pernambuco.[107] The attentive reader might have noticed that these events were typically very small in scale and certainly much less well attended than many of those in the capital, or São Paulo, or nearly any of the events that celebrated the raids of the centenary, including those in Pernambuco. But in isolation such items tended to depict the commemoration of the centenary as a success throughout the country.

For their part, the organizers of the exhibition were well aware of the limits and challenges of organizing events in many parts of the country, for they were familiar with the difficulties their delegates faced. In private correspondence they lobbied state officials to promote the fair and to cooperate with their representatives, as in the case of their appeal to the governor of Pernambuco cited above. In public, they insisted that the exposition was successful and that its success was due to the participation of every state and territory. But in making such claims organizers also acknowledged the differences that visitors would notice in the displays of various states as well as the possibility of regional tensions; therefore, they took care to depict these issues not as signs of failure but as reminders of the opportunities the exposition offered for the development and closer unity of the nation.

Thus, for example, in an article celebrating the economic development of São Paulo, the official magazine of the exposition insisted that the fair gave proof of the progress of every one of Brazil's states, while also granting that visitors would see examples of both "the productive greatness of the larger states" and "the limited enrollment" of the states of the South and the North. In the same piece it also insisted—in spite of all the evidence the exposition itself provided—that the fair proved that Brazilians shared a "unanimous convergence of knowledge, aspirations, and efforts" and, above all, that it displayed "a lack of egotism or a spirit of regional superiority." This assertion sat uncomfortably alongside the article's conclusion, which voiced the Paulista view of the centenary, announcing São Paulo's "brilliant display" in the exposition and suggesting that for other Brazilian states "the Paulista displays can serve as a lesson and an incentive." That is, the magazine said, the exposition displayed both national fraternity and Paulista preeminence, pairing condescension with encouragement.[108]

Given that this interpretation was advanced by the official gazette of the exposition, it is little wonder that some Brazilians felt alienated from the major events planned by the national government to celebrate the centenary, and it is not surprising that the exposition itself received mixed reviews. Many contemporaries counted it a failure, a sentiment acknowledged by the organizers themselves. As the exhibition's official magazine admitted in February 1923, while the Parque de Diversões was popular and entertainment areas and events well attended, "the pavilions are empty. The displays unstudied, unobserved. The section in the Praça Mauá, full of the most useful lessons for industrialists and agriculturalists, receives not one visit!" It blamed the expense and difficulty of transportation and the unbearable weather of the summer, but it admitted that such circumstances "fill the heart with bitterness."[109]

Five months later, in the event marking the exhibition's end, the minister of justice and internal affairs, João Luís Alves, insisted that the fair had demonstrated "the prodigious economic progress of Brazil." He acknowledged its critics when he noted and rejected "the idea that the Exposition was a failure," pointing to the number of countries that participated in the fair and the number of people who visited it, and being careful not to scrutinize too closely what kinds of activities attracted those visitors once they entered its gates. Similarly, while he also mentioned the number of exhibitors from the various states, in doing so he highlighted not only the scale of the Brazilian contribution but also the exposition's display of regional difference, for between them the federal capital and the states of Minas Gerais, São Paulo, and Rio de Janeiro accounted for more than 40 percent of the total number of Brazilian exhibitors.[110]

At the same event, Mário de Lima, who served as the commission's representative in Minas Gerais, argued that the exposition had made Brazilians conscious of all they could accomplish in spite of their doubts, because it displayed the progress that had been made in the national project of exploration, development, and unification. Stating that this project brought the republic's "civilizing work to all corners of the country," showing "a few sparks of the intense flame of progress that illuminates the coast," Lima depicted the interior as uncivilized and flattered the self-image of the coastal cities, by which he implied not a Fortaleza or a Natal but the major centers of the Southeast, especially Rio de Janeiro and São Paulo. The exposition, he said, brought together "inhabitants of every state," and together they demonstrated, "amid hostile voices, the capacity of the Brazilian, so unjustly questioned by cosmopolitan prejudice in comparison to what is ours."[111] Apparently, it did not occur to Lima that some Brazilians might see his speech itself as hostile to their ways of life and their claims on the nation. Thus, even as the organizing commission tapped Alves and Lima to celebrate the exposition as it closed its gates, in spite of their hopeful assertions they alluded to what many in their audience knew: the fair displayed not only Brazil's progress but also its challenges, among which the unevenness of national development and regional tensions were impossible to ignore.

Playing the Nation, but Not Together

Government organizers and their partners in the private sector approached athletics and team sports events much as they did the exposition and congresses dedicated to historical inquiry, religious practice, and medicine. They used these events to make the country's centenary a venue for articulating and sharing their vision of Brazil and Brazilians before an audience at once foreign and domestic. If the events functioned as organizers hoped they would, the foreign audience would learn that Brazil was modern and full of opportunity, closely attuned to the requirements of Progress and eager to work with foreign friends to develop the country's vast resources and meet its potential. Brazilians, meanwhile, would take away a sense of their nation's distinctive identity and their own responsibilities for helping it meet its glorious future, which meant both embracing modernity and setting aside the social, ideological, and regional differences that divided them from their fellow citizens.

The international exhibition was, of course, the centerpiece of the efforts undertaken by the national government, the most ambitious and expensive, but athletic competitions were in their own ways especially important. Within a generation of their introduction to Brazil in the late nineteenth century, modern sports had become dominant in the landscape of Brazilian popular culture, with rowing, athletics (track and field), volleyball, basketball, and tennis attracting admirers amid the hegemony established by football. One reason for the extraordinarily rapid growth of interest in such activities was advocates' insistence that football and other athletic practices would make Brazilians better citizens, better workers, and better soldiers, able to confront the demands and meet the opportunities of the modern world.[112] It is no surprise, then, that centenary celebrations all over Brazil included sports and athletics events. In the capital, government administrators worked with athletes and sports administrators to organize several major events, which like the exposition featured both national and international components. For example, in 1922 Rio de Janeiro hosted almost the entirety of the country's first-ever "national" football tournament, the Campeonato Brasileiro de Seleções Estaduais, as well as the sixth edition of the Campeonato Sul-Americano de Futebol. There were also three major athletics competitions, one for Brazilians, one continental (the Jogos Olímpicos Latino-Americanos, the first of its kind), and one for soldiers and sailors (the Jogos Mundiais Militares). These events and others, such as high-stakes horse races and athletics displays put on by Boy Scout troops, made Brazilians' interest in sports a central feature of celebrations of the centenary.

Indeed, perhaps more than any particular commercial or artistic display at the exposition, any monument, or even the most stirring address, sporting events offered the surest means of making the centenary what official organizers hoped it could be, a celebration of Brazil's strengths and a forecast of its bright future. First, sports linked Brazil to Western modernity in palpable ways, both because contemporaries understood them to be the practices of scientifically minded, cosmopolitan nations and because in organizing centenary athletics events Brazilians worked closely with well-respected international organizations, including the Young Men's Christian Association (YMCA) and the International Olympic Committee (IOC). Related to this, sports competitions allowed Brazilians to take the field and track alongside foreign rivals and friends as equals, regardless of the country's relative influence in the international order, whereas one of the exposition's themes was Brazil's underdevelopment. Second, like the raids of the centenary, the character of sporting events helped make explicit the hopes and assertions of centenary celebration organizers insofar as athletes did not display or speak their claims but instead performed and embodied them. Every jump, every pass, every sprint could be depicted as the enactment of Brazilian identity and proof of Brazilian accomplishment, and organizers and their partners in the press made sure to do so. As Eric Hobsbawm has written in reference to the attraction that "representative" football teams hold for nationalists, "the imagined community of millions seems more real as a team of eleven named people," to which it is important to add that those in the grandstands of athletic venues are more than audience members; they help make the spectacle of sports competitions into performances of identity and belonging.[113] Centenary organizers worked with sports administrators to give contemporaries the chance to imagine Brazil through its athletes and their performance of nationality. They sought to ensure that the athletes were especially skilled, strong, and agile and also that they had the right social profile and demeanor to embody the version of Brazil organizers hoped to portray. Moreover, as they did with the exposition they took seriously the importance of setting and space, enlisting the capital's leading sports organizations in the construction of new venues and the improvement of existing ones in order to offer athletes and fans the proper stages for their performance of the values of the centenary.

As was the case with the exposition and other centenary events, however, planners confronted various challenges that threatened the promise offered by the sporting events of the centenary. There were financial and logistical issues, administrative failures and missteps, and, most troubling of all, clashes over identity and nationality that turned Brazilians against one another and also threatened to make athletic competition into diplomatic crisis. On one hand, these problems were nothing new in Brazilian and South American sport, which had been riven by regionalist, nationalist, and organizational conflicts almost from the very beginning of modern sports' history on the continent, and the centenary sports were successful enough that they helped lay the groundwork for the future growth of the Olympic movement in the region, among other contributions. On the other hand, in the moment, many contemporaries understood that the sporting events of the centenary failed to deliver the benefits organizers hoped they would, and the events seemed to reinforce and even exacerbate the regionalist tensions that other centenary commemorations had helped reveal, much as the exhibition itself did.

In some respects, the sporting events organized to celebrate the centenary seem to have been a success. The Fluminense Football Club constructed the country's first sports stadium in 1918, in part to play host to the first major international sporting event held in Brazil, the 1919 South American football championship. The project reinforced the club's position as one of the capital's most important sports and social institutions and benefited from the support and assistance of national and city authorities. Three years later, Fluminense again hosted the football championship, along with many other centenary sports events, and again its leaders worked with civic authorities and sports administrators, this time to expand and improve the stadium, among other projects, which meant that in time for the centenary Brazil could boast one of the continent's largest and best-appointed athletics venues, a modern venue for a modern nation.

As it was when the Fluminense stadium first opened, in 1922 the reopening of the stadium was especially satisfying because the Brazilian national team, the seleção, won the South American football championship, defeating Paraguay 3-0 in the final match. Before then, the stadium had hosted many matches of Brazil's first national football championship, which pitted state select teams and one representing the federal capital against one another and ended in an exciting match between the representatives of the country's two strongest centers of sporting practice, the capital and the state of São Paulo. Following a similar structure and sequence, in August Fluminense hosted a track and field meet and other athletic events for Brazilian athletes, with the best among them qualifying to represent Brazil in the Jogos Latino-Americanos in September. These "Olympic" games were the first of their kind in the region, and required Brazilian organizers to work not only with their counterparts in Uruguay, Chile, and Argentina but also with the IOC and the YMCA, which helped plan and administer them. As César R. Torres has demonstrated, both international organizations considered the games successful, and the IOC sought to build upon them to expand the reach of the Olympics movement in Latin America.[114] Finally, in the military games, many of which also took place at the Fluminense stadium, Brazilian soldiers and sailors competed against Latin American as well as English, American, and Japanese athletes, giving contemporaries proof of one of the organizers' most ambitious claims, that the centenary meant

Brazil was ready to take its rightful place among the most advanced of nations.[115] These were some of the most well-attended events of the entire centenary schedule. The YMCA estimated that 162,000 people attended the events of the Jogos Latino-Americanos and the military games, which as José da Silva points out was a "a significant quantity for the era, as attendance amounted to nearly 15% of the city's population."[116] The football tournaments attracted even more attention, for not only did they attract tens of thousands to the Fluminense stadium, but, because of the extraordinary popularity of the sport, newspapers throughout Brazil covered them extensively and provided real-time updates to fans at their offices during many matches.[117]

Beneath this seeming success, however, were conflicts, controversies, and failures that lessened the events' capacity to realize the aims organizers hoped they would achieve. Some of these had to do with the venue itself. In 1918 and 1919 Fluminense had to weather fierce criticism of its first stadium project, in part because some residents objected to its appearance in their tony neighborhood of Laranjeiras, and in part because the club sought and received government support in the form of generous loans and the award of publicly owned land adjacent to its property. The expansion of the stadium and the construction of a new gymnasium for the centenary events raised some of the same challenges and questions, though fewer complaints. Again Fluminense's plans required land parcels not under its control, and again the city government saw fit to transfer them to the club. These included not only city-owned property but also privately held land, which prompted one property owner to sue in hopes of halting construction; the attempt failed. Construction was also expensive, and there were disputes over whether the club or the government would take responsibility for the costs. Although the club did secure government financial assistance, even then there were arguments over whether that assistance constituted a grant or a loan to be repaid. The records of the club and authorities are unclear on the point, but the club secretary, Mário Pollo, asserted that in completing construction and hosting the centenary games Fluminense had "assumed responsibilities which rightly pertained to the government" and it was "absolutely clear" that in 1922 Fluminense had made "sacrifices on behalf of our Brazil."[118] Pollo's claims of Fluminense's sacrifices elided the clear and significant benefits the club gained through the construction of the stadium and its expansion, but he was correct that the club took on a leading role in the centenary's most important sporting events, and did so at the request of the government's own officials and organizers.[119]

In fact, organization of the athletics events of the centenary was in some respects quite irregular, and contemporaries found it both confusing and controversial. Early on, organizers planned track and field and other "Olympics" events, but only for Brazilian athletes. Torres shows that they expanded their vision to include South American competitors and others at the urging of YMCA and IOC officials, and further that, although in retrospect these officials depicted what became known as the Jogos Latino-Americanos as a great success, in private conversations they acknowledged disappointments and irregularities, some of which they orchestrated themselves. Centenary planners tasked the most prominent national sports body, the Confederação Brasileira Desportos (CBD), with organizing the games, but whether because of bureaucratic inertia, mismanagement, or the economic crisis through which Brazil was suffering, by late 1921 little had been accomplished in preparing for the games.

YMCA and IOC officials grew frustrated with what they perceived to be the CBD's failings and they seriously considered withdrawing support for the event, a step that would have challenged Brazilians' claim that the celebrations were proof of their country's accession into the first rank of Western nations. Instead, representatives of the international organizations appealed directly to Carlos Sampaio, the city mayor and exhibition superintendent, and worked with him to marginalize the CBD through the creation of a new organization called the Comissão Organizadora dos Festejos Desportivos do Centenário. As Torres points out, though the new commission was able to accomplish much and oversaw the administration of not only the Jogos Latino-Americanos but also several other national and international competitions, the intervention of the YMCA and IOC helped breed among local administrators confusion and competition, which "arguably were not in the best interest of Brazilian sport."[120] That is, proud Brazilians could boast that in the centenary Brazil had hosted the very first "Olympic" games in Latin America, but centenary organizers paid for the privilege, the cost including infringement on Brazilian sporting sovereignty and preferential treatment for the aristocratic Fluminense Football Club.

These were not the events' only organizational irregularities and challenges. Some involved rivalries among sports administrators in the participating countries, such as the dissatisfaction of the mostly Spanish American Confederación Sudamericana de Atletismo with the administration of the games, which it had reluctantly transferred to Brazilian direction after lobbying by the IOC.[121] For their part, many athletes complained about the quality of the referees assigned to their events. Individual athletes and whole teams abandoned their competitions to protest what they saw as biased or incompetent refereeing, including, for example, the Argentine basketball team during a game against Uruguay, and the Paraguayan football team during a match against Argentina.

2.5. "South American Brotherhood," *A Careta*, 7 October 1922. The caption reads, "What some build by hand, others break with their feet!" In the South American football championship, the Latin American "Olympics," and the Brazilian competitions organized for the centenary, controversy on and off the playing fields threatened organizers' hopes to use sports to communicate their message of peace, cosmopolitanism, and modernity. Courtesy Charles E. Young Research Library, University of California, Los Angeles.

Such was their dissatisfaction with the organization and arbitration of the events that the entire team representing Chile withdrew from Jogos Olímpicos Latino-Americanos, while the controversies that surrounded the South American football championship led Congressman Carlos Garcia to propose the prohibition of international football matches in Brazil, as well as a prohibition on government support for the Brazilian national team should it play such matches abroad.[122]

While tensions among international organizations and administrators and athletes in neighboring states were significant, just as important for Brazilians were issues that highlighted and exacerbated the regionalist character of Brazilian sports during the period. First, centenary athletics events were plagued by arguments and backbiting between Paulistas and Cariocas. The rivalry was a permanent feature of Brazilian sports in the early twentieth century, most famously compromising Brazil's participation in the first two football World Cup tournaments. Before then it was apparent in 1922, despite the fact that, as Maurício Drummond points out, organizers worked in various ways to use the centenary events to attempt to forge peace between the two. For example, the CBD (which remained in charge of the football tournaments of the centenary even after the intervention of Carlos Sampaio and his new commission) scheduled the final match of the national football tournament in São Paulo rather than in the capital, and it arranged for international matches for a second-string Brazilian select team against teams from Argentina, Paraguay, and Uruguay to be held there even while the Campeonato Sul-Americano continued in Rio de Janeiro. Thus, 1922 saw the oddity of Brazil winning the Copa Roca against Argentina in São Paulo *and* the South American championship final match against Paraguay in Rio de Janeiro on the same day, 22 October.[123]

On-field success did not produce the camaraderie and resolution organizers hoped for. Fans in Rio de Janeiro made a practice match between Paulistas and Cariocas organized to help coaches decide who should join the seleção for the international tournament into a spectacle of anti-Paulista sentiment; newspapers and magazines accused organizers of showing preference to players from their own cities; and, most concerning to contemporaries, athletes themselves said they were victims of administrators' poor choices, which they attributed to regionalist bias. The matter came to a head when the seleção's star forward, the Paulista Arthur Friedenreich, gave an interview to Rio de Janeiro's *Correio da Manhã* in which he accused the Rio de Janeiro–dominated CBD of incompetence in training the team and neglecting its duty of care for the players from São Paulo. He said the administrators treated them as if they were "simply football players, that we have no other social role and that we do not merit any consideration." The CBD, Friedenreich said, failed to provide them proper equipment and access to practice facilities, financial assistance so that they could live comfortably in the capital during the competition, which lasted more than a month, and proper medical care. Friedenreich said he therefore had to turn to friends and acquaintances to help him recover from an injury he sustained in a match against Chile. "Naturally," he concluded, the Paulista contingent "is disgusted," and some were considering a return home before the end of the tournament.[124]

While Friedenreich's fellow Paulista, the defender Amílcar Barbuy, verified his claims, the leaders of the CBD rejected the accusations, calling them "fundamentally false."[125] The administrators chose not to offer a substantive rebuttal or address the players' concerns, at least publicly, leading predictably to Cariocas and Paulistas lining up in support of their fellow citizens. The two groups tolerated one another and saw out the tournament, but victory did not convince them to put aside their differences; instead they added the centenary dispute to the growing list of annoyances and grudges that characterized their long-running rivalry.[126]

Moreover, organizers' attempts to use sports to celebrate the centenary and display Brazil as they imagined it could be were troubled by problems other than the rivalry between Cariocas and Paulistas. The organizers of the Campeonato Brasileiro de Seleções Estaduais and the Brazilian centenary "Olympics" saw them as opportunities to build the national community, the centenary providing the chance to think and act in novel and more encompassing ways about Brazilian sport and the nation itself. There were no regular national sporting competitions in Brazil before 1922. Most leagues and competitions were organized as contests among teams from the same city or town, with a few bringing together athletes from neighboring locations, as was the case with the São Paulo city league, which also included the Santos club. In rare instances teams and individual athletes traveled to challenge rivals elsewhere, but, aside from ad hoc efforts to organize "Brazilian" teams for participation in international events, the only sustained effort Brazilians undertook to build a "national" sports community in the years before 1922 consisted of halting and irregular attempts by football administrators in São Paulo and the capital to organize a competition between teams from their cities. The events organized for the centenary were planned specifically for the celebration of Brazil's independence but they were also designed to take advantage of the celebratory moment to build a national sports community on a more sustained basis.

While competitions helped set down foundations for the future, things did not work out as planners hoped, in part because, like past efforts, the events of the centenary were far from national ones. Consonant with contemporary practice, the great majority of the athletes and football players to participate in the competitions were white or near-white, all were men, and they came from just a few places. The "Campeonato Nacional," as the Brazilian "Olympic" games were called, which organizers used to choose the Brazilian athletes who would represent the nation in the Jogos Latino-Americanos, included athletes from only a handful of places. There were forty-six from São Paulo, twenty-three from the city and state of Rio de Janeiro, and seven from Rio Grande do Sul, along with eighteen sailors affiliated with the Navy sports league (Liga de Sports da Marinha), which was based in the capital.[127] The first "Brazilian" football championship cast a wider net, and included select teams representing São Paulo, the state of Rio de Janeiro, the federal capital, Paraná, Rio Grande do Sul, and Bahia. Further, while all the contests of the Campeonato Nacional took place in Rio de Janeiro, some matches of the football championship took place outside it. Still, though, aside from Bahia, all the teams came from the South and Southeast, and the competition served mostly as a prelude to the predictable final championship match, which pitted Cariocas against Paulistas, who won 4-1 on 13 August in São Paulo. The teams played again in Rio de Janeiro a few days later so that coaches and administrators could decide which players would join the Brazilian seleção for the South American championship; that is, as it was in the past and, with rare exceptions, would continue to be the case for many years into the future, the 1922 seleção was constituted exclusively by footballers from Rio de Janeiro and São Paulo.

Thus, events labeled "Brazilian" and designed to promote the notion of a national sporting community in fact reified regional distinctions. They pitted athletes designated not Brazilians but Cariocas, Paulistas, Gaúchos, and so on against one another. They reminded Brazilians of the dominance of Rio de Janeiro and São Paulo in athletic accomplishment and representation because of administrators' decision to hold the majority of the events in those two cities. And, despite the names with which administrators branded the events, they were far from national competitions, with much of the country left out as Cariocas and Paulistas resumed their endless struggle for supremacy.

The regionalist character of these events was especially apparent in Pernambuco and neighboring states, where local athletes complained that their compatriots to the south exhibited a very narrow view of the nation and organized a separate set of competitions for the northern and northeastern players they said were excluded from so-called Brazilian competitions. Pernambucanos agreed with Paulistas, Cariocas, Gaúchos, and other Brazilians about the benefits of modern sports, and they agreed that the celebration of the centenary should include athletics competitions, football tournaments, and other sporting events. A year before the centenary date they were already discussing how to incorporate sports into their centenary celebrations, for example, in a "festival of Olympianism" at the Theatro Santa Izabel, and by early 1922 they were making plans and raising money for special competitions in track and field, football, rowing, water polo, swimming, tennis, and other activities.[128]

At that time administrators of local clubs and leagues also discussed the invitations they had received from the CBD to participate in the "national" competitions and tournaments to be held in Rio de Janeiro, but the discussions did not proceed very far, and they quickly decided Pernambucanos would not travel south. Sports administrators pointed to rivalries between local clubs as well as lukewarm support from the sporting public, which, they said, meant the city and state lacked the financial resources and the "spirit of solidarity" necessary to organize representative teams for the national events.[129] Octávio Moraes also described organizers' disappointment in the region's young people, who in his view were not committed enough to physical education and activity but were instead stuck in "a torpor" from which they needed waking. He said he and other sportsmen hoped to use the centenary events to stoke local interest, and regretted that they had not achieved all they had hoped in time to be able to accept the CBD's invitation.[130] While they may have believed this to be the case, it is also true that there was enough cooperation and interest among sports athletes, enthusiasts, and administrators that they were able to organize a number of sporting events for the centenary and to obtain significant financial resources to do so.

Further, even as they pointed to local and regional reasons for the decision not to participate in the centenary sporting events organized for Rio de Janeiro, Pernambucanos also blamed southerners for their plight, which they said was the plight of the entire region of which Pernambucanos often depicted themselves as the natural leaders. Thus the *Diario de Pernambuco* criticized the administrators of northern sports leagues, who the paper said "forget to perform their duties," and also "the highest leaders of national sport," who had "abandoned" northern athletes and sportsmen.[131] It said that those adminstrators left "the despised and forgotten North to confront difficulties" and left it to its own devices.[132] The journalist and organizer Cicero Brasileiro de Mello was more specific, saying that the CBD in particular evinced "little interest" in northern sporting life and that its "neglect" was compounded by the "lie" that the North did not possess good and accomplished athletes who could compete against their compatriots in the south.[133]

Aside from, perhaps, financial assistance, it is not clear exactly what these critics expected or hoped to have received from the CBD and other nominally national organizations. In 1922, they also wanted the imprimatur of these organizations for their own events, which they saw as opportunities both to give the lie to southern assumptions and to build sports communities in the northern and northeastern regions. Given that the participation of northern states in events in the national capital was "difficult," the *Diario* said of the Campeonato do Norte that "we see no more noble and patriotic way for the states of the North to commemorate the centenary of Brazilian independence than by gathering their youth for this great athletics challenge."[134] Similarly, Mello called it "a patriotic undertaking" that would bind northern and northeastern sporting communities together and thereby "react" against southern neglect.[135] And the *Jornal do Recife* called the idea "commendable," though it worried about the level of competition organizers could hope to obtain, given that sports had developed unevenly in the region, Pernambucanos enjoying the reputation of "leading practitioners of sport in the Brazilian Northeast," despite the complaints of figures like Octávio Moraes.[136]

These commentators were working out how they understood the regions of Brazil and Pernambuco's own place in the nation, as the *Diario* and Mello referred to the "North" and the *Jornal* increasingly used the newer designation of "Northeast." It seems that in sports as in other contexts, the coming of the centenary prompted these reflections and helped contemporaries define the region. Southern and southeastern authorities, though, had their own notions, and when Pernambucano administrators requested their endorsement for the "northern" games "national" administrators rejected the request; according to the *Diario*, the southerners stated that "Pernambuco's plans will greatly harm the centenary Olympic Games to be held in Rio de Janeiro next September."[137] The CBD and other administrators were vague about the character of the injury they feared, and it is difficult to know what Brazilians in the capital and elsewhere thought of Pernambuco's plans, which received very little attention outside the North and Northeast. These authorities likely understood Pernambucanos as undermining their hopes of organizing competitions that could be called national ones, compounding the many other challenges they faced with an explicitly regionalist threat. Financial difficulties and administrative missteps and rivalries (some of which were inflected with regional tensions) were already jeopardizing organizers' plans in a variety of ways, not least in terms of their plans for sports and athletics events, and Pernambuco now purported to speak for and organize an entire region, making it clear that in sports as in so much else Brazil was a country of parts rather than a unified national community.

For their part, Pernambucanos were disappointed in their putative national leaders, but they did not give up, and instead pressed ahead with their plans. Using the institutional reach and resources of Recife's leading sports organization, the Liga Pernambucana dos Desportos Terrestres, they made plans and raised funds from private donors and they also lobbied the governments of the city and state, both of which agreed to provide financial support. It should be recalled that these governments had denied such support to exhibition organizers, but the city provided 5 contos de réis and the state allocated 20 contos, which contemporaries said was the first award the state government had ever made to promote sporting activities.[138] They reached out beyond Recife to invite the participation of athletes in more than a dozen cities and towns in Pernambuco and in the states of Pará, Maranhão, Ceará, Rio Grande do Norte, Paraíba, Alagoas, Piauí, and Bahia. They also contacted the governments of these states directly in order to request financial assistance for organization of the events, even though their fundraising had been successful enough that by mid-July they were already able to commit to cover the transportation and lodging costs of the state delegations that accepted the invitation.[139]

By the middle of 1922 it had become clear that athletes and administrators in Pernambuco and many other states had no intention whatsoever of participating in "national" sporting events, and that the Campeonato do Norte would proceed with or without the approval of the CBD. Perhaps in order to save face, or because, as the *Diario* put it, "the argument of the members of the Confederação was flawed in itself," in late July the CBD relented and gave its sanction for the event. Regardless of the reason, this was, according to the *Diario*, cause for regional pride: local leaders' success in not only organizing the competitions but gaining CBD support for them was best understood as "a victory for Pernambuco."[140]

When September came, there were very few official events to celebrate the centenary in Recife, but the city did play host to a variety of sporting events, many of which were of an exclusively local nature and matched events held throughout the republic, such as a track and field meet, a crew tournament, and a football championship for city clubs. As in the national capital, soldiers also joined in, both as participants in the track and field meet and in a meet exclusively for the members of the twenty-first battalion of light infantry stationed in Recife. Beginning on Independence Day, the city also hosted an intermunicipal football tournament for select teams from throughout the state and, a week later, a series of matches between the state select teams of Pernambuco, Paraíba, and Rio Grande do Norte. A team representing Piauí had declared its intention to participate as well, and was still planning to compete as late as 17 September, but due to travel difficulties, the team never arrived in Pernambuco.[141]

To be sure, this roster of events did not match organizers' ambitions. Only around half of the towns and cities invited to participate in the intermunicipal football tournament did so, and the interstate tournament included teams from only three of the nine states Pernambucanos hoped would join. However, in certain respects their efforts seem to have been successful, at least in relative terms, and they certainly were significant. Organizers were not able to convince every town in Pernambuco or every state in the North and Northeast to send athletes to compete in their events, but the CBD and its partners in the national government were also unable to meet their own goals, despite all their resources. Teams from only five of twenty states joined the capital's own team in the "national" football championship, and athletes from only three states, the capital, and the navy participated in the "national" Olympics meet. Meanwhile, conditions were especially challenging for sports administrators in Recife, where political violence and the intervention of federal forces had resulted in the suspension of the city football championship earlier in the year and where the city's other centenary celebrations were quite limited.[142] Given these circumstances, the fact that Pernambucanos were able to organize centenary sporting events seems just as important as their relatively modest character.

Furthermore, contemporaries saw Recife's centenary athletics events as successful, in purely sporting terms and in terms of building the sporting community. The track and field meets, the crew competition, and, especially, the football tournaments were among the best-attended of all the centenary events, much to the delight of those who worried that Pernambucanos did not dedicate enough attention to sports and other forms of athletics and that those who did were not quite as sporting as one might hope. Local newspapers noted that attendance was strong throughout the weeks of the competitions, and the *Jornal do Recife* took special notice of the many fans who came to the city to cheer on athletes from their own towns, such as when teams from Olinda and Caraurú faced one another in the intermunicipal tournament's semifinal match, thus helping fulfill one of the organizers' goals: to bring together Pernambucanos from throughout the state.[143] In the *Diario*, A. Fernandes focused on the football tournaments' capacity for promoting camaraderie among Brazilians. He wrote that although some worried that football in Brazil was degenerating into a "school for brutality," the centenary events attested to the public-spiritedness and sense of fair play of Pernambucanos and their guests. He wrote that the games of the centenary "are realized in an atmosphere of mutual affection," and that it was important "to salute the correct way in which those who see in [sport] a means to improve the qualities of the raça are practicing it in this Centenary year."[144] The columnist saw Recife's centenary sports as a surprising and significant accomplishment to be celebrated.

Finally, just as the events in the capital helped build a foundation for future "national" competitions, the competitions in Recife helped Pernambucanos build the sports and cultural community of the North and the newly designated "Northeast." Pernambucanos saw themselves as the natural architects and leaders of this community, and they used the centenary as a venue for articulating and advancing the project. Their plans for the "sporting festivals" of the centenary were part of these efforts, which is one reason that CBD support was so important in 1922. As far as Pernambucanos were concerned, the sanction of national sports authorities confirmed the accuracy of their surmise that Pernambuco spoke for and was the natural center of the region that would come to be called the Northeast.[145]

This did not mean that Pernambuco or the region was apart from the nation; after all, Pernambucanos held these events to honor the nation's centenary. Rather, Pernambucanos organized their centenary sports to display their sense of how the state and region fit into the whole national community, to show that it was distinctive and coherent, that it did not depend on the southern states, and that it, too, was Brazilian. Recognizing and attempting to strengthen Pernambuco's connections beyond the region, local sports administrators sought the approval of the CBD for their Campeonato do Norte and reminded it of its responsibilities beyond the Southeast. Meanwhile, Cicero Brasileiro de Mello championed the idea of the tournament and also traveled in advance of Pernambuco's sporting events to learn from athletes and administrators in São Paulo, which many contemporaries acknowledged as possessing the most advanced and accomplished sporting community in the country. Like most advocates of sport, he insisted that sporting life was intimately and directly connected to the civic and economic health of every modern people, and thus he explained to a newspaper in Bahia that he traveled to São Paulo because it was "a power with a bright future and in its amazing display of technical ability Brazilians find the proof of their progress and their hegemony."[146] That is, Brazilians had much to learn from the way Paulistas organized and played sports, not only in order to build their own athletic organizations and improve their own athletic performances but also because lessons in sports were lessons in every aspect of modernity. Expressed by a leading figure in Recife's sports and sports journalism, the sentiment flattered Paulistas' self-image as the leaders of the nation, while also asserting Pernambuco's role in organizing and guiding its own region; after all, it was Recife, not, say, Salvador, that was organizing the "northern" championship.

Once centenary sporting events in the Southeast began, Pernambucanos and other Brazilians in the North and Northeast were happy to celebrate both their own accomplishments and "Brazilian" victories in the Jogos Latino-Americanos and the Campeonato Sul-Americano, each of which competitions local newspapers covered closely and in detail. The *Diario de Pernambuco* and the *Jornal do Recife* reported on each event and each football match, like almost every other publication in the country with particular attention to the matches of the national seleção in the South American championship. And like those other publications, they read deep meaning into Brazilians' victories. More than two weeks after the final match of the South American championship, the *Jornal do Recife* celebrated the seleção with a front-page photograph and the call, "Viva Brazil!"[147] Just as commentators said that Pernambuco's own events and its own regional tournament attested to the state's progress toward civic and "racial" health, so too they celebrated the athletes representing the nation for more than their sporting accomplishments. The editors of the *Jornal* asserted that the development of Brazilian sports affirmed the progress of the country as a whole, and that, even before the seleção won its championship, the victories of 1922 announced its "renaissance." They pointed to Brazilians' accomplishments in the Jogos Mundiais Militares and the Jogos Latino-Americanos, stating that although the country was enduring many political and economic difficulties, these athletes, this "hopeful youth of Brazil," gave their compatriots great confidence in its present and its future.[148]

In many respects, then, the sporting events organized for the centenary were like the international exhibition and its adjuncts, including the horticulture and livestock expositions and the many congresses organized for the occasion. Brazilians depicted the sports of the centenary as essential to the celebration of the great event. As athletes and as spectators, they enjoyed football and other sporting pursuits, so it was fitting that they would be included in the celebrations. More important, through sports Brazilians told the stories they wanted to tell about the nation and themselves, and sports offered the opportunity to tell them in a public, performative way. Football fields and swimming pools functioned in the same way as did exhibition pavilions and lecture halls, offering Brazilians venues in which to stage spectacles of order and progress, identity and the nation. These were closely managed so that actors, roles, and performances would hew closely to organizers' expectations and broadcast the messages they hoped to share with foreign and domestic audiences.

However, just as much as the exposition did, sporting events presented political leaders and celebration organizers with a number of challenges. These figures faced quotidian difficulties having to do with finance and organization, including how to pay for new facilities and how to administer hundreds of matches, games, and events on a scale that was unprecedented in Brazil. More significant, centenary sports revealed the deep-seated tensions among Brazilians about what it meant to be Brazilian, who belonged to the national community and who did not, what roles they ought to play within it, and who was to decide such essential questions. Thus, the centenary sports joined with the exposition to display the ongoing political and social marginalization of women, working people, and people of color, while also helping to bring into the open—and to exacerbate—the regionalist tensions that organizers in Rio de Janeiro had hoped to leave behind with their "international" and "national" events. On the football field and in the exposition, Cariocas and Paulistas carried on their rivalry, while Pernambucanos, Gaúchos, Paraibanos, and others displayed their own dissatisfactions with a status quo that seemed to relegate to them the roles of bystanders to and followers of southeastern hegemony.

In the end, the major public events of the centenary were performances of unity and fracture, modernity and underdevelopment. Above all, they were performances of inquiry. In the variety of architectural styles of the exhibition; in its maps and statistical displays; in the pavilions highlighting São Paulo's modernity and Rio Grande do Norte's underdevelopment; and in the attempt to build a national sporting community where only local competitions had existed, events organizers demonstrated that they understood the centenary as an opportunity to bring Brazilians together, as the editors of the exposition magazine said, in order to "know their country better, to know it well, to throw light on all the corners of its territories, to keep their eyes open in all directions." Organizers' prejudices and the challenges they faced limited the success of this enterprise, but, clearly, they helped open up space for inquiry in the physical space of fields and pavilions, posing questions that would continue to be asked in the ensuing years. Indeed, even those who did not accept the invitations offered by planners in the national capital joined in the project. Gaúchos debated how they fit into the national community and even whether they belonged to it, while Pernambucanos staged their own performances of identity, which some called "northern" and others began to call "northeastern" and all called Brazilian. These questions were not answered in 1922, but the centenary lent urgency to Brazilians' engagement with them, and the exposition and the centenary sports were essential, for they put the inquiry on display.

Chapter 3

The Uses of Independence and Other Histories

In the arguments made by the editors of *O Separatista* and other supporters of Rio Grande do Sul Governor Borges de Medeiros against the republican state and their local rivals in 1922 and 1923, they drew on the past in explicit ways, claiming they followed their forebears in the nineteenth century to justify their criticisms and demands. In particular, they emphasized the importance of the separatists of the Revolução Farroupilha and also the state's leaders in the early republic, especially Medeiros's patron, the strident federalist Júlio de Castilhos, called the "Patriarch" of Rio Grande do Sul. That this should have been the case is of course unsurprising. The commemoration of the events that brought about the country's political independence called forth consideration of the past, as it always did, and the significance with which contemporaries imbued the centenary as well as the scale of the celebrations they planned to mark it showed that history and History gained an extraordinary purchase in 1922. Brazilians performed their appreciations of the country's past and debated its meaning in a variety of venues, in scholarly circles and far beyond them.

The country's preeminent historical institution, the Instituto Histórico e Geográfico Brasileiro (IHGB), took a leading role in this regard: it organized a series of lectures focused on independence, which began in January and continued into 1923; it convened an international academic conference drawing together scholars of the history of the Americas; and it sponsored the publication of commemorative works, such as reproductions of historical documents and scholarly monographs. Almost all the states of Brazil had their own historical and geographic institutes in 1922, and they followed the example of the national organization, often focusing on how independence unfolded in their own states and regions, and many of these groups played prominent roles in planning local events to celebrate the centenary. The centenary also saw initiatives in the country's museum culture, the most prominent of which were the new Museu Histórico Nacional, which was attached to the international exhibition in the capital, and the grand reopening of the Museu Paulista (commonly known as the Museu do Ipiranga), which in 1922 discarded its previous focus on natural history to concentrate on the history of the state and nation, with a particular interest in independence.

Beyond the venues of professional and academic history, many other Brazilians took the opportunity of the centenary to comment on and debate the independence story and the nation's past. From President Epitácio Pessoa and his ministers to members of congress allied with and rival to his government, from governors and state deputies to mayors and other local officials, government leaders took advantage of the centenary celebrations to comment on Brazilian history, their interpretations often conveniently matching their own political interests. Every magazine and newspaper narrated the country's independence, with many inviting scholars to contribute essays and some publishing special numbers dedicated to historical subjects. And many of the private and public celebrations of the centenary were explicit in their attention to independence and other histories, including formal processions by students and soldiers, Carnival parades and the marches to celebrate the raiders of the centenary, the erection of monuments, the installation of plaques and other markers, and the inauguration of new parks, schools, hospitals, and other public and private works.

The power of these performances of memory was in the seeming significance of the moment and also in their variety. That is, the centenary demonstrated that Brazilians disagreed about the meaning and events of independence, with every scholar, museum director, politician, newspaper editor, and, indeed, every citizen and resident their own historian. Here the Brazilians of 1922 joined their forebears, who began to argue about the story of independence almost immediately after 1822, with confusion and disagreements even over which date should serve as the new nation's independence day.[1] Emilia Viotti da Costa, Hendrik Kraay, and Noé Freire Sandes, among others, have demonstrated the lack of consensus among nineteenth-century Brazilians about the relative importance of various actors and events. As these authors show, Brazilians used arguments over the independence story to engage in debates about the character of Brazil, about the legitimacy of the state and other institutions, and about who belonged in Brazil and who did not.[2] A narration of independence events focused on Pedro could be a way of focusing attention on the country's Portuguese roots and the importance of the national state, as was the case with the highly influential historian Francisco Adolpho de Varnhagen, for example.[3] Meanwhile, those who focused on the efforts of José Bonifácio de Andrada, Joaquim Gonçalves Ledo, and other counselors included some who looked to ratify Pedro's importance by emphasizing his partnership with Brazil-born advisers and others who used them to challenge the emperor's significance, thereby focusing on the differences between Brazilians and Portuguese, or in order to critique the imperial state.[4] And there were other stories to tell and events to commemorate, such as the Inconfidência Mineira, the Revolução Pernambucana, and Salvador's Dois de Julho, each one employed to make arguments about Brazil's past in order to shape its present and future.

Such arguments continued throughout the imperial period, with advocates of official and revisionist histories competing for influence over Brazilian memory, as could be seen in the equestrian statue of Pedro I unveiled in Rio de Janeiro in 1862. In an attempt to reconcile Brazilians with the unpopular former emperor and assert the continuing importance of the monarchy and the central government, conservative partisans commissioned the statue, which conflated Pedro's declaration of independence on 7 September 1822 with his acceptance of the constitution on 25 March 1824, so that rather than the sword he raised to make the Grito do Ipiranga, the statue depicts Pedro holding the constitution aloft. As Kraay shows, the attempt did not keep the liberal critics from attacking their rivals' history and labeling the statue a "bronze lie," for they remembered Pedro as an unwilling partner in constitutional governance and they rejected the attempt to rehabilitate his memory.[5] Instead, they advanced José Bonifácio as the "Patriarch of Independence," and the debates over the nature and meaning of independence continued.

A different sort of challenge emerged after 1889. While monarchists like Eduardo Prado and Joaquim Nabuco used the memory and celebration of independence as a means of critiquing the new republic, the new regime's architects and advocates struggled to come to terms with how they should relate to the founders of the state they had seized. They tried various approaches, including expanding on the relatively new idea of celebrating the 1789 Inconfidência Mineira and other "precursors" of independence, which served to begin the story decades prior to Pedro's interventions. For example, in his important 1893 text, *Festas Nacionaes*, Rodrigo Otávio Langgard de Menezes depicted Pedro as a counterrevolutionary and advocate for Portuguese influence who frustrated the ambitions of Brazilian patriots. The author rejected the notion that 7 September 1822 should be understood as marking the country's independence, which by then had been "consummated and recognized as a fact." He argued that 7 September was a convenient date on which to commemorate the political separation of Brazil from Portugal but also a reminder of the beginning of the struggle against the monarchy, which he called "an anachronistic lapse in the history of Brazil."[6] Although Menezes's book became required reading for young people during the early years of the republic, it was difficult to convince Brazilians to reconsider the significance of the date that had been the most important civic holiday in the national calendar in the nineteenth century.[7] José Murilo de Carvalho shows that leading governmental figures, scholars, educators of the republic promoted the Inconfidente Tiradentes as a martyr to independence and one of the great national heroes, situating him in contrast to Pedro and also to the protagonists of the Revolução Pernambucana, the liberation of Salvador, and other more violent and democratic episodes of the independence story.[8]

Brazilians continued these arguments throughout the first decades of the republican era, but the centenary was especially important as it prompted many among them to train their attention on the story of independence and what it might reveal about the character of the nation. As Noé Sandes writes, it initiated "a moment for refounding national memory," when scholars, political actors, and many others engaged in an intensive and wide-ranging project of history, memory, and identity, beginning with the publication of several new and revised and republished works by professional scholars.[9] Historians have done much important work on the historiography of the centenary, focusing especially on the IHGB, and have shown how its scholars attempted to use the centenary to forge the consensus that had been lacking in earlier times. Many of these scholars gained attention beyond the lecture halls of the institute, as their contributions were published not only by the IHGB but also in the contemporary periodical press. There their works joined comments and essays by figures like the director of the Arquivo Nacional, Luís Gastão d'Escragnolle Dória, and the prolific Elísio de Carvalho, so that academic and public historians played important roles in shaping popular understanding of and conversation about independence during the centenary period.

But of course the debate was not only a scholarly one, and it is essential to look beyond academic circles in order to understand the ways that memory and history shaped the performance of identity in 1922, to public venues like the new Museu Histórico Nacional, to broadsheet newspapers and popular magazines, and to events like the erection and inauguration of the many monuments completed for the centenary. If we adopt this more ample view it becomes clear that, as much as they helped bring Brazilians together through their shared history, centenary events revealed Brazilians' continuing disagreements and in some respects exacerbated the disputes of memory. These disputes tended to fall along two registers, one having to do with place and the other with time. On one hand, they came freighted with tensions over the relationship between region and nation, especially in terms of how Brazilians in the Southeast and those in the North and Northeast narrated the events of independence and explained their significance. On the other, they fell according to perceived connections and disjunctions between tradition and modernity, with some Brazilians focusing on the continuities that survived independence and others depicting the independence period as a watershed moment ushering in the possibility of profound change.

Such differences of interpretation and emphasis resulted in noise, contradiction, and fracture, which meant that rather than working to make the independence story part of a harmonious national story about the past, the centenary helped remind Brazilians of their differences with one another in their own day. Contemporaries recognized this difficulty, and some feared that it might represent a fundamental breakdown of the national community. This helps explain the activities of the IHGB in 1922 and 1923 as it sought to offer the public a consensus view of independence, which among other characteristics aimed to elide the major differences of interpretation that defined Brazilian scholarship and popular memory. And it also explains why many of those engaged in the projects of memory in 1922 used the centenary to search the past for the tools to promote harmony and order.

That search led some influential figures to a rediscovery of the country's first emperor and the imperial era, which republican historiography had gone to great pains to critique and reject. Related to this, as chapter 4 shows in more detail, was the work of some scholars and other figures who narrated independence as a story of Brazilians and Portuguese working together, a "Luso-Brazilian" triumph that did not mean a permanent rupture between the two peoples. Finally, the search led other Brazilians to the Catholic Church. The church was especially energetic in the celebrations of the centenary, during which, among other efforts, it organized a successful Eucharistic Congress in the capital as well as sometimes enormous outdoor masses of thanksgiving and parades throughout the country. Through these efforts Brazil's Catholic clergy and laity claimed the centenary and the nation, and they justified the claim through their own particular rendering of the Brazilian past. Led by figures such as the president of the IHGB, Afonso Celso, they argued that this history must be acknowledged and claimed, so that in Brazil's second centenary the church could play its historic role in "promoting and consolidating harmony among Brazilians," as Celso put it.[10]

Still, while the possibility of using the past to bring Brazilians together in the present was attractive to many, neither the activities of the IHGB, nor the work of Lusophile scholars and Portuguese residents, nor the claims of the church kept Brazilians from continuing their arguments about independence and other episodes of the nation's history. The goal of crafting a shared history and, through it, a cohesive national community, was a long way from realization in 1922, and the centenary celebrations exacerbated the problem by giving Brazilians rare opportunities to put their disagreements on display. Indeed, such were their disagreements over how to understand the country's past that many Brazilians did not accept the idea that they should celebrate independence at all. Rather, they joined their compatriots in the performances of commemoration, but their celebrations often related to independence only in a notional sense. Instead they preferred to celebrate other events and other histories, claiming these were more important than was independence in the making of the nation, and therefore more worthy of remembrance, regardless of the nominal reasons for the festivities of the centenary year.

Building Consensus in Rio de Janeiro

The first centenary of 1922 came on 9 January, which was the hundredth anniversary of the "Fico," when Pedro, who was serving as his father's regent in Brazil, rejected the order of the Lisbon Cortes that he return to Portugal, ostensibly in order to facilitate Brazil's return to colonial status in the aftermath of the Napoleonic crisis. In some respects, the story of the Fico matched the Grito do Ipiranga, concentrating attention on Pedro and his role in Brazilian independence. For those suspicious of Pedro and his legacy, however, the Fico was more attractive than the Grito because Pedro's announcement came after he had been delivered an appeal to remain in the kingdom, orchestrated by leading liberal activists and signed by eight thousand subjects; these were the "nation" and the "people" the prince referenced when he declared, "If it is for the good of all and makes the nation happy, I am ready! Tell the people that I will remain." That is, the Fico fit nicely into one of the major interpretations of independence offered by nationalists, that Pedro did not make or lead independence, but instead simply accepted the judgment of the Brazilian people and the fact of their distinctive and sovereign character.

The national government declared the Dia do Fico a public holiday in 1922, and Brazilians throughout the country observed the date, for the most part in a modest and reserved way. Newspapers published appreciative editorials and short columns narrating the event, officials made public pronouncements, and schools convened their students to mark the occasion. There were much larger events in Rio de Janeiro, which had been the scene of the events of January 1822. While the Grito had taken place along a streambank in São Paulo, the Fico had occurred in the capital when Pedro accepted the petition organized by José Clemente Pereira and Joaquim Gonçalves Ledo, so its celebration gave Rio de Janeiro the opportunity to assert that it too had served as "the stage of one of the most important steps toward Independence," in the words of Carlos Leite in the *Jornal do Brasil*.[11] The city government organized a variety of events to mark the occasion, including the publication of primary materials collected by the city archive, the decoration of the route the petitioners took as they brought their appeal to the prince, and a series of public celebrations including representatives of every major institution in the city. Organizers used these events to initiate their centenary project to reconcile Brazil's present with its many pasts and to synthesize various interpretations of independence and the character of the nation. But there was also evidence of the discord and the disagreement that would challenge and frustrate their hopes.

Thus, on one hand, organizers festooned the city with symbols and imagery of the independence era, including the flags and coats of arms of the United Kingdom of Portugal, Brazil, and the Algarves and of imperial Brazil. But they also took care to include the emblems of the republic, and they mixed republican symbols with royal and imperial ones, "on purpose," according to the *Correio da Manhã*, "to show that both groups together made the history of the people which now remembers the story of Independence in one single commemoration" (see fig. 3.1).[12] This attempt at synthesis characterized all the events of the celebrations. For example, organizers began the official program with a Catholic mass and called on several speakers to offer remarks that emphasized the role played by the church in independence, but they also included representatives of the Positivist Church, which was so important to the foundation and character of the early republic. On the other hand, there were those who questioned the propriety of celebrating the Fico. The Partido Republicano Nacional worried that authorities intended to restore the Dia do Fico to the nation's calendar of civic holidays, as it had been in the imperial period, and, while the Liga da Defesa Nacional participated

3.1. One of the events celebrating the centenary of the Fico, at the Igreja da Imperial Irmandade de Nossa Senhora do Rosário e São Benedito dos Homens Pretos, on 9 January 1922. Note organizers' intentional mingling of imperial and republican imagery. Photograph by Augusto Malta. Courtesy of the Instituto Moreira Salles.

in the celebrations, other nationalists worried about the fact that many of the protagonists in the drama of the Fico were Portuguese.[13] As Victruvio Marcondes put it in *Gil Blas*, Brazilian patriots must beware the "mystifiers" and "Portugalizers" who sought to use such celebrations to confuse Brazilians' sense of their own history in order to help Portugal and the Portuguese resident in the country to "recolonize" it, culturally and economically; he recommended that Brazilians instead focus their attentions on Dois de Julho and its story of conflict and liberation.[14]

Advocates of the official view confronted such sentiments in a variety of ways. Mayor Carlos Sampaio assured the Republican party that the declaration of the Dia do Fico as a holiday was a onetime event, while Escragnolle Dória complained that José Clemente was not afforded *more* attention from the organizers of the events, lamenting the fact that his grave was not one of the sites chosen for the celebrations and had not been adorned to match other locations in the city.[15] The *Correio* took a more aggressive tack. It depicted the independence movement as a partnership between Brazilians and Portuguese, such as José Clemente, who embraced the Brazilian cause, and it attacked the critics of the celebrations of the Fico both for their Lusophobia and their attempts to rewrite history, calling them "'nationalists' with no sense of nationalism." For the paper, the celebration of the centenary of the Fico was obligatory, for it reminded Brazilians that Pedro had served as "the convergence point for the nationalist movement," helping to ensure its champions would not turn on one another; he had been "the singular figure which Brazil needed at that moment to consolidate its political unity." Those who questioned the importance of the Fico attempted an "impossible disfigurement" of the historical record, which must be rejected by all right-thinking Brazilians.[16]

Finally, in the first talk in the IHGB's "Ano da Independência" lecture series, Supreme Court justice Augusto Olímpio Viveiros de Castro also took up these themes, asserting the importance of the event but also acknowledging the hesitation of some Brazilians to join in its celebration. He mentioned Pedro and José Clemente, but the protagonists of the event, in his telling, were the Brazilian people. Focusing on leaders and residents of Rio de Janeiro, São Paulo, Minas Gerais, and Rio Grande do Sul, he emphasized the actions of the Brazilians who prevailed upon Pedro to abandon his reluctance and embrace the local cause, which made the Fico "an exclusively Brazilian accomplishment." He conceded that the Fico "is not a Republican occasion" and that independence under the Portuguese prince "delayed the Republic for 67 years," but he asked his republican friends to accept the benefits of the process as it unfolded, ratifying one of the major thrusts of contemporary historiography in arguing that Pedro's guidance helped ensure Brazil's territorial integrity and lessened the necessity for violence in achieving independence.[17]

Measured in terms of attendance and the reactions of print media of the capital, the celebrations of the Fico were a success, but they also set a conflicted pattern for the performances of history and memory that followed in the ensuing months and continued until celebrations of the centenary of the liberation of Salvador on 2 July 1923. That is, while official organizers and their partners in the IHGB and other institutions told a story aimed at crafting consensus and synthesizing sometimes competing histories of independence and Brazil, others rejected the official project and instead insisted on their own historical interpretations. In fact, even in official circles in the capital, significant displays of disagreement demonstrated just how difficult forging a unifying consensus would be.

As the IHGB lecture series continued, with historians narrating each of the major and minor episodes of 1822, the speakers developed some of Castro's main themes. They emphasized the cooperation between the prince and his adopted people, led and embodied in their narrative by José Bonifácio, whose activities were the subject of the second lecture, given by Artur Pinto da Rocha on 16 January to mark the formation of

Brazil's first governing ministry. Thus, among other subjects, they recounted Pedro's role in meeting the Portuguese squadron sent to quell the separatist movement (the subject of a lecture by Moreira Guimarães), his journey to Minas Gerais (by Alfredo Valadão), and, of course, the Grito do Ipiranga (by Afonso Celso), but they also made sure to emphasize the actions of José Bonifácio and other counselors, who helped guide Pedro and inculcate in him a sense of Brazilianness and responsibility, for example, in naming him "Defensor Perpétuo do Brasil" (the designation the subject of the lecture by Laudelino Freire). Together, the lecturers worked to rehabilitate the memory of Pedro without depicting him as a solitary hero or joining his nativist critics in disparaging his contributions.[18]

This approach also had the effect of reconciling Portuguese and Brazilian actors in the drama of independence—Pedro and José Clemente, José Bonifácio and Gonçalves Ledo—rather than emphasizing the conflict between Portuguese and Brazilian peoples. Organizers reinforced this theme by asking series speakers to focus on the events of 1822, rather than the longer and broader story of the Brazilian nation's emergence and its struggle for sovereignty. Over the course of the previous hundred years, and especially after the foundation of the republic in 1889, Brazilian historians had discovered what they characterized as a series of precursors to independence, such as the Guerra dos Mascates (Pernambuco, 1711), the Inconfidência Mineira (Minas Gerais, 1789), the Revolta dos Alfaiates (Bahia, 1798), and the Revolução Pernambucana (Pernambuco, 1817). And there were those episodes narrators often included in recounting the story of Brazilian sovereignty that came after 1822, including, of course, the liberation of Bahia in 1823 but also the struggles against Pedro, such as the secessionist Confederação do Equador movement in 1824 and the emperor's abdication in 1831, which in many tellings ratified independence.

The IHGB and its speakers acknowledged these events, but their inclusion in the story of independence tends to lend it a more violent cast, one making the relationship between Brazilians and Portuguese more adversarial, which had been a major impulse in the early republican years and continued to characterize depictions of independence among nativists and nationalists in the 1920s. For example, Tiradentes, the martyr of the Inconfidência, had emerged in the late nineteenth century as the quintessential nationalist and republican hero, but the IHGB recitation of independence made him only one of the story's heroes, and not the most important, for the 1922 lecture series focused attention on 1822, especially the actions of Pedro and José Bonifácio. The organizers of the IHGB's centenary efforts aimed at reconciliation in their narration of Brazilian history, of Portuguese and Brazilians and also of past and present, through the narration of a story of continuity linking the colonial, imperial, and republican periods.[19] A focus on the violent episodes pitting Portuguese against Brazilians in the eighteenth and early nineteenth centuries would make such a project difficult; the focus on the events of 1822 helped the scholars avoid the challenge.

The IHGB's approach had two further effects. First, the focus on the events of 1822 emphasized the role of the wealthy, powerful, and well educated. The narration of the story of independence in which the protagonists were the prince and the polymath José Bonifácio left only minor and secondary roles for the more socially diverse characters of the stories of, for example, the Revolta dos Alfaiates and the liberation of Salvador; as Hendrik Kraay shows, Baianos tended to depict the part played in independence by their forebears as much more democratic than the official story, though during the centenary many among them were more willing to acknowledge the leadership of the prince and his counselors, as will be discussed below.[20]

Second, almost all the lectures in the IHGB's centenary series focused on events and actors in the Southeast, which in the speakers' telling was not simply a geographic place, but an essential contributor to the independence story. In Alfredo Valadão's narration of Pedro's journey to Minas, he claimed the experience of the country's interior had "Brazilianized" the prince, a process that was reinforced by his travels through São Paulo, during which he made the Grito along the Ipiranga.[21] Meanwhile, although the series acknowledged Bahia in Miguel Calmon du Pin e Almeida's lecture on the Battle of Pirajá, its focus on 1822 afforded very little attention to the North and Northeast, for the key events that took place there, such as the Revolução Pernambucana and the liberation of Salvador, came before and after 1822. The institution did acknowledge the North and Northeast when in 1923 it mounted a second lecture series, whose speakers covered independence-era events in the region, but it was designed to be separate and distinct from the centenary series and it was less coherent and much more limited. Beside lectures on Pará, Maranhão, and Bahia, it also included one on the role played by Brazilian naval forces in establishing independence.

Indeed, even the IHGB's major effort to celebrate the liberation of Salvador, the publication of *História da Independência do Brasil* by the Baiano Pedro Calmon, its release timed to mark the event's centenary, helped promote the sense of the precedence of the Southeast. Calmon covered the "precursor" events that preceded 1822, including those in Pernambuco, and he dedicated a chapter to Dois de Julho, but he tended to emphasize "the significance of the central provinces as the stage of the principal events that led to Brazil's political break from Portugal," as Eduardo Käfer has observed.[22] As we will see, the approach of the IHGB and its partners did not keep Pernambucanos, in particular, from insisting on their region's importance to the winning of independence and the formation of the nation. Still, it is a reminder that there were costs to the choices made by the IHGB and its partners in offering an official narrative that deemphasized the distinctions between Portuguese and Brazilians and between the republic, the empire, and the colony, including especially the potential to exacerbate regional differences.

The IHGB's approach to the centenary was of a piece with its character and work during the era. Having been closely allied to the imperial state, in 1922 it still carried the traditionalist sensibilities of its leading members, including its long-serving permanent president, Afonso Celso, and permanent secretary, Max Flieüss, who was the principal architect of centenary initiatives, including the lecture series. However, these figures also helped lead the institution to make a grudging peace with republican authorities in the early twentieth century, in part as a way of resolving serious financial difficulties. The two aspects of its institutional personality came together in the centenary, with the IHGB overseeing public displays emphasizing the role of the emperor in the unfolding of independence and affirming the importance of the central state by serving as an eager partner of the national government's plans for commemoration. Just as important, in the years leading up to the centenary, the institution had also committed itself to patriotic education and the building of the national community. For example, another of the IHGB's initiatives in the centenary year, alongside arranging lecture series, publishing historical documents and monographs, and organizing an international congress of historians of the Americas was publishing the monumental *Dicionário Histórico, Etnográfico e Geográfico do Brasil*. In its way a contribution to the spirit of inquiry on display in the centennial exposition and an assertion of the institution's mission to define Brazilian identity, the first of several planned volumes of the encyclopedia was published in 1922. The IHGB saw it, in the words of historian Lucia Guimarães, as an opportunity "to offer a panoramic view of the *nation's energies* and *of Brazilian unity*."[23]

The IHGB and like-minded Brazilians thus aimed to use the centenary to offer Brazilians a coherent, unified narrative of the country's past that provided them the means of creating community in the present, making the regions of Brazil integral parts of the whole, and reconciling the republic with its predecessor regimes. In the ensuing years, the IHGB and its scholars continued the project, leading some among them to the historical and cultural interventions of the Vargas state, with Getúlio

3.2. Banner illustrating the publication of the regulations of the fourth Exposição Nacional de Gado, *A Exposição de 1922*, September 1922. Here the artist linked the republic to the empire by including images of President Epitácio Pessoa (top center) and the two emperors, Pedro I (bottom left) and Pedro II. Courtesy of the New York Public Library.

Vargas inheriting the paternalistic role once inhabited by the emperors.[24] In the context of 1922, these initiatives were also important because their messages did not remain confined to the IHGB and scholarly circles. In fact, because many of the scholars involved in the work of the IHGB were active in various centenary venues, they helped promote the institution's vision of the centenary in many other public performances of memory in Rio de Janeiro in 1922. Above all, the institution's interest in conciliation—between Brazilians and Portuguese, between the republic and the empire and its founding prince—and its focus on 1822 and the Southeast characterized much of what occurred in the capital during the centenary celebrations.

Much of the press in the capital contributed to this project, as it had during the celebration of the Fico, the effort led by the magazine *Illustração Brasileira*. One of the roster of magazines published by the editing house behind the popular satirical weekly *O Malho*, the *Illustração* was an influential, highbrow monthly, named the "official journal" of the government's centenary commission in 1921.[25] Thus, it promoted the exposition and other major events that took place in the capital, including the IHGB's historical congresses, special publications, and lecture series, all of which the magazine covered in glowing terms. The magazine published transcriptions of some of the IHGB's lectures, and it expanded its own offerings on historical subjects in 1922. It offered space for scholars who disagreed with the IHGB's approach, such as Francisco de Assis Cintra, who was a critic of both Pedro and José Bonifácio, and presented a more republican interpretation in a regular column, but in general it gave readers a version of the synthesis the IHGB was using the centenary to develop, both in theme and approach, with a preference for documentation and the minute narration of events.[26] It therefore included columns in which historians emphasized the contributions of both the institutional church and the Masonic order in the story of independence, as well as events prior to 1822 and in the Northeast, while the dominant narrative offered in its pages focused on Pedro and José Bonifácio, the capital and the southeastern region, and the immediate context of the early nineteenth century, especially the independence year.

For example, in a major series that began in September 1921 and ran for a year, Mário Behring told several stories he labeled "The Forerunners of Independence." However, rather than the Guerra dos Mascates, the Inconfidência Mineira, the Revolta dos Alfaiates, and other events often depicted as the "precursors" of independence, Behring focused on 1822 and the actions of government and military officials in Lisbon and Rio de Janeiro, and much of his material came directly from the contemporary and retrospective writings of José Bonifácio.[27] Further, while Behring made sure to acknowledge the importance of the Inconfidência and Tiradentes, calling him "The Forerunner," this assertion came in a November 1922 article in which he specifically rejected the possibility that the 1710 Guerra dos Mascates could be understood as significant to the history of Brazilian sovereignty.[28] Behring's dismissal of the importance of the conflict and the purported heroism of Bernardo Vieira de Melo and other localist leaders was a rejection of one of the most treasured claims made by Pernambucanos on the history of Brazil and its independence, including, for example, in an article by Mário Melo in the very same issue of the *Illustração*.[29] That is, even while the magazine offered Melo, Assis Cintra, and others the chance to offer their own interpretations, the main thrust of the historiography offered by the "official" magazine of state centenary organizers was a methodical narration of the story of the Southeast and of Pedro and José Bonifácio, peaceable and respectable.

The Guerra dos Mascates and its ethnic tensions made for an uncomfortable fit in the effort to deemphasize the differences between Portuguese and Brazilians, an effort the *Illustração* also joined. For example, while Assis Cintra emphasized the difference between Portuguese and Brazilian interests in the independence era, Reis Carvalho insisted on their brotherhood in "A Independencia do Brasil," one of the *Illustração*'s most comprehensive and detailed historical offerings, published on the date of the centenary.[30] With a nod to synthesizing competing narratives, Carvalho began the piece with brief references to seventeenth- and eighteenth-century events throughout the country (from the Revolta de Beckman to the Inconfidência Mineira), but focused on the period after 1820 and especially on the work of José Bonifácio. Similarly, he acknowledged Luso-Brazilian tensions—saying, for example, that Brazil was "one of the most oppressed" of all American colonies and that the Emboabas and Mascates conflicts were "characterized by hatred between the Portuguese and those born in the country"—but he rendered independence not as a rupture but as a parting. He wrote that "the Portuguese raça divided itself between the Portuguese of Europe and the Portuguese of America: two peoples, politically distinct but morally united."[31] Here Carvalho expanded on a theme he had developed in an earlier article on Brazilian holidays, reminding his readers that while Brazil had its own great history and its own heroes Brazilians must continue to celebrate Portugal and "the cooperation of the Portuguese raça in the making of Brazil," for example, through the commemoration of discovery each year.[32]

Much of the press in the capital joined the *Illustração* in developing these themes for a more popular audience. *A Exposição*, the official magazine of the centenary fair, joined in the attempt to build consensus by publishing pieces on the events of the seventeenth, eighteenth, and nineteenth centuries that were purported to be the precursors of independence, but its narration of independence itself focused readers' attentions on the heroes of 1822 and Luso-Brazilian brotherhood. In the most important of its historical essays, the magazine stated in its special September edition that "Pedro I and José Bonifácio made independence. United, Brazilians and Portuguese accomplished it together." It was for this reason that Brazil's independence could be celebrated by both peoples; as the magazine put it, "still united, Brazilians and Portuguese celebrate today—the Brazilian people and the Portuguese people and both governments, indissolubly connected by the same traditions, the same destinies, the same aspirations, and the same ideals."[33] While other publications were unwilling to go quite as far, many joined the IHGB, the *Illustração*, and *A Exposição* in developing these key themes, of independence as largely peaceful, of the partnership between Portuguese and Brazilian actors, and of respectful reappraisal of the prince, despite the years of criticism he had endured in the nineteenth century and under the republic.

The sister publications of the *Illustração Brasileira* extended the reach of its approach and interpretation, for example, in *O Malho*'s centenary editorial, which focused on Pedro and his relationship to patriotic Brazilians and gently questioned the importance of Tiradentes, and in the painstaking narration of the prince's movements through São Paulo by Eugenio Egas published by the popular monthly *A Leitura para Todos* as the main historical feature in its September 1922 issue.[34] The influential *Revista da Semana* also helped spread this message, which was unsurprising given that in 1922 its director was the Portuguese Carlos Malheiro Dias, whose main contribution to the commemorations was the monumental *História da Colonização Portuguesa do Brasil.* In its centenary edition the magazine promoted the consensus advanced by the IHGB and others that in making the Grito, Pedro distilled the desires of the Brazilian people, and that once Portugal had completed its civilizing "mission" independence was a natural outcome rather than a conflicted one; Pedro's sword, the magazine said, "did not threaten enemies" but instead "saluted liberty."[35] It furthered these themes in a variety of ways, on one hand using the centenary to promote Luso-Brazilian friendship, as chapter 4 makes clear, and on the other encouraging respect for Pedro through items such as Alice de Serpa's analysis of the emperor's handwriting, in which she found qualities "great and worthy of passing on to posterity."[36] In fact, a regular contributor and the director of the national archive, Escragnolle Dória, went even farther than its editors would go: he followed his earlier demand for more attention to José Clemente by asserting in his historical essay for the centenary edition that Pedro had, in fact, made independence. He wrote of the prince, "He tears the Portuguese ribbon from his hat, unsheathes his sword, takes the oath and demands it from others. Brazil was born."[37]

Finally, major broadsheet newspapers joined in the effort, with the *Correio da Manhã* returning to the theme it had taken up in its coverage of the celebrations of the Fico, for example, in Mucio Leão's independence-day depiction of the prince as "fiery and colorful," with the "soul of a knight and the heart of a poet" and his assertion, "I will not accept any explanation for the actions of d. Pedro aside from worthy ones—worthy, let us understand, from the national point of view."[38] Elsewhere, the *Jornal do Brasil* asserted that "without question we owe much to the rebel prince" and it also published, among other comments, Carlos Leite's appreciation that "Pedro was the strong arm that accomplished what we were thinking, what we wanted," and Oswaldo Orico's characterization of the emperor as a "chivalrous and bold prince, complicated and audacious" and his observation that—rightly—"contemporary affection kisses the Prince's statue."[39] In its own "chronological synthesis" of Brazilian history, prepared for 7 September, *O Imparcial* lauded Brazil's Portuguese legacy, and while it mentioned the broader context of independence, it focused on Pedro and José Bonifácio and reprinted the effusive praise a contemporaneous publication had offered the prince.[40] *A Noite* published two editions on the date of the centenary, with the regular edition insisting on the importance of the prince's actions by calling 7 September

1822 "our nation's greatest date," and the full front page of the special centenary edition dominated by a narrative written by the monarchist historian José Francisco Rocha Pombo, a minute examination of Pedro's movements in August and September, which led to the Ipiranga.[41] A few publications struck dissonant notes.[42] But for the most part the written narrative offered to the Carioca public matched what began in January with celebration of the Fico and its rendering of independence as the work of a handful of great men. Chief among them were José Bonifácio and Pedro, the prince rescued from the attacks of nativists and largely protected from the critiques of many of the previous hundred years.

Beyond lecture halls and printed pages, Cariocas staged many other performances of memory. Among these was the new Museu Histórico Nacional. Despite its ambitious name, the museum began as a modest enterprise, two galleries mounted at the centenary exposition, "half hidden in the depths of the Pavilhão das Grandes Indústrias," in Noah Elkin's description.[43] But it was significant, for several reasons. First, it demonstrated the acknowledgment of the importance of history by the national state, which critics had often accused of neglecting it. Second, the museum endured, ensuring the persistence of the displays of 1922 as it expanded in the succeeding decades. Third, in the central and largest venue of the centenary celebrations, the museum narrated a history of Brazil that in some ways echoed and in others challenged the project of synthesis and consensus pursued by the IHGB and its partners, putting on display Brazilians' differences about the character of their country and its past. Unlike nativist and republican critiques of that project, the new museum began as an exhibition of the vision of its first director, Gustavo Barroso, who was a champion of Brazil's colonial inheritance, a critic of the republic, and a nostalgic for the empire.[44]

The idea for a national historical museum was an old one, and over the years various notions had been put forward about its proper location, mission, and character. In the centenary year alone, for example, advocates had advanced proposals for a military museum, a museum housed inside the national archives, and a museum directed by the IHGB. Barroso had been advocating for his vision of a historical museum for a decade before 1922, beginning with a column published in the *Jornal do Commercio* titled "The Cult of Nostalgia" ("Culto da Saudade"). He criticized his fellow Brazilians and the republican state, arguing that their lack of interest in the past weakened the nation and threatened its distinctive traditions, and he advocated for a national historical museum as a venue for confronting these problems.[45] He envisioned a museum where Brazilians could visit the past by inspecting its objects and where they would have an opportunity to pay their respects to the country's great men and their great deeds; his idea for a museum would invite not inquiry or scrutiny but instead awe and pride. When Epitácio Pessoa selected him to lead the museum effort a month before the centenary date, Barroso was left with little time, but there was also little doubt of the kind of display he would offer the public. When the museum's two halls, "From Colony to Monarchy" and "From Monarchy to Republic," opened in October in a small, modest ceremony, as the *Jornal do Brasil* put it, visitors found them dominated by "mementos of the wars in which Brazil took part and the belongings of the emperors."[46]

The first thing the visitor might take note of was the museum's frame. Its halls sat within the Palácio das Grandes Indústrias, which was one of the exhibition's attempts to display Brazil as a modern, progressive nation and one of its principal venues modeled in the neocolonial style. So too were the museum's rooms remodeled in a "colonial style."[47] Inside that frame, the visitor was invited to appreciate the nation's military glories, through images of its great soldiers and examples of their weapons, and its imperial heritage, including an equestrian statue of Pedro II and a variety of objects that had belonged to the emperors and their family. Even in its acknowledgment of slavery the museum told an imperial story, for it ended in the display of the pen used by Isabel to sign the Golden Law in 1888, and the museum celebrated the family's return to Brazil to participate in centenary events by putting on display the rudder of the ship on which they had sailed into exile.[48] The museum grew and expanded its vision in the ensuing years, but from the first day Barroso shared his perspective on Brazilian history, which was more dedicated to tradition and order than were all but the most conciliatory of the contributors to the IHGB lecture series. As Júlia Furia Costa summarizes his approach, in the museum Barroso "sought to demonstrate the continuity between Brazil as a Portuguese state and as a nation" and he wanted to ensure that the celebrations of the centenary would not depict independence as "a break from Portugal."[49] He rejected the republican interpretation of independence and its heroes, such as Tiradentes, in favor of a story of João VI and Pedro, and thus also the attempt to bring together "precursors" and the great men of 1822.[50] In Barroso's vision for the centenary, it was only the latter who ought to be celebrated.

As chapter 4 shows, Carlos Malheiro Dias and other Portuguese living in Rio de Janeiro, along with President António de Almeida and officers of the Portuguese state, did much to promote the themes advanced by Barroso and the museum. In February 1922, the Portuguese ambassador broke ground on the Portuguese exposition pavilion by calling Brazilian independence "a parting, with no loss of blood," and when Almeida arrived in September he said that Pedro declared Brazil's independence "in the name of everyone, Brazilians and Portuguese, given that the Portuguese also rebelled against Portugal, for liberty, for rights, for justice."[51] Barroso's fellow Brazilians also joined in these efforts, none more prominently than Epitácio Pessoa. He offered his most expansive remarks on the process of independence in welcoming Almeida to Brazil ten days after the centenary date, and in the public and crowded setting of the presidential palace he described independence just as Barroso, Almeida, and Dias would have liked. In spite of—or perhaps because of—rumors that he harbored anti-Portuguese sentiments, Pessoa asserted that "the Independence struggle was not a struggle of Brazilians against Portuguese, but of Brazilians and Portuguese together, against the retrograde and impolitic position adopted by the Libson Cortes." He said that because of the Portuguese king's promotion of the economic and cultural development of the country, "no one worked harder for the independence of Brazil than did D. João VI," and that when Pedro declared independence the act "was the logical consequence of his father's actions." What followed, according to the president, was not a war against Portugal, but a "protest" against "the follies of the Libson Cortes." Significantly, he did not mention José Bonifácio, Gonçalves Ledo, or any other individual actor, but instead said of Pedro that "he established independence." He concluded by stating that because Portugal had done so much to prepare Brazil for independent life, and the Portuguese had done so much to help Brazil achieve independence, "7 September 1822 is, then, a Luso-Brazilian date, a day of the Raça."[52]

This view echoed throughout the public performances of memory in the capital, in both subtle and obvious ways. For example, in the scheme the government commission adopted to finance the exposition, the Bonus da Independência lottery, every ticket was illustrated with a print of Pedro Américo's iconic depiction of the Grito do Ipiranga, and not, say, of the Battle of Pirajá or Dois de Julho or any of the Brazilian advisers who worked alongside Pedro to make independence. Another example had to do with the imperial family itself. One of the early steps the national government took to mark the centenary came in 1920, with the revocation of the banishment of the imperial family by republican leaders; and when the descendants of the emperors visited Brazil to participate in the celebration of independence, they were met with an enormously positive public response consisting of gigantic crowds and a huge outpouring of grief when news arrived that the Count d'Eu, the consort of Princess Isabel, had died during the journey.[53] Furthermore, when teachers took up the mandate by the capital's director of public instruction to offer their students a centenary lecture focused on independence, they tended to offer an appreciation of the cooperation between Portuguese

3.3. Postage stamp commemorating the centenary, based on Pedro Américo's *Independence or Death*. The painting had become the iconic image of the prince's Grito do Ipiranga by 1922. Courtesy of Wikimedia Commons.

and Brazilians in the making of independence. Alzira Caldas de Azevedo, for example, reminded her pupils that Brazilians revered Gonçalves Ledo and others who were Brazil-born, as well as Pedro, who was a foreign prince but, she said, had already come to identify with the Brazilian cause before 1822. Azevedo's story of independence was more in line with the synthetic consensus interpretation advanced by the IHGB, as she included references to the Inconfidência Mineira and the Napoleonic crisis, but she focused on 1822 and, above all, on Pedro.[54]

Finally, among other performances of memory, it is worth considering an intriguing one that took place on 27 September, as it brought together many of the themes developed in the capital's other venues through the centenary year. On that date, a group of well-to-do women—members of Rio de Janeiro's "highest society," according to both the *Jornal do Brasil* and *O Brasil*—paid a formal visit to the equestrian statue in the Praça Tiradentes, where they staged their reverence for Pedro. Organized by Vera Caracas and Corina Barbedo, the women began by displaying their commitment to the idea of national union; there were twenty-two of them, twenty to represent each of the states of Brazil along with one to represent the Acre territory and another the national capital. They chose the statue, according to the *Jornal*, to ensure that Cariocas would not have "forgotten Pedro I" in their celebrations of the centenary, marking their admiration by placing a heart-shaped arrangement of flowers at its base.[55] They communicated their conformity with a patriarchal, hierarchical interpretation of Brazil and its past in their social profile—they retired to the tony Confeiteria Colombo for a tea after the visit to the statue—in their focus on the emperor, and in their choice of speaker, the writer Lia de Santa Clara, who as a Portuguese immigrant also helped convey the group's comfort with the Luso-Brazilian narrative apparent in so many other events of the centenary in the capital. Santa Clara began by commenting on the group's sensibility about questions of sex and gender, saying that she was sure the women were not feminists "but feminine," that one of the reasons for their respect for Pedro was that the women found in him "many qualities that are irresistibly attractive to the fairer sex," such as his tempestuousness and ambition, and that they knew their own power lay in their understanding and display of love. She said that in judging Pedro the group did not take an interest in the political or social questions taken up by historians, but instead saw in him "simply the agent of your independence," which he himself had "initiated." In fact, Santa Clara did not mention José Bonifácio or any other "Brazilian" partners of the prince, so that the event offered the most uncomplicated version of the independence story, leaving no doubt of its hero.[56]

On one hand, this small event reflected some of the themes apparent in the first celebrations of the centenary in Rio de Janeiro, as the women followed the commemorations of the Fico to the Praça Tiradentes and the figure of Pedro I. Further, in bringing together Brazilian and Portuguese celebrants, the organizers staged a performance of Luso-Brazilian affinity that was among the goals of historians like Max Flieüss, writers like Carlos Malheiro Dias, and politicians like Epitácio Pessoa. Indeed, perhaps the best way to understand the choices official Brazil and its partners made in staging displays of the past is to view them as performances of conciliation, of Portugal and Brazil, of different interpretations of Brazilian history, of the colony, the empire, and the republic, of the past and the present. These choices were both ideological and political. While Lusophile and traditionalist celebrants like Gustavo Barroso took the opportunity of the centenary to perform their nostalgia, Pessoa and others anxious about the conflicted context in which the centenary events unfolded—regionalist and separatist tensions, the controversial presidential election, military uprising—looked to the past for examples of legitimacy and, above all, order.[57]

On the other hand, when the group stated its fear that the emperor might be forgotten, it acknowledged that many Brazilians questioned his significance and might reject the project of his rehabilitation that characterized many of the capital's centenary events. After all, the critique of Pedro had been a major theme of Brazilian and especially republican historiography for decades before 1922. Thus, while Flieüss and the IHGB advanced the notion of synthesis and consensus, Barroso and the Museu Histórico asserted a more Lusophile interpretation, which included an implicit critique of the republic, and *Gil Blas* and the Partido Republicano Nacional announced their annoyance at what they alleged was a failure of patriotism among those who rehabilitated the colony and the emperor. Those challenges were especially apparent beyond the capital, but they were also displayed within it. In fact, the IHGB president Afonso Celso publicly expressed his discomfort with certain aspects of the project in a widely reproduced article, titled "With No Loss of Blood?" A direct reaction to the Portuguese ambassador's depiction of events, in the piece Celso rejected the notion that independence had been achieved in an essentially peaceful manner, calling it a common but "false assertion." He enumerated all the minor and major clashes Brazilians and Portuguese had engaged in during and after 1822, and argued that these amounted to a real war of national liberation, with "all of the characteristics of real wars."[58] First published in the *Jornal do Brasil*, the text was reprinted by *Gil Blas* in the capital, as well as, among other venues, in *O Combate* and the *Revista Nacional* in São Paulo, the *Jornal do Recife* in Pernambuco, and *O Nacionalista* in Rio Grande do Sul. Conciliation and consensus were among the most prevalent notes struck in the celebrations Cariocas staged to mark the centenary, but there were dissonant ones as well.

The choices Cariocas made in how to commemorate independence were surely in part a function of the circumstances of the centenary celebration: marking independence in 1922 implied a focus on 1822. Still, Gustavo Barroso, Afonso Celso, and Victruvio Marcondes, among others, reminded them that other choices were available, different ways of narrating the history of independence and Brazil. They made this point in the capital and even in the venues of official celebrations; it was further clarified in the performances of memory that unfolded beyond Rio de Janeiro. Brazilians in other parts of the country celebrated the centenary, but when they did so they focused much less intently on the events and figures of 1822. In fact, some among them chose not to celebrate independence at all.

The Story of São Paulo, the History of the Nation

In certain respects, public performances of commemoration in São Paulo matched those in the capital. Given that the celebrated events of

7 September 1822 occurred in São Paulo, and that José Bonifácio was a native of the province, it is little surprise that many Paulistas joined their Carioca counterparts in making much of the immediate story of independence surrounding the actions of the prince and his advisers. The single largest centenary day event in the city was a civic pilgrimage to the neighborhood of Ipiranga, where Governor Washington Luís inaugurated a new monument to independence. The official party then visited the newly reopened Museu do Ipiranga, which for the centenary had traded its former role as a museum of natural history for a new one, as a historical museum dedicated to the story of independence and the state. After this visit, the group traveled to Santos, where it participated in the inauguration of another monument, this one dedicated to the Andradas—José Bonifácio and his brothers, Martim Francisco and Antônio Carlos, both of whom joined their more famous brother in the politics of independence and the early empire. Each of these events focused celebrants' attention on the events of the 1820s, the region of the Southeast, and the "patriarchs" of independence, much as did many of the events that took place in the national capital.

On the way back to the capital, however, the governor and his traveling companions made several more stops, each of which extended the chronology of the commemorations, forward and backward from 1822. First, still in Santos, they attended the inauguration of the Palácio da Bolsa Official do Café, the opulent new construction housing the coffee exchange, a monument to the industry that had built the state's enormous wealth and to its claim to lead the country's present and future. Then they visited the Monumentos da Estrada, a series of markers and structures built along the highway connecting Santos and the capital, each one telling the story of São Paulo from the time of its earliest colonists to the late nineteenth century. The monuments narrated the Paulista past as a story of progress and, more important, they conflated the history of São Paulo and the history of the nation. As Paulista organizers used the exposition to illustrate, one of the dominant themes of the centenary celebrations in São Paulo was the notion that São Paulo *was* the nation, Brazil's natural leader and the manifestation of its ideal character. In their rituals of memory, Paulistas extended this project beyond the exposition. Their performance of history during the centenary included the celebration of independence itself, especially those parts of the independence story that emphasized the role and contributions of São Paulo. But, even more than independence what Paulistas celebrated in 1922 was the history of the Brazilian nation, which, in their rendering, was synonymous with Paulista history, from its earliest times to the birth of independent Brazil along the banks of the Ipiranga, to their own, prosperous day.[59]

3.4. Three of the celebrations of the centenary in São Paulo: the inauguration of the Monumento à Independência (top), the Monumento aos Andradas (bottom left), and the Cruzeiro Quinhentista. *A Careta*, 23 September 1923. Courtesy Charles E. Young Research Library, University of California, Los Angeles.

The Monumento à Independência do Brasil was not completed in time for the date of the centenary; construction continued until 1926, and there were further changes in later decades, when the interior space within the pedestal structure was transformed into a crypt to hold the remains of Pedro I and his empresses, Maria Leopoldina and Amélia. Enough of the work had been carried out by 1922 that the monument could be inaugurated, however, and Paulista authorities made its construction central to the city's commemoration of the centenary and its christening a major event. Situated near the hill purported to be the site of the Grito, the monument comprises a granite staircase and plinth and several bronze sculptures in statue and relief, which exemplify the synthetic, consensus narrative of independence advanced by the IHGB and its partners. At the top of the structure is the largest sculpture, called the Marcha Triunfal da Nação Brasileira, depicting a group of men and women, some dressed in classical garb and some portrayed as indigenous, joining an allegory of Liberty driving a Roman chariot.

Though the monument commission organized by the state government preferred the design proposed by the Italian Ettore Ximenes, its decision did not meet with much popular support when it was announced in 1920, in part because it did not tell the independence story, so several other sculptures were added to the main one. At the base of the plinth are statues to four of the leading figures of the independence movement: Hipólito José da Costa, who advocated for independence through his London-based *Correio Brasiliense*; Joaquim Gonçalves Ledo, whom the monument labels "leader of the Independence movement in Rio de Janeiro"; and, ensuring that the visitor would understand the importance of São Paulo in the events of 1822, José Bonifácio—"the Patriarch of Independence"—and his fellow Paulista Diogo Antonio Feijó, who championed Brazil's cause in the Lisbon Cortes. The monument also includes two other statues that promote the synthesis narrative, one to the Inconfidentes and one to the Pernambucano revolutionaries of 1817. Finally, it presents three sculptures in bronze relief, one portraying the Battle of Pirajá and the other two focused on Pedro and his movements on 7 September 1822—the Grito do Ipiranga, the depiction based closely on Pedro Américo's iconic painting, and his entrance into the city the same day.

After an artillery salute, the official celebrations began with a pilgrimage to Ipiranga and the new monument; as the *Correio Paulistano* described the scene, beginning at dawn all roads leading to the neighborhood were busy with the movement of "the polymorphous and polychrome multitude, of men and women of every class, every age, every race who live and work here."[60] Tens of thousands attended the inaugural event, including Governor Washington Luís and his party, the formed ranks of the members of the Força Pública, hundreds of musicians, and twelve thousand Boy Scouts who had camped at the site the night before. Together, they staged a performance of memory focused on Pedro, the Grito do Ipiranga, and, above all, the contributions of São Paulo to the story of independence and Brazil. It was in part a musical affair, including performances of the national anthem, the "Hino da Independência" (composed by Pedro I), and the new "Hino do Centenario," by H. de Macedo and Savino de Benedictis, which focuses on the actions of the prince, from the Fico to the Grito.[61]

A second performance of the national anthem came at the unveiling of the monument's relief depicting the Grito, after which Washington Luís and the official party visited the original on which the monument's rendering had been based, for Pedro Américo's painting dominated the Salão de Honra in the reopened Museu do Ipiranga. There they found an elaboration of the consensus story of independence, the central gallery including images of Pedro, José Bonifácio, Gonçalves Ledo, and Feijó, as well as José Clemente Pereira, Maria Leopoldina, and the Baiana soldier Maria Quiteira de Jesus Medeiros. On the way to the main gallery visitors—according to the *Correio* numbering fifty thousand on centenary day—found images of and references to many of the other events and personages of the most expansive version of the independence story and its purported precursors. These included the Ouro Preto revolt of 1720, the Inconfidência, the Revolução Pernambucana, debates in the Lisbon Cortes, the Fico, Pedro's expulsion of Portuguese naval forces, the Battle of Pirajá, and Dois de Julho, as well as the brothers Andrada, Thomas Cochrane, Joana Angelica, and Januario Barbosa. The director, Affonso de Taunay, made clear his ambition to offer an ample, inclusive narrative of independence, and his regret that the museum could not depict many of the other actors of the independence story, because "there was no way of discovering their likenesses," a challenge that he attempted to meet by including their names on bronze plaques mounted alongside the images that told the story.[62]

From the museum, the governor and his party traveled to Santos for the inauguration of the monument to the Andradas and the Palácio da Bolsa Official do Café. Like the Monumento à Independência and the Museu do Ipiranga, the Monumento aos Andradas focused celebrants' attention on the consensus narrative of independence, for while both José Bonifácio and Martim Francisco were active in the capital as the events of the 1820s unfolded, Antônio Carlos had participated in the Revolução Pernambucana in 1817 and in 1822 was one of Brazil's representatives to the Cortes. The inauguration event's official orator, the historian Eugenio Egas, helped make the case as well. While offering effusive praise for the contributions of Martim Francisco and Antônio Carlos and claiming that José Bonifácio was one of the great American liberators, comparing him to San Martín, Bolívar, and Washington, he also acknowledged the importance of the prince and depicted independence as largely peaceful and strictly political. Like many of the historians most active in the public celebrations of 1922, Egas argued that both José Bonifácio and Pedro were necessary to independence, their partnership essential to and emblematic of the larger movement. Neatly summarizing this interpretation, he told the crowd that "two great men made it—the prince was the intemperate youth, thirsting for glory and great deeds; José Bonifácio calm, thoughtful, and prudent at an older age, ambitious to see Brazil become autonomous. D. Pedro is action, Bonfácio discretion; the prince is the sword, Bonifácio the book. And, thus, they were the most important and most typical of the men who made Independence." As was the case with historians in Rio de Janeiro who made similar arguments, Egas paired his emphasis on the partnership between the Brazilian statesman and the Portuguese prince with the assertion that independence was limited in its aims and did not entail anti-Portuguese sentiment. José Bonifácio was the vital figure, he said, because he represented those who sought "to separate politically from Portugal, the mother country, but only politically, for we did not want to loosen other ties, as Portugal is also 'our happy and beloved patria.'" Indeed, far from depicting independence as conflicted, Egas's inauguration speech was explicitly Lusophile. He said, "Portugal is always and will always be our pride, our raison d'être, the touchstone of our strength, the very foundation on which the strong and powerful qualities of the Luso-Brazilian raça are built."[63]

Whether such a "race" existed in 1822 or 1922 was the subject of much debate during the centenary year, and the argument played out in a variety of settings, from the events surrounding the Libson–Rio de Janeiro air raid and the visit of António de Almeida to observations about Portugal's contributions to the exposition. Indeed, to a great extent this debate helped define what the long-standing arguments about history that surfaced in 1922 were about. That is, as much as they were about the relative importance of events, personages, and causes of independence, such disputes were about identity and nationality, about whether Brazilians were part of a larger Lusophone family or a people not only politically but culturally distinct, and about the character of the distinction where it existed. Many republicans and contributors to the IHGB's centenary efforts argued that the Brazilian nation had already existed by the turn of the nineteenth century, well before political sovereignty came, while more conservative and traditionalist figures like Gustavo Barroso emphasized the continuities between the colonial and national periods and between the peoples of Brazil and its mother country. The focus on 1822 in the IHGB lecture halls and Rio de Janeiro more broadly helped Cariocas elide these differences and aim at a consensus view of independence, but as they remembered the past, Paulistas engaged issues of identity in much more explicit ways.

While Eugenio Egas made clear his views on these matters, the performance and display of memory and history at other events in São Paulo tended to offer a different, opposing view, which claimed that a distinctive Brazilian nation had existed for many more than one hundred years, and that the nation was specifically, essentially Paulista. Thus, on one hand, the monuments to independence and the Andradas and the Museu do Ipiranga offered a narrative of independence focused on Pedro and his advisers, while acknowledging the "precursors" of their activity. On the other, to a great extent independence itself was not the main subject of the ceremony inaugurating the independence monument, the newly reopened museum, or the Monumentos da Estrada connecting Santos and São Paulo. Instead of independence, many Paulistas used the centenary to remember and celebrate the history of their own state. In their story, the protagonists were not the Inconfidentes or the Pernambucano revolutionaries or the liberators of Salvador, or Pedro, or even José Bonifácio; the protagonists of their story of Brazil were the Paulista people, the most important of whom were the bandeirantes.

The bandeirantes were explorers and slave-hunters who set out from São Paulo for the interior of the continent in the sixteenth, seventeenth, and eighteenth centuries. They had little to do with the independence movement celebrated in 1922. But by the early twentieth century they had come to embody the story Paulistas liked to tell about themselves—not of brutality and enslavement but of bravery and initiative. Antonio Celso Ferreira shows that this careful narrative was the result of decades of work by historians and other intellectuals to construct a distinctive Paulista identity and to depict their state "as the central actor in Brazilian history" and found heroic expression in "the epic of the bandeirantes."[64] The centenary provided a powerful site for promulgating these efforts, and the drive to build São Paulo's celebrations around the bandeirantes and, through them, to claim Brazil's history, began almost as soon as Paulistas began discussing the great date.

For example, Alphonso Pinto made the case in 1916 in the *Revista do Brasil*, the enormously influential journal of Paulista identity and nationalism. Pinto argued that São Paulo's centenary celebrations ought to be "essentially historical" and that they should celebrate the heroes of 1822. This was not enough, however, and he insisted that Paulistas should also take the opportunity of the centenary to celebrate the foundation of their own city and the bandeirantes, whom he called "intrepid argonauts" and "heroic expeditionaries." Together, he said, the foundation of São Paulo, the bandeiras, and the declaration of the country's independence were "the backbone of the history of Brazil, which in its general lines can almost be said to be the history of S. Paulo on a larger scale."[65] Pinto continued to make the case for including the bandeirantes in the celebrations of the centenary in the following years, for example, in a speech sponsored by the Liga Nacionalista de São Paulo in 1917.[66] José Francisco da Rocha Pombo joined Pinto in the pages of the *Revista* and made the argument even more plain. For him São Paulo had always been "the heart of our nationality" and "the center of our entire history," in great part because it had witnessed some of the first and most successful initiatives to colonize the country's interior, first by the Jesuit missionaries of the sixteenth century and then by the bandeirantes. Of the bandeirantes, he wrote that their example was essential to the work of building Brazilian nationalism; it was "so important that on its own it would be enough to renew the national idea." As far as he was concerned, the Jesuits and the bandeirantes had made the region and thereby had made the nation, and because of them Brazil should focus its centenary celebrations on São Paulo itself. He mentioned the Grito do Ipiranga only in passing.[67]

These figures were joined by many others. For example, two different groups decided to mark the centenary by erecting a monument to the bandeirantes. One was a group of Portuguese residents of the city and the other a group of native Paulistas. Chapter 4 analyzes the controversy that emerged over their competing plans, which were rooted in competing views of the identity of the bandeirantes and thus meant that neither project was completed in time for the centenary. In fact, the Paulistas' preference, for the now well-known monument designed by Victor Brecheret, was shown in model form to great acclaim in 1920, but it was not completed and inaugurated until much later, as part of São Paulo's celebration of its four-hundredth anniversary. Still, the groups agreed on the importance of the bandeirantes and the appropriateness of their presence in the centenary. The leader of the Portuguese initiative, the architect Ricardo Severo, called them "the unshakeable foundation of our nationality," while Menotti del Picchia argued that he and his fellow Paulistas must celebrate the bandeirantes for they were the "heroic founders of our nationality."[68] The monument had to wait, but the people of São Paulo were certain that the bandeirantes must play a central role in the celebrations in 1922.

When the centenary day arrived and celebrations began at the Monumento à Independência, participants in the ceremony inaugurating it heard the "Hino do Centenario" and the "Hino da Independência" and saw the Grito do Ipiranga in bronze relief. When they turned their attention to the official speaker for the event, however, the state deputy Roberto Moreira spoke very briefly about Pedro and the independence movement. Instead, he narrated all of Brazilian history, focusing on the period before 1800 and two main subjects, the conquest of the interior and differences between the Portuguese and those who were Brazil born. In Moreira's telling, the thousands who gathered at the foot of the monument were there to celebrate Brazil and, he said, "as you know, Brazil was made by Brazilians, or, more accurately, by Paulistas." The Portuguese were responsible only for initiating the process of discovery and colonization; they "settled only on the maritime coast" and failed to explore beyond it. In his own way echoing those Brazilians who used the raids of the jangadeiros to pose questions about the character and location of the "real" Brazil, Moreira suggested that the true nation lay away from coastal settlements. To make Brazil, he argued, was the work of the domination of the interior, the work of the bandeirantes. In the florid language and heroic tones with which many Paulistas spoke of the bandeirantes, Moreira said:

> The Paulistas were those fearless leaders of the bold "bandeiras" during which, tramping through the wild backlands, delving into thick and intractable jungles, crossing immense and cascading rivers, climbing steep and rough mountain ranges, overcoming fevers, hunger, beasts, and Indians, they rode the nation's rafts to the farthest points, points that have been ratified as ours through the diplomatic genius of Rio Branco. Without these titanic strikes by the Paulista bandeirantes, Castilian domination of South America would be almost total. That is to say, the Brazil in which we were born and live would not exist, this great and beautiful Brazil, whose future will bring so much glory to civilization and the right.

Brazilians thus owed their country to São Paulo, and Moreira easily connected the past to the present, shifting from the third person to the first, as in his claim that Paulistas conquered the interior and then made it their own; "we," he said, "made it and, conquering the land, we opened it, we built it, and we defended it."

As he continued, Moreira mentioned the flashpoints of Portuguese–Brazilian conflict and difference—the moments when "Brazilians" defended Brazil against not only indigenous groups and Spaniards but their own colonizers—such as the wars of the Emboabas and the Mascates—and he distinguished between the ambitions of the "Portuguese captains" and the "nationals, committed to freeing the land of foreign influences." He offered perfunctory remarks on independence itself, but depicted Pedro as despotic, his removal marking the beginning of Brazil's era of true liberty. Finally, like his fellow Paulistas who mounted the state's displays at the centenary exposition, he argued that the best testament to the nation at the centenary was São Paulo itself, which showed Brazilians what they could be. The city was "this fantastic jungle of domed and gilded towers, these smoking chimneys, this huge, dense, overflowing, confused mass of houses spilling into the lowlands, perched on the hills, and dotting their slopes, attesting in a material way to the monumental progress of S. Paulo, of Brazilian civilization, of the greatness of the patria." He called Brazilians to embrace their bright future and to accept that the descendants of the bandeirantes would lead them to it, for they had already accomplished so much; as Moreira said, "we believe in this greatness, ladies and gentlemen, for it is real and manifest."[69]

Moreira's use of the past to map a path to the future was a common rhetorical strategy among many of the centenary celebrants in 1922. The planners of the inauguration ceremony for the Monumento à Independência reinforced the point in their encouragement of the participation of the Boy Scout troops. As the *Correio* reporter covering the event put it, the twelve thousand scouts who had camped out at the monument site offered "the crowd, delirious with enthusiasm, a complete vision of tomorrow's Brazil." Each scout, according to the writer, was "a little Brazil." Together, they were "immense Brazil, embodied by them, living in them, present in their gallantry, in the childlike beauty of their bearing." They were "our greatest pride and our greatest hope," their inclusion making the inauguration event about much more than independence; as Moreira had put it, the celebration was of Brazil itself, especially its past and its progress as they were embodied by São Paulo.[70]

Though the reopened Museu do Ipiranga did not address the future in an explicit way, it did approach the centenary as an opportunity to engage with a history much broader and longer than the coming of independence. Under the direction of Affonso Taunay, the museum was remade as a historical institution between 1917 and 1922, after having focused primarily on natural history in the years after its original opening in 1895. It closed for renovation in 1920 and reopened in time for the centenary, offering a narrative of independence focused on Pedro and José Bonifácio while also acknowledging the longer story of "precursors" and contributors; its new independence displays understandably attracted some contemporaries' attention in 1922. However, when the museum reopened it did not offer visitors an experience focused primarily on the events of Ipiranga in 1822 or independence more broadly. Instead, the new museum dedicated itself to offering a specific lesson in Brazilian history, one that Adolpho Pinto, Rocha Pombo, and others had helped design in the years leading to the centenary. As Taunay put it, "the history of São Paulo is the history of Brazil itself."[71]

In her study of the work of Taunay and the institution, Ana Cláudia Fonseca Brefe shows that Taunay saw narrating independence as an important part of the institution's mission; he was intent on emphasizing the contributions of São Paulo, as the location of the Grito and in the contributions of Paulistas like the brothers Andrada, whose monument project in Santos he also helped guide as a member of the organizing commission. But, she writes, for Taunay, "the proclamation of Independence on Paulista soil, besides being a climactic moment in Brazilian history, was the result of a historic process initiated in the earliest period of colonial Brazil by the first forays made by the inhabitants of São Paulo to explore and conquer national territory, then undefined."[72] Thus, Taunay focused his scholarly work on uncovering the history of the bandeiras and contributing to Paulista intellectuals' work in rendering the bandeirante as the preeminent embodiment of the spirit of São Paulo; they were pioneering and energetic, and they had founded the Brazilian nation hundreds of years before the actions of Pedro in 1822. This view also informed Taunay's work in the organizing commission for the Monumento à Independência, where he was instrumental in the choice of Ximenes's classical design, which influential critics like Monteiro Lobato found too universalist. Taunay read the design differently, seeing its classical language as a means of projecting his sense of the epic, ancient character of Brazilian and Paulista history.

The visitor's experience of the museum culminated in a viewing of Américo's *Independência ou Morte*, but not before its numerous references to the bandeiras had impressed on them the notion that Paulistas had made Brazil by exploring, knowing, and conquering much of its territory. Some of these displays were not installed in time for the centenary events, such as the ornamental vases situated in the museum's central stair, which contained water from the rivers navigated by the bandeirantes. Still, the lesson could hardly be missed, for the entrance was dominated by monumental marble sculptures of the bandeirantes Fernão Dias Paes Leme and Antônio Raposo Tavares, while the interior displayed bronzes of Francisco de Brito Peixoto, Manuel Preto, Manoel de Borba Gato, Francisco Dias Velho, Bartolomeu Bueno da Silva, and Paschoal Moreira Cabral. Together, the sculptures offered a sense of Paulistas' expansive view of their claims on the nation, for the men depicted in them embodied the bandeirantes' efforts in Goiás, Mato Grosso, Minas Gerais, Paraná, Rio Grande do Sul, and Santa Catarina, educating the visitor to understand the incorporation and development of Brazil's interior and the histories of some of its prosperous and well-populated regions as part of the story of São Paulo.[73]

For Taunay and other prominent Paulista intellectuals, the project of the bandeirante carried a political and cultural valence in the local context, for it was a way of advocating for an older, more traditional, and more rural São Paulo, as opposed to the industrial metropolis that had emerged in the first decades of the twentieth century. As both Antonio Ferreira and Barbara Weinstein emphasize, their work to promote the cult of the bandeiras was highly racialized. On one hand, these figures acknowledged the roles played by indigenous and mixed-race members of the expeditions, while on the other, they claimed a fundamental whiteness of the bandeiras and used their alleged significance to discount the influence of people of African descent in the making of the region and nation.[74] Also important, along with their anxiety about the challenges modern urban life had brought in the form of class conflict and gendered tensions, was the possibility of losing what Adolpho Pinto called the "old Paulista genius" and "the characteristics of our raça" in a state and city of immigrants." "If we want to save them from drowning and disappearing forever under the alluvial sediments of immigrantism," he wrote, Paulistas must rediscover their past, in particular the early Jesuit missionaries and the bandeirantes, and they must do so at once. The centenary, he said, was the most opportune venue in which to begin.[75]

In the broader Brazilian context, the Museu do Ipiranga's focus on the bandeirante helped Taunay join his fellow Paulistas in finding the justification and explanation for São Paulo's contemporary national hegemony in the past, beginning with the Jesuits and bandeirantes, extending through the independence era and apparent in their own day through its prosperity and its modernity. Taunay expanded the museum's work to narrate a Paulista history of Brazil in the years after 1922, for example, through the Museu Republicano "Convenção de Itu." An annex of the Museu do Ipiranga, the museum opened in 1923 in the Paulista town where prominent activists had met in 1873 to plan a republican future for Brazil. The museum thereby conflated the history of Brazilian republicanism with the movement as it unfolded in São Paulo.

The occasion of the centenary helped focus the attention of the public and public authorities on the power and utility of the past, and Taunay took advantage of the opportunity. As Brefe puts it, in Taunay's approach to the celebrations of 1922, "one notices a lively effort to place the centenary of Independence in a long tradition that sees São Paulo not in a supporting role, but as the main character in the great episodes of national history."[76] Taunay used the centenary to advance this project, in the museum and in his roles in the independence and Andradas monument initiatives, and he found many partners in the extraordinary circumstances of 1922. Few were as explicit in asserting that the story of São Paulo was the history of Brazil as were the designers and advocates of the monuments placed along the Caminho do Mar, which linked the state capital to Santos and were inaugurated by Washington Luís as he and his party traveled home from the coast on the centenary date.

Among the many infrastructure projects undertaken by governments at all levels to mark the centenary, the improvements to the Caminho do Mar were not the most ambitious or the most commented on. However, as part of those improvements the state contracted the architect Victor Dubugras to design a series of structures and historical markers along the road, thus making the Caminho itself into a kind of monument. Each of these Monumentos da Estrada marked a particular event or phenomenon that helped shape the history of the region, from the time of the earliest settlers to the republican era. Traveling from Santos to São Paulo, the first is the Cruzeiro Quinhentista, a large cross celebrating the explorers and settlers of the sixteenth century, such as João Ramalho, Martim Afonso de Souza, José de Anchieta, and Mem de Sá, whom Dubugras honored in Portuguese tiles at the base of the cross. The next of the markers inaugurated on the centenary date was one of several honoring the work of Bernardo José de Lorena, the governor who installed the first stretch of paved road in the region in 1790, a decorative arch and staircase called the Padrão do Lorena. Beside Lorena, again in tiles, the site invites visitors to recall the life and work of the muleteers who linked the coast to the interior and helped drive São Paulo's development. Third is the Rancho da Maioridade, a two-story building designed as a stopping place for travelers. It is named for the stretch of road it sits upon, the Estrada da Maioridade, which was widened and improved under the direction of provincial governor José Carlos Pereira de Almeida Torres in the 1840s, so named to honor the ascension of Pedro II to the imperial throne and the declaration of his "majority" in 1840. The building's decorative panels depict Pedro's visit to São Paulo in 1846, as well as some of the era's statesmen, including the brothers Andrada. Finally, the Pouso de Paranapiacaba is another building designed for travelers' rest, this one in the region where the São Paulo Railway installed its first tracks to carry the state's indispensable coffee to the coast in the 1860s; the site thus highlights the economic development of the state in the late nineteenth century and the republic that Paulista political actors used their wealth to engineer.[77]

Each monument tells its own story, introducing travelers to an episode or era in Brazilian history and inviting them to remember its heroes, but the project's design meant that the monuments' deeper significance was in the way they work together to narrate the past in the same way that Roberto Moreira did in his speech at the inauguration of the Monumento à Independência and Affonso Taunay in his work to remake the Museu do Ipiranga. The official inauguration event took place at the Pouso de Paranapiacaba, where the state deputy Júlio Prestes gave a lengthy address on the project and each of the individual monuments, in which he emphasized the ways in which the Caminho monuments presented the history of the nation as the history of São Paulo.[78] First, just as organizers emphasized the significance of Ipiranga by placing the independence monument there and remaking the museum rather than opening a new venue to promote its pedagogical mission, Dubugras situated the Caminho monuments in specific locations of purported historical significance.[79] Prestes emphasized the point, and offered lengthy descriptions of the region's geography, including long quotations from travelers who had visited the region in the past, such as the seventeenth-century Jesuit Simão de Vasconcellos and the nineteenth-century scientists John Mawe and Hercules Florence. The land—its resources, rivers, and soil—were fundamental to the story, he argued, and therefore to its commemoration. Prestes made much of early explorers' commitment "to know the land," as well as the way that Paulista nature had shaped and changed them, serving as the seedbed for "the raça that aimed to discover, to demarcate, to grow, to populate, and to make Brazil great." He also made sure to emphasize the continuing importance of the land, especially in the ways that the region's mineral wealth and farmland made possible São Paulo's prosperity and Brazil's progress.

Second, Prestes's comment about the "raça" nurtured by the land was one of many he offered about the national lessons he read in the Caminho monuments, which echoed Moreira's assertions about the differences between coastal and inland settlements and Taunay's commitment to the idea that the bandeirantes embodied a distinct and ancient nation. The Caminho monuments established the movement from the coast into the interior as fundamental to the story of São Paulo, and, Prestes asserted, this movement distinguished Brazilians from Portuguese in essential ways. Like Moreira, he asserted that the Portuguese discovered but did not make Brazil, because they remained on the littoral, "without the necessary knowledge of the land" that they claimed. Rejecting the idea of a "Luso-Brazilian" nation, Prestes emphasized the importance of race, especially the mixing of Europeans and the indigenous, while making sure not to mention the historical fact of the African presence in São Paulo. Thus, he spoke of the "melding of the races" that had produced the caboclo, "the result of the breeding of two races, making him, with the superior qualities of the Portuguese and the resilience and hot bloodedness of the savage, ready for adventure and ready to bring forth our nationality." Prestes thereby distinguished the Brazilian nation from the Portuguese and found the distinction in the earliest years of the colonial era. As he put it, the history recounted in the monuments showed that "our progress was not accidental, our civilization was not the work of foreigners, our culture not the product of one hundred years." Political sovereignty was incidental to the more important story of the nation, and the centenary was merely an opportunity for the celebration of Brazil, which was much more than one hundred years old in 1922.

Prestes also joined with Moreira, Taunay, and many other Paulistas in insisting that the history of São Paulo was the essential narrative in the history of Brazil, for the raça seeded in the interior of the state was the "the raça which conquered and made Brazil, which discovered and demarcated its frontiers, which sowed and reaped our freedoms, which fought for our progress, and which glories in our civilization." Thus, the monuments claimed not only the region's early explorers and settlers in the Cruzeiro Quinhentista and the Padrão do Lorena but also Pedro II and his advisers—the Rancho da Maioridade celebrated the brothers Andrada, as well as some of the second empire's non-Paulista statesmen, such as the Duque de Caxias and Senador Vergueiro—and, like the Museu Republicano, the republic itself at the Pouso de Paranapiacaba. As Prestes put it, the monuments commemorated "the social mission of the Paulista in the making of our nationality."

Making the point even more explicit, Prestes concluded with a passage situating the Paulista within the larger Brazilian nation, and, again like Moreira, Taunay, and the planners of the state's displays at the exposition, insisting that the Paulistas' "mission" was an enduring one. He said that the monuments served as a reminder of the contributions of "our raça," which continued to be both an example and natural guide to the country, a mission embodied in Washington Luís, "the irrepressible moral representative of our energy, our sense of justice and our rights, our culture, our conscience, and our aspirations." As the governor guided São Paulo, he "guide[d] the Patria and the Republic, to the glory of American civilization." Here Prestes insisted the monuments both marked and collapsed time, which helps explain the fact that the Caminho monuments did not reference independence in an explicit way and that in a speech of over six thousand words Prestes barely mentioned independence. As Prestes explained it, the monuments were an "ex-libris of our history" and part of Paulistas' "cult of the past," but they also "connect in themselves ideas and life, time and space, explaining the present."[80] The monuments, that is, like the Paulistas' engagement with history throughout the centenary year, narrated the past and used it to justify São Paulo's claims to hegemony in contemporary Brazil.

Júlio Prestes won the contested presidential election of 1930, but he never took office. It had been seized by Getúlio Vargas in his "revolution" that same year. Prestes went into exile and worked to oppose Vargas, including by supporting São Paulo's Constitutionalist rebels in 1932. In fact, he might be considered to have helped lay the groundwork for the rebellion ten years before, in his speech at the Pouso de Paranapiacaba. While Paulista business and commercial figures used their displays and pavilions at the centenary exhibition to stake their claims on Brazil's present and future, Prestes, Roberto Moreira, and Affonso Taunay justified those claims by staging a particular reading of the past. If, as Taunay said, "the history of São Paulo is the history of Brazil itself," and if contemporary Paulistas had inherited the "mission" to guide the country's destiny, as Prestes asserted, they could hardly do otherwise than see their state as exceptional and themselves as the rightful leaders of the nation. The Constitutionalist forces of 1932 depicted themselves as modern-day bandeirantes and the central characters of the story of Brazil, a role they had been taught to inhabit over the course of decades, culminating in the extraordinary performances of memory of 1922.[81]

Thus, although in some ways Paulistas' engagement with history and History during the centenary year echoed the approach undertaken by important figures in the national capital—from the articulation of a cumulative, synthetic version of the story of independence to the interest they took in Pedro and José Bonifácio—the clearer notes were discordant. Despite the hopes of many prominent figures in Rio de Janeiro, including the members of the IHGB, who had been tasked by the national government to lead Brazil's performances of history in 1922, few Paulistas seem to have adopted the views advanced by Eugenio Egas in his speech at the inauguration of the Monumento aos Andradas. Instead, following Moreira, Prestes, and Taunay, Paulistas challenged the significance of 1822 and the notion of Luso-Brazilian amity, and they claimed their story was the story of Brazil.

Paulistas' challenge to the interpretation offered by narrators in the capital was to be expected, given the well-worn, well-known rivalry between Cariocas and Paulistas, which they enacted in many venues of the centenary, from the exposition to the football field. Many other Brazilians also rejected the approach advocated by the IHGB and its official partners, and, though they did not accept Paulistas' particular interpretation of the past, their own performances of memory helped mark centenary history with difference and discord. Nowhere was this perspective as apparent as in the Northeast.

The Northeast, Cradle of Brazilian Liberty

As in São Paulo, in the Northeast Brazilians celebrated the events of 1822 but they also used the centenary to assert the importance of other aspects of the nation's history, which many deemed more meaningful than the story of Pedro and José Bonifácio; for some, these episodes were more important than the story of independence itself. Thus, though Bernardino de Souza, the president of the Instituto Geográfico e Histórico da Bahia, said in 1919 that Baianos ought to "join with all of Brazil in the commemorations of the seventh of September 1922," he also called on them to reserve "all of your efforts for the brilliant commemoraton of Dois de Julho in 1923, *the true centenary of our independence*."[82] Even more clear in their suspicion of the importance of 1822 were many Pernambucanos, who the Instituto Archeologico e Geographico Pernambucano (IAG, now called the Instituto Arqueológico, Histórico e Geográfico) described as marking the centenary with "perfunctory events, ordinary, the kind that after two or three days the people forget, since no stamp of originality makes them memorable."[83] They preferred to remember their own story of liberty, which they tracked from the seventeenth-century struggle against Dutch occupation to the eighteenth-century Guerra dos Mascates to the nativist, nationalist, and regionalist conspiracies, rebellions, and wars of the nineteenth century that preceded and succeeded the events of 1822. Theirs was a story of Pernambuco as the cradle and timeless ideal of Brazilian liberty and nationality, told in the context of the centenary celebrations of 1922 and in the larger and more elaborate celebrations of the centenaries of the Revolução Pernambucana in 1917 and the Confederação do Equador in 1924. Indeed, the commemorations of these centenaries seem to have done much to contribute to the emergence of the idea of the discrete region called the Brazilian "Northeast," with Pernambuco as its leader and Recife as its capital. Displays and performances of memory and history were essential to this process, for they helped distinguish Pernambuco not only from the Brazil of the hegemonic Southeast but also from Bahia, its chief rival for the leadership of the region.

Cariocas and Paulistas made their own claims on the story of independence, in the Fico and the Grito and the brothers Andrada. Mineiros did the same, presenting Pedro's 1822 visit to the province as essential to his becoming Brazilian and, of course, enjoying Brazilians' wide acceptance of Tiradentes as the most important "martyr" to the independence cause, while Piauí, Maranhão, and Pará pointed to the battles that took place in their regions. Bahia was the site of a series of naval battles, the most important of which was the Battle of Pirajá, but for Baianos and for Brazilians at large, none of the violent episodes of the independence war rivaled the significance of the liberation of Salvador on 2 July 1823. In his essential work on the memory of Dois de Julho, Hendrik Kraay shows that Baianos began to use the liberation story very soon after independence, the holiday providing a convenient means of negotiating local, regional, and national identities and loyalties. Framing the liberation of their capital as more heroic and more inclusive than the doings of the prince and his court, Baianos used the celebration of Dois de Julho to draw appealing contrasts between their own community and what they depicted as a distant, aristocratic (and later oligarchic) national state, which over the years became identified most closely with the commemoration of 7 September and, later, the foundation of the republic on 15 November. Because it was a more violent episode than the Fico and the Grito and other events that unfolded in the Southeast, Dois de Julho helped Baianos articulate a nationalist discourse that often took on Lusophobic tones. And because it was central to the story of national liberation, many Baianos used it to claim a Brazilian identity and to reject Africa and the African influences that they feared defined Bahia, as many outsiders said they did. Hence the central emblem of Dois de Julho was the armed caboclo striking tyranny; like Júlio Prestes and many of the admirers of the jangadeiro raiders, Baianos found the caboclo a convenient figure. Neither Portuguese nor African, neither imperial nor pacific, their armed caboclo allowed Baianos to avoid confronting difficult questions of ethnicity while helping establish their own claims on the past and their own distinctive regional and national identity.[84]

Kraay shows how celebrations of Dois de Julho changed over time and discusses the uses to which the holiday was put by various groups with different and sometimes competing interpretations of Bahia's past and present. For example, in 1895 middle- and upper-class Baianos erected the Monumento ao Dois de Julho in Salvador, partly as an attempt to enact a measure of discipline on the lower orders; celebrations focusing on the site of the monument, they hoped, would be less difficult to control than the marches and festivities that ranged throughout the city. Such efforts continued throughout the republican period, as with the prohibition in 1920 of the bands of revelers who announced the holiday's coming in the days leading up to 2 July, sometimes in ways local elites found unruly. As Wlamyra Ribeiro Albuquerque has noted, what disturbed the city fathers who banned the practice and criticized other popular events "was the autonomy exercised by the popular classes to highlight or attribute their own meanings to the Dois de Julho celebrations, thus offering alternative readings of civic practice."[85]

Such alternative readings of citizenship might threaten their power in the present, and they also complicated Baiano elites' attempts to use Dois de Julho to shape the way outsiders viewed the city, a project they pursued with particular vigor in preparing for its centenary. Knowing that Salvador and Bahia would enjoy extraordinary attention in 1923, city and state officials partnered with cultural and business leaders to use the celebration of the centenary to assert an image of Bahia as respectable and modern, with modernity defined in the careful way it was in the country's leading cities, its challenges to social, gendered, and racial hierarchies ignored or marginalized. On one hand, they redoubled their efforts to discourage popular activities they disliked, such as maxixe performances and working-class parades. On the other, they organized a program which echoed the approach taken by their counterparts in Rio de Janeiro in 1922, from the dispossession of unsightly properties and other urban "improvements" to celebrations populated heavily by soldiers and students and a commercial exposition complete with a "parque de diversões" to encourage attendance, just as in the centenary fair in the capital.[86]

Dois de Julho could offer Baianos a means of asserting a narrative of independence which challenged those focused on Pedro, José Bonifácio, and events in the country's Southeast and therefore the national dispensation built upon them, but it could also serve as a means of binding Bahia to the national state, and official and institutional actors tended to assert this interpretation at the centenary. In this view, Dois de Julho did not challenge the legitimacy of the story of the prince. Rather, it ratified and legitimized that story, with historians depicting Pedro and his court as embodying elite perspectives and the liberators of Salvador representing the will of the Brazilian masses in joining with Pedro to free Brazil. Albuquerque shows that Baiano leaders sought to use the centenary to remind Brazilians what they owed to Bahia and its contributions to independence, not to challenge the memory of independence as it was advanced in the capital and among prominent historians.[87] It was easy to make this case given that the significance of Dois de Julho was so widely accepted by scholars and institutions throughout the country and they included it in their centenary efforts, with Bahia's contributions highlighted by, among others, Affonso Taunay in the Museu do Ipiranga and the IHGB in its publication of Calmon's *Independência do Brasil*. Thus, though as Bernardino de Souza suggested Bahia dedicated greater effort to public performances of memory in July 1923 than in September 1922, the state did participate in the major initiatives to celebrate the centenary in the capital, with over four hundred exhibitors showing their wares at the Rio de Janeiro fair and a *seleção baiana* the only state team outside the South and Southeast which participated in the "Brazilian" football championship organized for the centenary.

While Baianos and Pernambucanos shared certain perspectives about the past and their states' roles in contemporary Brazil, centenary events played out very differently among the latter. As the previous chapter showed, Pernambucanos participated in the centenary fair only in a "modest" way, with fewer than half the number of exhibitors that Bahia enlisted, and they rejected the invitation to participate in the athletics events organized in the capital, instead organizing their own Campeonato do Norte. The celebrations of the centenary in the state were also modest, and they would have been even more limited had it not been for the intervention of Catholic leaders who organized religious festivities to mark the occasion. The conflicted political scene in the state surely contributed to these circumstances, as Pernambucanos fought one another and against federal forces sent to quell the unrest which characterized the state during 1922. It also seems that Pernambucanos' suspicion about the importance of 1822 and of the dominant narrative of Brazilian history contributed to their lack of interest in the holiday; after all, they were very willing to celebrate the centenary raiders when they had the opportunity to do so in 1922 and 1923, and they were eager to celebrate the historical episodes they found significant, including during September 1922.

Noé Sandes points out that the Pernambucano challenge to the dominant interpretations of Brazilian historiography and memory had been established well before centenary period. In the nineteenth century, Pernambucano scholars worked to offer "a republican and anti-Portuguese national image," which they found embodied in the history of their own region, beginning with the struggles against the Dutch and the Guerra dos Mascates, and continuing with the Revolução Pernbambucana of 1817 and the Confederação do Equador of 1824. This image and narrative contrasted sharply with the view advanced by influential southern historians like Francisco Adolpho de Varnhagen, who depicted the Pernambucano revolution as "antinational" and the monarchy as the essential institution in the making of Brazil, leaving the Pernambucanos "marginalized in a regional discourse," as Sandes puts it.[88] The coming of the republic seemed to legitimize Pernambucanos' interpretation of Brazilian history, but much to their chagrin the IHGB and other influential historical institutions lighted upon Tiradentes and the Inconfidência Mineira as the new emblems of the nation, so that, while they did acknowledge the 1817 movement, they did not afford it and other events in Pernambuco the kind of attention that Pernambucanos demanded. When Gonçalves Maia complained in the 1923 edition of the magazine of the IAG—that the notion of Tiradentes as "the precursor of the republican idea in Brazil and its first martyr" was "a powerful historical lie" and that Brazilians should instead celebrate Bernardo Vieira de Melo and the other rebels of Olinda in 1710—he was summarizing decades of annoyance and pride among many of his fellow Pernambucanos.[89]

This was the dominant perspective of Pernambucanos' engagement with the past during the celebrations of the centenary of Brazilian independence: distinctive, regionalist, and sometimes combative. Pernambucanos acknowledged Pedro and José Bonifácio, and in 1923 they celebrated the centenary of Dois de Julho, but they were much more interested in commemorating the past of their own state and region, which the state's leading historical institution made clear. The IAG oversaw elaborate celebrations to commemorate the centenary of the Revolução Pernambucana in 1917, beginning to plan for the anniversary as early as 1913. Over the course of four days in early March 1917, the IAG helped organize several events in Recife that looked to the state's present and future, including a horticulture exposition, a football tournament, and the inauguration of a literacy campaign, and it led the city, state, and region in a multifaceted commemoration of the revolution, which it called "the most perfect and complete" political movement in the history of Brazil.[90]

The effort began on 5 March with the inauguration in the town of Jaboatão dos Guararapes of a new school named for the 1817 revolutionary Domingos José Martins; it was the first of more than thirty new schools that were opened throughout Pernambuco to celebrate the centenary and carried the names of the "martyrs" of 1817. The next day was the centenary date, which began with a reenactment of deacon Bernardo Luiz Ferreira Portugal's 1817 blessing of the flag of the revolutionaries by the Archbishop of Olinda and Recife, Sebastião Leme da Silveira Cintra, the flag having been adopted as the state flag of Pernambuco in 1917 at the prompting of the IAG. The archbishop then celebrated an outdoor mass, which was followed by a lecture on the contributions of the clergy by the canon José Pereira Alves, one of the IAG's official orators. The celebrations continued with a ceremony to lay the foundation stone for a monument to the revolution, a "civic-military" parade including students, soldiers, and sailors, and the opening of the horticultural exposition. The day's events ended in a formal gala at the Theatro Santa Izabel featuring performances of patriotic music, including a hymn to the revolution, and a series of lectures, by the archbishop, General Joaquim Inácio, and the historian Oliveira Lima, who insisted, contrary to the assertions of scholars like Varnhagen, that the revolution was "a national movement."[91] The IAG oversaw similar events at the theater the next two nights, the first featuring historical lectures by local scholars and scholars representing the citizens of other regions that had participated in the 1817 movement, the second inaugurating the activities of the literacy campaign. Finally, the institute ordered bronze medallions struck to mark the centenary, with one side listing the names of the martyrs of the revolution and the other its flag and the lion that served as the emblem of the state, it printed archival documents related to the revolution, and it published several historical works on the movement.[92]

As this summary suggests, though the IAG had many partners in the celebration of the centenary of the 1817 revolution, under the leadership of its energetic permanent secretary, Mário Melo, the IAG was the engineer and principal organizer of Pernambuco's impressive commemoration program. Five years later, the situation was much different. The IAG did make plans to celebrate the centenary of independence, but because the state government did not make once-promised funds available to pay for their realization, the organization canceled its plans and withdrew completely from any commemoration of the event. Without the guidance of the state's most important historical institution, many residents of Recife worried that their state would find itself embarrassed and left open to charges of a lack of patriotism when the centenary date came, and they appealed to the IAG to reconsider. Melo wrote to the editors of the state's major newspapers in August 1922 to acknowledge their anxiety, but, he said, the institution saw the inability or unwillingness of the state government to provide the monies it needed to pursue its plans as decisive, and so "the Instituto, seeing that all its efforts were wasted and that any further attempt would be useless, decided to cross its arms."[93]

This was no bluff. A month later, Recifenses and other Pernambucanos did celebrate the centenary, as the Catholic Church, business leaders, and others worked to fill the role left vacant by the IAG, but the celebrations were not what many hoped they would be, and they noticed the institution's absence. For example, one of the only major public events that took place in Recife on 7 September was a parade through the city center by its students. As they marched past the IAG building, they found it "completely closed," according to the *Jornal do Recife*, "as if nothing new was happening on that occasion, when the people, united in the same feelings of freedom, offered its meaningful tribute to independence day." The paper lamented the "unpleasant impression" made by the IAG's appearance, and said that "at the least, the noble old establishment ought to have been open and adorned as an example to the masses and also to pay its respects to the popular cause during that praiseworthy moment."[94] Instead, the institution remained closed throughout the period of the centenary celebrations, and the only activity it undertook to mark the centenary was the publication of a special edition of its journal that mentioned independence only very briefly and instead offered a series of essays about the history of Pernambuco, including Melo's lengthy "Chorographia de Pernambuco," Vicente Themudo's history of the 1817 revolution, and pieces by J. A. Correia de Aranio, Xavier Pedrosa, and Samuel Campello about the ethnographic, literary, and theatrical history of the state, respectively.

The perspective adopted by the IAG had to do with financial considerations, but also with its members' interests and their interpretation of the Brazilian past. The IAG began the centenary year with the inauguration of a new monument, an obelisk at the location where the Forte Real de Bom Jesus had stood. The Forte, also called Arraial Velho, had been an important site in the seventeenth-century fight against the Dutch forces occupying the region, a conflict that Pernambucanos depicted as one of the most important episodes in the history of Brazil, perhaps more important than independence itself. At the monument's inauguration Mário Melo rehearsed the themes Pernambucanos tended to develop in discussing the struggle, the most important of which was that it was not a struggle of Portuguese against Dutchmen but instead one pursued by *Brazilians*, who, Melo said, had been "nearly abandoned by the metropole." Thus, like the Paulistas who saw in the bandeirantes proof of the antiquity of Brazilian nationality, Pernambucanos saw in their own history the origin story of the Brazilian people. As Melo put it, "this is the year in which the country will celebrate the first centenary of its political independence. Independence could not have come about if there had been no Brazilian nationality. And the cradle of Brazilian nationality . . . was the Arraial do Bom Jésus. It was here, in this stretch of land in Pernambuco, that the idea of the nation arose."[95]

Mário Melo was extraordinarily active in promoting the idea that Pernambuco's story was the essential narrative of Brazil, including through advocating the importance of the Revolução Pernambucana and, even more directly, in questioning the significance of the actions of Pedro and the southern events of the 1820s. He made the case in numerous historical works, some of which he presented to a national audience, for example, in an essay published in the *Illustração Brasileira* in late 1921. Melo argued that "the cry of Pedro I at the Ypiranga was no more than a confirmation of what our ancestors had already accomplished." He pointed to the fight against Dutch occupation, the Guerra dos Mascates, the 1817 revolution, and the event that inspired the essay: the armed expulsion of Portuguese soldiers from the province in 1821, usually called the Convenção do Beberibe. According to Melo, the Convenção meant that "for we Pernambucanos 7 September does not possess the great significance afforded it in the other states. With D. Pedro or without D. Pedro; with 7 September or without 7 September; with the cry of the Ypiranga or without the cry of the Ypiranga, Pernambuco would have been independent, even if it had broken away from Brazil."[96] That is, on the eve of the centenary year, Melo presented to the Brazilian reading public the provocative suggestion that Pernambucanos questioned the importance of the centenary the country was soon to celebrate, and he also raised the specter of one of many Brazilians' greatest worries, the possibility that regional differences might mean fracture and separatism.

As chapter 2 showed, concern about regionalism and the territorial integrity of Brazil seemed merited in 1922, in Rio Grande do Sul where the editors of *O Separatista* and other regionalists set the stage for the violence surrounding the gubernatorial elections of that year and the "revolution" of 1923, and in Pernambuco itself during the fight over control of the state government, which ended in armed intervention by federal forces. Pernambucanos opposed to the intervention found in the state's history a useful set of rhetorical devices to articulate their anger and frustration, and they depicted their own resistance to extralocal control as the latest chapter in the long story that included not only the various struggles against the Dutch and Portuguese but also the separatist movement of 1824, the Confederação do Equador. Such examples would give Pernambuco's modern citizens the tools they needed to retain their sovereignty.[97] As Barbosa Lima Sobrinho put it in Rio de Janeiro's *Jornal do Brasil*, history taught Pernambucanos that no other region "surpassed it in the fight against foreigners," and that "the worthiest traditions of their native land" meant they would remain "jealous of their autonomy" against all enemies, who in the past had been foreigners and in his own day were the representatives of the national government.[98]

The immediate political conflict that had produced the intervention was at least temporarily resolved by September, but Pernambucanos' anger at Epitácio Pessoa persisted. So too did their conviction that the distinctive history of their state and region was more important than the story of 1822, a conviction that was reflected in their efforts to commemorate the centenary. According to Mário Melo, even the IAG's limited effort, the publication of a special edition of its *Revista*, "will not be perfect," because only a few of those invited to contribute to the volume had submitted texts; in comparison, the volumes prepared to celebrate the centenaries of the 1817 revolution and 1824 confederation were much more expansive.[99] As noted above, the IAG had planned more extensive efforts to mark the centenary, but its plans also signaled the doubts Melo had expressed about the significance of 1822. The IAG intended to use the vast majority of the 150 contos de réis it had requested of the state government to celebrate the centenary to complete the monument to the 1817 revolution, which suggests that the frustrations of Melo and the IAG were not about the government's failure to celebrate the centenary of independence itself but instead because of its failure to honor Pernambuco's past as it should.

Furthermore, although the IAG had abandoned most of its plans for commemorations of the centenary and closed its doors on independence day, its historical perspective was reflected in the ways that Pernambucanos observed the centenary. As was the case with their counterparts in São Paulo, one feature of Pernambucanos' celebrations in 1922 was that they did not focus their efforts on remembering independence itself. Instead, they used the occasion to narrate the story of Brazil as they preferred to remember it, in which Pernambuco was its "cradle" in a double sense: it was the home both of the Brazilian nation and the Brazilian republic. Thus when newspapers printed histories and essays to mark the centenary and speakers rose to address crowds gathered for public events during the days set aside to celebrate the holiday, readers and listeners found references to Pedro and José Bonifácio, as well as constant reminders of Pernambuco's own nineteenth-century contributions to the breaking of Portuguese rule, in the Conspiração dos Suassunas and the Pernambucano revolution and the Convenção de Beberibe. It was rarely the case that such narratives did not also include assertions of the importance of events that came later, the inclusion of which in centenary stories helped render Pernambuco as the essential defender of Brazilian liberty, such as the stands taken by the architects of the Confederação do Equador and the 1848 Praieira rebels against the power of the imperial state. Writers and speakers also made sure to begin their stories much earlier than the nineteenth century, with the struggle to liberate the region from Dutch control—the importance of which was widely accepted by Brazilian historians—and, somewhat more controversially but more important to Pernambucanos' 1922 activities, the Guerra dos Mascates.

As is mentioned above, the prominent southern writer Mário Behring had dismissed the significance of the Mascate war in his series of articles in the *Illustração Brasileira* on the precursors to independence. Instead, he narrated it as an economic struggle pitting landowners against merchants, arguing that "the people, the real people" preferred the latter, in great part because the former were led by slaveholders including Bernardo Vieira de Melo, whom Behring depicted as "really unlikeable, the mercenary soldier type, without scruple, who made the clash of arms a business."[100] Pernambucanos, however, saw the landowners as the heroes of the story and the merchants as its villains, and read the struggle as evidence of their forefathers' Brazilian patriotism and their rejection of monarchy in favor of republicanism. As Melo put it in his own essay for the magazine, "The Contribution of Pernambuco to the Independence of Brazil," the Mascate war was "the first outburst of Brazilian nativism." He described Vieira de Melo as "the sower of the republican idea in Brazil," and said that despite the failure of the "nativist" cause, the war helped make "Pernambuco the garden in which the tree of liberty was cultivated [and] which watered its roots with the blood of martyrs, the tree flowering in 1822 and bearing fruit in 1889."[101]

Public displays of reverence for the "Brazilians" who fought in the war thus figured prominently in Pernambucanos' celebration of the centenary of independence. In Olinda, events organizers flew the original 1710 flag of the city's senate, which had organized the war effort, and one of the major public celebrations was a Te Deum celebrated at the cathedral, highlighted by a speech in which Eustachio de Queiroz focused on the war and Olinda's role as the "cradle of independence."[102] Two months later, on 10 November, Olinda staged a major celebration to commemorate the anniversary of Vieira de Melo's "cry of the republic" in the senate, the program much more developed than those staged in Olinda and Recife to celebrate the Brazilian republic on the 15 November holiday.[103] In Recife, the Guerra dos Mascates was a constant point of reference in public celebrations of the centenary. For example, in the program organized by the Instituto de Sciencias e Letras for its special centenary meeting, lectures by Ulysses Sampaio, Samuel Campello, and Costa Rego Júnior on Pernambuco's nineteenth-century contributions to the independence movement were joined by others on the "restoration" war against the Dutch by Maviavel do Prado and on the Mascate war by Raul Monteiro. There were no lectures on southern events, not the Inconfidência Mineira and not any of those that involved Pedro and his advisers, suggesting to attendees that the independence story was a Pernambucano one. Indeed, when the institute's vice president, the inevitable Mário Melo, offered the opening remarks of the evening, he said that the "fruit" of independence "was harvested by people who did not plant it." In his telling, by 1822 independence was "a ripe fruit," for Pernambucanos had prepared the ground in the struggle against the Dutch and watered it with the blood of martyrs in the episodes of 1801, 1817, and 1821; they had planted the "seed" of independence, he said, in 1710.[104]

For most Pernambucanos interested in history, the single most important episode in the story of independence was the 1817 revolution, which they saw as establishing the state's importance as advocate both for the nation's liberty and its republic. One way that this view was made manifest in 1922 was in regard to the state flag, which a 1917 decree had changed to an adapted form of the one flown by the 1817 revolutionaries, the result of a successful initiative led by the IAG. In 1922, a consistent and central feature of 7 September events throughout the country was the ritual pledge of allegiance to the national flag by schoolchildren, and hymns and odes to and histories of the banner were common as well. Inspired by such displays of patriotism, on the centenary date Paraná's governor, Caetano Munhoz da Rocha, asked the legislature of his state to celebrate the event by abolishing the state's flag and anthem and suggested to his fellow state governors that they work to do the same, which he said would serve as "a gesture so patriotic that it will further strengthen the ties of the Federation."[105] Throughout the country Brazilians joined in what Capitão X called a campaign for "just one flag and just one hymn" in the *Revista da Semana*. As he put it, the campaign was welcome and timely, for on one hand, "we commemorate the centenary of Independence, which marks the beginning of the development of Brazilian unity, enjoying liberal and free institutions," and on the other, some Brazilians needed reminding of the importance of national unity, which was threatened by 1922's fraught presidential election and the separatist movement active in Rio Grande do Sul, among other places.[106] The editors of the magazine concurred, calling the display of twenty state flags at a purportedly national exposition an "aberrant" image, "undermining perfect national unity," and many citizens, including almost every state governor and legislature, indicated their support for the effort.[107]

Pernambucanos were not among them. For example, at the request of his counterpart in Paraná, the director of the Recife law school shared Rocha's call with his faculty and students, but they announced themselves "almost unanimously against the idea" and instead asserted that the school should be "the advocate for the conservation" of the 1817 banner.[108] The *Diario de Pernambuco* took notice of the debate, and made its own position clear in an elegant way, reprinting the 1917 decree establishing the revolutionary banner as the state flag.[109] As was so often the case, it was left to Mário Melo to explain the thinking of many Pernambucano partisans. Pernambucanos rejected the appeal to abolish their state flag "because to renounce the Pernambuco flag would be to renounce the heroes of 1817, forefathers of our political independence, [and] it would be to renounce one of the most brilliant pages in the history of Brazil." They were unanimous in their rejection of the appeal, according to Melo, because the flag was an essential emblem of the best traditions of the state and treasured "in the heart of the people."[110] Whether such unanimity existed it is impossible to say, but it does seem clear that the centenary celebrations of 1917 had prepared many Pernambucanos to embrace the story and symbols of the 1817 revolution as a crucial part of their inheritance in what they understood as the cradle of Brazilian nationality, liberty, and constitutional government.

Finally, that this perspective informed Pernambucanos' experience of the centenary is illustrated in one of the themes some of them developed in 1922: the notion that Brazil was not actually free or autonomous, that the independence Brazilians were celebrating was a fiction. Months before the centenary date, Clodomir Silva made the case in an essay in the *Jornal do Recife*, arguing that because Brazil did not have its own language, because foreign agents dominated its commerce, because its currency was weak, and because it was a peripheral actor in world affairs, it was not independent. He said that it was an immature country, which "lives to make merry and to work for foreigners, and to look at itself in the depths of the abyss at the edge of which it finds itself."[111] The intervention of federal forces in local politics prompted others to join him in expressing doubt about the quality of Brazilian liberty and sovereignty, and, as chapter 2 demonstrated, to question the exposition and other major efforts undertaken to mark the date by the national government. When September came, Pernambucanos returned to the theme, and to the searching, critical interpretation of Brazilian history that it implied.

In the *Diario de Pernambuco*, José Simões Coelho argued that Pedro's seeming accomplishment in 1822 masked Brazil's continued commercial and financial dependence, which had not changed in the intervening century. He went on to point out other failures Brazil had suffered in its first hundred years, one of which was its failure to know itself, so that it could improve itself. For this failure he blamed southern Brazilians, who, as sports administrators had said of the Confederação Brasileira Desportos, "ignored" the people of the North. Northern challenges thus remained unresolved, northern potential unrealized, and Brazil's independence unreal.[112]

Pernambucanos informed by this view used it to rationalize the meagerness of both their contributions to the exposition and the centenary celebrations in their state. What Brazilians could celebrate at the centenary, they said, was only the opportunity to learn from the failures of the previous century, to begin again and realize the broken promises of independence. Rather than joyous celebrations and reverent commemorations of the independence era, such an outlook implied projects like Recife's Hospital Centenário and the IAG's literacy campaign, the beginnings of an ambitious program of reconstruction. While many Pernambucanos approached the centenary in this manner, it was particularly and prominently apparent among the younger generation. It defined one of the most important public events of the centenary date, the gala at the Theatro Santa Izabel hosted by the Recife law school, which Robert M. Levine has described as "the very center of the Northeast's cultural universe."[113] After the usual music and pageantry, the school director Netto Campello offered a narrative of Brazilian independence in which he emphasized that to Pernambuco "is due national unity, inculcating it with the blood of its martyrs, who were forerunners of the independence of the republic and of liberty, 'the backbone of race and nationality.'" His was a celebratory speech, proud of the state and region but happy to hail

7 September as a "glorious date."[114] He was followed to the lectern, however, by Cussy d'Almeida Júnior, whom the student body had chosen as its official orator, and who offered a much less hopeful view.

Weeks before his address, d'Almeida had taken to the pages of the *Jornal do Recife* to join in the attack on the centenary celebrations as the Pessoa government's attempt to impress foreign dignitaries and as a waste of resources. These visitors would be shown Brazil's "poetic and enchanting receiving room, marvelous Rio," but the image was deceptive, for it did not afford a view of the North, "the south's spurious brother," which had been forgotten by "the nefarious action of false republicans and the mismanagement of their governments." Instead, the government preferred to put on "truly ostentatious bacchanals" while the country "marches unconsciously toward decadence."[115] In his speech on 7 September, d'Almeida continued his attack on the Pessoa government, focusing on what he depicted as transgressions against constitutional rights, including the ongoing state of seige and the "press law" limiting speech rights, then under consideration and promulgated in 1923.

The focus of the speech, though, was retrospective. D'Almeida spoke of the promise of Pedro's declaration of independence, but argued that the promise had never been realized, that Brazil's independence was a fiction and its leaders had failed to build a stronger, better educated, and more prosperous nation in the previous hundred years. The fall of the empire and the installation of the republic had not resolved these issues. "What have we accomplished in these one hundred years of independence?" he asked. "What have we done in education, in the administration of the economy, in the most important areas of social development?" He answered that all Brazilians had done in their independent life had been to play at politics—"politiquice"—accomplishing nothing. And so it was left to d'Almeida and his fellow students to save the nation, through urgent, radical action. As far as he was concerned, Brazil required nothing less than the complete remaking of its political system.

This was not a call to rebellion from the margins or from below, not a call from the emerging labor movement that had brought the city to a standstill with a general strike the previous month. It was a devastating critique of the status quo from the halls of one of the most influential institutions in the region, offered during the commemoration of the centenary by the city elite and published in a major newspaper. And the message was clear: modern Brazilian history was a narrative of failure and the Brazilian centenary no cause for celebration. Concluding with a return to 1822, d'Almeida ended the speech by calling on his classmates to do what Pedro had not and perhaps could not: "Let our cry be stronger, more incisive, more energetic and virile than that of the Ypiranga: the resurrection of liberty."[116]

Pernambucanos thus approached the centenary much as did the champions of the jangadeiros and the organizers of the Campeonato do Norte, among others. All these northern and northeastern Brazilians found in the centenary an extraordinary opportunity to define their sense of their region and its relationship to the nation as a whole. Scholars like Mário Melo and commentators like José Simões Coelho joined in this work through an explicit engagement with history and memory, drawing on the region's heroic past to define Pernambuco and the region as a whole as the cradle of Brazilian liberty and the defender of Brazil's authentic traditions in the face of what they saw as the failures of contemporary life. The appearance of federal military forces in Recife and, especially, the unique circumstances of the centenaries of 1917 and 1922 helped Pernambucanos realize the usefulness of their story. They found in those circumstances that history could be a valuable tool in pursuing their ideological and political goals in the present and imagining the future of their state, region, and country. They would remember the lesson in the coming years, their sense of the distinctions between the Northeast and the rest of Brazil becoming only more acute.

"Christo ou morte!"

Because of the choices of the state government and organizations like the IAG, some Pernambucanos worried the state would find itself embarrassed by the meagerness of its centenary events, but other actors intervened so that, in the words of the *Jornal do Recife*, citizens could say their state had celebrated the centenary "in a dignified way." At the forefront of these efforts were the archbishop of Olinda and Recife, Miguel Valverde, and the Catholic Church, which meant that one of the main features of the centenary as it was marked in Pernambuco was its religious inflection. Valverde and the church organized a series of special events to celebrate the centenary, including an outdoor mass, a Te Deum service, lectures on religious and civic issues, and significant charity works.[117] Even the Hospital Centenário, one of the few major projects undertaken by civic authorities, seems to have begun as a Catholic initiative.[118] The result, the *Jornal* said, was to join "the holy soul of the church that rules us through the sentiments of religion to the patriotic soul of the whole of Pernambuco, both vibrating with the same intensity and feeling with the same enthusiasm the immortal eloquence of that hundred-year-old liberty that was implanted in our land for all time." The paper made sure to register its disappointment in the state government and others who hold "a share of responsibility in situations that say something about our civic roles and our love of the nation," but it said that because of the intervention of the church, Pernambucanos could be proud of their centenary program.[119]

Government and civic actors elsewhere were of course much more committed to organizing events to celebrate the centenary, and they benefited from the fact that Valverde's efforts were matched by his counterparts throughout Brazil. Many private organizations were engaged in the celebrations of 1922, such as the business community organized through local chambers of commerce, and they sometimes engaged in their own selective narrations of Brazilian history, as did some of the immigrant groups discussed in chapter 4, but few were as prominent and ambitious in their efforts as the institutional Catholic Church. As the book's introduction notes, its best-known effort was the project to construct a monument atop one of the capital's iconic morros, which eventually produced the statue of Christ the Redeemer on the Corcovado peak, dedicated in 1931.[120] Ten years earlier, the idea for what the *Revista da Semana* called the "Monumento Catholico do Centenario" had yet to take on its definitive shape, with advocates suggesting a statue of Christ, a cross, and a chapel, or its definitive location, some suggesting Corcovado and others, the Pão de Açucar.[121] Indeed, those familiar with the completed statue would find the original design unrecognizable, of a naturalistic depiction of Christ holding a cross and globe (see fig. I.1).[122] Although the project was not completed in time for the centenary, it was widely discussed in the capital and throughout the country, and served as a symbol of the ways that the faithful and church officials approached the moment of commemoration. That is, in the words of the archbishop of Rio de Janeiro, Sebastião Leme, (formerly the archbishop of Olinda), they aimed to use the centenary to "reintegrate" the church into Brazilian life to ensure that, "as we enter our second century of political autonomy, the notions of faith and spirituality are reborn in the Brazilian soul."[123] The statue would help them pursue this project, for it would be, in the words of one of its critics, "an image of their God installed prominently in the Federal Capital."[124]

The idea for such a monument was an old one, but none of the earlier efforts had come to much, and when members of the city's Circulo Catholico revived it as a centenary project they, too, faced initial difficulties. Because the city was administered as a federal district, Corcovado and the other potential sites fell under the jurisdiction of the national government; it would thus be necessary to gain its permission to build the monument. But the republic had adopted a neutral line on religious matters, one that many Catholics interpreted as antagonistic and anticlerical, and the finance minister Homero Baptista rejected planners' request for permission to build the monument. Inside and outside government, however, for the most part the project seems to have been met with support and encouragement. For example, in a well-received speech on the floor of the national congress, Geraldo Vianna called it a "sublime achievement" and contemplated the city's visitors, for whom it would be "the most compelling reason for their visit to the nation's capital in the year of the Centenary."[125] Meanwhile, Afonso Celso, who besides serving as president of the IHGB also served on the project planning committee, noted that the press largely supported it, as reflected in the approval of publications as different as the *Revista da Semana* and its enemy *Gil Blas*, the former calling it "triumphant" and the latter saying "no idea for celebrating the centenary of our independence could be more worthy."[126]

After a series of appeals and a petition signed by tens of thousands of supporters, Epitácio Pessoa indicated his own support, and planners received permission to move ahead with the project. Though the situation prevented the monument from being completed in 1922, approval did come in time for the arrangement of a ceremony laying the monument's foundation stone during the centenary celebrations, the theme of which was the conflation of Catholic faith and Brazilian patriotism. In his remarks, the monument's original designer and engineer, Heitor Silva Costa, took note of all the place names that announced Brazilians' abiding Catholicism, and the keynote speaker, Raphael Pinto, discussed the role of the faith in integrating all Brazilians. Students who had gathered to sing the patriotic anthems and religious hymns also offered a song composed for the occasion, in which they announced that the monument would remind all those who visited the national capital: "We Brazilians proclaim / That Jesus is our King / And we all obey / His sacrosanct Law."[127]

The church developed its centenary program and worked to make the symbolic concrete through a variety of other events, the most important of which was the Congresso Eucharistico, held in the capital over the course of five days in late September and early October. Echoing the aims of the monument project, the congress sought to confront the difficulties the church had faced in the recent past. Members of the laity and the clergy came from all over the country to consider its overarching theme, "the Christian restoration of Brazil through the Eucharistic vitality of Christ." They discussed practical matters, such as methods of encouraging young people to attend mass and how to organize Catholic social action initiatives. They heard lectures on cultural questions, such as the relationship between the Eucharist and the fine arts. They also debated the role of the church in Brazilian life and how to expand its in-

3.5. Eucharistic Procession, Rio de Janeiro, 1 October 1922. *A Careta*, 7 October 1922. Courtesy Charles E. Young Research Library, University of California, Los Angeles.

fluence, for example, in sessions dedicated to the practice of Catholicism in the armed forces, among children in public schools, and in prison and hospital settings.[128] Public celebrations during what the church called the "Semana Eucharistica" extended the influence of the congress beyond lecture halls and the capital, such as prayer meetings and outdoor masses, including one in Rio de Janeiro's Campo de Sant'Anna for thirteen thousand children. To close the event, in a massive display of the power of the church in Brazil, Catholic communities throughout the country held Eucharistic processions that included hundreds of thousands of participants. The event gave Recife, for example, "a Christian afternoon," as the *Diario de Pernambuco* put it, and it seems that at least 100,000 people participated in Rio de Janeiro's procession alone, according to the count conducted by the *Jornal do Brasil*, though the *Correio da Manhã* counted twice as many in what it called "the most brilliant and eloquent affirmation of religious faith ever seen in Brazil."[129]

A few contemporaries voiced doubts about these activities, including members of other religious communities.[130] But Brazilians seem to have welcomed the church's participation in the centenary celebrations, and all over the country the press reported on its events with detailed, positive coverage, even as the events rarely celebrated independence in an explicit way, and participants often did not even mention it. Of course this may have been because, as many sympathetic commentators pointed out, so many Brazilians were practicing Catholics. However, as organizers, participants, and commentators also noted in their acknowledgment of the republic's purportedly anticlerical bent, a positive reception of the church's efforts was certainly not assured. It is important to note that these efforts were part of a broader initiative of Catholic activism aimed at reviving the influence of the church, led by officials such as Archbishop Leme, who had earlier joined in efforts to celebrate the centenary of the Revolução Pernambucana, and laymen including Afonso Celso. Another important figure was Jackson de Figueiredo, who in 1921 began publication of the Catholic magazine *A Ordem* and released *Do nacionalismo da hora presente*, in which he argued that Catholicism was the only feasible basis for building the national community.[131] In the centenary year he organized the Centro Dom Vital, a lay group aimed at gathering intellectuals and cultural figures to work at reinserting a Catholic perspective into Brazilian public life, and he helped organize some events of the Eucharistic congress. Later, he went on to lead his fellow Catholics into the public square through direct political engagement, culminating in the founding of the Liga Eleitoral Católica in 1932.

Leme, Celso, Figueiredo, and their partners focused on the present and the future of the faith and the church in Brazil, but to a great extent their efforts during the centenary were couched in retrospective terms, aimed at reminding Brazilians of the church's importance to the story of the nation. This work entailed using centenary events to celebrate the roles that individual clergy and the faithful had played in key episodes of national history, including in the independence movement, and, more important, to assert that the church and the faith had made Brazil, defining its character, unifying its people, and ensuring its persistence. A force for community, liberty, and learning, Catholics said, the church had been essential as Brazilians in the past confronted their challenges. As *A Cruz* put it in its historical overview of the nation at the centenary, "we owe almost everything we are to the Catholic Church."[132] Furthermore, these activists argued that the church could serve the same role again as Brazilians faced the challenges of the country's second century, from the fissures of regional difference to the changes effected by modern life; indeed, following Figueiredo, they often argued that the church was the only institution that could do so.

Nowhere was the Catholic narrative of national history as palpable in centenary celebrations as in Pernambuco. The institutional church took the lead in organizing celebrations in the state capital and helped organize events throughout the state, which offered participants and observers a sense of the church's importance in the region, in the past as well as the present. Thus the church offered masses and engaged in significant charity works, and it also opened up space for historical work, such as the inclusion of the speech by the priest Eustachio de Queiroz in the Te Deum held at the Olinda cathedral and its display of the Olinda senate flag, which the cathedral held in trust. Recife's Circulo Catholico hosted a series of lectures that ran throughout 1922, some of which focused on historical subjects, such as the talk given by the archbishop in late September on the importance of the faith to the events of 7 September 1822.[133] This work was made easier by the fact that Pernambuco's great claim to the independence movement, the 1817 revolution, is also often called the Revolução dos Padres, such was the extent of the involvement of Catholic priests in its leadership and development. When Pernambucanos who supported the church's efforts to organize centenary celebrations narrated independence, they made sure to mention 1817 and, specifically, the leadership provided by clerics. For example, in his centenary essay A. Fernandes, the leading columnist for the *Diario de Pernambuco*, depicted the Grito do Ipiranga as simply "the echo of our heroes' ambitions," naming two lay leaders and three clergymen, João Ribeiro Pessoa de Melo Montenegro, José Inácio Ribeiro de Abreu e Lima (Padre Roma), and Miguel Joaquim de Almeida e Castro (Padre Miguelinho), whom he made sure to identify as priests.[134]

Another favorite among local narrators was Joaquim da Silva Rabelo, the friar Caneca, who participated in the Revolução Pernambucana and also helped lead the Confederação do Equador movement seven years later. Choosing not to mention its lay leaders, the *Jornal do Recife* identified Caneca as one of the "principal heroes" of 1817 in its 1922 commemoration of the revolution, the others in its telling the priests Ribeiro and Roma.[135] Indeed, drawing a straight line from 1817 to 1824 to the Praeira revolt of 1848, in the early 1920s the paper was consistent in its depiction of not only independence but also the republican movement as the work of these clergymen and their lay partners and followers; like Fernandes, who presented Pedro as having been inspired by the 1817 revolutionaries, the *Jornal* called Deodoro da Fonseca "the happy successor of Frei Caneca [and] of João Ribeiro." It mentioned "other" leaders, but only the priests by name.[136] Caneca's efforts in the Confederação and its campaign against the imperial government only confirmed the paper's understanding of him as a "great Pernambucano hero" and one of the state's "most illustrious and devoted sons" in its centenary-year commemoration of his death.[137] Elsewhere, in the space afforded him by the *Jornal do Brasil* to comment on the church's centenary congress, the Pernambucano historian Ulysses Brandão presented the Confederates of 1824 as the forerunners of the republican idea and insisted that they had been animated principally by their faith, arguing that their break with the empire was due to their rejection of its guarantee of freedom of religion. According to Brandão, who developed the argument in a monograph on the Confederação, published by the IAG to celebrate the centenary of the movement in 1924, the congress reminded Brazilians that the country owed "its independence, its unity, and its culture to the Catholic, apostolic, Roman religion," and the story of the Confederação do Equador reminded them of the costs of forgetting.[138]

Brandão's inspiration for his short essay was a historical lecture given at the Congresso Eucharistico by his fellow Pernambucano, the priest Pereira Alves, in which he called on his fellow Catholics to rally around a "cry," not the famous one offered by Pedro, "Independence or death!" but another, "Christ or death!" For Brandão and Alves this call better characterized the full sweep of Brazilian history than the prince's cry in 1822, and it was more important in the present.[139] At home, Alves was one of Pernambuco's leading public intellectuals. In 1922 he served as president of the Olinda city council, he was a member of the IAG and the Academia de Letras de Pernambuco and one of the most prominent participants in local commemorations, at which he did much to promote the notion that the history of Pernambuco and the history of Brazil were fundamentally Catholic stories, the nation's triumphs the triumphs of the faith. For example, he served as the official speaker for the IAG's 1922 celebration of the end of the Dutch occupation of Pernambuco, which Alves said should be understood as a celebration of the centenary, which was an occasion when Brazilians must "remember the great work of the builders of our brasilidade," such as those who fought for the region's "restoration." Besides emphasizing the Pernambucano perspective that their region was the cradle of Brazilian civilization, the key theme of his speech was that Brazilians must understand that its fundamental basis was its Catholicism. Though he acknowledged "I am not in the pulpit" and said "I have not come here to preach morality," he emphasized the religious faith of those who led the fight against occupation and he made clear that he viewed the struggle as a war of religion and its commemoration, a religious ritual. In celebrating the sites of Brazilian victories, he said, "Tabocas, Casa Forte, [and] Guararapes are not tombs; they are altars." Concluding with a comment on the monument at the Arraial Velho that the Instituto would soon dedicate, he said the Arraial too was "an altar." The monument would be "a symbolic embodiment of our religious worship. It is erected in honor of the creators of Brazil, the apostles of the nationality, the Pernambucanos who only kneeled before God."[140]

Alves developed the theme throughout 1922, erasing any distinction between civic and religious community and depicting Brazilian history as a story of Catholicism. As he said in one of his centenary speeches, love of the fatherland was "imposed by the Catholic conscience," because "love of the Patria is not only a civil law, a law of nature, but also God's law, a law of the Church, a law of our collective conscience."[141] In June, when he was called to celebrate a mass marking the arrival of Sacadura Cabral and Gago Coutinho in Recife and to pray for the success of their raid, he joined many contemporaries in drawing a parallel between the aviators and their sixteenth-century predecessors in visiting Brazil. The pilots reminded Brazilians, he said, that when Pedro Álvares Cabral claimed Brazil for Portugal he was also claiming it for Christ, depicting Brazil as foundationally, inherently Catholic; using its oldest Western name, he called it the "promised land of Santa Cruz!"[142] Thus, the priest argued, Brazil was rooted in its Catholic identity from the very beginning and it was saved for Catholicism by faithful Pernambucanos, whose example endured, to inspire the patriots of the independence generation and those of the generation of the centenary, if only the latter would accept the guidance provided by the faith. Alves carried the message to the Congresso Eucharistico as well as to the bishoprics he took up in the aftermath of the centenary. He became bishop of Natal in late 1922 and bishop of Niterói five years later, during which mandate he participated in a variety of activities linking the church to the Vargas state, especially via his continuing interest in history, such as in the Museu Imperial in Petrópolis, inaugurated in 1943.[143]

Along with their claims that the history of their region was the essential history of Brazil, then, Pernambucanos were also at the forefront of the effort to use the centenary to promote the view that Brazil was a fundamentally Catholic country, their conviction revealed in their commemorations and narratives of the past. Under Archbishop Valverde the institutional church helped create the context in which this effort could be pursued, and members of the clergy like Alves were joined by lay figures in the region's leading cultural institutions in making the centenary a performance of memory characterized by both regional pride and Catholic faith. Even the IAG, which had so clearly rejected any significant role in the centenary events, joined in the effort, as three of the nine essays in the special centenary edition of its *Revista* were on religious matters; José Baratta's ecclesiastical history of Pernambuco, at more than one hundred pages, was one of the longest pieces in the volume.[144] But Pernambucanos were not alone in the effort to narrate Brazilian history as a Catholic story. They were joined by many others.

As with the histories offered by Cariocas, Paulistas, and Pernambucanos, those engaged in the Catholic effort presented Brazilians with a coherent, carefully edited story of the nation from its beginnings to the present day. Like Alves, they often began with discovery and exploration, for example, by citing the mass celebrated by Cabral and his crew and by using its earliest name; as the *Jornal do Brasil* put it in one of its many lengthy, appreciative pieces on the Congresso Eucharistico, Brazil had been the "Land of Santa Cruz from its birth."[145] They cited the importance of Catholic missionaries in the work of colonization and pacification, especially the Jesuits, with architects working in the neocolonial style citing the influence of their constructions, and Paulistas stressing the importance of José de Anchieta, Manuel de Nobrega, and their "Catholic method of colonization," in the words of Júlio Prestes during his speech inaugurating the Monumentos da Estrada.[146]

Of course, they emphasized the role of the faithful in the independence movement, depicting Tiradentes as a martyr of both the nation and the faith and emphasizing the participation of religious figures in the events of the nineteenth century. Beside the participation of the clergy in the Revolução Pernambucana, they also called for Brazilians to remember the heroic stand of the nun Joana Angélica de Jesus in Salvador and the role of the faith in Pedro's thinking and actions; for example, several publications claimed that the prince's confidant and confessor, Belchior Pinheiro de Oliveira, was especially influential in convincing him to declare independence.[147] Like other histories, the Catholic narrative of independence was also offered in the public celebrations of the centenary. Organizers throughout the country worked with the church to include Te Deum masses as part of celebratory programs, and clergy offering the masses used them as opportunities to emphasize the church's contributions. For example, the official celebrations of the Fico in Rio de Janeiro began in the Rosario church, with a mass offered by Olympio de Castro, whose sermon, according to the *Illustração Brasileira*, focused on the essential role played in Brazilian history by Catholicism, "the religion of the majority of Brazilians and which in every historical moment has dedicated its beneficent works to our destiny."[148] Elsewhere, the archbishop of São Paulo, Duarte Leopoldo e Silva, offered a series of lectures on the role of the clergy in independence and in the longer history of Brazil, including one that was part of a series of talks hosted by the national capital's Associação dos Empregados no Commercio to celebrate the centenary.[149] The bishop's "patriotic lectures" were published the next year under the title *O Clero e a Independencia*.

As Soares d'Azevedo noted in an essay on "The Catholic Church in the Centenary," the purpose of the work undertaken by figures like Leopoldo e Silva was to remind Brazilians of the historic and continuing importance of the church in the making of Brazil. Alves and Leopoldo e Silva and their partners sought to remind Brazilians of the work of the faithful in creating and liberating Brazil, and also in shaping the empire, in the abolitionist movement, and during the republic, despite some republicans' attempt to "marginalize the whole Christian epic," as d'Azevedo put it. Indeed, like other Catholic narrators, d'Azevedo considered the republican era one of the most important episodes in the church's history in Brazil, for it saw the church's continuing importance to the nation, for example, in challenging the "savagery" of the indigenous tribes of the interior and in providing assistance to the urban working class, and because it helped demonstrate the missteps and failures of the republican system. Republican culture and laws caused many Brazilians not to know or to have forgotten the role played by the church as the country's perpetual "guardian angel," but the centenary provided the faithful with the opportunity to remind their compatriots of the church's importance, showing them its significance in the present by offering them a history of its accomplishments and influence throughout the country's past.[150]

Like many Catholic narrators of the centenary, d'Azevedo made explicit his view that the work of history was not only one of recognition and memory. It was also part of a larger project aimed at contemporary politics and culture, which the organizers of the Congresso Eucharistico distilled as "Brazil's restoration in Christ"; d'Azevedo summarized their aims by echoing those who saw the centenary as a venue for discovery, writing, "What the Church can display during the commemorations of the Centenary is something more important than an artifact: it is Brazil itself." He hoped that the process of discovery would lead Brazilians to renew their commitment to the faith and produce concrete changes, such as the restoration of Catholic catechism in public education.[151] Another who used the centenary to trace the Catholic influence on Brazil to the present day was the historian Brandão, who saw the centenary as an opportunity to highlight the errors of the republic. Having shown the roles played by the clergy and the faithful in earlier periods, he attacked the republic's separation of church and state, which he claimed grew out of its founders' attempt to import a system designed for "a people of another raça, of another religion and other customs." "The provisional government of the Republic erred in this regard," he said, undermining the church's historic role as the guarantor of national community. He feared that the ultimate consequence of the separation would be "the destruction of national unity," as some states continued to be guided by the faith and the church, and some embraced Positivism and other novelties.[152]

The centenary experience left both writers hopeful of the eventual triumph of the Catholic project. According to d'Azevedo, the success of the congress showed that Brazilians shared his conviction that the country's governing system was republican but Christ was the "nation's king," while Brandão asserted it indicated that a new Catholic political party would be "invincible," especially if women were to gain the franchise.[153] Afonso Celso struck a similar chord, making explicit the continuity between past and present, and the utility of memory in shaping contemporary Brazil. As he had done throughout the previous decades Celso tried to use the centenary to emphasize the importance of Catholicism to Brazilian history and to elucidate the dangers he saw in the republic's religious policy, but as he also insisted, the centenary indicated that Brazilians were ready to confront those dangers and remake the relationship between the state and the church. He joined Brandão in depicting the faith as one of the most important forces in the historical construction of the national community, and he noted the risk to the national union caused by anticlerical policies, offering one of two major addresses at the Congresso Eucharistico on the subject (the other was offered by F. de P. Lacerda de Almeida, of the Rio de Janeiro law school).[154]

Taking up the theme of his fellow Catholic activist Figuieredo—and his fellow historians in the IHGB—during the centenary year Celso used his regular column in the *Jornal do Brasil* to suggest that what Brazilians needed most urgently was community, for the national family was threatened by a crisis of division and difference. Fortunately, he said, the faith "can advance and consolidate unity among Brazilians," and he rejected those who saw conflict between church and state because, "in Brazil, Catholic and patriot ought to be synonyms." He drew confidence from the fact that although the organizers of the official celebrations in the capital had neglected to include religious ceremonies among centenary events, "the Catholic heart and conscience of the nation" ensured the centenary would display Brazilians' patriotism and faith.[155] This was most obvious in the success of the congress but could also be seen in the celebrations of the Fico, in the campaign for the monument on Corcovado, and in Brazilians' warm reception of the embassy sent by the Holy See, which Celso said was "warmer" than that afforded to any other foreign visitor to the centenary.[156] Celso was active in all these efforts, and he told his readers they proved that in spite of the challenges threatened by modern society and modern government, Brazilians continued to be what history showed they had always been, faithful. Brazil was "the immense country, the great nation, which lives in the New World, under the Southern Cross, was born and matured under the shadow of the Cross; it was baptized with the name of the land of Santa Cruz; the cross blazes through its history; it carries the cross in its conscience; [and] it sees in the cross the certainty of its future."[157]

Catholic activists like Afonso Celso approached the centenary with a clear sense of the uses of the past. In narrating Brazil's story they found the means to reclaim the influence they believed the church had lost with the foundation of the republic, and they insisted that history's lessons showed that the faith was the only way to build the national community. Throughout Brazil, citizens, immigrants, and visitors took advantage of the window to the past opened up by the centenary celebrations to offer their own narratives of national history, often with one eye fixed on the present and the ways that history could be used as a tool for working out questions of power and identity in their own day. Their challenge was that there were so many stories to tell and so many storytellers. They emphasized different episodes and different characters, and they offered different, often competing interpretations of national history based on those choices. This meant that the performances of history enacted during 1922 did not amount to the kind of consensus the IHGB hoped to construct. Instead, they helped exacerbate Brazilians' differences in the present, especially as the events of the centenary put those differences on display.

As this chapter has shown, Brazilians disagreed in their views of Pedro and his advisers, and, related to this, they disagreed over the parts played by elite and popular actors in the independence era, the latter exemplified in disagreements about the meaning of the liberation of Salvador. As they made those disagreements known, they signaled they did not share a singular view of the central state's role in independence and in the country's early history, or, indeed, in their own time. Some of those involved in the performances of memory of 1922 presented independence as largely a peaceful affair, a parting rather than a violent break, while others emphasized violent episodes like the Battle of Pirajá and depicted independence as a war of liberation. All such arguments inevitably had as much to do with contemporary opinions about the country's Portuguese inheritance and the place of Portuguese residents in Brazil as they did with the historical record itself, and, as chapter 4 demonstrates more fully, the centenary proved an important venue for a close examination of Luso-Brazilian relations, past and present.

Elsewhere, to consider only one other example, the painter Georgina de Albuquerque drew attention to the gendering of the independence story through her painting *Sessão do Conselho de Estado*. In the painting, a rendering of the meeting of Pedro's advisers on 2 September 1822, Albuquerque emphasized Maria Leopoldina's role in advising the prince and agitating for independence. It was included in the art exhibition and contest organized as part of the official events of the capital, where it was well received, winning one of the contest prizes and then being installed in the new Museu Histórico, where it helped Gustavo Barroso emphasize the importance of the crown in the early history of the nation. Along with Affonso Taunay and others who sought to draw attention to the actions of Joana Angélica and Maria Quitéria, Albuquerque also drove the work of challenging narratives of independence that were focused—often exclusively—on Pedro and other male actors. Though these efforts were only beginning to gain momentum in 1922, they represented another suggestion of the challenge the IHGB and others faced in building consensus about national history.

Above all, Brazilians' differences over history had to do with how to understand the workings of region and time in the making of Brazil. Cariocas and Paulistas played out their ongoing rivalry in the centenary's venues of memory, from the pages of their books and their lectures to museum halls and monument projects, though both groups agreed that the most important episodes of independence took place in their region. Pernambucanos challenged the claims that both groups made on the past, insisting on the great significance of the 1817 revolution and other events, partly in order to challenge the power of the southeastern elite in the present day. For example, during the centenary celebrations they were even more likely than Baianos to assert the importance of Dois de Julho, depicting it as an edifying example of liberation and popular action, which they used to continue their dispute with Epitácio Pessoa, even after he had left the presidency.[158]

Brazilians also disagreed about the longevity of the independence movement, with prominent figures like Max Flieüss and Gustavo Barroso insisting on the significance of 1822 and Alphonso Pinto and Mário Melo explaining independence as a process that unfolded over a much longer period. The latter figures demonstrated that Brazilians' disagreements over history and historiography went far beyond independence itself, and many of the performances of memory in 1922 had very little to do with independence at all. Paulistas celebrated the bandeirantes, and Pernambucanos celebrated those who fought to drive out the Dutch, both groups claiming that the centenary was an occasion for remembering the origins of the nation, which they found in the stories of the heroes they championed. A similar process was at work among the activists who used the centenary to offer a Catholic history of Brazil rather than focusing on the actors and events of the 1820s. Unable to agree even on what the nation ought to be celebrating, Brazilians made the commemorations of the centenary into a discordant patchwork of narratives that exhibited their disagreements about the past and their arguments in the present.

If there was a signal amid the noise of competing narratives and memories, it was that many of those who engaged most fully with the past in 1922 seem to have done so in order to alert Brazilians to the dangers of modernity and urge them to heed the call of tradition. Republicans worried about the way the centenary celebrations encouraged a reassessment of the empire, but many Cariocas longed for the legitimacy Pedro seemed to have embodied and they insisted on celebrating him and his legacy, for example, by reviving the commemoration of the Fico and warmly welcoming members of the royal family who visited Brazil in 1922. While some Paulistas used the centenary to boast of São Paulo's development and bright future, others were especially interested in using the region's early settlers and the bandeirantes to confront what Pinto had called the "sediments of immigrantism" and the other dangers of modern life that confronted them. Inspired by the success of their Congresso Eucharistico, lay Catholics and officials spoke in confident terms about the future of the church in Brazil, but they made sure to emphasize that its position remained precarious, for modernity's government seemed to threaten the faith, and they used the centenary to call for a return to it. Pernambucanos also confronted the unsatisfying circumstances in which they found their region in 1922 with a nostalgic rendering of its past, using the centenary to label Brazil's modern history a failure and to call for Brazilians to recognize that a better future lay in the recovery of the country's authentic traditions, that is, in the traditions maintained in the Northeast.

These figures understood that Brazil confronted a crisis in their own day, of regionalist tension, social strife, and the weakness of the political system, which might result in what Ulysses Brandão labeled "the destruction of national unity." Some symptoms of the crisis shaped the experience of 1922 in obvious ways, such as the controversy over the presidential election, the Copacabana uprising, and the regionalist flashpoints that brought violence to Pernambuco and Rio Grande do Sul. Others were less controversial in the moment but potentially more threatening to the status quo; the foundation in 1922 of both the Brazilian communist party and the Federação Brasileira pelo Progresso Feminino, for example, suggested the ways that the country's experience of modernity was challenging its social order.

The trouble for those who used the centenary to call Brazilians to return to tradition was that they did not agree on exactly what that return ought to entail or what they hoped their fellow citizens would take from the history lessons they offered. Afonso Celso and Pereira Alves, for example, insisted on the church's importance to national history, but both also rejected the notion that Pedro was an essential figure in the independence story, and Alves also injected his Pernambucano patriotism into his historical work. Elsewhere, Gustavo Barroso used the Museu Histórico Nacional to insist on the importance of the emperor to independence and the preservation of Brazilian unity, while Mário Melo used the centenary to remind Brazilians of the longevity of the republican idea in Brazil. These disagreements helped make dissonance, not consensus, the most apparent characteristic of the displays of memory in 1922. Still, the historical work these traditionalists undertook ensured the continuing significance of the centenary. As they used the centenary to offer implicit—and sometimes explicit—critiques of contemporary Brazilian life and to offer Brazilians carefully crafted, edifying historical examples of ways to meet the challenges of the present, they shaped Brazilian memory in profound ways. In the ensuing years their views found purchase in a variety of contexts, from the completion of the monuments to Christ in Rio de Janeiro and the bandeirantes in São Paulo, to the Regionalist movement that came to define Pernambuco and the Northeast, to the impressive celebrations with which Brazilians marked the centenary of Pedro II's birth. Above all, they informed the many cultural and historical interventions of the Vargas state.

Chapter 4

Citizens of the Patria(s)

Immigrants and the Centenary

In October 1918, the architect Ricardo Severo gave the keynote address as his fellow Portuguese residing in the city of São Paulo gathered to commemorate the foundation of the Portuguese republic eight years earlier. Despite the occasion, he began on a pessimistic note, acknowledging the "callous skies of cataclysm" under which contemporaries lived, as war, disease, hunger, and financial shock threatened them with disaster at every turn. Moreover, Severo said that the crisis was even worse than it seemed, for he detected a broad "abandonment of tradition," which left them unmoored amid modernity's challenges and confusions, and he said the problem was especially apparent in Brazil. He did not, though, refer to the decline of religion, which so vexed Catholic activists like Afonso Celso. Instead, he worried about what he perceived as Brazilians' abandonment of the country's Portuguese inheritance, which they must rediscover if they were to build a healthy and peaceful country. Restoring that inheritance was Severo's project, and he insisted that the main responsibility for it belonged to the Portuguese themselves. "Our mission in Brazil is not ended," he said, "and it has not lost its active character; it is still closely linked to the ethnic constitution of Brazilian national identity, and our role in this country remains fundamental, as essential actors, conservators of the basic principles of the nationality, which is fundamentally Portuguese."

In asserting that Brazilian identity was "fundamentally Portuguese," Severo challenged the arguments of nationalists who saw a clear distinction between the two peoples—one that they saw rooted as far back in the past as the seventeenth century. He also questioned those who asserted the importance of other groups, including not only indigenous peoples and Africans but also Italians and other "new" immigrants, who were particularly important to the making of contemporary São Paulo. Severo knew that his view was not shared unanimously, and he therefore took the opportunity of addressing his fellow Portuguese to urge them to take up the mission he believed was surely theirs. He called on them to establish a "Casa Portugueza," a civic and cultural center where they could come together regardless of their towns of origin, social stations, or politics. They must join together and organize themselves in a formal way, so they might help one another as well as undertake the mission to lead Brazil back to its authentic self. Under one (tradition-inspired) roof, the "Casa" would provide educational and leisure opportunities and space for all the community's many social, cultural, and commercial groups. It would be, Severo said in another speech promoting the idea a year later, "a true monument of the Portuguese colony of S. Paulo, a temple of patriotism and a grand statement of Portuguese nationality, erected in honor of our country, and at the same time a monumental gift to the Brazilian land, as a testament to the contribution of the colony to its progress."[1]

Portuguese residents of São Paulo did open the "Casa de Portugal," but not until years later. As Severo acknowledged in 1919, many Portuguese in Brazil were either indifferent to or ignorant of their responsibilities to one another and to Brazil, and building the immigrant community was therefore a project that would take time and effort to complete. Severo worked to build the community and remind Brazilians of their inheritance in the ensuing years, most notably in his own field, where he was one of the leading figures in the movement to establish the neocolonial school as Brazil's "national" style of architecture.[2] He also took a prominent role in organizing Portuguese residents of Brazil to celebrate the independence centenary, which he saw as a rare and crucial opportunity. For Severo, for other Portuguese, and for Lusophile Brazilians, the centenary offered the prospect of bringing together the Portuguese of Brazil, promoting Portuguese immigrant interests and Luso-Brazilian affinity, reminding Brazilians of the historic and continuing importance of Portugal in the making of Brazil, and pushing back against anti-Portuguese sentiment among Brazilian nativists. Together and alongside the government of Portugal, they worked to make Brazil's independence centenary as much as possible a *Portuguese* event.

For his part, for example, Severo helped organize the community's reception of the numerous distinguished Portuguese visitors who came to Brazil to celebrate the centenary, such as President António de Almeida and the raiders Sacadura Cabral and Gago Coutinho. He oversaw the completion of Portugal's Pavilhão das Indústrias at the international exposition, a "traditionalist" building that organizers hoped would become home to a "Casa de Portugal" after the fair.[3] He was also the leading advocate and spokesman as the Portuguese of São Paulo came together to erect a monument to mark the centenary. This group considered monument projects to the bandeiras and the Portuguese language before settling on a work that would celebrate the Luso-Brazilian "race," an attempt to enshrine Severo's view that Brazil was "fundamentally Portuguese." Through such initiatives, Ricardo Severo and his fellow Portuguese claimed the centenary. Through it, they claimed Brazil.

They were not alone. Many other immigrants saw the opportunities the centenary offered them, to make themselves into communities, or "colonies," to use the telling term preferred by Severo and many other contemporaries, which would allow them to promote their common interests more effectively.[4] Most important, they sought to use the centenary to insist that they belonged in Brazil. Besides the Portuguese, who were active throughout the country and especially in the coastal cities where Portuguese merchant interests were active, the largest and most prominent of these colonies was that of the Italians residing in São Paulo; having made a number of the neighborhoods of Brazil's most dynamic city fully their own, they sought to confirm their claim in the centenary. Others active in the celebrations included groups of German, Japanese, and Syrian immigrants in the South and Southeast, as well as smaller numbers of British and American citizens who resided in Brazil's major cities and served as representatives of their home governments or home-based commercial interests. Like Severo and the Portuguese, these groups engaged with the centenary in three main ways. First, they welcomed their home nations' representatives in centenary events, figures such as Almeida and the Italian prince Giovanni Luigi Alliata di Montereale (known as Prince Alliata), organizing sometimes enormous public receptions as well as all manner of events in the private spaces of the colonies. Second, they helped ensure the countries' successful participation in the centenary fair, promoting the event, providing assistance with their pavilions, and even helping to fill those buildings with their own products. Third, colonies of immigrants and other foreign residents in Brazil came together to make the memory of their participation in the centenary permanent by erecting monuments, which always aimed at celebrating Brazil but also always memorialized the colonies themselves. Through such activities immigrants became ubiquitous, significant figures in the centenary, making it a venue for building their communities and performing their sense of identity and citizenship. This chapter therefore focuses on their activities, in particular on the Paulista Italians and the Portuguese in that city and in the capital.

To a very great extent, these groups were encouraged in their activity, both by governing authorities and by their Brazilian neighbors. As Frederick Pike has shown in his study of "Hispanismo" in Spanish America, the Spanish state hoped to use the independence centenaries of various Spanish American states in the 1910 decade to attempt to gain practical benefits from renewed ties and to reinforce its own legitimacy at home.[5] A similar process was at work as the young Portuguese republican state approached Brazil's centenary, for building strong relations with Brazil was the centerpiece of its foreign policy.[6] Other governments also understood the exposition and various centenary events as opportunities to promote closer relations between themselves and Brazil. All these governments found willing and valuable partners in their own citizens who resided in Brazil in 1922. For their part, Brazilian governments at the local, regional, and national levels were also eager for the participation of the immigrants and other foreigners resident in the country. Their willingness to participate in the fair and other official events as well as their work to undertake their own initiatives enlarged the scale and scope of the celebrations and confirmed the significance of the occasion, even as Brazilians like Mário Melo and Cussy d'Almeida Júnior doubted its importance.

These celebrants also faced several challenges as they approached the centenary, however. Immigrants were objects of intense interest for their Brazilian neighbors, who measured and commented on every action and utterance immigrants offered to celebrate the occasion as a way of considering whether and how they fit into Brazilian life. Many Brazilians considered immigrants essential to the great project of national development and viewed their participation in the centenary as proof of their successful adjustment to the country and its bright future. Others doubted certain immigrants could ever become part of the national community. Such Brazilians tended to react ungenerously to those immigrants' plans to participate in the centenary, and sometimes took offense at what they saw as the foreigners' use of the occasion to make inappropriate claims on Brazil. The kind of response immigrants were likely to get depended on their nationality, the region of Brazil in which they lived, and the ways they chose to participate in the centenary. As the chapter demonstrates, immigrants were sensitive to these issues, and their sense of how their neighbors might react to their activities informed their choices as they participated in the centenary celebrations.

To navigate the centenary, immigrants also had to resolve the difficulty Ricardo Severo had noticed, that organizing their colonies was neither easy nor inevitable. Some immigrants did not see themselves as members of such communities, whether because they considered themselves Brazilians or, say, Lombards rather than Italians, or because they rejected national commitments in favor of class-based identities. Some were alienated from organizing efforts owing to political differences, for example, as Portuguese monarchists and republicans carried their conflict to Brazil. And some simply lacked the resources of time and money to participate in collective action. If an immigrant colony were to come together to seize the opportunities the centenary seemed to offer, individual members would have to be convinced to participate, to give money to monuments campaigns and festivities celebrating visitors from home, and to turn out at community events in order to impress the public and make plausible the colony's claims. It was wealthier members of the colonies, men like Severo, who arrogated to themselves the responsibility for leading this effort, for gathering the community together and assigning its members their "proper" roles. There were, unsurprisingly, difficulties and a few failed initiatives, but contemporaries tended to agree that they were generally successful in their efforts, and immigrant centenary events largely reflected the preferences of the respectable classes, their sense of the meaning of the occasion and the colony's place in Brazil.

Indeed, one consequence of the centenary celebrations among immigrant groups seems to have been the strengthening of the positions of such figures, another reason Brazilian authorities welcomed the participation of immigrant colonies in the year's festivities. The work of organizing immigrant colonies helped reinforce their national identities and connect them more fully not only to one another but also to their countries of origin. Hundreds of thousands of Portuguese and Italians resident in Brazil participated in the centenary as Portuguese and Italians, and they were joined by thousands of others who made up Brazil's other colonies. The centenary thus made immigrant communities more coherent and distinctive than they were earlier, which helps explain the surge in the 1920s and 1930s in the establishment of immigrant organizations throughout Brazil, often in partnership with the governments of their mother countries. In 1922 some Brazilians worried about this prospect, anxious that the centenary might show that the country's immigrants were not assimilating to their new home, and that, in fact, the problem was worsening. However, while immigrants were enacting and performing their nationalities, they were also abandoning or at least setting aside other possible identities, such as Gaúcho regionalism in Rio Grande do Sul and working-class consciousness in industrial São Paulo. In other words, the centenary might reinforce differences between immigrants and natives, but in immigrant communities it also seemed to ratify the legitimacy of traditional authority and hierarchy, a relief to authorities confronting the country's many other fractures.

The centenary thus proved to be a testing time for immigrants, of both opportunities and hazards. It offered a rare chance to make public and legible their assertions that they belonged in Brazil and that they remained loyal to their home nations. It gave them new venues for building their own colonies and working out how community members ought to fit into them. It also offered others the chance to scrutinize how immigrants were adjusting to life in Brazil and to announce their own expectations and demands—Brazilians anticipating performances of gratitude and admiration, representatives of the immigrants' old countries hoping for nostalgia and cooperation. Immigrants and their erstwhile compatriots joined Brazilians in seeing the centenary as an exceptional and momentous occasion. They knew that the celebrations might be fleeting but the claims they made on one another through the celebrations would persist.

Organizing the Immigrant Community

Much of the work of immigrants' performance of identity took place before visitors arrived, exposition pavilions opened, or monuments were unveiled. In every city and town where immigrants would host visitors from home, where they intended to erect commemorative markers, and where they produced goods they hoped to display at the fair, they met to discuss their plans and organize their participation in the celebrations. These people of course interacted in more quotidian moments, but as with other groups interested in the centenary, the celebrations provided an urgent rationale for interaction and organization. Further, because of the public-facing nature of these celebrations, the centenary helped reinforce immigrant identities, and not in any sort of haphazard way. Instead, planning for the centenary afforded the respectable classes among immigrant communities opportunities to define immigrant identities according to their own preferences and to attempt to enact discipline on the lower orders among their compatriots resident in Brazil.

Some of this planning occurred months and even years in advance of visits, inaugurations, and openings, and well beyond the sites where they were to take place. For example, Portuguese residents of Recife expected that Sacadura Cabral and Gago Coutinho would come to their city, the aviators' first planned stop on the mainland, while their counterparts in São Paulo had to hope to convince them to travel to their city after the raid had been completed. The aviators arrived in Recife in early June and they visited São Paulo in early July, but Portuguese residents in both cities began meeting to discuss the raid and how best to honor the visitors in early April, only a few days after the months-long raid started and well before even the most optimistic projections of their arrival in Brazil.[7]

Gathered together again in the weeks before António de Almeida arrived in Brazil, the Portuguese in São Paulo generated an appeal for him to visit them and developed both a roster of events should the appeal succeed and a fund to pay for them. On this occasion they were disappointed, but their planning meant they had the time and money to organize a trip to Rio de Janeiro for a small group among them, and they delivered the statesman a congratulatory message and expensive presents, and took part in many of the events held in Almeida's honor in the capital.[8] Meanwhile, the Portuguese in Recife hoped to convince Almeida and his party to make a brief stop in their city as they steamed up the Brazilian coast before turning east for home, and they made detailed plans for several events to celebrate a possible visit. The ship stopped in Recife for only a few hours, however, and the president did not come ashore. But the Portuguese adapted quickly and took a leading role in the brief but, in their view, meaningful celebration of the visitors that took place at the city docks and aboard ship. They sent three commissions including dozens of their number to accompany city and state officials to meet Almeida and offer him proof of their esteem.[9]

A crucial aspect of this work was that it was organized; in fact, it was institutional. Any immigrant who wanted to could go to the docks to salute a visitor from home, to the inauguration of a monument, or to the exposition grounds to visit the pavilion of the old country, and immigrant organizations and publications encouraged them to do so. But to interact more intimately with visitors or participate in a more formal way in parades and other events of the colony, it was essential that they join in the work of committees organized by middle-class and wealthy immigrants to plan for the events, and participation in the committees was contingent on one's standing in the local community and among one's fellow immigrants. Prominent businessmen and well-known figures such as journalists, artists, and teachers had little trouble joining, and often took leadership roles in these ad hoc groups, but others could become involved only because of institutional connections, such as membership in cultural centers or affiliation with immigrant hospitals or charities. Those unconnected to such organizations and without cultural or financial capital were largely relegated to places in the crowd.

Foreign consuls and ambassadors played important parts in organizing their compatriots in Brazil, first, by liaising with home governments as intermediaries between visitors and immigrants, and second, by hosting or even convening the meetings at which the latter group planned for the centenary. In Recife, the committees organized to receive the Lisbon and New York raiders were presided over, respectively, by the Portuguese consul, Pedroso Rodrigues, and the United States consul, Charles Cameron.[10] Rodrigues's counterpart in São Paulo was José Augusto de Magalhães, who filled a similar role there and also led the group of Portuguese in São Paulo who traveled to Rio de Janeiro to salute the Portuguese president.[11] Also active in events in São Paulo were Italy's consuls in the city, Ugo Tedeschi and Bruno Zucculin. They helped organize the participation of Italian residents in a variety of events, including the centenary exposition and the erection and inauguration of a monument to the Brazilian composer Carlos Gomes, offered by the Italians of São Paulo to celebrate the centenary.[12] Besides these figures, the countries' ambassadors in the Brazilian capital, of course, played important parts in helping immigrants plan for and participate in the many events that took place there and involved their home countries, though there the Brazilian diplomatic apparatus was present and the commission organized by the national government specifically for the centenary celebrations was more active than its regional equivalents, thus leaving less space for immigrant communities' own organizations.

The character of the group that dubbed itself the "Commissão Executiva da Colonia Portugueza" and organized to oversee preparations to receive the Portuguese aviators in Recife gives a sense of how prominent immigrants helped the diplomats shape the colonies' centenary events. Besides Pedroso Rodrigues, this commission, which held its meetings at the Gabinete Portuguez de Leitura, included Pereira de Souza, the director of the Banco Nacional Ultramarino; Zenobio Lins, the president of the city's Associação Commercial; Diogo Salgado, the vice president of the Associação dos Empregados no Commercio; Cruz Ribeiro, the president of the Liga dos Desportos Nauticos; and José Júlio Rodrigues and Heitor Maia, both professors at the Escola de Chimica e Engenharia.[13] The *Jornal do Recife* depicted this group as "representative" of the city's Portuguese community, but also as constituted by "the majority of its most influential members." And while there was room in the group's organization for the large number of Portuguese traveling sales representatives in the city, they came together as a subcommission "of their station" to do the publicity work "indispensible to the proper reception to which the aviators have an indisputable right."[14] Ensuring their influence over the way that the immigrant community—and the city at large—would interact with the raiders, the commission remained in permanent session throughout the months of the raid, and reconvened in early August to arrange events when it learned that Sacadura Cabral would visit Recife again on his way home to Portugal.[15]

The group formed by Italians in São Paulo to defend the "the prestige of the Colony and the good name of Italy" by planning an appropriate reception for the Italian exposition commissioners on their visit to the city had a similar character. The group, which sought to speak for all the Italians of São Paulo, coordinated its plans with the Italian government and ensured a certain amount of representativity and respectability by making room for the participation of individuals according to the organizations of which they were members. Indeed, the group contemplated using the occasion of the centenary to form a Federazione delle Società Italiane, which suggests the extent to which centenary events reinforced immigrant identities and forged a specifically Italian identity rather than say, Piedmontese or Calabrian. Its presiding officer was the head of the Umberto I immigrant hospital, Davide Picchetti, and its members included representatives of the community's veterans groups (the Reduci di Guerra and the Reduci Garibaldini); its literary and artistic institutions (the Unione Artistica Ricreativa del Cambucy and the Dante Alighieri, Circolo Italiano, and Galileo Galilei centers); its commercial establishments (the Unione Viaggiatori); its regionalist organizations (the Lega Lombarda and the Società Trinacria); its schools (the Istituto Medio and the Federazione delle Scuole Italiane); its mutual assistance societies (the Società di Mutuo Soccorso di Barra Funda, the Società di Mutuo Soccorso di Agua Branca, and the Assistenza Civile); and its sports clubs (the Ítalo and Palestra Italia clubs), among others.[16]

Through such organizations, leading figures attempted to control participation in the centenary and imbued it with hierarchies of wealth and education even as they worked to bring together "all" Portuguese or "all" Italians in a city or a state. From the position of leadership they filled or assumed, moreover, they worked not just to include but to obligate their compatriots to participate in centenary events. Community leaders said immigrants were duty bound to celebrate Brazil in order to demonstrate their gratitude for the opportunities it provided them and to formally mark the connection between their old countries and their adoptive home. They also used their events as tests of loyalty, a means of demanding proof that immigrants continued to remain faithful to the mother country.

The editors of the newspaper *Fanfulla*, the largest and most influential of the Italian-language publications of Brazil, summed up this point of view in an editorial introducing its coverage of the centenary celebrations in August 1922, arguing that Italian immigrants could take pride in their contributions to Brazil's accomplishments in its first hundred years as an independent nation, which meant that "Brazil's celebration is also the celebration of the Italians." And they were sure that their compatriots would offer proof of their pride, gratitude, and sense of belonging in Brazil: "The Italians who reside in this Republic, always ready to fulfill their responsibilities, will be unanimous in the fulfillment of this joyful new duty. Dedicated to the daily work of the great development of this country, they will be dedicated as well to celebrating the progress it has achieved." Far from demonstrating a change in their loyalties, the editors said, these celebrations would be grounded in the immigrants' continuing "affection for the great Mother whom you left beyond the sea," a nostalgia that deepened their sense of the importance of nation and made immigrants from every region in Italy, every class, and every creed the ideal "witnesses and participants" in the "sacred apotheosis" that was the centenary. Italians in Brazil were both outsiders and insiders, both Italians and future Brazilians, and there was no question of their eager participation in the celebrations, which were a test of their patriotism the editors were sure they would pass. To ensure this, the editors signed off by offering their assistance in organizing Italians' plans and asserting the paper's role as the voice of the immigrant community.[17]

The kind of activity *Fanfulla* called for was on display on 20 September 1922, when Italians in São Paulo gathered for the traditional commemoration of the anniversary of the unification of Italy at the home of the Società Italiana di Beneficenza. The organization's directors took advantage of the coincidence in timing to include the Brazilian centenary in the year's celebrations, tying Italian immigrants to Brazil and weaving old and new loyalties together. The celebrations, which the *Correio da Manhã* said were the biggest the Italian community of São Paulo had ever held, included immigrant and native organizations, speeches by members of both communities, and both Italian and Brazilian music, amounting to a performance of Italians' ties to both nations. As the group's president said when he spoke of "Italians' obligation" to work for the greater glory of Brazil, a country he called "the most welcoming in the world," immigrants must demonstrate their willingness to honor their old and new homes, which he called their "two patrias."[18]

Such was the ubiquity of the rhetoric of duty in Italian immigrant circles in 1922 that another of the community's publications, the much smaller *Il Pasquino Coloniale*, depicted immigrants as exhausted by and at least a little resentful of the demands of their middle-class and wealthy "leaders." It made the point in a pair of cartoons published in July 1922, when *Fanfulla* and other community institutions were issuing regular

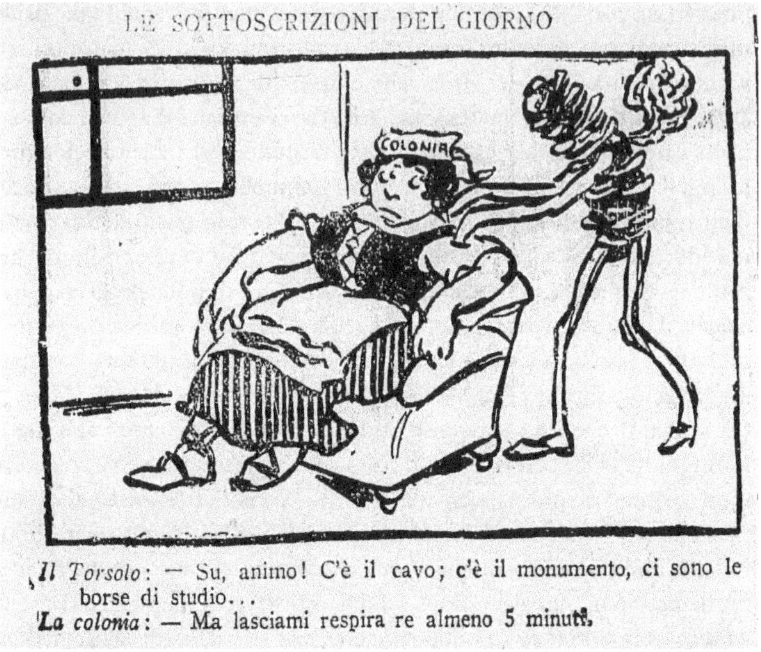

4.1. "Today's Donation," *Il Pasquino Coloniale*, 15 July 1922. In the cartoon, *Il Torsolo* cajoles *La Colonia*, saying "Come on! There's the cable; there's the monument, there are the scholarships . . ." *La Colonia* responds, "Just give me five minutes to catch my breath." Courtesy of the Acervo da Fundação Biblioteca Nacional—Brasil.

calls for contributions to fundraising campaigns for the monument to Carlos Gomes as well as a submarine telegraph cable between Italy and Brazil and other projects. In the first cartoon, the Italian consul in São Paulo addresses a crowd gathered at his window and, in the "voice of authority," reminds them that participation in the monument and cable campaigns are "two obligations" they must perform. The men are attentive but also clearly anxious, if not dubious.[19] The second cartoon suggests the consequences of these demands. In it, "Il Torsolo," the paper's lampoon of those who would speak for the community as a ridiculous and half-rotten "core," attempts to rouse the "Colonia" to its responsibilities, saying, "Come on! There's the cable; there's the monument, there are the scholarships . . ." Slumped in an armchair and clearly exhausted, the Colonia (depicted as it always was in the paper's cartoons as a peasant woman) asks to be allowed to catch its breath, "for just five minutes" (see fig. 4.1).[20] Returning to the theme in October in its coverage of the inauguration of the monument, *Il Pasquino* suggested that, far from a well-organized, public-spirited effort, it was characterized by competition among immigrant organizations and community leaders for pride of place in the event.[21] The mass of immigrants, meanwhile, participated only grudgingly, resentful of what one columnist called the self-important "grandees" (*graúdos*) who sought to speak for them and obligate their financial contributions and participation.[22]

Doubt, hesitancy, and even apathy surely characterized the views of many immigrants living in Brazil as they considered the centenary celebrations, but these attitudes were rarely expressed in such explicit and public ways. Activists acknowledged doubt and the possibility of a lack of interest when they employed the rhetoric of obligation in attempting to convince their compatriots to participate, which was as prevalent among the Portuguese as among Italians. As early as 1920, Portuguese residents of Rio de Janeiro and São Paulo were discussing how best to commemorate the centenary, with many of their ideas focusing on the erection of one or more monuments. Commenting on plans that were just being sketched out at that point, the Portuguese A. Duarte Silva said he preferred a more restrained acknowledgment of the centenary, but explained that many of his compatriots felt they should do more than celebrate the event. They thought they "should make a display" of their appreciation for Brazil and "make it eternal in marble."[23] Two years later, the Portuguese in Rio de Janeiro and São Paulo still planned marble records of their participation in centenary celebrations, and, although none of the monuments they intended to erect in the two cities was ever completed, the conviction that Portuguese living in Brazil were duty bound to participate in the year's patriotic events was undiminished.

Portuguese business and commercial figures, teachers, medical doctors, and sports administrators joined Portugal's diplomats in communicating to their compatriots in Brazil that they must take part in the events of the centenary and that it was especially important for them to offer a proper reception for António de Almeida and other visitors from home. This meant attendance at rallies, parades, and parties honoring the travelers, as well as contributions to fundraising campaigns to pay for the events and other proofs of loyalty. For example, when a group of Portuguese in Brazil decided to donate a hydroplane to Portugal as a way of honoring Cabral and Coutinho, they made all the claims typical of contemporary reaction to the event, from the aviators' links to the Age of Discovery to the notion that their accomplishment marked the rebirth of the Portuguese nation. Organizers of the campaign said that every loyal Portuguese must celebrate "these two supermen," as one planner called the aviators, and the best way to do so was to give Portugal the "wings" that would help it meet the future. He acknowledged that their compatriots had been asked repeatedly for public displays of allegiance, but said that this project was more important than any other because it was meant to celebrate an accomplishment of extraordinary import. "Not one Portuguese can shirk this duty," he wrote, "which is more imperative than any of those they have been called to fulfill."[24] Though it seems unlikely that every Portuguese did participate in the campaign, it is clear that many did, with contributions coming from all over Brazil and from large, well-funded institutions as well as individuals with much more modest means.[25] The campaign was a great success, raising over 400 contos de réis, which was more than enough money to purchase the hydroplane dubbed the *Sagres* as an allusion to Portugal's history of exploration.[26]

Loyalty, Disloyalty, and the Centenary

Though often unspoken, there were tensions here, for although many immigrants and other foreign residents understood the centenary as prompting them to consider notions of duty, obligations to Brazil and to their mother countries did not fit together nearly as neatly as many figures active in immigrant communities asserted. This was partly because in 1922 some Brazilians were busy constructing a nationalism more demanding than the one that had characterized the early years of the republic. A more strident nationalism was building before 1914, and then the war helped convince many influential figures that Brazil's traditional cosmopolitanism and emphasis on cordiality in foreign affairs was ill-suited to the dangers of the modern world.[27] Activists who were convinced Brazil must do more to promote war readiness and citizens' commitments to the nation promoted a variety of new projects during the war years, organizing young Brazilians in Boy Scout troops and older ones in shooting clubs, and they founded two prominent, explicitly nationalist groups, the Liga da Defesa Nacional and the Liga Nacionalista de São Paulo.[28] These groups maintained a generous disposition toward Brazil's diplomatic allies, shown, for example, in their fundraising for the work of the international Red Cross in France, Belgium, and Italy, but they also helped prepare the way for a more aggressive, even ethnocentric postwar nationalism by joining with other Brazilians in ostracizing and persecuting the country's German residents.[29]

The centenary gave nationalists a venue to showcase their views and to subject Germans and other immigrants to tests of their loyalty to Brazil. *Gil Blas*, the Rio de Janeiro magazine founded in 1919 closely associated with the nativist Ação Social Nacionalista organization, was especially eager to use the centenary as a proving ground—for Brazilians as much as for the foreign-born—and it found that many failed to offer the requisite proofs of fidelity; as was its habit, it was especially willing to doubt the country's Portuguese. The magazine's writers made room in their nationalist project for immigrants, such as "the German, the Italian, and the Pole" who, Mário Deval said, "settle the interior of the country and develop its agriculture, thus contributing to the rise in our productivity, that is, in our wealth."[30] Deval was rehearsing a sentiment common among Brazilians enthusiastic about the benefits of migration that was ubiquitous in centenary events involving immigrants. At the inauguration of monuments, the openings of pavilions of the countries most important to Brazilian immigration, and the hundreds of centenary events at immigrant organizations, the immigrant as laborer, essential to building Brazil, was a favorite theme of native and immigrant speakers alike.[31] Those writing for *Gil Blas* were no different and were particularly well-disposed toward Italian immigrants. They emphasized Italians' contributions as physical laborers in both agriculture and industry, for which "Brazilians ought to be very grateful." They pointed to cultural connections and "affinities" shared by Brazilians and Italians as fellow Latin peoples, for example, by sharing in Italians' celebration in 1921 of the six-hundredth anniversary of Dante Alighieri's death. And, they argued that Italian immigrants demonstrated that they understood their obligations during the centenary year, evincing what the magazine's editors called "a firm sense of their obligations to our country and grateful for Brazilian hospitality," shown most clearly by the work of those in São Paulo to erect the monument to Carlos Gomes.[32]

As far as *Gil Blas* writers were concerned, the activity of these Italians in the centenary celebrations was especially important because of what they saw as a glaring contrast between Italian and Portuguese efforts. As chapter 1 mentions, these writers suspected that Portuguese residents in Brazil sought to use the centenary to undermine Brazilian nationalism and promote a Portuguese identity for Brazil, which the magazine specifically and categorically rejected. *Gil Blas* saw this plot in everything from reactions to the Lisbon raid and the Almeida visit to proposals put forward by Portuguese communities in various cities in Brazil for the construction of centenary monuments, none of which satisfied the nationalists. The fact that the Portuguese state made it a special priority to use the centenary to promote stronger diplomatic ties with Brazil was sure to annoy a magazine like *Gil Blas*. Even worse was the notion of a formal political arrangement, a Luso-Brazilian confederation, which activists such as Ricardo Severo had been discussing in the years leading up to 1922; they saw the centenary as an excellent opportunity to advance the idea, and championed it in several public events, but in doing so they also attracted the ire of Brazilian nationalists.[33]

Gil Blas was already advancing a strongly anti-Portuguese editorial line, and because of such activities, its attacks against Portugal and especially the Portuguese in Brazil intensified in 1922. It rejected the possibility that the centenary could be a celebration shared by Portuguese and Brazilian citizens and that independence itself could be understood as a Luso-Brazilian triumph due to the roles played by Pedro I and other Portuguese-born participants in the independence movement. For the magazine, the centenary was a celebration of the rejection of Portugal and the legacies of colonialism, under which Brazilians were "victims," while Pedro and other Portuguese active in Brazilian politics during the independence era were, at best, secondary to more influential Brazilian figures like José Bonifácio or, more usually, hindrances to the development of the Brazilian nation. Indeed, the magazine called the forced abdication and exile of Pedro in 1831 "the origin of Brazilian Nationalism."[34]

The magazine therefore bristled at the Portuguese inflection of many centenary events, such as planners' decision to allow the staging of bullfights in the capital, and it encouraged António de Almeida *not* to visit Brazil during the celebrations, "for everyone's good and the happiness of the *two* nations."[35] It was more annoyed by the Portuguese resident in Brazil, whose plans to erect a monument to Camões as a way of marking the centenary the magazine deemed inappropriate, the poet irrelevant to the story of Brazil; whose response to the Lisbon raid it saw as a bad-faith attempt to exploit Brazilian hospitality, when in reality the raid was a "disaster"; and who contributed to the revisionism advanced during the centenary, which held that the independence struggle was neither violent nor national but rather a regrettable political dispute among members of the same "national" family.[36] To its usual depictions of Portuguese employers in Brazil as exploitative of native labor, of Portuguese publishers as manipulative of the Brazilian reading public, and of Portuguese salesmen as cheaters of Brazilian consumers, the magazine added new attacks in response to these activities. According to the periodical, during the centenary Portuguese residents showed that, unlike their Italian counterparts, they lacked dedication to and gratitude for their opportunities in Brazil. More important, the Portuguese were working in ways that were actively destructive of the Brazilian nation, in the place of which they were attempting to construct a false but, for some, seductive Luso-Brazilian unity.

The magazine's editors and writers railed against this notion and the ways they saw it manifested during the centenary. Among other efforts, *Gil Blas* ran several pieces on the history of independence, always emphasizing the violence of the movement, the roles played by leaders born in Brazil, and the perfidy of Portuguese loyalists.[37] In scathing essays its writers rejected proposals for any kind of formal political arrangement between the two countries, while its editors paired a grudging acceptance of the success of Almeida's visit with a reminder that his efforts to formalize closer relations between the two republics yielded little of substance.[38] Other contributors emphasized the differences between Portuguese and a distinctive "Brazilian language," rejected the idea advanced by one Brazilian writer that Portugal was the "perpetual metropole" of Brazilian letters, and insisted that the most important goal of Brazil's next hundred years must be economic independence, specifically the removal of Portuguese influence over Brazilian commerce.[39] Finally, the magazine rejected not only the idea for a statue to Camões, but in even more aggressive terms, the proposal of Portuguese residents of São Paulo for a monument to "A Raça," meaning a national identity shared by all Lusophone peoples, especially Brazilians and Portuguese. There was no such "race," wrote the Ação Social Nacionalista member Victruvio Marcondes, who argued that the very idea of it was ridiculous and offensive because it overstated the contributions of the Portuguese to Brazil, elided the differences between the two peoples, and ignored the roles played by people of indigenous and African descent in making the Brazilian nationality. He called the monument "a veritable Greek gift" and its advocates "troublemaking members of the corrosive party," the Portuguese seeking to use the centenary to destroy Brazilian nationalism for their own purposes and for the benefit of Portugal.[40] As Mário Deval put it in his own attack on Portuguese efforts in the centenary, Brazilians must be wary of such ideas and "alleged blood ties," which were "truly insidious traps" and that "we must avoid at all costs."[41]

The editors and writers of *Gil Blas* were left frustrated that many Brazilians failed to respond as they hoped to what the magazine depicted as the disloyalty of Portuguese citizens resident in Brazil. The magazine's writers and like-minded figures do seem to have influenced the centenary, though, as various commentators noted the Lusophobia expressed in some nationalist circles and discussed the ways in which it might affect centenary events. Chapter 3 covers one such episode, the controversy over the celebration of the Fico in January 1922, which left the *Correio da Manhã* complaining about "'nationalists' with no sense of nationalism" and their "Lusophobic outbursts."[42] Later, *O Malho* noted the Lusophobia of certain politically active figures in the capital, calling their hostility to Portugal and Portuguese residents of Brazil an "idiotic and ridiculous campaign," but it expressed confidence that Cariocas' response to the Lisbon raiders would illustrate their rejection of the nativist call.[43] And early the next year the Portuguese-run *Revista da Semana* looked back on the centenary with contentment while acknowledging that some

Brazilians did continue to exhibit nativism and xenophobia. Fortunately, these appeared only in "certain unhealthy parts of the social body" and not "in the highest levels" of Brazilian thought and the Brazilian state.[44] This was more likely a hopeful statement than a confident one, given that Epitácio Pessoa had been president during the largest of the centenary celebrations. In his public pronouncements Pessoa articulated strongly pro-Portuguese views and called independence day "a day of the raça" during Almeida's visit, but before those events accusations of Lusophobia had become sufficiently common and loud that he felt obligated to address the issue directly. He told Lisbon's *O Seculo* that he rejected "the murmured insinuation that I am hostile to the Portuguese people and their interests," and that he felt confident the centenary would put an end to such talk.[45] Even then, his objections did not keep *Gil Blas* from assuring its readers that he shared the magazine's outlook and continuing to depict him as a leader of its nationalist movement.[46]

Immigrants and other foreign residents also noted that some Brazilians harbored suspicions about their loyalties, and they wrestled with how they should navigate the sometimes-conflicting demands of the centenary. This was apparent, for example, in Rio Grande do Sul, where many immigrants were active in the celebrations, but, because of the distinctive ways that Gaúchos and other Brazilians related to immigrants from different countries, immigrants interpreted their centenary duties in different and even contradictory ways. As was typical of immigrant groups in many other places in Brazil, Italians, Spaniards, Syrians, and others among the foreign born organized themselves and put on special events dedicated to the centenary which featured speeches, music, and symbolism designed to highlight what they understood as the special relationships between their countries of birth and their adoptive home. However, the experience and activity of German and Portuguese residents was quite different, in comparison both to other communities and to one another, as can be seen in two texts produced in reaction to the centenary, one a speech by a German immigrant and public official asserting German commitments to Brazil, the other an essay by a Portuguese resident of Porto Alegre calling for the revival of Portuguese identity among immigrants in danger of the solvent of acculturation.

German immigrants and Brazilians of German descent knew that many Brazilians doubted their loyalty and sought to use the centenary celebrations to prove that they understood their obligations to Brazil. Jacob Kroeff Netto was a businessman and in 1922 was serving as a deputy in the state legislature. He gave the keynote address at a major centenary event in the city of São Leopoldo in the state's German immigrant heartland. Like other immigrants active in the commemorations, he spoke of the historic and contemporary contributions his forebears had made to Brazil, for example by citing the role played by the country's first empress, Maria Leopoldina of Austria, in the events of 1822 and by emphasizing the labor provided by German colonists in Rio Grande do Sul. But the focus of his speech was to reject what he depicted as "false prejudices" about the Germans of Brazil and the idea "that we are insufficiently 'Brazilians and patriots.'" These preconceptions and this doubt he blamed on the horrors of the Great War, which had produced among many Brazilians a powerful suspicion of immigrants of German descent, and the suspicion had lingered despite being "unreasonable, harmful, and unfounded."[47]

Kroeff said that the centenary was the exact right moment to face these questions in a forthright manner and to insist that the Germans of Brazil were not simply resident in the country but were immigrants and true Brazilians. He acknowledged and defended immigrants' sympathy for Germany and their work to maintain their distinctive identity, for example by continuing to speak German and to instruct their Brazilian-born children in the language, arguing that honoring their forebears in this way was a duty of inheritance which did not inhibit their commitment to Brazil. In this, Kroeff articulated a perspective common among members of other immigrant groups, as seen, for example, in the *Fanfulla* editors' assertion that Italians' memory of Italy made them better "witnesses and participants" in both the centenary celebrations and in the project of building Brazil.

But the editors of *Fanfulla* did not need to confront the kind of doubt faced by Kroeff and the community he spoke for, and they were therefore much less defensive and much less insistent in their claims of loyalty than was Kroeff. Kroeff was himself born in Germany but said he expressed the "affective feelings of the good children we want to be in this beloved Brazil." Unlike many commentators with connections to the immigrant communities of Brazil, he left no room for dual loyalties, no "two patrias" as the president of the Società Italiana di Beneficenza would have it. For German immigrants, Kroeff argued, Brazil alone was the "land of our birth, of our childhood, of our dreams, our hopes, our loves, our future, of our lives, in short, which we are ready to sacrifice if it were necessary in order to defend the integrity and the honor of our beloved Patria." They would continue to honor and respect their roots, just as would Italians, and Portuguese, and Englishmen, and Frenchmen, but, he insisted, German immigrants "are and want above all to be Brazilians, Brazilians in practice and in our hearts, for which desire we have already given many proofs during the difficult moments our dear and beloved Brazil has faced." Finally, he closed by calling on his audience not only to accept as Brazilians immigrants from Germany and their children, but also to work to build a nation that rejected distinctions based on national origin, for, he argued, one of Brazil's greatest challenges in its second centenary was "the challenge of unification and the adoption of our own sense of national identity, today so complex and varied and in fact so natural and necessary in a new country, with a settlement and immigration system like ours." Unlike the Italians and Portuguese described above, that is, Kroeff did not see the centenary celebrations as an opportunity to remind Germans of old loyalties but instead as a call to commit to one, renewed pledge to Brazil; such a pledge would build a stronger Brazil and, Kroeff clearly hoped, it would ease the scrutiny which afflicted German immigrants and their descendants.[48]

In many parts of Brazil, such as the Rio de Janeiro of *Gil Blas*, Portuguese residents faced the kind of scrutiny that worried Kroeff. The centenary served to intensify some Brazilians' doubts about their loyalty but, as another resident of Rio Grande do Sul said, it also revived among immigrants a sense of the importance of their own distinctive communities. In a series of articles published in Porto Alegre's *Correio do Povo* in October 1922, the Portuguese Theophilo de Barros Corrêa de Mello Neves argued that the centenary celebrations had demonstrated that the city's Portuguese residents had become *too* integrated into the Brazilian context. Neves began the series on the defensive, noting that while the city's Italians, Germans, and other foreign born had been conspicuous in their centenary activities, the Portuguese did in fact participate, despite what readers might have believed, because "they did not provide any outward proof that was worthy of attention of their attachment to the celebrations." He reported that some locals read this as apathy and "a demonstration of disrespect," but insisted this was not the case. Instead, he said, because of the cultural "intermingling" between them, the Portuguese in Porto Alegre celebrated alongside and among Brazilians; the connection between the groups was so intimate "that it is difficult to know where the Brazilian begins and the Portuguese ends." It was therefore easy to miss the Portuguese commitment to celebrating the centenary, which sowed doubt about Portuguese loyalty and fueled Lusophobia.

Neves granted the doubters some ground, for he argued that while the Portuguese identified in the closest possible terms with Brazilians in a cultural sense, they were still Portuguese in their political identity, and in fact that they were "the most difficult to assimilate of all peoples."[49] Thus, he outlined a dilemma for the Portuguese in Porto Alegre and in other parts of Brazil—of how to manifest their affinity for Brazil and Brazilians while maintaining their Portuguese identity and loyalty to the mother country—which was a very different proposition than those outlined by Jacob Kroeff, *Fanfulla*, and Neves's fellow Portuguese in other places. Kroeff rejected the possibility that German-Brazilians faced such a dilemma, insisting that his brethren were fully committed to Brazil, while *Fanfulla* and many other immigrant voices felt comfortable allowing for the possibility of multiple loyalties. Unlike these others, Neves realized the existence of a tension, revealed in the centenary experience, between the demands of immigrants' roots and continuing connections to home and their duties to Brazil. He knew, furthermore, that they confronted this tension within the immigrant community and also outside the bounds of the community, as Brazilians observed and sometimes doubted them.

Despite his unique perspective on the challenges faced by immigrants in Brazil, Neves had a familiar solution to this dilemma—organization. He argued that the Portuguese of Porto Alegre must learn from the centenary experience, especially the suggestion that they failed to pay the respect due to Brazil's great nationalist moment and to organize themselves. They would thereby obtain a venue to build the immigrant community as well as a platform from which to prove themselves to their Brazilian neighbors. On one hand, such an organization, which Neves wanted to call the "Liga Portugueza" and was much like Ricardo Severo's contemplated "Casa Portugueza," would bring together all Portuguese immigrants, regardless of religious or political commitments, and their existing groups, such as the Vasco da Gama sports club and the Beneficiencia Portugueza, in order to help recent immigrants adjust to Brazil, to promote Portuguese commercial interests, and to celebrate Portuguese holidays, "all the patriotic and utilitarian" needs of the community.[50] He lamented that the community possessed no proper venue to observe its "civic rituals," such as celebrations of the Libson raid and the visit of the Portuguese president, and hoped a league would serve such a role in the future. On the other hand, the league would face outward, toward Porto Alegre, Rio Grande do Sul, and Brazil. It would organize Portuguese residents and immigrants for participation in Brazil's civic rituals, in order to avoid the misunderstandings of the centenary celebrations, and it would also help build goodwill by teaching Brazilians about Portugal and the roles the Portuguese played in historical and contemporary times. For example, he hoped the league could advertise the hard work performed by Portuguese immigrants and teach Brazilians about their forebears' activity in the colonial period, perhaps through the erection of a monument to José Marcelino de Figueiredo (Manuel Jorge Gomes de Sepúlveda), the Portuguese founder of Porto Alegre.[51]

It is not clear how Neves's fellow Portuguese responded to his prompting in the moment, though the Casa de Portugal cultural and civic center did open in Porto Alegre in the next decade. In the meantime, in his essay Neves demonstrated the significance contemporaries assigned to the centenary experience, the celebrations much more than mere parties and more meaningful than the civic holidays of most years. Neves understood that in the centenary immigrants and other foreigners residing in Brazil faced a real, substantive dilemma, a test of loyalties that had no clear and obvious answer likely to please everyone. There were opportunities here: for minority groups to prove their dedication to Brazil, as Kroeff asserted; for migrants to demonstrate they had not forgotten their duties to their mother countries, as leaders of the hydroplane fundraising campaign said; for the strengthening of bonds connecting immigrants to one another, as a new Liga Portugueza in Porto Alegre or a Federazione delle Società Italiane in São Paulo might do; and, as in the proposal for a monument to "A Raça," for making arguments asserting the historic and continuing affinity between the cultures of Brazil and immigrants' countries of origin. But there were also dangers: that immigrants' performances of a commitment to Brazil would annoy those expecting proofs of their continuing loyalty to home, and vice versa, that Brazilians would reject immigrants' notions of the proper ways to celebrate the centenary; and that strengthening immigrants' sense of distinctive community would result in difficulties in the process of adjustment to Brazil.

This helps explain the urge manifested by many immigrants and foreign-born residents who saw themselves as leaders to attempt to organize their compatriots. As the *Pasquino Coloniale* pointed out, some of these figures saw that they might benefit personally from the performances of loyalty enacted by their compatriots residing in Brazil, if only in the abstract but still meaningful sense of publicity and prestige. They also seem to have understood the possibilities and hazards of the centenary experience, if Brazilians could be convinced of the value immigrants contributed to the nation, for example, or if Brazilian nationalists came to believe immigrants had failed tests of loyalty. They therefore worked to present to the public a pleasing, well-orchestrated performance of immigrant commitment to the centenary. As was typical of the mostly middle-class and wealthy perspective inhabited by these businessmen, diplomats, journalists, and educators, they worried that many of their compatriots could not be trusted to meet the demands of the moment. Through organization, these figures sought to enact a certain amount of discipline on hundreds and in some instances thousands of individuals, the majority of whom were working class, who otherwise might participate in the centenary as individuals, or inappropriately, or not at all. Through organization, they also hoped to ensure that their activities would be made acceptable and legible to the larger Brazilian public.

Claiming a Place in Brazil

These issues of organization and obligation, of doubts and arguments about immigrants' loyalties, were prevalent throughout the centenary year, and especially apparent in those moments when Brazil's foreign-born communities took center stage in commemorative events. On several occasions the centenary was an expression of the experience of foreigners residing in Brazil: at ceremonies to open the exhibition spaces of countries that had large numbers of foreign residents in Brazil; during visits to Brazil by prominent figures from home countries; and in the inauguration of monuments erected by immigrants and the foreign born. Each of these events took on its own character, depending on which group took the protagonist's role, the particular event being staged, and the ways in which the group had organized itself for the centenary. Alongside these differences, one thematic thread remained consistent, whether the group was made up of Italians, Portuguese, Japanese, or Germans, and whatever their activity. Like Brazilians, immigrants and the foreign born imbued the centenary with deep meaning. And like those Brazilians who were sometimes or often left out of dominant narratives of the nation and its peoples, such as the jangadeiros, these groups used the centenary to stake a claim to the country, a claim they often rooted in the past and insisted was especially justified in Brazil's present and future. The exhibition, the visits of prominent figures from home, and centenary monuments afforded them opportunities to articulate that claim—in speech and symbol, and also in a substantive and physical sense, as they occupied public spaces and made them into stages for the performance of belonging.

Renewing Ties

One of the principal ways that immigrants interacted with the commemorative events of 1922 was by participating in events celebrating the journeys undertaken by the raiders of the centenary. They were among the thousands and tens of thousands who gathered in public squares, filled theater halls, and contributed to fundraising drives to salute, see, and hear from the centenary's biggest heroes. Immigrant publications knew their readers were as interested in the raids as were readers of papers and magazines aimed at Brazilian natives. For example, São Paulo's Italian-language *Fanfulla* made sure to cover the Lisbon–Rio de Janeiro raid and interviewed the aviators during their visit to the city.[52]

Unsurprisingly, immigrant communities were especially engaged with raids undertaken by their erstwhile compatriots. American residents of Brazil took the lead in organizing receptions for Euclides Pinto Martins and his several American companions, Italians paid closer attention than others to the efforts of Luigi Longobardi to complete a river raid from São Paulo to Asunción, Paraguay, and, of course, the Portuguese in Brazil took an extraordinary interest in the centenary's most celebrated raiders, Sacadura Cabral and Gago Coutinho. Moreover, many other visitors came to Brazil to take part in the centenary exposition, the largest number coming from nations that constructed their own pavilions.[53] Those nations sent special diplomatic delegations to Rio de Janeiro, and the official representatives were accompanied by artists and musicians who would take part in events related to the exposition as well as journalists sent by their editors specifically to cover it. In the capital and in various places of interest to their home governments, these traveling parties met with immigrants and other nationals residing in the country, who often served as their hosts and guides in Brazil. The Italian Prince Alliata and the United States secretary of state, Charles Hughes, among the most prominent of these visitors, received an extraordinary amount of attention, both from their Brazilian hosts and their compatriots living in Brazil.

Immigrants and foreign residents of Brazil had many reasons to be drawn to visits by prominent figures from their home countries. Some indulged in nostalgia, others felt obligated to participate, and many surely were attracted simply by the excitement of festivities and parades. Most important was that the visits were opportunities for immigrants to perform national identity as they understood it. Some took part in events related to the visitors to show they were still loyal subjects and citizens of their mother countries, whereas others wanted to be understood as immigrants and future Brazilians who did not forget their roots and could help forge closer ties between their once and future homes. From parades to events at community institutions like hospitals and cultural centers, visits by diplomats and other dignitaries afforded Portuguese, Italians, and other foreigners in Brazil rare and public chances to display their perspectives on belonging and citizenship. Had the visitors come in other years and for other reasons, they would certainly have enjoyed enthusiastic receptions from their compatriots in Brazil, but the centenary lent added weight and significance to the interactions, since it dealt so clearly in history, nationality, and identity, and it afforded an outsized stage for the display of those ideas.

As with the raids, the most celebrated of the foreign dignitaries, diplomats, and others to visit Brazil for the centenary celebrations was Portuguese, President António de Almeida. In fact, Almeida's visit to Brazil was perhaps the only event of the centenary celebrations to approach the scale and intensity of those surrounding the Lisbon raid. And, as with Cabral and Coutinho, Portuguese immigrants and residents helped take the lead in planning for Almeida's visit and in making his many public and private appearances successful, at least as judged by attendance and media coverage. The scale of these events and the attention afforded Almeida's visit exceeded what was typical of the many visits made by foreigners whose compatriots lived in Brazil in 1922, and the visit is therefore worth focusing on here, both because of the significance contemporaries assigned to it and because it distilled the most important characteristics of the ways that immigrants and other foreigners residing in Brazil approached such visits.

Almeida was the first Portuguese head of state to visit independent Brazil, having been preceded in the country only by Maria I and João VI, who had come in 1808, fleeing Napoleonic forces during the war for the Iberian Peninsula. The majority of Brazilian commentators welcomed him, despite the position of *Gil Blas* that he should not come. After his arrival on 17 September, their enthusiasm only grew, largely because by all accounts Almeida fulfilled every expectation, given his reputation as an effective and powerful speaker. His address to the national congress on 20 September was widely depicted as one of the great triumphs of the centenary, "magisterial," in the assessment of the *Jornal do Brasil*.[54] Indeed, even *Gil Blas* grudgingly admitted the visit's success and not only called Almeida "likeable" and "eminent" but also agreed with other commentators that he was "the foremost speaker of the raça," which was a remarkable admission given that the magazine had always rejected the idea of a "raça" shared by Portuguese and Brazilians as absurd and offensive.[55]

Almeida's visit to the centenary exposition on 24 September was an enormous success, despite the fact that the completion of the Portuguese pavilions was months away. There was little special about the visit itself. Almeida and Epitácio Pessoa toured the fair together and exchanged the kind of effusive compliments to be expected from such a spectacle of diplomacy. But they were not alone, and they were accompanied not only by their respective staffs and prominent figures in Carioca society. They were met by what observers judged to be between 200,000 and 300,000 admirers, and Almeida seized the chance to cement his popularity among them. *A Noite* reported that "he plunged into a turbulent ocean of multitudes, coming into intimate contact with our people." As the paper interpreted it, the crowd was responding to Almeida as an individual, his fame as an orator, and his democratic manner. It was also using him to celebrate Portugal, for he was "the lively embodiment of the glories, the energies, and the aspirations of the nation of seafarers."[56] This

4.2. The crowd gathered to salute António José de Almeida during his visit to the centenary exposition, 24 September 1922. *A Careta*, 30 September 1922. Courtesy Charles E. Young Research Library, University of California, Los Angeles.

was exactly the kind of response Almeida and his government had hoped for when they planned his journey to Brazil, insofar as forging closer relations with Brazil was one of the main priorities of their foreign policy. Using the visit to lobby Pessoa on several matters, such as tariff rates, Almeida had to settle for minor agreements related to the labor rights and military responsibilities of immigrants and to copyright issues, and the two governments ultimately ratified only the copyright agreement. But, as with the Lisbon raid and Portugal's participation in the exposition, Almeida's visit does seem to have helped improve the country's reputation with the Brazilian public.[57]

Near the center and at the forefront of this and many other events of Almeida's stay were the Portuguese residing in Brazil. They attended events where Almeida interacted with the Brazilian public, such as his visit to the exposition and a reception at Brazil's presidential residence, and the president also set aside time specifically for his compatriots. He visited commercial and industrial figures (for example, at the Câmara Portuguesa de Comércio e Indústria do Rio de Janeiro), political activists (at the Gremio Republicano Portuguez), medical and charity workers (at the hospital of the Real e Benemerita Sociedade Portugueza de Beneficios), and those involved in intellectual and cultural pursuits (at the Real Gabinete Português de Leitura). In all these instances, the Portuguese of Brazil played crucial roles. They were hosts and speakers, they helped organize and finance the events, they filled seats and sidewalks as members of audiences and as spectators, and they were almost always subjects of discussion. Each event had its own character—such as focus on commercial relations at the exposition and an emphasis on immigrants' duty of charity to one another at the Portuguese hospital—but they delivered a consistent message: the Portuguese in Brazil remained Portuguese, but they also belonged in Brazil, which served as a homeland away from home.

Almeida delivered that message, for example, in his speech at the Real Gabinete Português de Leitura. He acknowledged the patriotism of his compatriots in Brazil, whose response to his visit had been overwhelming, moving him "to tears." He also noted their nostalgia for home, saying it did them great credit as true children of Portugal, but encouraged them to focus on the opportunities they enjoyed in their new home, suggesting about their homesickness "that they can alleviate it by loving Brazil."[58] Unsurprisingly, the most constant theme of Almeida's celebrated discourse during his visit was an emphasis on the two countries' natural affinity, and he depicted Portuguese immigrants as crucial to the work of forging a closer relationship between Portugal and its former colony. He discussed Brazil and Portugal as two distinct countries, emphasizing both their shared history—including Brazilian independence, which he described as the peaceful work of both Portuguese and Brazilians—and the possibilities of a closer present and future, speaking in his parting message of the two peoples as "partners in the same civilizing work, in which we have worked so closely together, Brazilians and Portuguese brothers forever, becoming ever closer."[59] In his telling the process by which the countries would become even closer than sister republics was already well underway because of the welcome Brazil had given to Portuguese migrants who were as dedicated to Brazil as to the country they had left behind. They were, he told the Brazilian president, "huge masses of workers" who "feel in Brazil as if they are in their own land" and "beloved sons of Portugal" who not only respected Brazil's laws and offered it their honorable labor, but were devoted to it "as if it were theirs."[60]

Despite his reputation and the hopes of anti-Portuguese activists, Epitácio Pessoa joined Almeida in going beyond diplomatic niceties to make the case that Portuguese citizens belonged in Brazil. Receiving Almeida at the presidential residence, he answered those who wondered at Brazil's eagerness to include Portugal in its centenary celebrations, insisting that the independence movement was the work of Brazilians and Portuguese together against the depredations of the retrograde Lisbon Cortes. He said the commemoration of 7 September was not a celebration of Brazil's triumph against Portugal but "a Luso-Brazilian occasion," and he went even farther, calling Brazilians and Portuguese "two branches of the same people," which explained why Portuguese migrants so often settled in Brazil. In his words, "the Portuguese who lived among us in 1822 did not feel—as they do not feel today—as if they lived in a foreign land."[61] Such was his confidence that Brazil was a fit home for Portuguese emigrants that he saw no controversy in accepting the prospect of offering them the right to Brazilian citizenship without obligating them to abandon their ties to Portugal, saying of his talks with Almeida that "the question of dual nationalities, which has preoccupied the minds of so many statesmen, has no meaning between two countries like Portugal and Brazil."[62] In the event, Pessoa overestimated the Brazilian congress's appetite for the agreements he negotiated with Almeida, but, though they were not ratified, they contributed to the sense that Almeida's visit was a success, not least for the Portuguese living in Brazil.

The Portuguese in Brazil basked in the attention they received from the presidents of the two countries during Almeida's visit, and they joined the politicians in delivering the message that they remained Portuguese but that Brazil was theirs as well. They were many of the "thousands and thousands of people" who met him when he disembarked at the Rio de Janeiro docks and accompanied him to the presidential palace, and they were among the hundreds of thousands who celebrated him at the exposition.[63] They also took charge of the visit in their own ceremonies, such as an event to celebrate breaking ground for the monument they intended to erect to commemorate the centenary, and in his visits to the various Portuguese institutions in the capital, many of which took place behind closed doors but at which crowds gathered to cheer as Almeida entered and exited.[64] Lest observers miss the lesson of their presence, speakers made the point explicit when they were given the stage at these events. Along with paeans to Brazil, to their homeland, and to Almeida personally, these figures made sure to assert the claims of Portuguese immigrants, on both their former home and on Brazil.

On one hand, as Almeida pointed out, these figures asserted their loyalty to and nostalgia for Portugal constantly and with a passion that touched him deeply; in the words of Eduardo Dias, who welcomed Almeida to the Gabinete Portuguesa on behalf of the Portuguese colony in Rio de Janeiro, theirs was more than the "inevitable nostalgia that any emigrant feels for his native land," because this was a sensibility felt "particularly among the men of our raça."[65] He and others said that this explained the commitment evinced by the Portuguese in Brazil to maintaining their ties to home. This commitment could be seen in many respects, such as the cultural work performed by the Gabinete, and in practical ways, such as the support the Câmara Portuguesa lent to Portugal's war efforts, the colony's assistance with Portugal's participation in the centenary exposition, and even in Almeida's negotiations with Pessoa, activities mentioned by the chamber president, Alexandre Herculano Rodrigues, as proofs of the colony's "solidarity" with their mother country when Almeida visited the group.[66]

On the other hand, these figures made explicit their sense of their place in Brazil. In the same speech at the Gabinete Portuguesa, Dias assured Almeida that "the Portuguese are quite happy in Brazil!" and that "Portuguese immigrants almost always seek eternal rest in the sacred land of Brazil," even as they carried "glaring in the retina the reflection of twilight in the august land of Portugal!"[67] At the same event, Carlos Malheiro Dias rhapsodized about the opportunities that the Portuguese had found and exploited in the country, depicting it as a "Brazilian Canaan."[68] Making the same point was José Augusto de Magalhães, Portugal's consul in São Paulo, who spoke for the Portuguese who traveled from the city to Rio de Janeiro to salute Almeida on behalf of their compatriots residing there. As he told Almeida at a public reception at the Guanabara Palace, where Brazil lodged its most esteemed visitors, "this colony lives as if it were in its own country."[69]

Portuguese residents of Brazil thus sought to use Almeida's visit to meet the challenge of Lusophobia and to strengthen their claims on Brazil. As chapter 1 mentions, before Almeida's arrival Portuguese immigrants had approached the Lisbon raid in much the same way, using it to announce their commitment to closer relations between Portugal and Brazil, to advertise their patriotism as Portuguese, and to claim belonging in Brazil. A good example of the dynamic can be seen in the march staged by Portuguese residents of Recife to celebrate the news that Cabral and Coutinho had survived their second crash. Local newspapers described it as an impromptu expression of relief, though the spontaneity of the event may have been overstated, since the papers also reported that it was organized and led by the Portuguese consul Pedroso Rodrigues, who was already doing much to organize the colony to receive the raiders. The *Diario de Pernambuco* counted thousands of marchers, "from the most prominent members of the Portuguese colony to its most humble," who were joined and followed by Brazilians, including the marching band of the state police.[70] As they marched through the streets of Recife's downtown, they gave "vivas and praise" to the aviators, to Brazil, and to Portugal, carrying hundreds of flags, of Brazil, of Portugal, and the Cruz da Malta banner of the colonial era, and at every stop they sang the national anthems of both countries. They made sure to visit the offices of the city's major newspapers, nominally in order to thank them for keeping them informed of news about the raid.[71] Perhaps not coincidentally, the local press reported on the march in glowing terms, the *Jornal do Recife* calling it an "improvised festival of patriotism, which took on an enchanting solemnity" and a "great patriotic march," and the *Diario de Pernambuco* describing it as a "quite brilliant procession," which at its conclusion at the Praça da Independência "was truly majestic."[72] And this was only the first in a series of extraordinarily successful events related to the journey of Sacadura Cabral and Gago Coutinho in Pernambuco, during the raid and after it, when Cabral returned to Recife in August 1922.

Not every visit met with such enthusiasm and adulation as those of Sacadura Cabral, Gago Coutinho, and António de Almeida, but the essential character of such visits was consistent throughout the centenary. Many of the biggest and most talked-about of the events surrounding these visitors took place in the national capital, but, as the example of the Portuguese parade in Recife shows, the visits were important wherever the travelers found their compatriots living in Brazil, and the extent to which each visit carried distinctive elements amid the general pattern had much to do with regional differences, as is to be expected given differences between the parts of Brazil and the irregular settlement of immigrants throughout the country. The Italian experience of centenary visits can help illustrate the point.

Many Italian dignitaries visited Brazil during the centenary year, including Prince Alliata and the head of the Italian mission to the exposition, Cesare Corinaldi. These visitors received a warm welcome when they arrived in Rio de Janeiro, and Epitácio Pessoa and other Brazilian leaders extended them every courtesy, treating them as proxies for their praise of Italian immigrants to Brazil in much the same way that they approached the Portuguese aviators and the Portuguese president. Italian residents of Brazil helped make their visits successful, both by organizing events to celebrate them in the Brazilian capital and traveling there from other parts of the country to pay their respects. The scale of their enthusiasm and their performances of nationality and belonging was made most visible, however, not in Rio de Janeiro but in the Italian capital of Brazil, the city of São Paulo.

The series of visits by major Italian visitors began in late July, when Enrico Caviglia, the soldier known as the hero of the Battle of Vittorio Veneto, arrived in São Paulo. He would later anger many Brazilians for remarks he made after his return home about the condition of Italian immigrants on São Paulo's coffee estates, which one Brazilian newspaper explained as a petty reaction to the cool response he received from Brazilians in Rio de Janeiro.[73] Whatever the truth of the matter, the small Italian colony living there gave him a warm welcome, but it was nothing compared to his experience in São Paulo.[74] A large, well-organized delegation met his train and led a parade throughout the city's Italian neighborhoods to a banquet in his honor. Besides a visit with the city chapter of Italian war veterans, he toured all the major institutions of the colony, its hospitals, mutual aid societies, and cultural centers, and he helped make the city's grand municipal theater an Italian cathedral when he gave a speech on the Italian experience of the Great War.[75] *Fanfulla* called his visit to the Leale Oberdan mutual aid society "a true festival of *italianità*," where he heard the group's president assert the immigrants' continuing loyalty to their homeland; as Andrea Caliò said, although many of Italy's children were "scattered and isolated in the most remote areas," they "cannot forget you, since your name is a reason for pride and goodness, for greatness and self-denial, and even far away they knew and will know how to honor you, to love you as a mother!"[76] Caviglia heard much the same a few days later when he visited another major Italian institution, the Palestra Italia football club, where the club's president, Eurico De Martino, emphasized its commitment to the Italian people even as they lived abroad, calling it a "highly patriotic fellowship that . . . contributes to the physical and intellectual development of the race [*razza*]." Echoing many of the Portuguese who greeted Almeida during his visit to Brazil, De Martino also claimed that his organization was vital to forging good relations with the Brazilian people, for sport "leads to the brotherhood of two peoples who are made to understand one another due to the the commonalities of their bodies and spirits."[77]

When Cesare Corinaldi and the exposition commissioners came to Brazil in September, many of these same residents of São Paulo participated in discussions about traveling to Rio de Janeiro to prove to the visitors their patriotism and the "unconditional respect of the Colony."[78] They were able to do more when Corinaldi came to their city in November, organizing an elaborate welcome and several celebratory events, such as a reception at the Camera Italiana di Commercio di S. Paolo, with which the Italian exposition commission had worked closely in preparing for the centenary fair. As the chamber president, Egidio Pinotti Gamba, said in welcoming Corinaldi, they believed his visit would not only "help to consolidate Italy's bonds with this friendly country"; for commercial and other reasons, it was of great importance "for the Italians of São Paulo and for Italy." That is, the members of the chamber might live in Brazil, but they were not Brazilians. They were "the Italians of São Paulo," and Corinaldi's visit helped them advertise the fact.[79]

Such was the character of events when prominent Portuguese and Italian figures visited Brazil during the centenary, whether they were famous figures such as Almeida and Caviglia or lesser-known travelers such as the Italian senator Augusto Setti, a member of the official Italian delegation to the centenary who traveled to Campinas in São Paulo, a visit highlighted by his interactions with the representatives of Italian organizations in the city. The visits were distinguished by regional differences such as the conspicuous influence of anti-Portuguese activists in Rio de Janeiro and the size of the Italian population of São Paulo, but they also followed a consistent script according to which immigrants announced their commitment to their homelands and their claims on Brazil in performances of identity and belonging. That these performances took place in public, on the stage set for the centenary, was a crucial fact; they were more than arguments in an immigrant newspaper and they took place both in the lecture halls of immigrant libraries and also far beyond them, making them harder to ignore and potentially much more powerful, as even *Gil Blas* had to attest.

Displaying Identity at the Centenary Exposition

Many of these visitors had traveled to Brazil to attend the centenary exposition. The event had both "national" and "international" sections, but it is clear that the exposition was the centerpiece of official activities for the centenary largely because of planners' hopes that it would attract foreign participation and attention. Thirteen countries opened pavilions on the fair's "Avenida das Nações," giving them opportunities to display their wares to Brazilians and to one another, as well as to make a formal demonstration of their intent to build stronger diplomatic and commercial relations with their hosts. Each sent official delegations of exposition commissioners, usually led by prominent statesmen. Because many of these countries counted their own among the residents of Brazil, planners' outward-looking perspective also made the exposition a venue in which these immigrants could claim public attention and space for themselves and reinforce their relationships and affinities with their mother countries.

Immigrants and other foreigners resident in Brazil claimed space at the exposition in a literal sense, taking over areas in the pavilions to display their own products; a few even constructed their own pavilions. Those who did not participate as exhibitors also claimed the exposition by helping organize the participation of home countries and by attending events focused on them, such as celebrations of the beginning of construction of the pavilions and of the formal inauguration of those spaces. Each nation that opened a pavilion at the exposition was also celebrated with its own day, for example, the "Dia da Inglaterra" and the "Dia do Japão," usually set up to coincide with the pavilion's opening. On these days organizers made the fairgrounds and surrounding areas celebrations of the country and its culture, hoisting its flag throughout the venue and hosting "typical" musical and dance presentations, among other events. For Brazilians and foreign exhibitors these were important opportunities to enact the rituals of diplomacy, and for organizers they were useful in attracting public attention to the fair. Immigrants and other foreigners resident in Brazil made special efforts on days assigned to their mother countries, in some cases traveling to Rio de Janeiro specifically to participate in the events and ultimately making these days into performances of belonging, claiming both their old and new homes.

Many immigrants and other foreign residents understood the opportunities the exposition offered and worked to encourage the participation of their compatriots. The activities of the Câmara Portuguesa de Comércio e Indústria do Rio de Janeiro suggest the kind of work such Brazil-based figures performed and how they sought to use the exposition to knit together Brazil and the mother country, the mother country with its citizens abroad, and those citizens with one another. Soon after the Brazilian government committed itself to organizing an international exposition to celebrate the centenary in late 1920, the chamber began discussing how best to encourage the participation of Portugal and Portuguese businesses, and in 1921, First Secretary A. J. Gomes Barboza traveled throughout Portugal to proselytize for the fair, well before the Portuguese government accepted Brazil's invitation to the event. In Lisbon, Coimbra, Porto, and other cities he met with government officials and representatives of dozens of commercial and cultural organizations in hopes of impressing upon them the significance of the centenary exposition and the necessity of Portugal's participation in it.[80]

As Gomes Barboza put it, the Câmara saw as one of its important tasks the strengthening of ties between Portugal and Brazil, and it viewed Portugal's successful involvement in the exposition as essential to that effort; in his words, "not a single Portuguese in Brazil can imagine that Portugal would not participate in this Exposition." He was therefore gratified when the Portuguese government announced it would accept Brazil's invitation and committed significant financial resources to the event (2,500 contos de reís). Still, he did not consider his mission complete, and stayed in Portugal for six months to continue helping to organize Portuguese participation, for example, by meeting regularly with the commissioners appointed by the state to oversee the country's involvement.[81]

Meanwhile, the members of the Câmara worked to bring together their compatriots in Brazil and ensure their support for Portugal's two pavilions, the Pavilhão de Honra, which housed historical and cultural displays, and the Pavilhão das Indústrias, a commercial venue. They held regular meetings of their members and helped advertise the event among Portuguese living in Brazil, often working alongside Portuguese diplomatic staff to ensure coordination of Portuguese efforts on both sides of the Atlantic. They reached beyond Rio de Janeiro, too, communicating with and eventually helping to organize the efforts of Portuguese chambers of commerce and their other institutions throughout the country as they contemplated how they might use the exposition to advance their interests.[82] The members of the chamber understood the commercial benefits the exposition seemed to offer them as individuals, but, like the immigrants and other foreign residents in Brazil described above, they realized the importance of an organized effort in their involvement in the centenary if they were to obtain those benefits. As the editors of the organization's *Boletim* put it in an early essay on the exposition, Portugal and the Portuguese in Brazil would only find success at the fair if every participant understood the opportunities it offered for their "particular and special interest," but, they argued, this was not the event's only benefit and perhaps not its most important one. Instead, what the exposition offered was a chance to advocate "for the *interests of all and of everyone*," an excellent opportunity for the Portuguese in Rio de Janeiro and throughout Brazil to recommit themselves to one another and to build their Portuguese colony.[83] The members of the chamber knew that the exposition came during a period charged with possibility, on the one hand, the menace of Lusophobia, and on the other, a chance for closer Luso-Brazilian relations and a more comfortable life for Portuguese in Brazil. They viewed concerted effort to participate in the exposition as the key to confronting the first and advancing the second, and thus they reached beyond the organization's usual remit to seize the opportunities offered by the centenary.

As Portugal's plans for the exposition advanced, the Câmara worked directly alongside its official exposition commission as it orchestrated the installation and promotion of the country's pavilions, and the group held several special sessions to hear from the lead commissioner, A. A. Lisboa de Lima, about the group's needs after he arrived in Brazil. At his request, the Câmara offered the commission various forms of support, from facilitating connections with Portuguese groups in other parts of Brazil to organizing a "Commissão de Assistencia" to help not only in mounting Portugal's pavilions but also in interacting with the local press.[84] Finally, the Câmara took on an important role when it came time to open the pavilions, advertising the inauguration events, coordinating the attendance of Portuguese resident in Brazil, and playing host to the diplomats and other official visitors who traveled to Rio de Janeiro for the exposition.[85]

Few organizations performed such varied activities as did the Câmara Portuguesa in joining foreigners living in Brazil to the participation of their mother countries in the centenary exposition, but many individuals and organizations contributed in their own ways to the same end. Commercial, financial, and industrial organizations were involved in this work, such as the Portuguese Banco Nacional Ultramarino and the Camera Italiana di Commercio di S. Paolo. Political, arts, charity, and even sporting institutions joined them, for they knew the exposition was much more than a trade fair. For such groups, the pavilions of Portugal could also be understood as the pavilions of the Portuguese of Brazil, the pavilion of Italy also belonged to the Italians residing in the country, and so on.

These immigrants helped appointed commissioners build their countries' pavilions, fill them, and promote them to the Brazilian public. However, this cooperation also made the exposition a venue for tension and potential conflict for immigrants and other foreign residents, between the possibility of becoming Brazilian and the opportunity to reinforce one's sensibility as Portuguese, Italian, or Japanese. On one hand, the exposition allowed for the layering and intertwining of old and new ties, for one could as easily visit Brazilian pavilions as foreign ones. On the other, any individual expositor and any particular firm contemplating the fair would have to make an explicit choice if they were to show their wares, whether to advertise an immigrant identity and seek admission to the "national" exposition alongside their neighbors in their states of residence, or to participate as a foreigner resident in Brazil in the pavilion of the mother country. The fair's rules did not allow exhibitors the option of participating in both national and international sections; they had to choose.

The exposition was of course a temporary event, and the choices exhibitors made need not define them in the future, but it is clear that contemporaries took this dilemma seriously. Evidence that both individuals and groups wrestled with the choice they were faced with, and its potential consequences, can be seen in a variety of places, including statements by the pavilions' organizers themselves. At the reception in his honor at the Camera Italiana di Commercio di S. Paolo, Cesare Corinaldi echoed his host, the chamber president Gamba, stating explicitly that the Italian contribution to the exposition was designed to display the productive capacity of the peninsula *and* of the Italians of Brazil. It was especially important, he said, that the pavilion highlight the "labor of the Italians of São Paulo," where so many Italians had settled, and he and his fellow commissioners relied heavily on the work of the chamber to organize its exhibition.[86] For their part, in their public remarks Lisboa de Lima and the other Portuguese commissioners announced that they would not have dreamed of including items produced by the Portuguese of Brazil in their own pavilion. Implying that the inclusion of such products would give offense to Brazilians because they were manufactured in their country, at the much-delayed inauguration of the pavilion, ambassador Duarte Leite Pereira da Silva stated that its organizers had not "presumed to display the products of our colonies in Brazil."[87]

However, despite the assertions of the commissioners and ambassador, there is more than a little reason to doubt their claims about Portugal's intentions in this regard. Rosália Augusta da Cunha Marques has shown that the government's appointed commissioners viewed the exposition with trepidation from the outset, worried that Portugal would display its own underdevelopment in Rio de Janeiro, able to show the country's wines, oils, and fish products, but little else. To enrich Portugal's offerings they planned expansive artistic and historical displays and also did expect to include items produced by the Portuguese colonies of Brazil, at least throughout the early stages of planning in 1921.[88] This helps explain why the Câmara Portuguesa de Comércio de S. Paulo informed the press in September 1921 that its members would participate in the international rather than the national section of the fair, or, in its phrasing, "in the exhibition of Portuguese products."[89] And it also helps explain Lima's work with and reliance on the Rio de Janeiro chamber in so many respects.

But Portugal's experience of the exposition was in many respects an unhappy one. Political and financial difficulties at home complicated efforts there, while in Rio de Janeiro bad planning, bad engineering, and, it seems, graft meant long delays in the construction of Portugal's two pavilions. Worse, in the early stages of construction of the Pavilhão das Indústrias, its main support columns fell and Portuguese and Brazilian workers turned on one another, leaving seven injured and one dead. These troubles led many Portuguese in Brazil to lose confidence in the official commissioners, and the Portuguese government eventually initiated legal proceedings alleging financial mismanagement and other crimes against both the pavilions' chief engineer, Malheiro Reimão, and the lead commissioner, Lima.[90] As a result, the Pavilhão de Honra did not open until December 1922 and the Pavilhão das Indústrias did not open until May 1923, around the time the exposition had originally been scheduled to close.

It is little wonder, then, that Portuguese business and commercial figures in Brazil would have been disposed to show their products in the "national" section, regardless of their early intentions, and that Duarte Leite would have been motivated to find a way to explain their absence from Portugal's pavilions. It is also very difficult to know the extent to which the displays in the pavilions of Portugal and other countries actually matched the statements organizers made in public settings, as exposition bookkeepers did not record the country of residence of each exhibitor or the provenance of the products they displayed. A definitive evaluation of the choices made by immigrants and other foreign residents in Brazil in 1922 would necessitate a close examination of the records of their firms, to the extent that such records exist. It is clear, however, that the particular organization of the exposition obligated them to make such choices, and that whether they were informed by practical concerns or a sense of identity and belonging, they were not always easy choices to make.

One Italian exhibitor regretted his original choice and sought permission to move his submission from the international section (and the Italian pavilion) to the Brazilian part of the fair. Eurico Mori was a chemist living and working in São Paulo, and he enrolled in the Italian pavilion to advertise insecticides for use in the agricultural market. By early 1923, he had decided he preferred to display the products alongside his Brazilian neighbors, however, and requested permission from fair administrators to remove the products from the Italian pavilion and place them in the national section. The administrators approved the request, asking only that Mori make a formal application for entry as an exhibitor "among national products."[91] When it came time for those administrators to conclude the exposition by announcing the judgments and awards decided on by the fair's juries, they listed Mori among the Brazilian participants in the event.[92]

Mori's case indicates that things may not have gone quite as smoothly as was suggested by Corinaldi and his partners among the Italians resident in Brazil as they attempted to use the exposition to bring emigrants and mother country together in a display of Italian industry. Another "Italian" effort helps illustrate the tensions and opportunities the fair presented to the country's immigrant communities, that of the Indústrias Reunidas Fábricas Matarazzo. The Matarazzo company was one of Brazil's largest and was producing a wide variety of merchandise in 1922, including foodstuffs, textiles, and metal products, the business having grown enormously from the early efforts of Francesco Matarazzo and his brothers, who had migrated to Brazil in the 1880s. The Matarazzo family and company seized on the exposition as an opportunity to display their success, participating in their own right and helping to organize the participation of the state of São Paulo.[93] Such was the scale of the company and its resources that it was able to capture much more attention than most other exhibitors; it could also avoid the choice faced by other people

4.3. Pavilion of the Indústrias Reunidas Fábricas Matarazzo. Photograph by Thiele and Kollien. Courtesy of the Instituto Moreira Salles.

and businesses with ties to Brazil and to their countries of origin. That is, rather than show its wares in the Italian pavilion or in the São Paulo section of the national fair, the company constructed its own pavilion.

But even carving out space of their own did not relieve the family and its company from the questions of identity faced by immigrants and other foreign residents as they contemplated the exposition and navigated centenary events. Even though its business interests were almost exclusively based in Brazil, and much of the family, including the company's general director, Francesco Matarazzo Júnior, had been born there, the family maintained strong ties to Italy in 1922, and these were apparent at the exposition. The items it displayed were produced in Brazil but housed in a pavilion designed by Italian architects in the form of an Italian medieval *castello*, its interior decorated with Italian art (see fig. 4.3).[94] More significantly, the company coordinated the opening of the "palazzo" with the opening of the Italian pavilion and "Italy Day," tying the family, the company, and their participation in the centenary to the efforts of Italians on both sides of the Atlantic.[95] Contemporaries noticed, and both Italian and Brazilian commentators depicted the pavilion as part of the Italian contribution to the exposition; for example, *Il Pasquino Coloniale* called it a demonstration of "the amazing accomplishments of Italian industry in São Paulo," and *Combate* focused on the Matarazzo company in its survey of the Italian contribution to the fair, drawing the merest distinction between Italian industry and "the prodigious rise of Italian industries in Brazil."[96]

Some immigrants and other foreign residents used the fair to cultivate closer connections with their countries of origin, while others took it as an opportunity to announce their adherence to Brazil. Still others tried out both approaches and shifted between identities, a dynamic that was clear in the case of Eurico Mori and also seems to have been at work among the Portuguese who helped organize the Portuguese industrial pavilion but then displayed their products alongside their Brazilian neighbors when Portugal's efforts foundered. The one consistent pattern among all these people was that they found in the exposition a venue for claiming Brazil, their claims exemplified and performed in the moments set aside to celebrate the participation of their mother countries: "Portugal Day" and other such "days," as well as celebrations of the beginning of construction and inauguration of their pavilions. Of course, these were events celebrating Portugal, Italy, Japan, and other participating countries. But they were also events for and of immigrants from those countries living in Brazil. These people had done much to organize the participation of their mother countries in the exposition, and they took on important roles during the events set aside for those countries.

Like many events of the centenary, these occasions had a ritual quality that the exposition planners did much to emphasize, beginning with the dedication of particular days to specific countries. For example, 28 October was Italy Day, 31 October was Japan Day, and 11 November was Portugal Day. The organizers then reframed the space of the exposition, festooning it with the flag and colors of each country to be celebrated, and requesting the collaboration of local residents and businesses in doing the same, so as to extend the stage beyond the exposition grounds and into the city. Finally, for each day they planned a series of events designed to celebrate the day's nation in "typical" ways, from concerts

4.4. Japan Day at the centenary exposition, 31 October 1922. Photograph by Augusto Malta. Courtesy of the Acervo da Fundação Biblioteca Nacional—Brasil.

of national music to dance performances to the participation of immigrants and Brazilians in the country's traditional dress, all of which was punctuated by speeches from prominent figures emphasizing that country's friendship with the Brazilian people.

The celebrations of Italy Day actually began on 27 October, with the inauguration of the Italian pavilion. Boy Scouts from the town of Amparo in the state of São Paulo, many of them the children of Italian immigrants, formed a guard of honor as Cesare Corinaldi and the Italian commissioners, prominent figures among the Italians resident in Brazil, and Brazilian statesmen arrived to open the building. Corinaldi and the city mayor, Carlos Sampaio, exchanged messages of congratulations and praise, after which they led a visit to the pavilion. Afterward came a performance of Pietro Mascagni's *Cavalleria Rusticana* by a visiting Italian company, with support from musicians and choralists from Rio de Janeiro. The next day's events began with calisthenic and marching exercises by the scouts in honor of Italy, followed by a flower parade, with Italian music played by eight marching bands. Prizes were awarded both for the decoration of the cars in the parade and for the children who rode in them wearing traditional Italian costumes. The parade paused for a ceremonial hoisting of the Italian national flag and ended in time for a concert of Italian music at the exposition's events pavilion and a fireworks display celebrating Italy and Brazil. Organizers attempted to extend the celebration not only by requesting that Cariocas decorate the city in the colors of the Italian flag but also by encouraging hotels, theaters, and cinemas to offer performances of Italian music.[97] Furthermore, to do their utmost to make the day a success, they offered free admission to the exposition. By all accounts they seem to have achieved their goal, *Correio da Manhã* reporting "extraordinary" attendance that day.[98]

This program was typical of the "days" dedicated to participating countries, although the scale of attention and attendance varied from one to another. Immigrants and other foreign-born residents did much to ensure the success of these days and similar events, such as celebrations to break ground for the pavilions. Brazilian commissioners and their foreign counterparts knew this and made sure to include them. When construction began on the Portuguese industrial pavilion, for example, there were speeches by Duarte Leite and the Brazilian justice minister Ferreira Chaves, who also served as the president of the Comissão Organizadora do Centenário da Independência do Brasil. Organizers also made a point of encouraging the participation of Portuguese immigrants and other residents in Brazil. They included the representatives of more than a dozen Portuguese organizations based in the capital in a formal way by asking them to sign the register marking the commencement of the construction project and inviting them to assist in the ceremonial raising of the Portuguese flag on the site of the future pavilion, an action by which they quite literally claimed Brazilian soil, at least for the duration of the exposition.[99] Once the exposition began, organizers reached out again to such figures and to all members of the "colonies" of the nations to be celebrated, "not only in this capital but in all the states," as they put it in their appeal to the Italians of Brazil, encouraging their attendance and asking for their support.[100]

Many did attend the events of those "days," and made them some of the most successful ones of the exposition. There, they found Brazilians both unusually well disposed to celebrate their countries of origin and willing to assert that they themselves were welcome and valued in Brazil. Brazilian speakers and journalists made sure to draw attention to the contributions of immigrant laborers and immigrant businessmen, including not only the often-praised Italians but also the Portuguese, who were so frequently the targets of Brazilian suspicion. Even they enjoyed the most complimentary tributes during these special moments, such as when the *Correio da Manhã* marked its coverage of the opening of the Portuguese arts pavilion with an appreciation for "the Portuguese merchants and industrialists who live in Brazil and contribute so much to our progress," and when the exposition's official magazine highlighted its coverage of

Portugal's industrial pavilion by calling attention to the excitement it generated in the "Luso-Brazilian soul" and the bonds between Portugal and Brazil, "united in the same ideal, by the same history, by the same blood, by the same sense of courage, by the same suffering."[101]

That is, it seems that the rituals of the exhibition promoted exactly the goal announced by the Câmara Portuguesa in 1921, which was to use the fair to bring Brazil and the mother country closer together, not least because of the benefits this might bring to the chamber's members and other Portuguese residing in Brazil. They reinforced the notion that immigrants and other foreigners could be at home in Brazil and claim it as their own while also maintaining their own distinctive identities. This does not mean they were not confronted with difficult choices related to these issues; they surely were, such as the one faced by exhibitors contemplating whether to seek admission to the national or international section of the fair. But the exposition opened up space, literally and figuratively, for these actors to engage with issues of nation and citizenship to a great extent on their own terms, making their own choices, rather than obligating them to abandon foreign identities, as *Gil Blas* and other nationalists would have hoped. When reporting to readers about Italy Day, the exposition's official gazette pointed out that because of the presence of Italian immigrants, parts of São Paulo and other states felt like "a Nation within the Nation!"—and, far from a lament, it depicted this circumstance in a wholly positive light.[102]

Belonging, in Stone and Bronze

While the exposition was a temporary affair, many contemporaries hoped to mark their participation in the centenary in a more enduring way, hence their plans to erect many monuments, of many types. Besides traditional forms of statuary and monumental architecture, there were also other structures and endeavors their planners depicted as monuments to the occasion, such as ceremonies to break ground for a future Brazilian capital in Goiás and for the Hospital Centenário in Recife, Pernambuco, and a few exposition buildings designed to be of permanent use after the fair's end. While many of these efforts were undertaken by Brazilians, others joined with them to help make 1922 a year of inaugurations and groundbreakings. Mexico's new revolutionary government gave Brazil a statue of Cuauhtémoc, for example, while the American chamber of commerce offered a monument celebrating the friendship between the American and Brazilian peoples.

Like the members of the American chamber, many groups of immigrants and other foreign residents sought to articulate their sense of the centenary through statements made in bronze and stone. These groups used monuments and statues to deliver another version of the message they consistently made as they approached the centenary. Each group used their monument initiative to announce that they were members of a discrete community and to call the members of that community together to decide how to turn their ideas about Brazil into reality and to raise money to hire sculptors and engineers and purchase materials. Each used their project to communicate in a clear and enduring way that the community celebrated Brazil as a land of opportunity, and gratitude was one of the most consistent themes of their discussions about their activities and their inauguration of completed monuments. And each used their monument to announce that they belonged in Brazil: they claimed a place in the country in senses both literal and figurative. On one hand, they claimed the site of the monument itself, which they sought to make into an enduring proof of their place in Brazil. On the other hand, many of these projects were much more specific than the Americans' appeal to "friendship" and instead highlighted the foreigners' sense of their own special relationship to a particular event, idea, or person in Brazilian history and culture, so that the monument was an assertion of a claim to Brazilian identity. Finally, when completed, each project was inaugurated in yet another organized ritual of belonging, joining celebrations of visitors from home and the exposition to make the centenary as much an occasion for immigrants and foreign residents as for Brazilian citizens. Structures like the Italian-donated monument to Carlos Gomes and a Portuguese-planned monument to the bandeiras were designed to make this notion much more enduring than a visit, no matter how celebrated, or displays at the fair, no matter how grandly presented, which may explain why they were also sometimes the most controversial of the efforts immigrants undertook as they participated in the centenary.

Immigrants used monument projects to demonstrate in clear and tangible ways that they were grateful for the hospitality Brazil offered them and that they admired the nation and its story. Besides saying as much—which organizers did constantly—they indicated that this was part of their thinking about these projects through their choice of subjects. Some erected the obelisks that in 1922 were still the most common language of celebration and commemoration, but others sought to make more evocative statements, often choosing to celebrate specific episodes in the Brazilian story. Thus, when a group met in June 1920 at the Câmara Portuguesa de Comércio de S. Paulo to discuss plans for a monument project that would be the centerpiece of their centenary efforts, they demonstrated their understanding of the history of Brazil and the treasured traditions of the state in which they lived by choosing the bandeirantes as the monument's subject.

Despite the bandeirantes' distance from the events the centenary purported to celebrate, the project's advocates joined with the Paulistas described in the previous chapter, calling the bandeirantes not only "heroes" but also "the prolegomena of independence." As Ricardo Severo put it when he introduced the idea to his fellow Portuguese, the events of 7 September 1822 constituted "an incident, a political event in the history of Brazil," but the work of the bandeirantes centuries earlier was a "monumental work, the unshakable foundation of [Brazil's] national identity," making a monument to the bandeirantes "the real monument to the independence of the Brazilian nation."[103] His audience, which the *Correio Paulistano* said was made up of "many of the most prominent members of the colony," accepted the proposal immediately, and at the same meeting organized a commission to pursue the project, with Severo as president.[104]

The counterparts of the São Paulo Portuguese in Rio de Janeiro took a similar tack in their project to erect a pantheon of the Brazilian nation. The pantheon was to be a "civic temple," where Brazil would celebrate the great heroes of the past as well as the great heroes of its future, interring their remains within its halls and erecting statues to immortalize them and to imbue visitors with the lessons of their patriotic lives.[105] When the president of the pantheon commission, José Antonio de Souza, met with Epitácio Pessoa to explain the nature of the project, he emphasized that its planners saw it as a means of proving the gratitude and esteem the Portuguese of Rio de Janeiro felt toward Brazil and a way of "demonstrating in an objective and lasting way the feeling with which they dedicate themselves to the joys of the Brazilian people."[106] He argued that the pantheon was their way of celebrating Brazil, rather than drawing attention to themselves, a theme picked up by Carlos Malheiro Dias in his remarks as the official speaker of the Portuguese colony at the groundbreaking and laying of the structure's foundation stone. Dias said that as they discussed the centenary the Portuguese of the capital struck on the idea of a pantheon because "its gratitude would be more adequately expressed in paying homage to the great Brazilians who, through their actions and their genius, in politics, arms, science, and literature, contributed in a prominent way to the greater glory of the Patria."[107] Like the monument to the bandeirantes, the pantheon might not focus on the centenary in particular, but it would, Souza, Dias, and their partners hoped, show in a tangible way the immigrants' gratitude and their acknowledgment of the essential elements and distinctive story of Brazil.

The Italians of São Paulo made a similar point in a different manner. They too chose a subject far removed from the independence story, but rather than celebrating a group of heroes as the Portuguese looked to do in the monument to the bandeiras and the pantheon, theirs was a monument to Brazil's great composer Carlos Gomes. Despite Gomes's distance from the nominal rationale for the centenary celebrations, contemporaries depicted this as a natural choice. Gomes enjoyed international renown as a master composer, and, as the composer of *Il Guarany*, he had translated one of Brazil's foundational myths to the stage. Like many of the bandeirantes, Gomes was from the state of São Paulo, born in the city of Campinas, and he had lived for a time in Italy. Finally, they said, Italian immigrants were the right group to celebrate Gomes because Italy was a country particularly attuned to the importance of the arts. In their manifesto to the Italian community of the city and state, the monument commissioners said that "for centuries [Italy] has held undisputed primacy in the divine art of sound," and their assertion was echoed by the city deputy mayor Henrique de Sousa Queiroz in his speech at the monument's unveiling, when he said that Italians "know how to cultivate good art" and that they resisted the "materialist standard" that dominated modern life."[108]

As in other instances, one of the prevailing themes of discussion about the Gomes project was that it proved the gratitude of the community that commissioned it. Both Brazilians and Italians insisted on this point. As the *Correio Paulistano* noted, the monument was "so highly expressive in its meaning that it surpasses the usual proofs demanded by courtesy." It was, instead, "a clear demonstration" of the friendship and affection Italian settlers felt for Brazil.[109] Similarly, the *Illustração Brasileira* spoke of the colony's "gratitude to a welcoming people" and its "sincere friendship and deep admiration for the Brazilian people," while the *Correio da Manhã* called it "one more proof" of its "high regard for Brazil."[110] This was exactly what its planners hoped the monument would communicate. *Fanfulla* reported that the commission viewed it as a "demonstration of the devotion of the Italians who have settled in this state" and the paper said it would demonstrate the views of "all the Italians," who would participate in the celebrations of 7 September but who also wanted to go beyond them, "who feel and want to offer a tribute to the welcoming nation that is more than an act of cold adhesion."[111] As was its wont, the paper's reference to the views of "all" Italians was certainly overstating the case, but there was enough financial support for the project that the commission was able to oversee not only the erection of the monument but also one more proof of Italians' gratitude, the creation of the Premio Carlos Gomes, a cash prize awarded every other year to the Brazilian who composed the biennial's best symphony.[112]

These monument projects were designed to offer enduring proofs of gratitude of communities of foreign descent to Brazil and their esteem for Brazilian traditions. However, planners also conceived of them as going much farther , even beyond the usual assertions that they amounted to permanent demonstrations of the friendship and affinity shared by these communities and the people of Brazil. Centenary monuments also served as embodiments of the communities' claims on Brazil and its history; they were monuments of belonging. Thus, just as much as the monument to Carlos Gomes was a demonstration of the respect the Italians of São Paulo had for Brazil's most accomplished and well-loved composer, it was also a demonstration of their own claim on the great man. Gomes's residence in Italy was a favorite subject of organizers, writers, and speakers, as was the fact that he and his Italian wife named one of their children Ítala, which commentators presented as the embodiment of the composer's love for Italy and its importance in his work.[113] Early in 1922 *Fanfulla* explained that among all the great Brazilians who might be celebrated, the organizing committee chose Gomes "because he loved Italy as his second homeland, having completed his studies in Italy and having received his triumphant baptism as a musician in Italy."[114] The committee hired Luigi Brizzolara, an Italian sculptor, to complete the work, which made the Italians' claim explicit. Besides Gomes himself, the monument includes figures representing music, poetry, Gomes's most important operas, and both Brazil and Italy as well as a dedication that read, in part, that it celebrated a "Great Brazilian Spirit / Who Joined His Genius / To Italian Inspiration."[115] When the time came for the monument's inauguration, *Fanfulla* went farther, saying that because of the influence of Italian art and culture on Gomes, his art "was also ours!"[116]

Italians in São Paulo used their celebration of Carlos Gomes to claim Brazil itself, an assertion that played out in the ritual of the monument's inauguration. First, the monument was installed in a prominent, privileged locale, in front of the lavish municipal theater in the city center. Next, the committee chose 20 September as the inauguration date, a day on which Italians celebrated the capture of Rome in 1870 and a major civic holiday for Italians in Brazil. When it decided to postpone the unveiling because of the death of Consul Ugo Tedeschi, it chose 12 October, which Tedeschi's replacement Bruno Zucculin made a point of reminding attendees was a holiday throughout the Americas in order to celebrate what he depicted as an Italian accomplishment.[117] The inauguration was a massive event, with thousands of attendees, many of whom arrived at the monument site as participants in a parade dominated by members of the Italian institutions of the city and state, including literary societies, mutual aid and laborers' groups, charities, schools, and political organizations.[118] Finally, in his keynote address, Zucculin drew a direct parallel between the composer and Brazilians of Italian descent, saying

4.5. Inauguration of the Monument to Carlos Gomes, São Paulo, 12 October 1922. *Vida Moderna*, 22 September 1922. Courtesy of the Acervo da Fundação Biblioteca Nacional—Brasil.

that "for Brazilians who are the children of Italians, Italy is their mother while Brazil is the spouse with whom they identify. For Carlos Gomes, Brazil was mother and Italy his spouse."[119] Here he joined with others in claiming Gomes for Italy and Italians, while also expanding his vision to assert the belonging of Italians and their children in Brazil, as well as Italy's continuing claims on their loyalty and affection. Amplified by a specially installed sound system, which ensured that the audience heard his claims, Zucculin said plainly what the organizers of the monument project sought to broadcast and make manifest, that Italians belonged in Brazil even as they—and their children—remained Italian.

Much of the commentary foreign residents and immigrants made during centenary celebrations followed the same pattern, identifying episodes and heroes in Brazilian history and society whom they could claim as their own in order to assert their own sense of belonging. Thus, for example, English residents drew attention to the role that Thomas Cochrane played as commander of the Brazilian imperial navy during the independence struggle.[120] Jacob Kroeff Netto did the same for his German-Brazilian compatriots when he cited the example of Maria Leopoldina, though his awareness of Brazilian suspicions made him careful not to suggest they retained any real ties to the mother country beyond their cultural inheritance, as some Italians and Italo-Brazilians could. Unsurprisingly, Portuguese commentators were especially likely to stress the influence and activities of their compatriots, including with respect to independence itself, where they cited Pedro I, of course, but also João VI and José Clemente Pereira, all of whom the writer Mota Assunção called "laborers for the Independence of Brazil" in the monthly bulletin of the Centro Republicano Português.[121] As António de Almeida did, they also tended to depict independence as a largely bloodless affair undertaken by Brazilians and Portuguese together, helping them not only to articulate a claim on Brazil but also to dispute the idea that independence had created any kind of distance between the two peoples.[122]

Many Portuguese also took the opportunity the centenary provided to make broader claims about the Portuguese influence in the making of Brazil and the importance of the Portuguese legacy in Brazil's present, a perspective they made apparent in their monument projects. One such project was not designed in stone and bronze but in paper and ink. Carlos Malheiro Dias edited and helped organize the three-volume *História da Colonização Portuguesa do Brasil*, whose scale and production matched its subtitle's claim that it was a "monumental commemorative volume for the first centenary of the independence of Brazil." Almost nine hundred pages long and illustrated throughout with well-produced, expensive images, including chapters that begin with pages mimicking the style of illuminated manuscripts, the book is not about independence but on the period from the late fifteenth century to the late sixteenth century, which Dias called the era of the "making of Brazil, the history of its infancy and its adolescence." Dias was able to bring together many leading Brazilian and Portuguese historians of the period for a work that "built the strongest foundation for the monumental edifice of Brazilian glory and carved into the edifice of the nationality the images of its heroes."[123]

Here again was the celebration of Brazil through its history and heroes, but its admirers also saw the book as an intervention in the debate about the role of the Portuguese in contemporary Brazil. It focused on a period of unquestioned Portuguese influence, before any of the events that Brazilians later depicted as the precursors of independence—before the fight against the Dutch for Pernambuco, before the bandeiras, before the Inconfidência Mineira—a weighty reminder of the argument that the basic character of Brazil was Portuguese. Assunção told the members of the Centro Republicano that the book would be "the Bible of the Portuguese" in Brazil, for it would confront misconceptions about the Brazilian past and, most importantly, the Lusophobia of the present. He wrote that of the efforts to educate the public the book project was "among the most necessary and most urgent," because it would combat "the lamentable ignorance of the illiterate and the studied or perfidious ignorance of privileged doctors and literary charlatans." It would be "the heroic remedy against these vermin" and a "prophylactic campaign" against anti-Portuguese prejudice, bringing about a brighter future for Brazil and for the Portuguese resident there; he concluded that "the Lusophile reaction will come, therefore, without any doubt" and the *História* would hasten its arrival.[124]

Though few advocates for centennial monument projects were as clear about their political purposes as Assunção was in his discussion of the *História*, many seem to have shared his general perspective. Thus, while organizers in Rio de Janeiro hoped the pantheon would become a civic temple for Brazilian heroes, they also expected it to serve as an enduring reminder of the country's Portuguese legacy. They tried to ensure this by the design of the pantheon complex, for its entrance would be "guarded" by the statues of two Portuguese, Pedro Alvares Cabral and Francisco Manuel Barroso da Silva, whom Dias called "two symbolic sentries" in his speech on behalf of the Rio de Janeiro Portuguese colony. Under their watchful eyes, he said, the temple would house both "the sacred ashes" of Brazil's greatest heroes and "the Portuguese heart" that "will beat eternally" within its walls.[125]

Similarly, while the bandeiras had become emblematic of the identity cultivated by the partisans of São Paulo, Portuguese planners for a monument to the bandeirantes sought to claim the story for themselves and their forebears. They planned to erect a monument crafted in Portugal by Portuguese artists, led by the well-known sculptor Teixeira Lopes, which only made sense, according to Ricardo Severo, because the bandeirantes may have come from São Paulo but they should be understood as Portuguese. He said that the bandeiras were the work of "native Brazilians, descendants of Portuguese, and Portuguese from the metropolis," and he went farther. He challenged popular memory by arguing that the "shared work" of the bandeiras should be celebrated alongside the conflict between the bandeirantes and the much-maligned "emboabas," the Portuguese migrants who came to Brazil after Paulistas discovered gold in modern-day Minas Gerais and whose presence led to several years of violent conflict in the region. Severo argued that this conflict, which he called "disagreements" and traditional historiography labeled war, joined the bandeiras to constitute "the prolegomena of independence."[126] The bandeiras became a Portuguese endeavor, and a violent clash between longtime residents of Brazil and Portuguese newcomers was made into a family squabble, at least as interpreted by one of the most prominent and active Portuguese in all of Brazil.

The Portuguese claim on Brazilian history and identity was especially apparent in the project for a Monumento à Raça, another centenary project led by Severo. When Portuguese residents of São Paulo announced plans for a monument to the bandeirantes they received support from the state governor Washington Luís and others.[127] However, critics insisted that a bandeirantes monument must be erected by Paulistas themselves, as in fact it was, eventually, with Victor Brecheret's Monumento às Bandeiras. Severo and his partners were undeterred and looked for other subjects worthy of a monument, considering, for example, a monument to the Portuguese language, before settling on a monument "to the raça."[128] Perhaps in hopes of avoiding conflict and confusion, they recruited both Paulistas and Portuguese, including consul José Augusto de Magalhães, in a "great Luso-Brazilian commission" to oversee the project.[129] Unfortunately, their efforts were even more short-lived than were the earlier plans to erect a monument to the bandeiras, which makes it difficult to know much about what they intended to communicate or accomplish in the monument. In one of its few public statements the commission stated that while it viewed the independence of Brazil as a "political fact, a result of natural political evolution," it also considered it essential to demonstrate its conviction that independence "had done nothing to affect the bonds of friendship that unite Portugal and Brazil." The centenary was the right moment to insist on the point, "in order to emphasize it better now" and to show that the relationship between the two countries went far beyond friendship; in Brazil, the commission said, "the raça proceeds steadily to fulfill its great historical destiny."[130] In other words, the monument would represent even more than the kind of tactile and enduring claims Portuguese residents hoped to make in their projects to construct a monument to the bandeiras and the national pantheon. It would memorialize the conviction of many Portuguese, and some Lusophile Brazilians, that there was no meaningful distinction between Portuguese and Brazilian people, that, in spite of Brazil's independence, they remained one nation, one "race."

It is no wonder, then, that the idea of a "Monument à Raça" irritated some Brazilian nationalists. As mentioned above, Victruvio Marcondes had much to say about the project, none of it complimentary and all of which he summed up in two incredulous questions: "A monument to the raça? But by God what raça?" That is, he could not even conceive of and certainly would not tolerate the notion that Brazilians and Portuguese were one nation, one people, one race. The monument, therefore, would memorialize a misreading of Brazilian culture and society, and Marcondes was unwilling to consider that its Portuguese organizers had anything other than destructive intentions. He accused them of taking advantage of the naïveté of the Brazilians willing to participate in the project and of a malicious and deliberate attack on Brazil through "mythmaking lies about the history of our people's development," which they would install under the guise of pretending to celebrate the Brazilian centenary. Finally, he argued, a monument to a Luso-Brazilian "race" would be a betrayal of the Brazilian patriots who fought for independence and would add to the misguided notion being proposed by so many Portuguese figures in 1922, that independence was a peaceful event that did not undo the unity of the two peoples. For Marcondes, a monument to independence ought to be one that memorialized Brazilians' victories against Portugal, such as at the Battle of Pirajá; he even doubted that Brazilians should celebrate the Grito do Ipiranga, and argued that a celebration of the Portuguese influence in Brazil would mean that "our glorious martyrs will have fought in vain" and that the centenary would become a celebration "of one hundred years of fictitious and deceitful emancipation."[131]

Such criticism may explain why organizers abandoned the idea of erecting a Monumento à Raça, just as they had abandoned their plans to erect a monument to the bandeiras. Menotti Del Picchia allowed that Severo and his partners had the best of intentions, and said they should be encouraged to celebrate the Portuguese legacy in Brazil by erecting a monument, but he argued that this must not be a monument to the bandeiras and he led the effort to discourage them from doing so in a series of columns in the *Correio Paulistano*.[132] He agreed that the bandeirantes, whom he called "demi-gods," ought to be honored at the centenary and that "Paulistas will not find in their history a more important episode to eternalize in blocks of marble."[133] However, the bandeiras were not, as Severo would have it, the accomplishments of Portuguese but of Brazilians, specifically Paulistas. The bandeiras were "really the greatest expression of [Brazil's] glorious and heroic past," and Paulistas themselves must control their memory and depiction.[134] In his words, "only a Paulista can understand [the bandeiras] in all of their majestic grandeur."[135] Del Picchia therefore advocated that the city and state erect the monument designed by Brecheret, who had been born in Italy, but who Del Picchia understood as a "Paulista" and whose model for the monument the critic called "a genuinely Brazilian work." He preferred that no monument be built if it were not Paulista; equally proud of Brecheret's achievement and annoyed that the Portuguese did not immediately cede to local desires, he called Brecheret's plans "the monument that the Portuguese killed but did not replace."[136] They could complicate nationalists' plans, that is, but they could not be allowed to displace them, so although no monument to the bandeirantes was erected in time for the centenary, Del Picchia and others among Brecheret's admirers celebrated when an important gallery displayed the sculptor's model, while the Portuguese eventually turned away from the project.[137]

The pantheon project does not seem to have agitated Brazilians in the way that the bandeiras and Raça initiatives did, which might suggest that the discord over the Portuguese monuments owed to the relative intensity of the nationalist movement in the capital and in São Paulo. It seems more likely that the two São Paulo projects were particularly irksome because they seemed to make the Portuguese claim on Brazil and its history especially apparent. Planners of the pantheon asserted the significance of the Portuguese legacy in an explicit way by placing Portuguese "guardians" at its entrance, but they left decisions about who belonged in the pantheon itself to Brazilians. António de Almeida, Mota Assunção, and other Portuguese emphasized the importance of Portuguese figures to the history of Brazil, including in the independence movement, but the vast majority of such claims were made in passing, and Carlos Malheiro Dias and the editors of the "monumental" *História* volume focused on the early years of Portuguese Brazil, avoiding the more conflicted episodes of the late colonial and independence periods.

In other words, it is possible that Brazilians were open to the idea of foreigners making claims on their history and assertions of belonging in the unique context of the centenary experience—of raids and visits and the exposition—but were more sensitive when the same figures sought to install their claims in explicit ways and in stone and bronze. Still, Brazilians' annoyance at the bandeiras and Raça monuments is glaring and noteworthy given that Brazilian commentators tended to accept and agree when Italians made their claims on Carlos Gomes. The Italian and Italo-Brazilian leaders of the Gomes project made clear their belief that Italians could claim Gomes as their own, and their monument, which included a figure representing Italy, made the claim explicit. But rather than resisting the assertion, Brazilian commentators accepted it and all that it implied about the place of Italians in contemporary Brazil. Thus, *O Estado de São Paulo* noted that Italy "with good reason claims a part of [Gomes's] glory," because it was in Italy that "he drank in the knowledge that completed his artistic training and it was in the Italian environment that his musical talent expressed itself in the many works that have established him in the history of the art." The *Illustração Brasileira* accepted the idea that Gomes considered Italy his "second patria" and made exactly the point that the monument organizers hoped to communicate, that the Italians resident in Brazil were very much like Gomes, at once Italian and Brazilian, for they "look on Brazil with equal affection." And in helping to inaugurate the monument, Henrique de Sousa Queiroz made the same point and used the same language, saying that the "children of Italy" had made Brazil "your second patria."

Finally, *Gil Blas* depicted the monument as proof that Italians were model immigrants, especially as compared to the hated Portuguese. Marcondes wrote of the contrast he saw between the Monumento à Raça and the Gomes monument, depicting the former as aggressive and anti-Brazilian and the latter as a selfless gesture by a group that was "more intelligent and progressive" than the Portuguese. Ignoring the statue of Italy and other claims that the monument included and its organizers made, he celebrated it as a gesture "honest and human: giving without receiving!" The magazine's editors agreed, saying that the monument proved that the Italians of São Paulo possessed "a solid understanding of their duties to our country and [were] grateful for Brazilian hospitality," another reason that while the Portuguese colony in Brazil was "*stupid and ridiculous*, . . . Brazilians should be very grateful for [the Italians'] valuable work in agriculture and industry."[138] It is clear that the organizers of the Gomes monument did indeed hope to gain by their initiative, but the anti-Portuguese campaign of these nationalists required otherwise, helping the Italian community avoid censure and making it easier for them to claim Brazil.

The consistent support Brazilians offered the Italian colony for the Gomes project is all the more remarkable because when the monument was unveiled contemporaries found that the likeness they saw bore very little resemblance to the man it depicted. The depiction was so unfaithful that Brizzolara decapitated the statue and installed a new, purportedly more accurate one, several years later. Still, though commentators mentioned the issue they tended not to dwell on it or suggest that it undermined the claims Italians were using the monument to make. Del Picchia, for example, praised the sculptor, saying that far from failure, he had "saved us" after a series of badly designed monuments the city had recently inaugurated: "Now we're better."[139] Similarly, in its review, the *Revista do Brasil* did not mention the question of rendering the composer's face, though elsewhere it reprinted a lampoon about it originally published in *Il Pasquino Coloniale*. Instead, it asserted that the monument was "the most beautiful scuplture among us today. Carlos Gomes is superbly styled, in an attitude that communicates the majesty of his genius." Further, notwithstanding its usual work to promote cultural nationalism—for example, it had published Adolpho Pinto's calls for a monument to the bandeiras and, later, an image of the Brecheret model that Del Picchia so admired—it did not object to the inclusion of a statue representing Italy in the Gomes monument. Instead, it said the statues of Brazil and Italy were "two beautiful designs, each constituting by itself a perfect monument."[140] As far as these critics were concerned, the monument was an artistic triumph and a welcome contribution from their Italian neighbors, despite its depiction of Gomes himself.

There were significant differences in the subjects of the monuments the Portuguese and Italian residents planned for the centenary. The Portuguese bandeiras and Raça projects made much broader claims on Brazil than did the pantheon, which focused on Brazilian heroes, or the Italian monument's focus on one individual Brazilian. Regional interests and differences may have contributed, especially in the case of the bandeiras, which Paulistas had come to regard as the central myth of their distinctive identity and therefore approached with the jealous sense of ownership seen in Del Picchia's arguments. There were differences in the process by which each initiative developed, for while the bandeiras project was a Portuguese initiative, the Gomes monument began in 1909 as an effort of Italians and Brazilians together, which Italian activists took over in 1920 due to the original effort's halting progress. They made sure to communicate with their Brazilian partners before they did so, and enjoyed local encouragement, including from the state governor, and they cooperated with the state government in setting up the Gomes prize once the monument expenses had been covered.[141] Ricardo Severo and his fellow Portuguese followed that model in the Monumento à Raça, which shows that partnership with Brazilians was not a failsafe, especially when the claims the initiative was making were ambitious ones. The different responses also corresponded to differences in Brazilians' views of different groups of immigrants. While 1922 saw an outpouring of Lusophile sentiment and a rediscovery and celebration of the Portuguese legacy, as seen in Brazilians' responses to António de Almeida and the aviators and to the Portuguese exposition spaces, it is also the case that anti-Portuguese sentiment was an important part of Brazilian discussions of national identity in the 1920s, as Victruvio Marcondes and other activists clearly demonstrated. Meanwhile, even as the visit of Enrico Caviglia made it apparent that Italians might not be perfectly well adjusted in Brazil, they continued to be depicted as model immigrants, not only by the industrialists and plantation owners who relied on their labor but also by the most aggressive nationalists.

Finally, it is important to consider that these projects took on an essential, distinctive form, which was itself an important reason that foreign residents and immigrants undertook them. Visits by diplomats, artists, business figures, and soldiers lasted weeks or, at most, a couple of months. The exposition lasted almost a year, and in a few instances its buildings had longer lives, but it too was designed to be temporary. These activities exemplified the special circumstances of 1922, and it is likely that Brazilians were more open than they might usually have been to the prospect of foreigners making claims on their history and asserting their sense of belonging in the special circumstances of the centenary celebrations. A monument in stone and bronze installed those claims in a much more enduring way than any speech or essay, any display or parade, which helps explain both the attraction they held for immigrant organizers and the sensitivity that Brazilian observers displayed in considering them. Nowhere was this as apparent as in the controversy over the monument to the bandeiras, where the defenders of the prerogatives of Paulistas to control their depiction were prepared to miss the chance to mark the centenary with a monument to the great endeavors rather than to cede to the vision of the Portuguese residents of the city. It can also be seen in the fact that many Portuguese and some Brazilians used the centenary to claim there existed a shared Luso-Brazilian race, and nationalists often objected, but their objections became more intense and antagonistic when a group of Portuguese made plans to erect a monument to the idea. The scale and seeming permanence of monument projects meant that the benefits they might afford their promoters appeared greater, but also that the stakes of the claims they made on Brazil seemed higher, and so all of those interested in questions of belonging invested them with greater significance than other forms by which immigrants and other foreigners participated in the centenary.

The monuments projects undertaken by immigrants and other foreign residents of Brazil thus exemplified the ways that the centenary opened up space for the practice of citizenship in early twentieth-century Brazil. Immigrants used them to claim Brazil, in ways both tangible and ideological. Completed monuments took hold of public space in Brazilian towns and cities, which were also given over to immigrants when the monuments were inaugurated, and they put on display immigrants' ideas about themselves and their place in the country. The projects also exemplified the extent and the limits of that space and of Brazilians' openness to immigrants' claims. Thus, Italians were able to set their claims in the marble and bronze of the monument to Carlos Gomes in São Paulo, and Brazilians celebrated their efforts despite the mischaracterization of the composer in its original version. Meanwhile, their Portuguese counterparts made ambitious plans for monuments to the bandeirantes, to the Luso-Brazilian "race," to the Portuguese language, and to Brazil's pantheon of heroes. But, at least in part due to Brazilians' objections, the only major centenary monument they completed was one dedicated to Sacadura Cabral and Gago Coutinho in Recife, inaugurated in 1927. The significance of the comparison ought not be overread, but it does seem an almost irresistible metaphor for the relative effectiveness of the immigrant groups' performances of identity and belonging in 1922. It is also a reminder that while the centenary offered immigrants rare opportunities to express themselves and make claims on Brazil it also presented them with difficult circumstances and significant problems, for contemporaries approached the centenary with utter seriousness.

Requiring long-term planning, significant investment, and purposeful organization, monuments projects were among the most important of immigrants' initiatives during the centenary celebrations, and where they were completed they were also the most enduring. Other efforts were important as well, from the work immigrants did to welcome distinguished visitors from home to their participation in the centenary exhibition. Together these efforts indicated that immigrants joined with Brazilians in acknowledging the significance of the centenary, and, in turn, for the most part Brazilians encouraged immigrants' participation in the year's celebrations, reading it as evidence of immigrants' gratitude and commitment to Brazil. There were indications of the anxieties of immigrant life, made evident in the defensiveness voiced by German commentators in Rio Grande do Sul and the biting criticism aimed at some Portuguese efforts, which came not only from the nativists of *Gil Blas* but also from less strident nationalists such as Menotti Del Picchia. The centenary put on display both the mutual esteem and the anxieties, the measure of each tracking closely with the character of the relationships Brazilian communities tended to have with the immigrant groups living in them. This goes a long way in explaining the distinctive experiences of Italians, Germans, and Portuguese as well as the differences these groups confronted in various parts of Brazil.

Part of the centenary's significance, then, is that it put on display immigrants' and Brazilians' prevailing attitudes about one another and the character of their interactions. It also affected immigrants' lives in concrete ways, especially by building the sense that they were members of discrete communities. Some efforts undertaken by immigrants suggest that many wanted to straddle old and new identities and even to forge them together. Italians' depiction of Carlos Gomes as at once Brazilian and their own might be understood in this way, and the impulse was especially clear in Portuguese initiatives to promote the idea of a Luso-Brazilian nation, as was the idea for the Monumento à Raça and much of the rhetoric characterizing the visit of António de Almeida. However, centenary events also sometimes seemed to necessitate a choice between identities: thus, for example, except in rare instances (like the Matarazzo company's construction of its own pavilion), exhibitors were obligated to designate their wares "national" or "international," while in Rio Grande do Sul, Jacob Kroeff Netto and Theophilo de Barros Corrêa de Mello Neves noted that some immigrants felt they had to perform one or another identity, lest they offend Brazilians' sensibilities.

The pressure to display immigrant identities came from Brazilians, from their former homes, and from within immigrant communities. Ambassadors, consuls, and members of special centenary embassies played important roles in organizing the participation of Brazil-based nationals in the centenary. Meanwhile, aware that many Brazilians expected immigrants to stage performances of identity, loyalty, and gratitude, and seeing them as opportunities to strengthen their own social standing, well-to-do and well-connected immigrants arrogated to themselves the task of overseeing those performances. They worked with diplomats and Brazilian officials to decide on a schedule of activities, they organized committees and raised funds, and they prodded their fellow immigrants to participate in events according to scripts they themselves composed. An immigrant might attend the centenary fair or watch a parade as an individual, but immigrants were also left with little doubt of their responsibilities and their assigned roles in "immigrant" events.

While we might expect Brazilian state authorities to have been uncomfortable with displays of potentially competing loyalties, they seem to have welcomed them, which might be explained if we consider authorities' own aims for centenary rituals and the particular circumstances in which the centenary unfolded. First, as official organizers were eager to internationalize the celebrations and they welcomed the participation of the peoples and governments of friendly nations, they helped to create the mechanisms for deepening immigrants' connections with their countries of origin. Thus, the participation of Portuguese and American groups in welcoming the aviators from Lisbon and New York, respectively, and the work of immigrant business groups to promote the fair helped increase the scale and significance of centenary events, ratifying organizers' claims of their success. Second, and perhaps more important, immigrants who were organized by their social betters within their own national "colonies" to perform roles assigned to them were unlikely to challenge the legitimacy and authority of Brazil's ruling classes, a boon to be embraced amid the difficulties of 1922, from barracks revolts to electoral disputes to labor trouble. The centenary might inhibit the process of immigrants' adjustment and assimilation that many Brazilians hoped it would hasten, but for the sake of successful centenary celebrations and for the maintenance of social order, immigrants could be encouraged to revive old ties and rehearse former national identities. The task of dealing with the consequences of these choices was left to the future, another of the tensions the centenary helped to expose and exacerbate, another way its celebratory air blew in winds of crisis and fracture.

Epilogue

The chapters of this book have noted some of the ways that the celebrations of 1922 echoed in the ensuing years, such as José Pereira Alves's continuation of his efforts at the Congresso Eucharistico to reconcile the state to the church after his appointment as bishop of Niterói in 1928, and the 1954 completion of Victor Brecheret's monument to the bandeirantes, which its advocates had hoped would be unveiled for the centenary. There were many other such echoes and instances, for the performances of citizenship and identity Brazilians staged to commemorate the centenary functioned not only as displays of the country and reflections of the attitudes and perspectives of its people. They had tangible effects that continued to shape Brazilian life well after 1922. As in the cases of Alves and Brecheret, the centenary brought individual people and groups to wider public notice, which, for example, helps account for Walter Hinton's ability to get work as a surveyor in the Amazon basin in the mid-1920s, and the political influence the jangadeiros from Rio Grande do Norte gained from their own raid. It also explains why a group of jangadeiros from Ceará chose to stage a raid on the national capital in 1941 as a way to seek recognition of their demands as citizens and laborers; they had apparently learned from their predecessors that such a performance of their claims on the nation could bear fruit.

These examples also point to the continuing significance of the performances of the centenary, beyond the careers of individual celebrants and the memories of specific events. Through their centenary efforts Alves and Brecheret exemplified the ways that the celebrations of 1922 exacerbated tensions in the relationship between tradition and modernity in twentieth-century Brazil. Alves was one of many figures in 1922 who argued that the republic had abandoned Brazil's traditions in its attempt to brand the country as cosmopolitan and advanced, and both the priest and the sculptor engaged with the past as a means of anchoring Brazilian modernity in its "authentic" character. Both were also involved in another of the most prevalent projects of the centenary, the scrutiny and celebration of Brazil's regional particularities, Alves as a champion of the North and Northeast and Brecheret as the quintessential artist of the bandeirantes. The raiders of the centenary also helped make it an effort to know Brazil, from north to south and coast to interior (which Hinton's work in the Amazon also continued), but, in addition, this effort deepened regionalist sensibilities and made it more challenging to build the national community. Finally, the jangadeiro raiders gained an extraordinary purchase on Brazilians' attention because they seemed to embody the "real," traditional Brazil and the distinctive qualities of their home regions, which drew attention to the nation's unresolved debates about matters of race and national origin, and the way they shaped what it meant and should mean to be Brazilian.

These tensions did not subside but persisted after the fair finally closed its gates in July 1923, contributing to the breakdown of political order in 1930 and setting the parameters of its reconstruction in the succeeding decades. As the book has shown, the tensions that defined the centenary experience—between tradition and modernity, between regional identity and national community, concerning questions of race and national origin, and between older and younger generations of Brazilians—could be both productive and dangerous, and they proved to be so. In order to track the ways that the centenary continued to shape Brazilian life, this epilogue thus focuses on each of these tensions in turn and some of the connections between the ways in which they played out during the centenary celebrations and in the circumstances of later years.

The distinctions and relationship between tradition and modernity were apparent throughout the celebrations of the centenary. The arrival in Rio de Janeiro of aviators flying the most technologically advanced airplanes and of fishermen sailing simple rafts was a jarring illustration of the point, which contemporaries developed by depicting the Portuguese raiders and the jangadeiros as embodiments of the possibility of integrating qualities that seemed irreconcilable. In their telling, the former suggested that the spirit of the age of discovery endured, and the latter that the traits generations of fishermen had to develop in their confrontation with difficult conditions could be harnessed to face the future. The centenary exhibition displayed Brazil's economic accomplishments and untapped potential in a language at once traditional and quite up to date. On one hand, the displays opened in a set of new constructions eclectic in style but dominated by neocolonial architecture. On the other, the campus stood on ground created through the destruction of one of Rio de Janeiro's oldest settlements, the buildings glowed with light produced by a cutting-edge grid of electric power, and organizers depended heavily on quantification and statistical analysis to tell the story of Brazil.

Brazilians used the centenary to celebrate the past, though they did not agree on which past they should focus on and they offered widely different interpretations of its meaning and relevance to their own time. While some looked to use the rituals of memory to strengthen traditional religious practice, to rehabilitate the colonial order, or to celebrate Pedro I and the empire he founded, often to criticize the republic that replaced it, others used the centenary to legitimize the republic by emphasizing what they viewed as the links between the past and the present. Finally, the tension between tradition and modernity was expressed in the ways that immigrants participated in the centenary and Brazilians' varied responses to their initiatives. Portuguese residents of Brazil used the centenary to remind Brazilians of their Portuguese roots, while also using the celebrity of Gago Coutinho and Sacadura Cabral and António de Almeida to assert that their presence in the country could help it build modernity, claims that nativist activists rejected out of hand, asserting instead that Brazil must cast off the Portuguese inheritance to realize its potential. The chief beneficiaries of such arguments in 1922, it seems, were the Italians who populated São Paulo and other regions in southeastern Brazil, whose own claims on the country received a much more welcome response from Brazilians, who tended to depict Italian laborers as essential partners in the project of economic development.

In the period after 1922 these debates and the expansion of initiatives begun for the centenary continued, including in the completion of monuments to the bandeiras and of Christ the Redeemer, both projects treating subjects centenary Brazilians understood as closely connected to national tradition in the language of modern art. The Brazilian modernist movement began before the centenary and flourished after it, with artists and critics like Tarsila do Amaral and Oswald de Andrade helping to define the 1920s and 1930s. Because of the Semana de Arte Moderna, however, the story of the modernist movement became anchored to 1922, and it is important to note the interest that many of its participants took in the centenary, seen not only in Brecheret's designs but also, for example, in Menotti Del Picchia's commentary on the public art produced for the celebrations and the involvement of Mário de Andrade in the debate over the neocolonial style that defined the exhibition. Like so many others, they seem to have understood the centenary as a rare opportunity to capture public attention for the matters that most concerned them, including what modernity meant in Brazil and how it related to the nation's past and its customs.

Though quite unlike the modernists in his sensibilities, the arch-traditionalist Gustavo Barroso followed a trajectory similar to theirs as he worked to encourage Brazilians to join him in a "culto da saudade" celebrating the Brazilian past. He began his advocacy well before 1922, but the centenary provided the circumstances for his appointment as director of the new Museu Histórico Nacional and its opening as part of the fair. Modest as it was during the centenary celebrations, the museum grew in scale and significance in the ensuing years, especially after 1930, when Barroso found a partner in the construction of his "culto" in the form of the Getúlio Vargas regime. Vargas embraced the opportunity to use the state to intervene in, and therefore attempt to define, the public performance of memory, overseeing numerous initiatives that promoted reverence for the Brazilian past and institutionalizing the effort by organizing the new Inspetoria de Monumentos Nacionais (now the Instituto do Patrimônio Histórico e Artístico Nacional) in 1933. Among many other efforts, two of particular relevance to the current work were the historic preservation of the town of Ouro Preto and the organization of a new imperial museum in Petrópolis. The former honored both the colonial inheritance and the Inconfidentes who conspired in the town and the latter completed the redemption story of the emperors, the two projects thus continuing work that had helped define the centenary celebrations, and, as in 1922, the government used them as a means of legitimizing itself, as Daryle Williams has shown. Williams shows that tensions between tradition and modernity persisted during the Vargas years, as Barroso promoted a view that rejected the modern, and modernist culture managers came to dominate in the Inspetoria and other parts of the state bureaucracy. As in 1922, these tensions were sometimes fruitful and always deeply meaningful because contemporaries understood the relationship between tradition and modernity as key to defining Brazil and brasilidade.[1]

Getúlio Vargas was similarly intentional in his drive to confront the challenge of regionalism that was so apparent in 1922 and the centenary helped exacerbate. Many contemporaries read the raids of the centenary as performances of Brazil's regions and regional identities. They saw the aviators coming from Lisbon and New York and less-celebrated raiders, such as those who walked or rode bicycles, as doing essential work in familiarizing Brazilians with regions of the country they did not know; they saw the jangadeiros from the North and Northeast as doing even more, not only spreading knowledge but in fact embodying the supposedly distinctive qualities of people from the region, such as resilience and bravery. The ways that regional identities played out in the major official initiatives of the centenary were much less felicitous. Fair organizers sought to use the event to help Brazilians know the country and they worked to ensure that every state and territory would be represented in its exhibition halls; sports administrators tried to do the same with the events they planned. But regionalist resentments and biases, including organizers' own, jeopardized their efforts, with the result that the fair and the sports competitions displayed and deepened those feelings, as demonstrated by the unwillingness of many Brazilians to participate in the fair and Pernambucanos' organization of their own sports competitions.

A similar process played out as Brazilians staged commemorations of the past. Historians and events organizers sponsored by the national state drew connections between "precursor" episodes, which took place in many regions of the country years and even centuries before independence, and the story of Pedro and his advisers, which unfolded in Rio de Janeiro, São Paulo, and the Southeast, part of an effort to use the centenary to promote a consensus interpretation of the history of the nation and its independence. However, as this project also included an emphasis on the significance of the prince and the elision of the differences between Portuguese and Brazilian actors and of the violence of the independence process, it tended to alienate Pernambucanos, who treasured an interpretation of their own region's history characterized by a rejection of monarchy and violent conflicts between the Portuguese and the native born. They scorned efforts at building a consensus narrative of independence, instead asserting that the centenary ought to be a celebration of Pernambuco's precedence in the story of Brazil, which was much like the claim offered by Paulista historians, who saw the value of an inclusive approach but largely followed Affonso Taunay's claim that "the history of São Paulo is the history of Brazil itself." These differences in interpreting Brazilian history were heavily informed by regional differences and regionalist outlooks, which also shaped how immigrants and other foreign residents of Brazil experienced the centenary. Thus, the assertion by the Italians of São Paulo that the centenary was an occasion to announce their loyalty to their "two patrias" was welcomed by many Brazilians, including nativist activists. Portuguese immigrants received a much more mixed response when they did the same, more generous in São Paulo, for example, than in Rio de Janeiro, and Germans and German-Brazilians in Rio Grande do Sul used the centenary to try to convince any doubters that though they were proud of their cultural inheritance they were loyal only to Brazil.

In short, the centenary did as much to display regional differences and intensify regionalist feeling as it did to forge a more cohesive, more united national community, and its effects seem to have contributed in direct and indirect ways to the mounting challenge regionalism became after 1922. Chapter 2 noted the connections between the centenary and one of the better-known examples of the regionalist episodes that unfolded in its aftermath, the so-called Gaúcho revolution of 1923. The "revolution" grew out of long-standing disputes in the politics of Rio Grande do Sul, including arguments over the relationship between the state and the national government, which the centenary moment and its rituals intensified. The conflict did not resolve these disputes, and the regionalist feelings that helped fuel it continued to define the Gaúcho scene, appearing in grand style when the state government oversaw a massive effort to celebrate the centenary of the separatist Guerra dos Farrapos in 1935. Some read this effort, which included a national and international commercial fair, as a means of situating the state more firmly within the national community, but it also worried Brazilians concerned about the continuing challenge of regionalism in the state and beyond it.[2]

The book has also focused on two other regions where the challenge was especially apparent, Pernambuco and São Paulo. In Pernambuco, the years after 1922 saw the crystallization of regionalist sentiments, formalized in the Centro Regionalista (1924) and its Congresso Brasileiro de Regionalismo (1926), best known for the promulgation of Gilberto Freyre's *Manifesto regionalista*, in which he insisted Brazil's authentic identity lay in the traditions of Pernambuco and its neighboring states.[3] As the book has shown, Recifenses, Pernambucanos, and their neighbors in the Northeast used the centenary to explore and promulgate the meaning of tradition and region, and though Freyre was not involved in the celebrations of 1922 it does not seem a coincidence that he and his partners found the ground well prepared in the aftermath. As was the case with Freyre's Northeast, which amounted to a claim on Brazil, not its rejection, regionalism did not have to mean separatism or a challenge to the nation. But it could seem threatening, which is how supporters of the Vargas regime read the Constitutionalist revolt of 1932, despite the Paulista rebels' view of themselves as defenders of the legal order. Their use of the emblems of local identity—especially the bandeirantes, which were such an important part of the centenary celebrations (including in the discourse of Vargas's future rival Júlio Prestes)—helped confirm the regime and many nationalists in their view that the revolt was an expression of regionalism and therefore a spasm of anti-Brazilian animus.[4]

Thus, Getúlio Vargas looked to co-opt Paulista economic interests by providing relief and support for the coffee industry, and he worked to confront the challenge of regionalism in a variety of other ways, concrete and symbolic. Amid the restructuring of the political order was the removal of governing authorities at every level, including state governors and legislators, the former replaced by appointed intervenors and the latter finding their assemblies reorganized and reopened, but briefly, and closed again with the establishment of the Estado Novo in 1937. That same year, Vargas presided over a public ritual of antiregionalism, a ceremony to burn the flags of the Brazilian states. Not content with the legal abolition of the flags, banned by the constitution of the new state, the ceremony announced and sacralized the decision to enact one of the failed initiatives of the centenary celebrations, to honor "one single flag." Beginning with an outdoor mass, it functioned as a ritualized performance of union and national community, each state banner burned in a large urn and a large flag of Brazil raised over the ashes.

A final example combined the physical and the symbolic. The project to construct a new national capital to break Brazilians' understanding of the country as a coastal republic is usually associated with the presidency of Juscelino Kubitschek, who oversaw its completion and inauguration. But it began long before Kubitschek's interventions, with commissions studying the problem and working on plans for the city throughout the republican period, including during the second Vargas presidency in the early 1950s. The organizers of the official events of the centenary were also attracted to the idea, and on 7 September 1922 arranged for the dedication of the Pedra Fundamental da Futura Capital Federal dos Estados Unidos do Brasil, an obelisk marking what was then planned as the site of the future capital, just to the north of the area that became Brasília. The ceremony was small and it did not begin the project in earnest, but it was reported on throughout the country, and therefore helped the state to demonstrate its interest in place and region and in performing the work of building the national community.

Among the most persistent and prevalent themes of the centenary celebrations, it is of course unsurprising that Brazilians, immigrants, and visitors would have been particularly concerned with issues of race and national origin. They were, after all, among the issues most commented on and worried about by nation builders throughout the country's independent life, guiding major decisions, such as how to pursue abolition and whether and how to promote immigration. The centenary arrived during a period of reassessment and innovation, not least because the Great War had shattered the assumptions shared by many Brazilians about the superiority of Western civilization and because the contemplation invited by the commemorative moment meant that questions about how Brazilians of different racial backgrounds and with roots in different places fit into the nation.

These kinds of questions made the raids of the centenary seem like deeply meaningful events, for Brazilians understood them as performances of racial identity and national origin. They said aviators from Portugal, the United States, and Brazil embodied the qualities they supposed were particular to each of those countries, although they engaged in the same kind of endeavor, long-distance flights, and they were even more convinced that the raids by the jangadeiros and other fishermen were significant in these terms. The fishermen, many contemporaries said, proved that Brazil's racial constitution meant not backwardness, as pessimists had alleged, but greatness, the raiders demonstrating the enormous potential of the Brazilian caboclo and its other mixed-race citizens. The organizers of the centenary exhibition focused on displaying evidence of the country's economic potential, but they also engaged with questions surrounding the racial identity and character of Brazil, for example, by offering an optimistic narrative of the country's progress according to the dictates of eugenicists in the Pavilhão de Estatística, and by partnering with medical professionals in several efforts focused on children's welfare, such as the Primeiro Congresso Brasileiro de Protecção à Infância. Their invitation to a group of Pareci speakers from Mato Grosso to stage a public performance at the fair, while one of the few official acknowledgments of the place of the indigenous in the nation, was also much noticed and another indication of the ways that issues of race and nation shared the fair with matters of industry and agriculture.

Chapters 3 and 4 showed how concerns about racial and national identity—conflated in contemporaries' use of the term "raça" to connote both concepts—were especially important in shaping how Brazilians remembered the past and navigated the present because the centenary encouraged particular scrutiny of Portugal's influence on Brazil, as a cultural inheritance and in the form of Portuguese living in the country. The vast majority of Brazilians celebrated Gago Coutinho and Sacadura Cabral and António de Almeida and praised the mother country in their comments about the visitors. But they were more conflicted as they looked to understand the roles of the Portuguese in the nation's past, including its story of independence, and in its present and future as residents and immigrants. Some Brazilians and Portuguese used the centenary as an opportunity to assert, as Ricardo Severo put it, that Brazil was fundamentally a Portuguese nation, arguing that independence was a Luso-Brazilian accomplishment and that the nation to be celebrated in 1922 was the "raça luso-brasileira," where Portuguese immigrants were very much at home. Others rejected both of these notions, often in quite strident terms, the argument appearing, for example, in Paulistas' insistence that the bandeirantes were Brazilian, not Portuguese; in resistance to revisionist historians' acknowledgment of the significance of Pedro and other Portuguese in the independence process; and in nativists' horror at the idea of a Luso-Brazilian confederation. Such critics tended to answer centenary Lusophilia by describing Brazilians as a multiracial people and to insist on the importance of immigrants other than the Portuguese, especially Italians. Italians were not blind to the opportunity such disagreements presented to their making claims on Brazil while maintaining their own distinctive identity, and thus contributed to the centenary's display of both national community and racial and cultural difference.

As Gladys Ribeiro has demonstrated in her extensive work on anti-Portuguese feeling during the First Republic, one reason that some Brazilians feared and resented Portuguese residents and immigrants was because of their efficient and effective organization, which made them a "true power" in the life of Rio de Janeiro and other major cities.[5] As we have seen, the centenary would only have intensified their apprehension in this regard. Portuguese and other foreigners residing in Brazil organized themselves to participate in the celebrations along national lines, and it does not seem a coincidence that the years after 1922 were characterized by a proliferation of new immigrant societies and organizations, especially among two of the groups most active in the centenary celebrations, the Italians and the Portuguese, whose Casa de Portugal cultural centers grew directly out of the community's centenary activities. Brazilian nationalists became increasingly apprehensive about the loyalties of the members of such organizations, not least the old and new groups that promoted a sense of *italianità* and support for Mussolini's Fascist state among Brazil's Italians, which seemed to constitute an existential threat when Brazil entered the war in 1942.[6]

Worried nationalists reacted to these challenges in several ways. The most well known of these were the efforts of the Fascist-inspired Ação Integralista Brasileira—led by Plínio Salgado, who had been active in the debates and celebrations of the centenary—and, with much greater effect, the Vargas government's campaigns aiming at the "nationalization" of the foreign born and their descendants. Among other initiatives, Vargas mandated that for every three employees two must be Brazil born; he attacked immigrant education by obligating schools to offer instruction only in Portuguese, delivered by Brazilians; he destroyed the foreign-language immigrant press; and, during the war, he took special aim at Japanese, German, and Italian communities, their activities surveilled, their loyalties tested, and their organizations obligated to "Brazilianize" themselves in name, language, and activities. Aside from the so-called Law of 2/3, the Portuguese largely avoided the brunt of such actions, and, combined with the slowing of immigration and populist measures pursued by the Vargas regime, anti-Portuguese sentiment seems to have declined in the 1930s, but the message was delivered, the centenary's welcome of immigrant identity confronted and withdrawn.[7]

Vargas also worked to build the national community, the project defined to a great extent by questions of race and national origin. In education, in the plastic arts, in forms of popular culture like music and sport, and in national and international exhibitions, Vargas and his partners in the state and outside it, from Gilberto Freyre to Candido Portinari, sought to show immigrants and the native born of all races how they defined national identity and to teach them the roles they were expected to play in making modern Brazil. Daryle Williams, Darién Davis, and Carmen Nava, among others, have shown the ways in which this project was both inclusive and limiting, on one hand promoting the sense that all belonged in the nation and advertising respect for the cultural expressions of Afro-Brazilians and other marginalized groups, and on the other communicating a clear preference for whiteness as the national norm and insisting on the traditional hierarchy of race and color.[8] Again, these efforts echoed and built on the rituals and the debates of 1922, for in some respects the centenary exacerbated the challenge of integration and nation-building but it also helped point nation builders toward a solution: among other ways it did this, the discourse surrounding the jangadeiros and the immigrants active in the celebrations held that Brazilians of color and of various national origins could indeed help build the country's future, as long as they accepted guidance by their racial and social betters. The lesson, and the solution it implied, seemed to require only the will of those responsible for guiding the nation, and Vargas offered himself for the role.[9]

Indeed, it is worth remembering that at least a few Brazilians active in centenary events were very clear that the solution to the challenges of building national community must be ambitious and radical, including the need to construct a new, more responsible, more active state. They argued that the milestone was not to be understood as an occasion for celebration but for regret, and that the time and space of the centenary rituals were essential because they allowed Brazilians to see the failure of both independence and the republic and the necessity of renovation. Thus, Pontes de Miranda and Brenno Ferraz, the writers mentioned in the book's introduction, saw Brazil as a country "gigantic but ill," its moral order "indolent," and they called for radical change, a "revolution in our ideas and our customs," in Ferraz's words.[10] As we have seen, others shared this perspective and used the centenary to announce it. It was especially prevalent outside the regions that dominated the national scene and, significantly, among prominent younger Brazilians who took part in centenary events; that is, it was heard in those regions where resentment about the political status quo was most apparent, voiced by those assumed to be the country's future leaders. In Porto Alegre, José Pereira Coelho de Souza told his audience at the centenary celebration of the Federação Academica that when he surveyed contemporary Brazil, what he noticed were "wasted efforts, lost and misspent energies," especially in the Amazon, in the Northeast, and in the South.[11] In the same city, Gastão Dias told his fellow students in the Gremio dos Estudantes de Agronomia e Veterinaria that Brazilians were "politically emancipated and economically enslaved," and that the illiteracy of the majority of Brazilians and the elitist attitudes of the dominant classes left the country badly fractured and unable to develop.[12]

Commentators in the Northeast offered similar critiques, angered as they were about the hegemony of the Southeast and its alleged ignorance of their own region. They complained about the intervention of federal forces in Recife in 1922, while also pointing out the country's failures to ensure the education and health of its citizens and its economic development and sovereignty. Among others, Clodomir Silva asserted that Brazil was neither mature nor independent, and José Euclides asserted that because of the region's poor moral and physical health, Brazil did not have the "right" to celebrate the centenary.[13] And these figures were joined by the region's younger generation of leaders. When Cussy d'Almeida Júnior took the stage to speak for his fellow students at the celebration organized by the Faculdade de Direito, he argued that because of the failures of the previous hundred years and the shortcomings of the country's governing classes, the independence they were gathered to celebrate was a fiction.[14]

Though pessimistic about the past and the present, what distinguished young commentators like Souza, Dias, and d'Almeida—and Miranda and Ferraz—from critics like Silva and Euclides was their confidence that the future could be bright. Like those Brazilians who saw the jangadeiros as evidence of the real but latent capacities of the country's working people, Souza asked his listeners to imagine wasted energies directed "to a common goal: the day when the Brazilian, who struggles and suffers the neglect of the politically powerful, will have the guiding hand which will lead and direct him." With such leadership, which Souza said must begin with his classmates and contemporaries, Brazilians would accomplish great things: "What an astonishing country," he claimed, "what a miracle of a nation we will present to the world!"[15] Dias and d'Almeida also spoke of the importance and responsibility of their own generation, who must use their training and patriotism to remake Brazil. Dias emphasized that it would not be the old Brazil that they would create; instead, they must work "for the sake of the new nation!"[16] Like Ferraz, who spoke of "revolution," d'Almeida was even more explicit. For the salvation of the nation and its republic, he said, "we have only one hope—a new Republic."[17]

Thus, though the rituals of belonging and nationality that Brazilians staged to celebrate the centenary were characterized as much by doubt as optimism, as much by disharmony as community, they also helped Brazilians begin to imagine how to become the people they hoped to be. Figures like Souza, Dias, and d'Almeida used the centenary to prepare the ground for the great national project they believed the country required, which they were sure could only be wrought by the "guiding hand" of a new, powerful national state. In the meantime, they and their compatriots were left to wrestle with the great challenge revealed and made more formidable by the centenary, the challenge of realizing Brazil's potential, which seemed at once so great and so threatened by discord and fracture.

Notes

Introduction

1. Raphael Pinto, quoted in "Christo Redemptor: A Cerimonia do Lançamento da Pedra Fundamental do Monumento," *A Exposição de 1922*, October 1922. This and all succeeding translations are mine.

2. Such metonyms thus lend themselves to the construction of the "invented traditions" that Eric Hobsbawm and Terence Ranger show are so important to modern nations. Hobsbawm and Ranger, *Invention of Tradition*, 9.

3. "Projectos: n. 225—1922," in Brazil, *Diário do Congresso Nacional*, 4 October 1922.

4. See especially Carvalho, *Os Bestializados*; Sodré, *O tenentismo*; Hahner, *Emancipating the Female Sex*; L. Pereira, *Footballmania*; and Brito, *História do Modernismo Brasileiro*.

5. Rappaport, *Ritual and Religion*, 216. See also Rappaport, *Ecology, Meaning, and Religion*, 213.

6. As Hendrik Kraay argues, it is important to acknowledge that participants use ritual practices not only for enacting their values but also for shaping and making them. He calls for a more ample view of the significance of ritual than does the influential Clifford Geertz, whose depiction of rituals as performances of values but not as opportunities to confront and possibly reshape them leaves "little room for politics," as Kraay puts it in *Days of National Festivity*, 4.

7. Scholars of Mexico have done much important work on civic rituals. See especially Beezley and Lorey, *Viva Mexico!*; Tenorio-Trillo, *I Speak of the City*;

and two articles by Michael J. Gonzales, "Imagining Mexico in 1910" and "Imagining Mexico in 1921." Beyond Mexico, see Beezley, Martin, and French, *Rituals of Rule* and two articles by Rebecca Earle, "'Padres de la Patria'" and "Sobre Héroes y Tumbas."

8. Along with Kraay's *Days of National Festivity*, see also Kraay, *Bahia's Independence*. Another especially important work on civic ritual in Brazil is Barbara Weinstein's *Color of Modernity*. In the book's second part, Weinstein analyzes the celebration of the quadricentennial of the founding of São Paulo, and shows how Paulistas used the celebration to assert their region's preeminence within the national community.

9. Oliveira, "As festas que a República manda guardar." The phrase comes from the epigraph of a text that helped justify the new calendar, Octavio's *Festas Nacionaes*.

10. Among the most important of these works are Levy, *Entre Palácios e Pavilhões*; M. Pereira, *1908, um Brasil em exposição*; Pesavento, *Exposições Universais*; and Rezende, "The Raw and the Manufactured."

11. Levy, *A exposição do centenário*; Wadsworth, "Brasil en 1922"; and Wadsworth and Marko, "Children of the Pátria." Among other works on the centenary, see especially Elkin, "Promoting a New Brazil," and Santos and Melo, *1922*.

12. Motta, *A nação faz 100 anos*.

13. In her book on Bahia, *Algazarra nas ruas*, Wlamyra Albuquerque is among the few scholars to have afforded focused attention on centenary celebrations outside of the Southeast.

14. Kraay, *Days of National Festivity*, 3. As Frederick Cooper argues in *Citizenship, Inequality, and Difference*, citizenship might be best understood as "the right to claim rights" (20) and "a construct to make claims" on the political community (46). The Brazilian case shows that civic rituals can function as extraordinary opportunities for people to make those claims and to enlarge or, to use Cooper's term, "thicken" the meaning of their citizenship.

15. Here and throughout the book, I used gendered language such as "fishermen" and "statesmen." I do so purposefully, in part to emphasize the highly gendered character of power and representation in Brazil during the 1920s. That is, all the fishermen discussed in chapter 1 were, in fact, men, the cooperatives to which the raiders of the centenary belonged monopolized by them. Women were of course active in politics, but their formal political rights were severely limited before they gained suffrage in 1932; the official representatives of the state discussed in the book, Brazilians and foreign visitors alike, were men. In the book I make note of instances when individual women or groups of women were involved in the debates and the rituals of the centenary. In general, though, the major public events of the centenary and the institutions that planned them were dominated by men, and the language used in the book draws attention to this fact.

16. On these efforts, see especially Hochman, *Sanitation of Brazil*; Stepan, *Beginnings of Brazilian Science*; Hardman, *Trem Fantasma*; Meade, *"Civilizing" Rio*; Bueno, *Política Externa da Primeira República*; Needell, *Tropical* Belle Epoque; and Bocketti, *Invention of the Beautiful Game.*

17. See, in particular, Greenhalgh, *Ephemeral Vistas*; Plum, *World Exhibitions*; and Rydell, *All the World's a Fair.*

18. Carvalho, "Brazil 1870–1914."

19. On debates over Eurocentric racial doctrines, see especially Schwarcz, *Spectacle of the Races*; Peard, *Race, Place, and Medicine*; and Stepan, *"Hour of Eugenics."*

20. See essential work by Gladys Ribeiro, including *Mata Galegos* and *O Rio de Janeiro dos Fados.*

21. See the classic series released by Stanford University Press, which includes Love, *Rio Grande do Sul* and *São Paulo in the Brazilian Federation*, as well as Levine, *Pernambuco in the Brazilian Federation* and Wirth, *Minas Gerais in the Brazilian Federation.*

22. As Weinstein argues in *Color of Modernity*, "far from being just a by-product or reflection of already-existing uneven development, I would argue that discourses of difference are generative of policies and decisions that consolidate and exacerbate regional inequalities" (2). On the generation of regional identities during the era, see also Albuquerque Júnior, *Invention of the Northeast*; Campbell, *Region Out of Place;* and Silva, *República em migalhas*, especially Janaína Amado, "História e Região: Reconhecendo e Construindo Espaços," 7–15.

23. Pontes de Miranda, "A Nova Geração," *O Jornal*, 28 July 1922.

24. Brenno Ferraz do Amaral, "O Momento: A Geração do Centenario," *Revista do Brasil*, September 1922.

25. As Marc Bloch pointed out in *Historian's Craft*, generation is an often indistinct category of analysis, as "the periodicity of the generations is by no means regular" (186). But as he also pointed out, it is potentially a fruitful one, and it seems to be especially useful in considering "times out of time" like the civic rituals studied here, when they might become particularly salient.

26. Coutinho and Cabral, *Relatorio da viagem aérea Lisboa—Rio de Janeiro.*

27. On these projects, see in particular Besse, *Restructuring Patriarchy*; Corsi, *Estado Novo*; Lesser, *Negotiating National Identity*; Pandolfi, *Repensando o Estado Novo*; Williams, *Culture Wars in Brazil*; and Wolfe, *Working Women, Working Men.*

Chapter 1: Fishermen and Aviators

1. The total number of visitors is not known because organizers did not count the number of visitors on dates when admission was free. There were

3,626,402 paying visitors over the course of the exposition's run. Elkin, "Promoting a New Brazil," 362.

2. Motta, *A nação faz 100 anos*, 72.

3. "A glorificação de um desastre!" and Arthur Gaspar Vianna, "A estocada no nacionalismo: O 'raid' Lisbôa-Rio," *Gil Blas*, 16 and 24 June 1922.

4. "O Penoso Raid," *Careta*, 29 July 1922.

5. "A inconsciencia das multidões," *Gil Blas*, 9 June 1922. See also Vianna, "A estocada no nacionalismo."

6. Now little used, the term also carries both of these connotations in other languages, including Spanish, Italian, and French. See A. B. Ferreira, *Dicionario da língua portuguesa*, 1453, which renders the second meaning of "reide" as "Longa excursão a pé, a cavalo, de automóvel, avião, etc." It seems plausible that Portuguese speakers adopted this meaning of the term not directly from English practice but from the French, who had significant cultural influence on Brazil and other countries in the late nineteenth and early twentieth centuries. The Centre National de Ressources Textuelles et Lexicales notes the use of the term in a sporting sense to refer to a long-distance journey testing equipment and travelers as early as 1886 (https://www.cnrtl.fr/etymologie/raid).

7. "O grande *phoco* internacional e as modernas borboletas . . ." *Careta*, 16 September 1922.

8. For example, *Gil Blas* claimed the flight had been a failure from the moment of the aviators' crash landing at the São Pedro and São Paulo archipelago, because, it stated (incorrectly), the archipelago was not part of Brazil. "A glorificação de um desastre!"

9. Benjamin Costallat, "O poema das jangadas," *Jornal do Brasil*, 24 September 1922.

10. E. Cunha, *Rebellion in the Backlands*, 89.

11. Weinstein also points out that commentators have thus been able to use the discussion of region as a way of alluding to thorny racial questions without breaching Brazilians' sense of etiquette and cordiality. Weinstein, *Color of Modernity*, 6. See also Kraay, *Bahia's Independence*, esp. 171–78.

12. See Marques, "A viagem do presidente António José de Almeida," and Miranda, "Um 'voo' entre Portugal e Brasil."

13. The first replacement aircraft was delivered by a Brazilian naval vessel, the second by a Portuguese one.

14. When they crashed again, also at the São Pedro and São Paulo archipelago, it was an English merchant vessel, the *Paris City*, that saved them and returned them to Fernando de Noronha.

15. Some of this support is detailed in "A heroica proeza," *A Voz do Mar*, 29 October 1922. The writer quotes the Baiano raiders as saying they decided to undertake the journey after an appeal that they do so by the commander of the Brazilian navy cruiser *José Bonifácio*, Armando Pinna. Under Pinna and the

ship's previous commander, Frederico Villar, the crew of the cruiser had worked to organize the fishing cooperatives that many of the raiders belonged to, a mission depicted by Giovanni Roberto Protásio Bentes Filho as a direct attempt by the national government to tie fishing communities to the national community. The raids might be understood, then, as a demonstration of the effectiveness of that project. See Bentes Filho, "Do Norte ao Sul."

16. For example, see reports of the Santa Catarina governor, Raulino Horn, offering assistance to the Sozzi brothers in "Um grande 'raid' R. G. Sul—R. Janeiro," *Correio da Manhã*, 2 August 1922.

17. Antonio Azeredo, quoted in "Ecos e Noticias," *Jornal do Brasil*, 23 September 1922. The reward for the jangadeiros was made official by Decree no. 4923 of 26 January 1924. *Diário Oficial da União*, 2 February 1924.

18. "Raid New-York–Rio: Gloria aos bandeirantes do Azul," and A. Fernandes, "Raid 'Hinton-Martins,'" *Diario de Pernambuco*, 28 December 1922.

19. The Natalense writer Luís da Câmara Cascudo claimed (in *No caminho do avião*, 19) that Martins had been raised in Rio Grande do Norte, not Pernambuco.

20. While Martins often stated that he wanted to be referred to only as a Brazilian, which was honor enough for him, he also objected in the strongest possible terms whenever it was put to him that Brazilians had been under the impression that the more famous Hinton had organized and led the expedition, or that Martins was little more than a passenger. See, for example, "Raid New-York–Rio," *Jornal do Recife*, 24 December 1922.

21. "Raid New-York–Rio: Gloria aos bandeirantes do Azul."

22. "Raid New-York–Rio," *Jornal do Recife*, 30 December 1922.

23. "Raid New-York–Rio," *Jornal do Recife*, 21 January 1923.

24. "Raid New-York–Rio," *Jornal do Recife*, 23 January 1923.

25. "Raid New-York–Rio," *Jornal do Recife*, 27 January 1923.

26. "Raid New-York–Rio," *Jornal do Recife*, 28 January 1923.

27. "Á espera do premio," *Careta*, 4 August 1923.

28. "O Ultimo Dia de Homenagens a Momo," *O Jornal*, 13 February 1923, and "Os tres cortejos de Momo," *Revista da Semana*, 17 February 1923. The raid was also celebrated in the carnival events for 1923 in Recife, by the Bloco Mocidade do Torreão, and José Candido da Silva contributed to the popularization of the raid with his ragtime song "De New York ao Rio." On the former, see "O mundo vae se acabá," *Jornal do Recife*, 4 February 1923; on the latter, see photograph, *O Malho*, 14 April 1923.

29. "O raid aereo Portugal-Brasil," *Diario de Pernambuco*, 18 April 1922.

30. "O 'Raid' New-York–Rio," *Jornal do Recife*, 12 August 1922.

31. *Folha do Norte*, reprinted as "Raid New-York–Rio," *Jornal do Recife*, 24 December 1922.

32. As Joel Wolfe points out in *Autos and Progress*, the 1920s was a key de-

cade in the growth of automobile culture in Brazil, but car ownership was then a privilege of the elite. See especially chapter 2, 33–59.

33. Bocketti, *Invention of the Beautiful Game.*

34. Mendonça, *O Sport está deseducando a mocidade brasileira*; and Proposal 225 of 1922, *Diario do Congresso Nacional*, 4 October 1922.

35. In *Autos and Progress*, Wolfe calls Brazil's first cars "curiosities of the elite," 13–32.

36. "Por Ares Nunca Dantes Navegados," *O Jornal*, 8 and 23 April 1922.

37. A. Fernandes, "De uns e de uns outros . . ." *Diario de Pernambuco*, 2 June 1922.

38. Carlos Chiaccio, "Portugal Continua . . ." *Revista da Semana*, 24 June 1922.

39. "Por Ares Nunca Dantes Navegados," *O Jornal*, 8 and 23 April 1922; and "O sextante e o corrector," *Revista da Semana*, 3 June 1922.

40. "Por Ares Nunca Dantes Navegados," *O Jornal*, 8 April 1922.

41. See, for example, "O sextante e o corrector," *Revista da Semana*, 3 June 1922.

42. "Rabiscos," *Fon Fon*, 29 April 1922.

43. J. R., "Pontos da vista," *A República*, 6 June 1922.

44. "O Centenario," *Correio Paulistano*, 25 August 1922; and "Il caso Longobardi," *Il Pasquino Coloniale*, 25 November 1922. *Il Pasquino Coloniale* rejected the idea that the raid had scientific value, instead calling it "a sporting trip with no aim whatsoever."

45. "Raid New-York–Rio," *Jornal do Recife*, 24 December 1922.

46. "O 'Diario' no Ceará," *Diario de Pernambuco*, 15 July 1922.

47. "Notas da Semana," *O Malho*, 17 February 1923.

48. "Echos: De vagar se vae ao longe," *Jornal do Brasil*, 16 September 1922.

49. General Jonathas Barreto, "A Jangada do Norte," *Revista da Semana*, 14 October 1922. Barreto had been the director of the Colegio Militar.

50. J. R., "Pontos da vista," *A República*, 6 June 1922; and "Ethopéa [*sic*] Nautica," *A República* (Natal, Rio Grande do Norte), 19 August and 21 September 1922; "A Odysséa dos Jangadeiros," *Revista da Semana*, 2 September 1922; and "Senhoras e senhores," *O Imparcial*, 11 December 1922.

51. "Do extremo norte ao Rio em simples Jangada!" *Careta*, 30 September 1922. See also "Os pescadores que commemoram o centenario," *O Malho*, 7 October 1922, and "Tres mezes, oscillando no mar alto," *Revista da Semana*, 9 December 1922.

52. These were the jangadeiros from Rio Grande do Norte, Sergipe, Paraná, and São Paulo, the others arriving later on. "A passeata dos jangadeiros," *O Jornal*, 1 October 1922.

53. Olavo Bilac, quoted in Elkin, "Promoting a New Brazil," 239.

54. See coverage in the *Correio da Manhã* in May 1904, including "Jan-

gada 'Brasil,'" 6 May 1904, which noted the difficulties faced by the project's proponents.

55. J. R., "Pontos da vista," *A República*, 19 August 1922.

56. "Salvé Alagoas," *O Progresso* (Penedo, Alagoas), 12 December 1922.

57. Ruy Barbosa, quoted in "O 'raid' victorioso das canoas," *A República*, 3 October 1922.

58. "Echos: De vagar se vae ao longe."

59. Epitácio Pessoa, quoted in "A epopéa dos pescadores," *O Brasil*, 1 October 1922.

60. For example, Santos Dumont helped take the lead in offering tributes to the aviators when they departed for home. "A partida dos aviadores portuguezes," *O Jornal*, 5 October 1922.

61. See, for example, "Looping the Loop: Os heróes dos ares," *Careta*, 24 June 1922.

62. Gustavo Barroso, "O abraço do futuro," *Fon Fon*, 17 February 1923.

63. "Raid aéreo Portugal-Brasil," *A República*, 21 April 1922.

64. "Os Dois Heróes," *O Malho*, 17 June 1922.

65. Ruy Barbosa, quoted in "O 'raid' victorioso das canoas."

66. "A Epopéa dos Jangadeiros," *A Exposição de 1922*, November 1922.

67. "As heróicas viagens dos jangadeiros," *Revista da Semana*, 23 September 1922.

68. "Noticeiro: Os Jangadeiros," *Revista Maritima Brazileira*, October 1922.

69. Alberto Maranhão, quoted in *Diario do Congresso Nacional*, 11 October 1922.

70. "As heróicas viagens dos jangadeiros."

71. "Raid New-York–Rio," *Jornal do Recife*, 7 December 1922.

72. "Raid New-York–Rio: Gloria aos bandeirantes do Azul," *Jornal do Recife*, 28 December 1922.

73. Barroso, "O abraço do futuro."

74. J. L., "O raid aéreo," *A República*, 17 May 1922.

75. "Raid New-York–Rio: Gloria aos bandeirantes do Azul."

76. "A glorificação de um desastre!"

77. Vianna, "A estocada no nacionalismo."

78. Photo caption, and "A Collaboração dos jornalistas portuguezes," *Revista da Semana*, 24 June and 27 May 1922.

79. Marquez de Denis, "Semana Elegante," *Revista da Semana*, 8 April 1922.

80. Capitão X, "Semana Militar," *Revista da Semana*, 29 April 1922. Emphasis added.

81. On the possibility of creating a formal political arrangement between the two countries, see Bettencourt-Rodrigues, *Uma confederação luso-brasileira*.

82. "Looping the Loop: Os heróes dos ares."

83. "Brasil-Portugal" and "Entre Brasil e Portugal," *O Malho*, 15 April and

1 July 1922. See also "Por Ares Nunca D'antes Navegados," *O Jornal*, 20 April 1922, in which the paper said the raid belonged to "our same raça, of Portuguese and Brazilians."

84. "O 'raid' aereo Portugal-Brasil," *Diario de Pernambuco*, 6 June 1922; Estaquio Gomes, "Salvé Portugal!" and Arthur Alves Barbosa, "'Hoje, absortos nos lusos milagres . . . '" *Jornal do Recife*, 6 and 7 June 1922.

85. "Notas da Semana," *O Malho*, 20 May 1922.

86. "Notas da Semana," *O Malho*, 10 June 1922.

87. Peard, *Race, Place, and Medicine*; and Stepan, *"Hour of Eugenics,"* esp. 153–69.

88. Kuhlmann Júnior, *As Grandes Festas Didáticas*.

89. Wadsworth and Marko, "Children of the Pátria," 71.

90. R., "A voz do povo," *O Jornal do Brasil*, 29 September 1922.

91. "Topicos & Noticias," *Correio da Manhã*, 3 October 1922.

92. "Ergue-te-Jeca!" *A Voz do Mar*, 29 October 1922.

93. "Quando elle quer . . ." *O Malho*, 7 October 1922.

94. Costallat, "O poema das jangadas."

95. Admiral Raja Gabaglia, then Inspector de Portos e Costas, said at an event celebrating the raiders that the nation was leaving behind "that sad and callow look of the rumored 'géca-tatú.'" Beside the raiders, he also pointed to the work of the Confederação Geral dos Pescadores and its Boy Scouts troop in preparing the sailors of the future, who, he was sure, would be not Jécas but "men who were capable and useful to Brazil." Raja Gabaglia, quoted in "A linda festa, em Jurujuba, offerecida pelo Ministro da Marinha e Inspector de Portos e Costas aos bravos pescadores," *A Voz do Mar*, 29 October 1922.

96. See, for example, Hermes Fontes, "Á gloria dos humildes," *O Imparcial*, 16 September 1922.

97. "Looping the Loop: Heroismo Brasileiro," *Careta*, 30 September 1922.

98. Costallat, "O poema das jangadas," and Maranhão, speech in the Camara dos Deputados.

99. "Duas jangadas de pescadores nortistas: A chegada emocionante desses heróes obscuros," *Correio da Manhã*, 12 September 1922

100. R., "A voz do povo," *Jornal do Brasil*, 29 September 1922; "A Victoria dos Pescadores do Nordeste," *A República*, reprinted from *O Brasil*, 4 October 1922; and Paulo Vianna, quoted in "A odysséa emocionante dos jangadeiros do norte," *Correio da Manhã*, 21 September 1922.

101. Fontes, "Á gloria dos humildes."

102. On the ways that Brazilians in the nineteenth and twentieth centuries used the term, see especially Campbell, *Region Out of Place*, 77; and Kraay, "Between Brazil and Bahia," 265–66.

103. "O 'Diario' em Alagoas," *Diario de Pernambuco*, 15 December 1922; and José dos Reis Lisboa, quoted in "A chegada dos pescadores conterraneos," *A*

República, 20 October 1922. *A República* introduced its readers to the discourse in its frequent reprints of material from the capital's *O Brasil*, for example, in "A Victoria dos Pescadores do Nordeste," *A República*, 4 October 1922. Similarly, Recife's *A Noite* reprinted Costallat's "O poema das jangadas" on 19 October 1922.

104. Aside from the thousands of reports that quoted them at length and the hundreds of talks the two gave about the raid, Cabral and Coutinho published an entire volume dedicated to the accomplishment: Coutinho and Cabral, *Relatorio da viagem aérea Lisboa*.

105. The raiders from Rio Grande do Norte were Benjamin Alves de Mendonça, Manoel Duarte, Francisco Candido de Oliveira, João Soares do Nascimento, Philadelpho Thomaz Marinho, Sebastião Paulino, João Miguel, Ignacio Pedro, Manoel Claudino da Silva, Manoel Claudino Filho, Manoel Reinaldo, and Manoel Olyntho. From Alagoas came Umbelino José dos Santos, Eugenio Antonio de Oliveira, Joaquim Fastilino de Sant'Anna, and Pedro Ganhado da Silva. The Paranaenses were Virgilio Faria, José Ribeiro, Manuel Carlos Rodrigues, Antonio Rodrigues, Joaquim Tigre, Domingos Voador, Olirio Ventura, Praxedes Magalhães, and Valentim Tempestade. The Baianos were José Gomes Cardoso, Antonio Reginaldo Nascimento, Manoel Francisco Silva, Belmiro Galdino Silva, Eleonato Santos, João Encarnação, Benevenuto Avelino Santos, and João Augusto Sequeira. The Sergipanos were Manoel Olympio Mangueira, Manoel Francisco dos Santos, Manoel Antonio dos Santos, Possidorio Francisco dos Santos, João Cupertino da Silva, José Francisco dos Santos, and José Lopes dos Santos. The Gaúchos were João da Encarnação Menfuturo and Waldemar Arrojado. I have been unable to identify the names of the raiders from São Paulo and Ceará.

106. Costallat, "O poema das jangadas" and "Senhoras e senhores."

107. Costa Rego, speech in the Camara dos Deputados, quoted in *Diario do Congresso Nacional*, 25 November 1922.

108. Fontes, Á gloria dos humildes"; Armando de Virgilius, quoted in "A Federação do Remo e os Jangadeiros do Norte"; "O 'Diario' em Alagoas," *O Diario de Pernambuco*, 24 December 1922; Armando Pinna, quoted in Maranhão, speech in the Camara dos Deputados; Deoclecio Duarte, quoted in "A Exposição Internacional: Homenagens aos jangadeiros norte rio-grandenses," *O Jornal*, 10 October 1922; and "Notas da Semana," *O Malho*, 7 October 1922.

109. Paulo Vianna, quoted in "A odysséa emocionante dos jangadeiros do norte." Others did the same in other locations; for example, José dos Reis Lisboa, the official orator of the José Bonifácio fishing cooperative, spoke frequently on behalf of the Natalense raiders. See, for example, "O Centenario: 'Raid' dos pescadores," *A República*, 24 August 1922.

110. "As heróicas viagens dos jangadeiros."

111. "A odysséa emocionante dos jangadeiros do norte."

112. Paulo Vianna, quoted in "A odysséa emocionante dos jangadeiros do norte." Emphasis added.

113. Paulo Vianna, quoted in "A odysséa emocionante dos jangadeiros do norte."

114. Diacon, *Stringing Together a Nation*, 14.

115. "Por Ares Nunca Dantes Navegados . . ." *O Jornal*, 9 May 1922.

116. For example, the Sergipanos traveled 790 nautical miles or 1,463 kilometers, according to the placard on their truck. Photograph, "Os jangadeiros acolhidos pelo Sr. Presidente da Republica," *Revista da Semana*, 7 October 1922.

117. "Raid New York–Rio," *Diario de Pernambuco*, 23 December 1922.

118. See, for example, "Raid New-York–Rio," *Jornal do Recife*, 27 and 28 January 1923. These editions were given over to coverage of the raiders' visit, with numerous articles on the journey and the raiders, as well as large photographs of the crew members, their airplane, and the Recifenses who gathered to celebrate their accomplishment.

119. The first part was "A Primeira Viagem Aerea de Portugal ao Brasil," *Revista da Semana*, 8 July 1922.

120. "Vespucio e a ilha Fernão de Noronha," *Revista da Semana* 10 June 1922. For another example of introducing readers to Fernando de Noronha, see also "Portugal-Brasil: O grande 'raid' aereo Lisbôa-Rio," *Fon Fon*, 22 April 1922.

121. "Ligando as Tres Americas pelo Ar," *Revista da Semana*, 17 February 1923.

122. "Da Bahia ao Rio, a Pé," *Revista da Semana*, 16 December 1922.

123. Affonso Celso, "Preciosidade desaproveitada," *Jornal do Brasil*, 31 August 1922.

124. See, for example, "O 'Jornal' no Rio Grande do Norte," *Jornal do Recife*, 28 December 1922.

125. The congressional daily recorded that this passage was particularly well received. Maranhão, quoted in *Diario do Congresso Nacional*, 11 October 1922.

126. "Commentarios: Raça Forte," *O Jornal*, 8 October 1922.

127. Costallat, "O poema das jangadas."

128. "Commentarios: Raça Forte."

129. Costallat, "O poema das jangadas."

130. Albuquerque Júnior, *Invention of the Brazilian Northeast*.

131. These episodes are discussed in chapter 2.

132. Longobardi claimed, for example, to have identified oil deposits in Mato Grosso. "Expedição italiana que percorreu parte do Brasil," *O Estado* (Florianópolis, Santa Catarina), 7 March 1923.

133. João Ninguem, "Azas a Portugal," *Diario de Pernambuco*, special edition, 15 May 1922.

134. Antonio Azeredo, quoted in "Ecos e Noticias." The award was formalized in Decree 4712 of 27 July 1923, 10 contos of the 200 contos de réis set aside

under amendment for the Sozzi brothers for their bicycle raid from Rio Grande do Sul. The Brazilian government awarded the Portuguese aviators 50 contos in Decree 4956 of 18 October 1922; and Walter Hinton and Euclides Pinto Martins 100 contos in Decree 4823 of 26 January 1924. *Diário Oficial da União*, 21 October 1922, 7 August 1923, and 2 February 1924. Also, the Rio de Janeiro city council awarded Anésia Pinheiro Machado 50 contos for completing her raid to the city from São Paulo. "Conselho Municipal," *Jornal do Brasil*, 4 November 1922.

135. Burns, *Flying Firsts of Walter Hinton*, 174–91.

136. "O 'Jornal' no Rio Grande do Norte," *Jornal do Recife*, 27 October 1922.

137. "Os heroes do mar," *A República*, 21 October 1922. On the dispute, see Cunha, "Pátria e dever." Cunha depicts the conflict as demonstrating the agency and complexity of the community of fishermen in Natal's cooperatives, who, he says, "were not only the happy patriots who celebrated Independence, but also those marginalized from society, insecure in their rights" (52).

Chapter 2: A Nation of Parts

1. Rezende, "The Raw and the Manufactured," 29.

2. Rezende, "The Raw and the Manufactured"; Motta, *A nação faz 100 anos*; and Elkin, "Promoting a New Brazil."

3. "As Industrias Manufactureiras de S. Paulo," *A Exposição de 1922*, nos. 14–15 (no month), 1923.

4. Rydell, *All the World's a Fair*; Plum, *World Exhibitions in the Nineteenth Century*; and Greenhalgh, *Ephemeral Vistas*.

5. Andermann, "Tournaments of Value," 333–34.

6. Rezende, "Of Coffee, Nature and Exclusion," 270.

7. Pesavento, *Exposições Universais*.

8. For example, exhibitions in 1861, 1866, 1873, 1875, 1889, and 1892 were organized to prepare for participation in major exhibitions hosted by London (1862), Paris (1867 and 1889), Vienna (1873), Philadelphia (1876), and Chicago (1892), respectively.

9. Andermann, "Espetáculos da diferença."

10. *Guia Oficial da Exposição Nacional de 1908*, quoted in Elkin, "Promoting a New Brazil," 203n18.

11. Levy, *Entre Palácios e Pavilhões*, 15.

12. Benchimol, *Pereira Passos*.

13. Kessel, *A vitrine e o espelho*.

14. Kessel, *Arquitetura Neocolonial no Brasil*; and Levy, *A Exposição do Centenário*.

15. Tenorio-Trillo, "Tropical Cuauhtémoc." See also Levy, *A Exposição do Centenário*, 223–25.

16. Levy, *A Exposição do Centenário*, 216. The statue of "Amicitia" was completed in time for the centenary, but it took several more years to complete the base, which was finally inaugurated only in 1931.

17. Armando de Oliveira, quoted in Kessel, *Arquitetura Neocolonial no Brasil*, epigraph, n.p.

18. Levy identifies Sampaio as an advocate for the neocolonial approach, but Kessel suggests that the mayor was ambivalent about the style. See Levy, *A Exposição do Centenário*, 44–45; and Kessel, *Arquitetura Neocolonial no Brasil*, 120–22.

19. Mário de Andrade, quoted in Kessel, *Arquitetura Neocolonial no Brasil*, 116. On Ricardo Severo, see J. Silva, "A construção do nacional."

20. Levy, *A Exposição do Centenário*, 172–79, 189–94, and 201–4.

21. Levy, *A Exposição do Centenário*, 235.

22. "Sete de Setembro," *A Exposição de 1922*, September 1922.

23. Elkin, "Promoting a New Brazil," 20.

24. The diorama is described in "Chronica da Exposição," *A Exposição de 1922*, September 1922.

25. Elkin, "Promoting a New Brazil," 19.

26. "A formidavel força economica e productiva do Estado de São Paulo," *A Exposição de 1922*, December 1922. Mônica Pimenta Velloso points out that for some nationalists—especially those in São Paulo who hoped to reorient the nation toward its interior—maps carried an almost spiritual dimension. She writes that for them "the map of Brazil was transformed into an object of civic and poetic worship, because through it it was possible to create national feeling." Velloso, *A brasilidade verde-amarela*, 52.

27. "O Pavilhão Britannico na Exposição Internacional do Centenario," *A Exposição de 1922*, nos. 14–15 (no month), 1923. Original in English.

28. Commissão Organizadora da Exposição—Delegacia no Estado do Pernambuco—Prestação de contas que faz o Dr. Jayme Castello Branco Coimbra, dos supprimentos na importancia de Rs. 17:500$000, remettidos pela Thesouraria da Commissão Organizadora, por intermedio do Banco do Brasil, Comissão Executiva da Comemoração do Centenário da Independência, 1921 a 1925, Código do Fundo, 1I, Seção de Guarda SDE, SDE 045, box 2417, Arquivo Nacional do Brasil.

29. Julio Azambuja, letter to Exms. Drs. Vice-Presidente e mais Illustres membros da Commissão do Ministerio da Agricultura na Exposição do Centenario, 22 September 1921, in folder Rio Grande do Sul: Delegado da Commissão Organizadora 35 I; and Julio Azambuja, letter to Exms. Drs. Vice-Presidente e mais Illustres membros da Commissão do Ministerio da Agricultura na Exposição do Centenario, 14 January 1922, and telegram response, 28 January 1922, in folder Rio Grande do Sul: Delegado da Commissão Organizadora 35 II, Comissão Executiva da Comemoração do Centenário da Independência, 1921 a

1925, Código do Fundo, 1I, Seção de Guarda SDE, SDE 045, box 2417, Arquivo Nacional do Brasil.

30. Wanderlino Nogueira gave a lecture on his raid "a pé" from Bahia to the capital in the Palácio das Festas in December 1922. "Da Bahia ao Rio, a Pé," *Revista da Semana*, 16 December 1922.

31. The commission awarded the institute 132 contos de réis. File "Verba para despeza orçada," Comissão Executiva da Comemoração do Centenário da Independência, 1921 a 1925, Código do Fundo, 1I, Seção de Guarda SDE, SDE 045, box 1177, Arquivo Nacional do Brasil.

32. The centenary commission awarded the Rondon commission a large sum to sponsor the publication of these works, ultimately amounting to 216 contos de réis. Files "Directoria de Contabilidade 1a Secção of the Secretaria de Estado da Justiça e Negocios Interiores" and "Verba para despeza orçada," Comissão Executiva da Comemoração do Centenário da Independência, 1921 a 1925, Código do Fundo, 1I, Seção de Guarda SDE, SDE 045, boxes 1177 and 2312, Arquivo Nacional do Brasil. On the life and career of Rondon, see Diacon, *Stringing Together a Nation.*

33. "A secção indígena na Exposição da Independencia" and "Zicunati," *Revista da Semana*, 21 April 1923 and 21 October 1922.

34. "Zicunati."

35. "A Epopéa dos Jangadeiros." On the children's performances and the Museu da Criança, see Wadsworth and Marko, "Children of the Pátria"; and Wadsworth, "Brasil en 1922."

36. As Noah Elkin writes, the fair organizers saw the event as an opportunity to show that Brazil could play a leading role in the attempt "to recapture the buoyant optimism of the pre-war *belle époque* and to restore shattered faith in the cosmopolitan ideals of liberalism and progress." Elkin, "Promoting a New Brazil," 257.

37. Padua Rezende, "A Exposição Nacional de 1922," *A Exposição de 1922*, July 1922.

38. Motta, *A nação faz 100 anos*, 71.

39. Motta, *A nação faz 100 anos*, 102.

40. Letter from João Maurico de Sampaio Vianna to Delfim Carlos B. Silva, 20 April 1922. Caixa 2348.

41. Letter from João Maurico de Sampaio Vianna to Delfim Carlos B. Silva, 14 June 1922. Caixa 2348.

42. Letter from Delfim Carlos B. Silva to João Mauricio de Sampaio Vianna, 17 June 1922. Caixa 2348.

43. "A formidavel força economica e productiva do Estado de São Paulo"; and "S. Paulo na Exposição de Flores e Fructas," *A Exposição de 1922*, January 1923.

44. Letter from Sampaio Vianna to Delfim Carlos, 20 April 1922. Caixa 2407.

45. "A formidavel força economica e productiva do Estado de São Paulo." The writer used the English "leader," further emphasizing the state's modernity.

46. Epitácio Pessoa, quoted in "A formidavel força economica e productiva do Estado de São Paulo."

47. Letters from José Garibaldi Dantas to Delfim Carlos B. Silva, 2 February and 27 April 1922. Caixa 2407.

48. Letters from José Garibaldi Dantas to Delfim Carlos B. Silva, 2 February and 24 May 1922. Caixa 2407. Dantas stated that the 50 contos contributed by Rio Grande was a contribution toward the construction of the Palácio das Indústrias, but this seems to have been an error; state contributions helped build the Palácio dos Estados.

49. Letter from José Garibaldi Dantas to Delfim Carlos B. Silva, 24 May 1922. Caixa 2407.

50. Letter from José Garibaldi Dantas to Delfim Carlos B. Silva, 27 April 1922. Caixa 2407.

51. Letter from José Garibaldi Dantas to Delfim Carlos B. Silva, 24 May 1922. Caixa 2407.

52. Letter from José Garibaldi Dantas to Delfim Carlos B. Silva, 24 May 1922. Caixa 2407.

53. Letter from Joaquim Pessôa Cavalcanti to Delfim Carlos B. Silva, no date. Caixa 2407.

54. Letter from Joaquim Pessôa Cavalcanti to Delfim Carlos B. Silva, no date. Caixa 2407.

55. Letter from José Garibaldi Dantas to Delfim Carlos B. Silva, 27 April 1922; and Letter from Joaquim Pessôa Cavalcanti to Delfim Carlos B. Silva, no date. Caixa 2407.

56. For example, see Sandra Jatahy Pesavento's demonstration of Rio Grande do Sul's interest in exhibitions in *Exposições Universais*, esp. 226–30.

57. Letter to the editor, "Exposição do Centenario," *Diario de Pernambuco*, 4 March 1922; and "A Exposição do Centenario," *Correio do Povo*, 22 July 1922.

58. Letter from Jayme Castello Branco Coimbra to Antonio Olyntho, 21 October 1921. Caixa 2419.

59. A. Fernandes, "De uns e de outros . . ." *Diario de Pernambuco*, 2 December 1922.

60. "O fracasso," *Jornal do Recife*, 26 January 1922.

61. Telegram from Jayme Coimbra to "Off Exposição Rio," 24 March 1922. Caixa 2419.

62. Telegram from Simões Lopes to the Governor of Pernambuco, 4 April 1922. Caixa 2419.

63. "O Assucar e a Exposição do Centenario," *Diario de Pernambuco*, 12 August 1922.

64. Letter from Jayme Coimbra to Delphim Carlos Silva, 23 May 1922. Caixa 2419.

65. See file labeled "Serviço de Films: Operador Comelli," April–June 1922. Caixa 2293.

66. In his yearly message to the state assembly, Medeiros highlighted the most impressive indications of the Gaúcho contribution, which included 739 items weighing almost 90,000 kilograms and worth over 442 contos de réis. "Mensagem apresentada pelo Presidente do Estado, dr. A. A. Borges de Medeiros," *A Federação*, 17 October 1922.

67. Letter from Julio Azambuja to Ildefonso Soares Pinto, 30 September 1921. Caixa 2417. Pinto served as president of the state commission.

68. Letter from Julio Azambuja to Exms. Drs. Vice-Presidente e mais Illustres membros da Commissão do Ministerio da Agricultura, Industria e Commercio na Exposição do Centenario, 8 October 1921. Caixa 2417. See also Letter from Julio Azambuja to Ildefonso Soares Pinto, 3 November 1921. Caixa 2417.

69. Letter from Antonio Olyntho to Julio Azambuja, 10 November 1921. Caixa 2417.

70. Letter from Julio Azambuja to Ildefonso Soares Pinto, 3 November 1921; Telegram from Julio Azambuja to Exposição Rio, 9 July 1922; and "Exposição do Centenario," *A Federação*, 27 April 1922.

71. Julio Azambuja, quoted in "Exposição do Centenario," *A Federação*, 27 April 1922.

72. Telegram from Julio Azambuja to Exposição Rio, 9 July 1922. Caixa 2417.

73. See, for example, "A Exposição do Centenario," *Correio do Povo*, 22 July 1922. Coverage in *A Federação* tended to be limited to wire stories written in Rio de Janeiro, and to focus on foreign pavilions and participation.

74. Maria Antonieta Antonacci depicts Medeiros as a committed positivist unwilling to use state resources on behalf of private interests, as he demonstrated when he refused support to Gaúcho ranchers during the economic crisis of 1921. This might explain his unwillingness to do more in support of the state's participation in the exhibition in 1922, though his broader policy of promoting economic development and diversification would seem to have been well matched to involvement in the event. Antonacci, *RS: as oposições*, 39.

75. On Pernambuco, see Levine, *Pernambuco in the Brazilian Federation*, 81–84. On Rio Grande do Sul, see Love, *Rio Grande do Sul*, 201–7.

76. "Commentarios," *O Separatista*, 6 September 1922.

77. See, for example, "O Separatismo em face da successão presidencial," *O Separatista*, 14 November 1922.

78. See, for example, Amaro de Azambuja Villanova, "Separatismo?" and "Ideologia separatista e o caracter rio-grandense," *Correio do Povo*, 7 September 1922 and 1 July 1923.

79. José Luiz de Almeida Martins Costa, "Separatismo," *Correio do Povo*, 20 August 1922.

80. Mem de Sá, "Liga Rio-Grandense Nacionalista," *O Nacionalista*, August 1922.

81. "Semana Militar," *Revista da Semana*, 19 August 1922.

82. J. R., "Commentarios . . ." *O Separatista*, 10 September 1922.

83. Amaro de Azambuja Villanova, "Separatismo?" *Correio do Povo*, 7 September 1922.

84. "Pró-Assis Brasil," *Correio do Povo*, 21 November 1922.

85. Untitled announcement, *O Separatista*, 6 August 1922.

86. Eduardo Pacheco de Andrade, "De cócoras, não!" *O Separatista*, 14 August 1922. For coverage of the episode, see also "Separatismo," *A Manhã* (Porto Alegre), 4 and 12 August 1922.

87. "Commentarios . . ." *O Separatista*, 6 September 1922.

88. Antonius, "Chronica: As Festas do Centenario," and "Commentarios . . ." *O Separatista*, 6 August and 6 September 1922.

89. Ponta Grossa, "Eis a festa" and "O fim da festa," *O Separatista*, 10 and 14 September 1922.

90. "As commemorações do Centenario," *Correio do Povo*, 2 September 1922.

91. Letter from "Um patriota" to the editor, *Correio do Povo*, 1 September 1922.

92. Fittingly, the paper was especially vexed by the new "lei da imprensa" approved in mid-1922 which limited the freedoms of speech and the press. "Um seculo de independencia politica," *Imprensa*, August–September 1922.

93. José Pereira Coelho de Souza, quoted in "As commemorações do Centenario," and Gastão Dias, quoted in "As commemorações do Centenario," *Correio do Povo*, 14 and 20 September 1922.

94. "Pela politica," *Jornal do Recife*, 18 June 1922.

95. Mário Rodrigues, "Monstros!" *Correio da Manhã*, reprinted in *Jornal do Recife*, 16 June 1922.

96. "Pela politica," *Jornal do Recife*, 18 June 1922.

97. A. Carneiro Leão, *Jornal do Brasil*, reprinted in "Ultima Hora," *Jornal do Recife*, 18 June 1922.

98. José Euclides, "Civilisação de fachada," *Jornal do Recife*, 14 September 1922.

99. A. Fernandes, "De uns e de outros . . ." *Diario de Pernambuco*, 3 June 1922.

100. A. Fernandes, "De uns e de outros . . ." *Diario de Pernambuco*, 19 August 1922.

101. "Congresso da Lavoura do Nordeste" and "Congresso da Lavoura do Nordeste Brasileiro," *Jornal do Recife*, 4 November 1922 and 7 January 1923.

102. Mário Melo, quoted in "Commemoração civica," *Diario de Pernambuco*, 28 January 1922.

103. "O triste caso de Pernambuco" and "O sr. Epitacio Pessoa utilize-se das carabinas do Exercito para entregar o governo de Pernambuco aos seus parentes contrabandistas e incendiarios!" *Correio da Manhã*, 27 and 30 May 1922.

104. "A Intervenção em Pernambuco," *Jornal do Brasil*, 24 May 1922.

105. "Boatos?" *Jornal do Brasil*, 25 May 1922.

106. "O Centenario nos Estados" and "Centenario nos Estados," *O Brasil*, both 10 September 1922.

107. "Écos do Centenario nos Estados" and "Écos do Centenario em Pernambuco," *O Malho*, 20 January and 10 February 1923.

108. "A Evolução Agricola e Industrial do Estado de São Paulo," *A Exposição de 1922*, November 1922.

109. "Chronica da Exposição," *A Exposição de 1922*," February 1923.

110. João Luís Alves, "Encerramento Official da Exposição Internacional de 1922," *A Exposição de 1922*, nos. 17–18 (no month), 1923. The federal district contributed 642 exhibitors, Minas Gerais, 878, Rio de Janeiro 341, and São Paulo 577. According to the data provided by the minister, all the other states combined to contribute 3,575, with only Ceará (1,000) and Bahia (433) participating at a level that matched the states of the Southeast. He stated that there had been 308 contributors from Paraíba, which was more than 100 fewer than Joaquim Pessôa Cavalcanti had claimed in his final report as the commission's delegate in the state.

111. Mario de Lima, "Encerramento Official da Exposição Internacional de 1922," *A Exposição de 1922*, nos. 17–18 (no month), 1923.

112. Bocketti, *Invention of the Beautiful Game*.

113. Hobsbawm, *Nations and Nationalism since 1780*, 143.

114. Torres, "Latin American 'Olympic Explosion,'" 1088–111.

115. Cancella, "O esporte e as Forças Armadas," 153–68.

116. José da Silva, quoted in Karina Barbosa Cancella, "As forças armadas e os jogos esportivos do centenário de 1922," in Santos and Melo, *1922*, 137.

117. João Manuel C. Malaia Santos, "O Rio de Janeiro e os jogos de 1922: economia de um projeto esportivo," in Santos and Melo, *1922*, 77–78.

118. Mário Pollo, "Historico do Fluminense Football Club," unpublished manuscript. Archive of the Fluminense Football Club.

119. On the stadium and its controversies, see Bocketti, *Invention of the Beautiful Game*, 51–57; and Santos, "O Rio de Janeiro e os jogos de 1922," 58–80.

120. Torres, *Jogos Olímpicos Latino-Americanos*, 129. Torres also narrates the preparations for the games, including the interventions of the international organizations and the tensions among Brazilian administrators (118–23).

121. The organization recognized the Rio de Janeiro games and named the athletics competitions the Third South American Track and Field Cham-

pionship, but in 1924 voided the results. See Torres, *Jogos Olímpicos Latino-Americanos*, 138.

122. "Projectos: n. 225—1922," *Diário do Congresso Nacional*, 4 October 1922. On the controversies that troubled the Jogos Olímpicos Latino-Americanos, see Torres, *Jogos Olímpicos Latino-Americanos*, esp. 126–27.

123. Maurício Drumond, "Os jogos esportivos do centenário: o ponto de vista da política," in Santos and Melo, *1922*, 15–36.

124. Arthur Friedenreich, quoted in "Os sports no Centenario," *Correio da Manhã*, 27 September 1922.

125. Confederação Brasileira Desportos, quoted in "Os sports no Centenario," *Correio da Manhã*, 29 September 1922.

126. See, for example, an interview with the vice president of the Associação Paulista de Sports Athleticos, Mariano Procopio, in "Os sports no Centenario," *Correio da Manhã*, 30 September 1922; and "Football: Os Paulistas na equipe nacional," *Correio Paulistano*, 6 October 1922.

127. Vicari and Mazo, "Commemorações do Centenário," 8.

128. "Pernambuco no Centenario" and "Foot-ball: Pernambuco no Centenario," *Diario de Pernambuco*, 9 September 1921 and 27 January 1922.

129. "Foot-ball: Pernambuco no Centenario."

130. Octávio Moraes, "A Campanha do Athletismo em Pernambuco," *Diario de Pernambuco*, 10 September 1922.

131. "Foot-ball: Pernambuco no Centenario."

132. "Football: Telegramma Auspiciosa," *Diario de Pernambuco*, 28 July 1922.

133. Cicero Brasileiro de Mello, quoted in "Foot-ball: Como Pernambuco pretende commemorar o Centenario," *Diario de Pernambuco*, 23 February 1922.

134. "Foot-ball: Pernambuco no Centenario."

135. Mello, quoted in "Foot-ball: Como Pernambuco pretende commemorar o Centenario."

136. "Sport," *Jornal do Recife*, 16 July 1922.

137. "Football: Telegramma Auspiciosa."

138. "Foot-ball: Como Pernambuco pretende commemorar o Centenario"; and "Varias" and "A Subvenção á 'Liga P. D. Terrestres," *Diario de Pernambuco*, 24 February and 9 July 1922.

139. The Liga commission invited the participation of sportsmen and athletes in the Pernambuco cities and towns of Olinda, Goyanna, Limoeiro, Timbauba, Jaboatão, Victoria, Bezerros, Caruarú, Garanhuns, Quipapá, Palmares, Gamelleira, and Barreiros. "Sport," *Jornal do Recife*, 19 July 1922.

140. "Football: Telegramma Auspiciosa."

141. "Sport," *Diario de Pernambuco*, 17 September 1922.

142. "Sport," *Diario de Pernambuco*, 25 June 1922.

143. "Sport," *Jornal do Recife*, 26 September 1922.

144. A. Fernandes, "De uns e de outros . . ." *Diario de Pernambuco*, 16 September 1922.

145. As Courtney Campbell has shown, Pernambucanos continued to look to sports to articulate their sense of themselves as northeasterners and as Brazilians in later years, for example, in their lobbying to host a match of the 1950 World Cup. Campbell, *Region Out of Place*, 121–34.

146. Mello, quoted in "Foot-ball: Como Pernambuco pretende commemorar o Centenario."

147. "Viva o Brasil!" *Jornal do Recife*, 9 November 1922.

148. "Um prenuncio de Renascença," *Jornal do Recife*, 13 October 1922.

Chapter 3: The Uses of Independence and Other Histories

1. See, for example, Lyra, "Memória da Independência," 177.

2. E. Costa, *Brazilian Empire*; Kraay, *Days of National Festivity*; and Sandes, *A Invenção da Nação*.

3. Sandes, *A Invenção da Nação*, 27.

4. E. Costa, *Brazilian Empire*, 37–39.

5. Kraay, *Days of National Festivity*, 166.

6. Menezes, *Festas Nacionaes*, 123 and 126.

7. Oliveira, "As festas que a República manda guardar," 182–84.

8. Carvalho, *Formation of Souls*, 59–82.

9. Sandes, *A Invenção da Nação*, 12.

10. Affonso Celso, "Écos do Congresso Eucharistico," *Jornal do Brasil*, 4 October 1922.

11. Carlos Leite, "O Centenario do 'Fico,'" *Jornal do Brasil*, 8 January 1922.

12. "O primeiro grande passo para a proclamação da independencia," *Correio da Manhã*, 9 January 1922.

13. "Como é para bem de todos . . . Commemora-se amanhã o centenario da historica phrase de Pedro I," *Correio da Manhã*, 8 January 1922.

14. Victruvio Marcondes, "O 'Fico,'" *Gil Blas*, 6 January 1922.

15. "Os que não queriam consagrar o 'Fico' . . ." *Correio da Manhã*, 8 January 1922; and Escragnolle Doria, "José Clemente Pereira," *Revista da Semana*, 21 January 1922.

16. "Desfiguração Impossivel," *Correio da Manhã*, 9 January 1922.

17. Augusto Olímpio Viveiros de Castro, quoted in "Commemorou-se hontem com grande solemnindade o primeiro centenario do 'Fico,'" *Correio da Manhã*, 10 January 1922.

18. Sandes, *A Invenção da Nação*, esp. 187.

19. Sandes, *A Invenção da Nação*, 186. The institution began this work with one of the first projects it undertook to celebrate the centenary, the posthumous publication of Francisco Adolpho de Varnhagen's *História da Independência* in

1916. The highly influential nineteenth-century historian had emphasized the connection to Portugal in his work on Brazilian history, depicting the nation as fundamentally Portuguese. The decision to publish his uncompleted study of independence set the pattern for the work the institution would undertake in 1922, for it depicted Pedro in a sympathetic light and the violent spasms of the Northeast as unproductive and even "antinational." Sandes, *A Invenção da Nação*, 27. In regard to this effort it is worth noting the historical work of the monarchist diplomat Manuel Oliveira Lima. In *O Movimento da Independência, 1821–1822*, he focused closely on the prince and his advisers while also looking to reconcile regional histories into a single national story. Wilma Peres Costa calls it "the most important and representative work published during the first centenary of Independence . . . without doubt." Costa, "A Independência na historiografia brasileira," in Jancsó, *Independência*, 68. See also Dutra, "Mirror of History," 84–87.

20. On earlier renderings of independence history in Bahia, see Kraay, *Bahia's Independence*.

21. Käfer, "Entre a memória e a história," 75.

22. Käfer, "Entre a memória e a história," 67. As the secretary of the Commissão Promotora dos Congressos do Centenário da Independência, Calmon helped organize the official events of the centenary.

23. Guimarães, *Da Escola Palatina ao Silogeu*, 101, emphasis in the original. The italicized phrases were offered by Jônatas Serrano in the *Dicionário*.

24. On this process, see especially E. Silva, "A República comemora o Império."

25. The first number with the designation was published on 7 September 1921.

26. As Sandes points out, in practice this choice meant a preference for narration rather than interpretation, but the choice of which episodes to narrate and which actors to focus on functioned as an argument in its own right—about what and whom were important to the story of independence and the meaning of Brazil.

27. Mario Behring, "Os Prodromos da Independencia," *Illustração Brasileira*, 7 September 1921–15 August 1922.

28. Mario Behring, "O Precursor," *Illustração Brasileira*, 15 November 1922.

29. Mário Melo, "A contribuição de Pernambuco para a Independencia do Brasil: A Revolução Republicana de 1710," *Illustração Brasileira*, 15 November 1922.

30. Assis Cintra, quoted in Käfer, "Entre a memória e a história," 57n63.

31. Reis Carvalho, "A Independencia do Brasil," *Illustração Brasileira*, 7 September 1922.

32. Reis Carvalho, "Os feriados brasileiros," *Illustração Brasileira*, 15 August 1922.

33. "VII de Setembro," *A Exposição de 1922*, September 1922.

34. The editorial suggested that among the Inconfidentes, Tiradentes was the most important, but that he was also an ineffective figure because of his lack of guile; he was, the magazine said, "the most humble and the most anonymous, the most ingenuous and the most sincere, and therefore the most awkward," so independence had to wait for a figure of action, that is, Pedro. "Cem annos de Independencia," *O Malho*, 9 September 1922. Eugenio Egas, "1822–1922," *A Leitura para Todos*, September 1922.

35. "Independencia ou Morte!" *Revista da Semana*, 9 September 1922.

36. Alice de Serpa, "Estudos graphologicos," *Revista da Semana*, 4 March 1922.

37. Escragnolle Doria, "A Viagem da Independencia," *Revista da Semana*, 9 September 1922.

38. Mucio Leão, "Literatura do centenario," *Correio da Manhã*, 7 September 1922.

39. "Centenario da Independencia," Carlos Leite, "O Centenario do 'Fico,'" and Oswaldo Orico, Pedro I e a lei da imprensa," *Jornal do Brasil*, 29 September, 8 January, and 10 October 1922.

40. "Independencia ou morte!" *O Imparcial*, 7 September 1922.

41. "A maior data da nossa patria" and "Rocha Pombo, "Independencia ou Morte!" *A Noite*, 7 September 1922 and 7 September 1922 special edition.

42. For example, *O Brasil* did not even mention the prince in its editorial for the centenary date. "Cyclo Historico Brasileiro," *O Brasil*, 7 September 1922.

43. Elkin, "1922, O encontro do efêmero com a permanência," 131.

44. R. Abreu, *A fabricação do imortal* and J. Costa, "O Culto da Saudade."

45. João do Norte (Gustavo Barroso), "Culto da Saudade," *Jornal do Commercio*, 22 December 1912. Barroso developed the argument in several pieces before 1922, for example, in the *Revista da Semana*, where he argued that "we cannot have national identity without love of the past and the lessons of past accomplishments." "Os Dragões da Independencia," *Revista da Semana*, 23 December 1916.

46. "Está installado o Museu Historico," *Jornal do Brasil*, 12 October 1922.

47. "Está installado o Museu Historico."

48. Elkin, "Promoting a New Brazil," 282.

49. J. Costa, "O Culto da Saudade," 59.

50. R. Abreu, *A fabricação do imortal*, 183–84.

51. Duarte Leite, quoted in "O Pavilhão de Portugal," *Illustração Brasileira*, 20 March 1922; and António de Almeida, quoted in "A saudação ao povo brasileiro," *America Brasileira*, Edição do Centenario, 1922.

52. Epitácio Pessoa, quoted in "Portugal—Brasil: As homenagens ao Presidente Antonio José de Almeida desde a sua chegada ao Rio," *Jornal do Brasil*, 19 September 1922.

53. See, for example, "O 'Marechal da Victoria,'" *Correio da Manhã*, 1 September 1922.

54. Alzira Caldas de Azevedo, quoted in "Prelecções sobe o 7 de Setembro nas escolas municipaes," *O Brasil*, 7 September 1922.

55. "Homenagem a D. Pedro I," *Jornal do Brasil*, 29 September 1922.

56. Lia de Santa Clara, quoted in "Uma tocante homenagem a Pedro I," *O Paiz*, 29 September 1922. Santa Clara was the pseudonym used by the writer Paulina Campelo Macedo, who wrote for the *União Portuguesa* and *O Paiz*, among other publications. On Macedo's career and her role in promoting Luso-Brazilian relations, see Cruz, "Paulina Campelo Macedo."

57. Elkin suggests that Pessoa's appointment of Barroso as director of the Museu Histórico should be understood in this context. Elkin, "Promoting a New Brazil," 279.

58. Affonso Celso, "Sem Effusão de Sangue?" *Jornal do Brasil*, 30 March 1922.

59. Marly Motta, "'São Paulo é a Cabeça da Nação': Historiografia Regional e História Nacional no Brasil Republicano," in Nunes and Freire, *Historiografias Portuguesa e Brasileira*, 336–37.

60. "O Centenario," *Correio Paulistano*, 8 September 1922.

61. Chernavsky, *A construção dos mitos e heróis*, 74–75.

62. These included the Pernambucano revolutionary José de Barros Falcão de Lacerda and the Franco-Brazilian military officer Teodoro de Beaurepaire. Affonso de E. Taunay, "O Museu Paulista," *Illustração Brasileira*, 25 December 1922.

63. Eugenio Egas, "O Centenario," *Correio Paulistano*, 8 September 1922.

64. A. C. Ferreira, *A epopéia bandeirante*, 269. See also Weinstein, *Color of Modernity*, 36–44.

65. Adolpho Pinto, "O Centenario da Independencia," *Revista do Brasil*, January 1916.

66. Adolpho Augusto Pinto, "O Culto do Passado e o Centenario da Independencia," *Revista do Brasil*, November 1917.

67. Rocha Pombo, "Factos e Ideas: A Terra Paulista e as suas Grandes Legendas," *Revista do Brasil*, July 1916.

68. Ricardo Severo, quoted in "Uma sympathica inciativa: Como a colonia portugueza de São Paulo pretende commemorar o Centenario da Independencia" and Helios, "Monumento das Bandeiras," *Correio Paulistano*, 28 June and 27 July 1920.

69. Roberto Moreira, quoted in "O Centenario," *Correio Paulistano*, 8 September 1922.

70. "O Centenario," *Correio Paulistano*, 8 September 1922."

71. Affonso Taunay, quoted in Brefe, *O Museu Paulista*, 64.

72. Brefe, *O Museu Paulista*, 58.

73. Brefe, *O Museu Paulista*, 116–17. See also Makino, "Ornamentação do Museu Paulista," 176.

74. A. C. Ferreira, *A epopéia bandeirante*, 137 and 146; and Weinstein, *Color of Modernity*, 39.

75. Pinto, "O Culto do Passado e o Centenario da Independencia."

76. Brefe, *O Museu Paulista*, 152.

77. Two other installations mark the sites of the Lorena road, the Monumento do Pico and the Pouso Circular, the first placed at the highest point of the original road and the other where the old road meets the modern highway. Finally, the monument at the Pontilhão da Raiz da Serra decorates a small bridge and marks the limit of the road between the Paulista plateau and the lowlands of the Baixada Santista; it was inaugurated in 1926.

78. Julio Prestes, quoted in "O Centenario," *Correio Paulistano*, 8 September 1922.

79. Brefe points out that Affonso Taunay was adamant about the importance of place, seeing Ipiranga as essential to Paulista and Brazilian history "long before it was the stage for the founding gesture" in 1822, because of its location as the gateway from the coast to the metropolis. Brefe, *O Museu Paulista*, 20. See also Velloso, *A brasilidade verde-amarela*, esp. 37–59. Velloso shows that many of the members of the influential "green and yellow" nationalist group, such as Cassiano Ricardo, were convinced that geography was the key to understanding Brazilian history and that it explained São Paulo's development and dominance. Furthermore, she shows, they joined their fellow Paulistas in lionizing the bandeirantes, "'geographic heroes,' that is, the Paulistas who built Brazil" (47).

80. Prestes, quoted in "O Centenario," *Correio Paulistano*, 8 September 1922.

81. On the way Paulistas enacted their distinctive regional identity in the revolt, see Weinstein, *Color of Modernity*.

82. Bernardino de Souza, quoted in Albuquerque, *Algazarra nas ruas*, 117. Emphasis in the original.

83. No title, *Revista do Instituto Archeologico e Geographico Pernambucano*, 1922.

84. Kraay, *Bahia's Independence*.

85. Albuquerque, *Algazarra nas ruas*, 83.

86. Albuquerque, *Algazarra nas ruas*, 117–23.

87. Albuquerque, *Algazarra nas ruas*, 112–17.

88. Sandes, *A Invenção da Nação*, 27.

89. Gonçalves Maia, "Uma formidavel mentira historica," *Revista do Instituto Archeologico e Geographico Pernambucano*, 1923.

90. Petition from the Instituto Archeologico e Geographico Pernambucano to the legislature of the state of Pernambuco, quoted in "O 1º Centenario da Rev-

olução Republicana de Pernambuco em 1817," *Revista do Instituto Archeologico e Geographico Pernambucano*, 1917.

91. Oliveira Lima, quoted in "Pernambuco: A solemnisação do Centenario no Recife," *Revista do Instituto Archeologico e Geographico Pernambucano*, 1917.

92. "Pernambuco: A solemnisação do Centenario no Recife."

93. Mário Melo, "O Centenario da Independencia e o Instituto Archeologico," *Jornal do Recife*, 16 August 1922.

94. "As festas do Centenario," *Jornal do Recife*, 9 September 1922.

95. Mário Melo, quoted in "Historia de Pernambuco," *Diario de Pernambuco*, 31 January 1922.

96. Mário Melo, "Pernambuco e a Independencia," *Illustração Brasileira*, 15 November 1921.

97. "Pela politica," *Jornal do Recife*, 18 June 1922.

98. Barbosa Lima Sobrinho, "A torva politicalha," *Jornal do Brasil*, reprinted in *Jornal do Recife*, 10 June 1922.

99. Mário Melo, quoted in "Commemoração civica," *Diario de Pernambuco*, 28 January 1922.

100. Mario Behring, "O Precursor," *Illustração Brasileira*, 5 November 1922.

101. Melo, "A contribuição de Pernambuco para a Independencia do Brasil."

102. Eustachio de Queiroz, quoted in "As festas do Centenario," *Jornal do Recife*, 13 September 1922.

103. "10 de Novembro," *Jornal do Recife*, 10 November 1922.

104. Mário Melo, quoted in "Commemoração do Centenario," *Revista do Instituto de Sciencias e Letras de Pernambuco*, April–September 1922.

105. Telegram from Caetano Munhoz da Rocha to Antonio de Souza, *Revista do Instituto Historico e Geographico do Rio Grande do Norte*, 1922.

106. Capitão X, "Semana Militar," *Revista da Semana*, 14 October 1922.

107. "Noticias e Commentarios: Uma Só Bandeira," *Revista da Semana*, 18 November 1922.

108. Netto Campello, "Extincção das Bandeiras Estadoaes," *Revista Academica da Faculdade de Direito do Recife* 30 (1922): 275.

109. "A Bandeira de Pernambuco," *Diario de Pernambuco*, 8 October 1922.

110. Mário Melo, "Relatorio dos trabalhos de 1922," *Revista do Instituto Archeologico e Geographico Pernambucano*, 1923.

111. Clodomir Silva, "Independencia," *Jornal do Recife*, 8 March 1922.

112. José Simões Coelho, "O Brasil de hoje a cem annos," *Diario de Pernambuco*, 10 September 1922.

113. Levine, *Pernambuco in the Brazilian Federation*, 63.

114. Netto Campello, quoted in "As Festas do Centenario," *Diario de Pernambuco*, 9 September 1922.

115. Cussy Júnior, "A Derrocada de um povo," *Jornal do Recife*, 15 August 1922.

116. Cussy Júnior, quoted in "As festas do Centenario," *Jornal do Recife*, 9 September 1922.

117. "Como o Archidiocese de Olinda vae commemorar o Centenario," *Diario de Pernambuco*, 12 August 1922.

118. "O Hospital Centenario," *Maria*, July 1922.

119. "O centenario," *Jornal do Recife*, 3 August 1922.

120. On the monument's conception, evolution, and completion, see Semenovitch, *Corcovado*.

121. "O Monumento Catholico do Centenario" and "Monumento a Christo Redemptor," *Revista da Semana*, 4 and 25 June 1921.

122. "As festas eucharisticas do Centenario: O que a Egeja vae fazer," *A Exposição de 1922*, August 1922.

123. Sebastião Leme, "A participação da Igreja na commemoração do Centenario," *A Cruz*, 18 June 1922.

124. Luiz de Barros, "Christo no Corcovado," *O Academico* (Recife, Pernambuco), 20 October 1922.

125. Geraldo Vianna, quoted in *Diario do Congresso Nacional*, 11 October 1922.

126. Affonso Celso, "O padrão de victoria," *Jornal do Brasil*, 6 October 1922; "O Monumento Catholico do Centenario," *Revista da Semana*, 4 June 1921; and Lucio José dos Santos, "Christo no Corcovado," *Gil Blas*, 13 January 1922.

127. Quoted in "Christo Redemptor: A Cerimonia do Lançamento da Pedra Fundamental do Monumento," *A Exposição de 1922*, October 1922.

128. "Centenario da Independencia" and "Congresso Eucharistico do Centenario," *Jornal do Brasil*, 12 August and 24 September 1922.

129. "Procissão Eucharistica," *Diario de Pernambuco*, 3 October 1922; "A grandiosa e inegualavel procissão da Eucharistia," *Jornal do Brasil*, 3 October 1922; and "A população carioca assistiu hontem a uma ceremonia verdadeiramente empolgante e grandiosa," *Correio da Manhã*, 2 October 1922.

130. For example, Laudelino de Oliveira Lima, an evangelical pastor, objected to the monument project because, according to one critic of his position, "he does not want to see Jesus Christ, not even painted." Pe. S. B. Van Esse, "A Imagem de Christo Redemptor," *Jornal do Brasil*, 24 September 1922.

131. In the book Figueiredo asked, "Given that Nationalism aims for the organization of all the country's strengths, which of these forces unifies us in the religious and moral sense—which is the one shared by the vast majority of Brazilians?" The answer, it was clear, was only Catholicism. Figueiredo, *Do nacionalismo da hora presente*, 31.

132. "100 annos de liberdade," *A Cruz*, 3 September 1922.

133. "Diario social," *Diario de Pernambuco*, 29 September 1922.

134. A. Fernandes, "De uns e de outros . . ." *Diario de Pernambuco*, 6 September 1922.

135. "6 de Março," *Jornal do Recife*, 7 March 1922.

136. "15 de Novembro," *Jornal do Recife*, 15 November 1921. See also "Parabens á Republica," *Jornal do Recife*, 15 November 1922.

137. "Frei Caneca," *Jornal do Recife*, 13 January 1922.

138. Ulysses Brandão, "As lições do Congresso Eucharistico," *Jornal do Brasil*, 14 October 1922.

139. Pereira Alves credited Francisco de Aquino Correia, the archbishop of Matto Grosso, as his own inspiration for the cry. "Congresso Eucharistico," *O Imparcial*, 27 September 1922. See also Olympio de Mello, "O Congresso Eucharistico," *O Imparcial*, 6 September 1936. In the column, Mello remembered Aquino's comment and the direct connection contemporaries drew between the cry of the Catholics and that of the prince.

140. Pereira Alves, "Commemoração civica," *Diario de Pernambuco*, 28 January 1922.

141. Mons. Pereira Alves, "No Centenario de nossa Independencia," *Mês do Clero*, April 1922.

142. Pereira Alves, quoted in "O Grande 'Raid' Prossegue: Pelos Céos do Cruzeiro!" *Diario de Pernambuco*, 8 June 1922.

143. See, for example, "O Centenario de Petropolis," *Jornal do Brasil*, 17 March 1943. Pereira Alves also organized a Eucharistic congress in Petrópolis for its centenary celebrations in March 1943.

144. José Baratta, "Apontamentos para a Historia Ecclesiastica em Pernambuco," *Revista do Instituto Archeologico e Geographico Pernambucano*, 1922.

145. "Congresso Eucharistico do Centenario," *Jornal do Brasil*, 29 September 1922.

146. Julio Prestes, quoted in "Centenario," *Correio Paulistano*, 8 September 1922.

147. See, for example, Assis Cintra, "Um sermão da Independencia," *Illustração Brasileira*, September 1922; Padre Belchior Pinheiro de Oliveira, "O Grito do Ypiranga," *Diario de Pernambuco*, 7 September 1922; and "Ás margens do Ypiranga," *Maria*, September 1922.

148. "9 de Janeiro: Centenario—'Fico,'" *Illustração Brasileira*, 20 January 1922.

149. "A Igreja Catholica na Historia do Brasil," *Revista da Semana*, 17 June 1922.

150. Soares d'Azevedo, "A Igreja Catholica no Centenario," *Illustração Brasileira*, 14 July 1922.

151. Soares d'Azevedo, "A Igreja Catholica no Centenario."

152. Brandão, "As lições do Congresso Eucharistico."

153. Soares d'Azevedo, "Rei da nação," *Correio da Manhã*, 29 September 1922; and Brandão, "As lições do Congresso Eucharistico."

154. "Congresso Eucharistico do Centenario," *Jornal do Brasil*, 24 September 1922.

155. Celso, "Écos do Congresso Eucharistico."

156. Affonso Celso, "A embaixada pontifícia," *Jornal do Brasil*, 24 August 1922.

157. Celso, "A embaixada pontifícia."

158. See, for example, Sobrinho, "A torva politicalha"; and "Dois de Julho," *Jornal do Recife*, 3 July 1923.

Chapter 4: Citizens of the Patria(s)

1. Ricardo Severo, "A 'Casa Portugueza' em S. Paulo," *Revista do Brasil*, October 1918; and Ricardo Severo, quoted in "Na Camara Portugueza de S. Paulo," *Correio Paulistano*, 2 December 1919.

2. J. Silva, "A construção do nacional."

3. "De Portugal: Agita-se em Lisboa a idéa de uma Casa de Portugal no nosso paiz," *Correio da Manhã*, 23 January 1923. The Casa did open in the capital in 1928, but in another locale, for the fair pavilion was an ephemeral structure and organizers decided that the renovation necessary to make it the Casa's permanent home was too expensive. The original design for the pavilion was the work of Alfredo de Assumpção Santos, J. Rebello de Andrade, and C. Rebello de Andrade. Severo took responsibility for its completion. Levy, *A Exposição do Centenário*, 228–29.

4. There are many important works on the immigrant experience during the First Republic. The most relevant to the present work are Alvim, *Brava gente!*; Lesser, *Negotiating National Identity*; and two works by Ribeiro, *Mata Galegos* and *O Rio de Janeiro*.

5. Pike, *Hispanismo*, 195–96.

6. On the Portuguese government's approach to the Brazilian centenary, see Marques, "A viagem do presidente António José de Almeida"; and Miranda, "Um 'voo' entre Portugal e Brasil."

7. "O raid aereo Lisboa-Rio," *Diario de Pernambuco*, 1 April 1922; and "Club Portuguez," *Correio Paulistano*, 2 April 1922.

8. See continuing coverage under the title "O Centenario," *Correio Paulistano*, esp. 4 and 28 September and 1 October 1922.

9. "O presidente de Portugal," *Jornal do Recife*, 3 October 1922.

10. "Raid New York–Rio" and "Raid Lisboa–Rio," *Jornal do Recife*, 9 May and 23 August 1922.

11. "Raid Lisboa–Rio" and "Dr. Antonio José de Almeida," *Correio Paulistano*, 8 April and 17 September 1922. In another example, the vice-consul of Portugal in Natal helped organize local celebrations of the Lisbon raid, which

took place even in the absence of the raiders themselves. See "O raid aéreo Portugal-Brasil" and "Raid Aereo Portugal-Brasil," *A República*, 11 May and 7 June 1922.

12. For example, Zucculin served as the official spokesman of the Italian community at the inauguration of the Gomes statue. "L'apoteosi di Carlos Gomes," *Fanfulla*, 13 October 1922.

13. "O Raid Lisboa–Rio" and "Raid Lisboa–Rio," *Jornal do Recife*, 1 April and 9 May 1922.

14. "O Raid Lisboa–Rio," *Jornal do Recife*, 1 April 1922.

15. "'Raid' Lisboa–Rio" and "Raid Lisboa–Rio," *Jornal do Recife*, 7 April and 3 August 1922.

16. "Cronaca Cittadina: La Commissione Commerciale all'Esposizione del Centenario e le Società Italiane di S. Paolo," *Fanfulla*, 20 September 1922.

17. "Cronaca cittadina: In Margine alla Cronaca—Per la celebrazione del Sette Settembre," *Fanfulla*, 26 August 1922.

18. "A commemoração do XX de setembro e do centenario, na Società Italiana di Beneficenza," *Correio da Manhã*, 22 September 1922.

19. "Un Vocc Autorevole," *Il Pasquino Coloniale*, 15 July 1922.

20. "Le Sottoscrizioni del Giorno," *Il Pasquino Coloniale*, 15 July 1922.

21. "L'Inaugurazione del Monumento di Gomes" and "La Fuga del Coreto del Monumento a Gomes," *Il Pasquino Coloniale*, 7 and 21 October 1922.

22. The columnist, Nasonelli, put a fine point on the critique in using the term "graúdos," a Portuguese word, in his Italian paper. "La chiacchiere di Nasonelli," *Il Pasquino Coloniale*, 21 October 1922. See also "La Fuga del Coreto del Monumento a Gomes."

23. A. Duarte Silva, "O Centenario da Independencia e a Colonia Portugueza de S. Paulo," *Correio Paulistano*, 23 July 1920.

24. João Ninguem, "Azas a Portugal," *Diario de Pernambuco*, special edition, 15 May 1922.

25. For example, while the Rio de Janeiro–based Real e Benemerita Sociedade Portugueza de Beneficios donated 1.5 contos de réis, Portuguese commercial employees in Recife raised at least 11 contos in their own right, proving, in the words of the *Jornal do Recife*, "how ardent is the patriotism among the more modest of the Portuguese colony of Pernambuco." *Relatorio da Real e Benemerita Sociedade Portugueza de Beneficios* (Rio de Janeiro: Typ. da "Casa Vallelle," 1923), 150; and "Raid Lisbôa–Rio," *Jornal do Recife*, 20 May 1922. Ultimately, the Portuguese community in Recife donated £4,000 sterling, while groups in Belém and Maceió each donated 10 contos de réis, those in Maranhão 5 contos, those in Fortaleza 4.5 contos, and those in Paraíba 760,000. "Os aviadores portuguezes," *Diario de Pernambuco*, 4 August 1922.

26. *Relatorio da Real e Benemerita Sociedade Portugueza de Beneficios*, 152.

27. See especially Skidmore, *Black into White*, in particular chapter 5, "The

New Nationalism," 145–72. See also Garcia, *Entre América e Europa*, 579–80; and Bueno, *Política Externa da Primeira República*, 484–86.

28. The Fluminense Football Club organized the country's first Boy Scout troop in 1916. The two nationalist leagues were founded the same year.

29. In the immediate postwar years, two new organizations appeared, the Propaganda Nativista (1919) and Ação Social Nacionalista (1920). On the evolution of the nativist movement, see Topik, "Middle-Class Brazilian Nationalism"; and Burns, *Nationalism in Brazil*.

30. Mario Deval, "O Momento Historico," *Gil Blas*, 7 April 1922.

31. For example, see speeches given by Cesare Corinaldi and Carlos Sampaio to celebrate the inauguration of the Italian pavilion at the international exhibition, covered in "O Dia da Italia," *A Exposição de 1922*, November 1922.

32. "A Colonia Italiana e o Centenario," *Gil Blas*, 17 February 1922.

33. Among others, these included the Brazilian law professor Spencer Vampré. See Bettencourt-Rodrigues, *Uma confederação luso-brasileira*, esp. 123 and 151–55.

34. "O 7 de Abril de 1831, inicio do Nacionalismo Brazileiro," *Gil Blas*, 7 April 1922.

35. Emphasis in the original. "Abaixo as touradas!"; "O nacionalismo, o auctor da 'A Mulata' e os lusitanoides desta banda . . ."; and "Faz que anda mas não anda . . ." *Gil Blas*, 23 July, 17 March, and 14 July 1922.

36. "A Colonia Italiana e o Centenario"; Arthur Gaspar Vianna, "A estocada no nacionalismo: O 'raid' Lisbôa–Rio"; Conde de Affonso Celso, "Sem Effusão de Sangue?" and "Os portuguezes sempre contra o Brazil," *Gil Blas*, 24 June and 22 September 1922.

37. See, for example, Celso, "Sem Effusão de Sangue?"; "O dous de Julho"; and "Os portuguezes sempre contra o Brazil," *Gil Blas*, 22 September 1922.

38. Victruvio Marcondes, "O monumento á 'raça' e o Trabalho de sapa da 'colonia'"; Antonio Torres, "União Luso-Brazileira: Carta aberta ao Dr. João de Barros"; and "Os tres turnos de uma commemoração festiva," *Gil Blas*, 16 June, 22 September, and 20 October 1922.

39. "A lingua brazileira," "Tu quoque, Almachio," and Deval, "O Momento Historico."

Gil Blas, 22 September and 7 and 14 April 1922.

40. Marcondes, "O monumento á 'raça' e o Trabalho de sapa da 'colonia.'"

41. Deval, "O Momento Historico."

42. "Desfiguração Impossivel," *Correio da Manhã*, 9 January 1922.

43. "Entre Brasil e Portugal," *O Malho*, 1 July 1922.

44. "Reveladores do Brasil," *Revista da Semana*, 3 February 1923.

45. "A Independencia, festa da raça," *America Brasileira*, October 1922; and Epitácio Pessoa, quoted in "Utlima Hora," *Jornal do Recife*, 14 June 1922.

46. *Gil Blas* implied that Pessoa shared its suspicion of Portuguese residents

in Brazil and also attacked those Portuguese who accused Pessoa of Lusophobia. See especially Vianna, "A estocada no nacionalismo," and "'Fim de luta?'—Não!'" *Gil Blas*, 24 and 29 June 1922.

47. On war-era views of Germany and German immigrants, see Luebke, *Germans in Brazil.*

48. Jacob Kroeff Netto, quoted in "As commemorações do Centenario," *Correio do Povo*, 19 September 1922.

49. Theophilo de Barros Corrêa de Mello Neves, "Os portuguezes em Porto Alegre," *Correio do Povo*, 4 October 1922.

50. Theophilo de Barros Corrêa de Mello Neves, "Os portuguezes em Porto Alegre," *Correio do Povo*, 5 October 1922.

51. Theophilo de Barros Corrêa de Mello Neves, "Os portuguezes em Porto Alegre," *Correio do Povo*, 7 October 1922.

52. "Nostra intervista con Sacadura Cabral e Gago Coutinho," *Fanfulla*, 22 June 1922.

53. All the foreign pavilions erected at the fair were organized as official initiatives of the governments of participating countries, except the "Chilean" pavilion, which was erected not by the Chilean state but by saltpeter producers based in Chile. Levy, *A Exposição do Centenário*, 147.

54. "O dia do presidente Antonio José de Almeida," *Jornal do Brasil*, 21 September 1922.

55. It allowed him the title, the magazine said, "without thereby abdicating our political program, which does not allow for confusion; and for that reason we cannot applaud any attempts at rough approximations, trade-offs, or inventions which are harmful to our Patria, even if they seem useful or necessary to anyone, including Portugal." "Os tres turnos de uma commemoração festiva," *Gil Blas*, 20 October 1922.

56. "Sentindo a palpitação de duas Patrias," *A Noite*, 25 September 1922.

57. Marques, "A viagem do presidente António José de Almeida"; and Miranda, "Um 'voo' entre Portugal e Brasil." See also P. Santos and Amorim, "As relações Portugal-Brasil na primeira metade do século XX."

58. Paraphrase of speech by António de Almeida, "A sessão do Gabinete Portugues de Leitura," *America Brasileira*, Edição do Centenario, 1922.

59. António de Almeida, quoted in "Saudação do Presidente de Portugal ao Brasil," *America Brasileira*, Edição do Centenario, 1922.

60. António de Almeida, quoted in "Portugal—Brasil: As homenagens ao Presidente Antonio José de Almeida desde a sua chegada ao Rio," *Jornal do Brasil*, 19 September 1922; and "Saudação do Presidente de Portugal ao Brasil," *America Brasileira*.

61. Epitácio Pessoa, quoted in "Portugal—Brasil: As homenagens ao Presidente Antonio José de Almeida desde a sua chegada ao Rio."

62. Epitácio Pessoa, quoted in "Brilhantes homenagens ao Dr. Antonio José

de Almeida no Gabinete Portugueza de Leitura: Como os portuguezes residentes no Rio receberam S. Ex.," *Jornal do Brasil*, 22 September 1922.

63. "Portugal—Brasil: As homenagens ao Presidente Antonio José de Almeida desde a sua chegada ao Rio"; and "Sentindo a palpitação de duas Patrias."

64. "Foi lançada a pedra fundamental do monumento que Portugal offereceu ao Brasil," *A Noite*, 25 September 1922. See also "Brilhantes homenagens ao Dr. Antonio José de Almeida no Gabinete Portugueza de Leitura." The *Jornal* noted that, outside the Gabinete, "in the street the people mounted an extraordinary tribute to the two presidents," Almeida and Pessoa.

65. Eduardo Dias, quoted in "Brilhantes homenagens ao Dr. Antonio José de Almeida no Gabinete Portugueza de Leitura."

66. Alexandre Herculano Rodrigues, quoted in "Parte Oficial," *Boletim da Câmara Portuguesa de Comércio e Indústria do Rio de Janeiro*, September–October 1922.

67. Eduardo Dias, quoted in "Brilhantes homenagens ao Dr. Antonio José de Almeida no Gabinete Portugueza de Leitura."

68. Carlos Malheiro Dias, quoted in "A sessão do Gabinete Portugues de Leitura," *America Brasileira*, nos. 9–12, Edição do Centenario, 1922.

69. J. A. de Magalhães, quoted in "Sentindo a palpitação de duas Patrias."

70. "O raid aereo Portugal-Brasil," *Diario de Pernambuco*, 13 May 1922.

71. "Raid Lisbôa-Rio," *Jornal do Recife*, 13 May 1922.

72. "Raid Lisbôa-Rio," *Jornal do Recife*, 13 May 1922; and "O raid aereo Portugal-Brasil," *Diario de Pernambuco*, 13 May 1922.

73. "Un'accusa sciocca," *Il Pasquino Coloniale*, 16 December 1922. The Italian paper rejected the accusation made by *Rio Jornal*, arguing that regardless of his experience the general could never be so petty.

74. "Um heroe da grande guerra: Chegará amanhã ao Rio bravo General Caviglia," *Jornal do Brasil*, 6 August 1922.

75. "Cronaca cittadina," "A S. Paolo," and "La nostra guerra rievocata dal gen. Caviglia nella sua conferenza al Municipale," *Fanfulla*, 26 and 30 July and 4 August 1922.

76. Andrea Caliò, quoted in "Cronaca Cittadina: Le visite del generale Caviglia—Il Ricevimento alla 'Leale Oberdan,'" *Fanfulla*, 2 August 1922.

77. Eurico De Martino, quoted in "La nostra guerra rievocata dal gen. Caviglia nella sua conferenza al Municipale."

78. "Cronaca Cittadina: La Commissione Commerciale all'Esposizione del Centenario e le Società Italiane di S. Paolo."

79. Egidio Pinotti Gamba, quoted in "Il Soggiorno del Grande Uff. Cesare Corinaldi a San Paolo," *Fanfulla*, 15 November 1922.

80. A. J. Gomes Barboza, "Relatório," *Boletim da Câmara Portuguesa de Comércio e Indústria do Rio de Janeiro*, March–April 1922.

81. Barboza, "Relatório."

82. "Associações," *Correio Paulistano*, 4 September 1921.

83. Emphasis in the original. "Portugal no Centenario da Independencia do Brazil," *Boletim da Câmara Portuguesa de Comércio e Indústria do Rio de Janeiro*, March–April 1922.

84. "Parte Oficial," *Boletim da Câmara Portuguesa de Comércio e Indústria do Rio de Janeiro*, September–October 1922.

85. The Câmara also helped organize an event celebrating the initiation of construction on the pavilions, in February 1922. "Exposição Nacional," *Illustração Brasileira*, 20 March 1922.

86. Cesare Corinaldi, quoted in "Il Soggiorno del Grande Uff. Cesare Corinaldi a San Paolo."

87. Duarte Leite Pereira da Silva, quoted in "Chronica da Exposição," *A Exposição de 1922*, no. 16 (no month), 1923.

88. Marques, "A viagem do presidente António José de Almeida," 20–22.

89. "Associações," *Correio Paulistano*, 4 September 1921.

90. Marques, "A viagem do presidente António José de Almeida," 119–23 and 148.

91. Letter from Delfim Carlos to Eurico Mori, 21 February 1923, Arquivo Nacional do Brasil, Comissão Executiva da Comemoração do Centenário da Independência, 1921 a 1925, Código do Fundo, 1I, Seção de Guarda SDE, SDE 045, Caixa 2348.

92. Mori won a silver medal for his insecticides and was listed among prize winners from São Paulo in the Brazil section, rather than among international entrants, as he would have been had he continued to display the products in the Italian pavilion. *Diário Oficial da União*, 23 September 1923.

93. Francesco Matarazzo served as a member of the commission organized by the state government to oversee São Paulo's participation in the exposition. "Esposizione del Centenario dell'Independenza del Brasile," *Fanfulla*, 14 January 1922.

94. "Le maravigliose affermazioni dell'industria italiana di San Paolo," *Il Pasquino Coloniale*, 30 December 1922.

95. The pavilion was inaugurated on 29 October 1922, two days after the inauguration of the Italian pavilion and the day after Italy Day. "All'Esposizione del Centenario: La Solenne Inaugurazione del Padiglione della Ditta Matarazzo," *Fanfulla*, 30 October 1922.

96. "Le maravigliose affermazioni dell'industria italiana di San Paolo," and "Os Italianos e o progresso do Brasil," *O Combate*, 8 November 1922.

97. "Na Exposição Internacional," *Correio da Manhã*, 22 October 1922.

98. "Na Exposição Internacional," *Correio da Manhã*, 29 October 1922.

99. "Exposição Nacional," *Illustração Brasileira*, 20 March 1922.

100. "Na Exposição Internacional," *Correio da Manhã*, 17 October 1922.

101. "Chronica da Exposição," *A Exposição de 1922*, no. 16 (no month), 1923.

102. "O Dia da Italia," *A Exposição de 1922*, November 1922.

103. Ricardo Severo, quoted in "Uma sympathica inciativa: Como a colonia portugueza de São Paulo pretende commemorar o Centenario da Independencia," *Correio Paulistano*, 28 June 1920.

104. "Uma sympathica inciativa."

105. Carlos Malheiro Dias, "O Pantheon Nacional," *Revista da Semana*, 7 October 1922.

106. José Antonio de Souza, quoted in "Centenario da Independencia," *Jornal do Brasil*, 31 August 1922.

107. Dias, "O Pantheon Nacional."

108. Comitato Esecutivo per il Monumento a Carlos Gomes, quoted in "Cronaca Cittadina," *Fanfulla*, 11 October 1922; and Henrique de Sousa Queiroz, quoted in "Carlos Gomes: A inauguração do monumento ao grande compositor brasileiro," *Correio Paulistano*, 13 October 1922. See also "Carlos Gomes," *Correio Paulistano*, 12 October 1922.

109. "Carlos Gomes," *Correio Paulistano*, 12 October 1922.

110. "Monumento a Carlos Gomes em São Paulo," *Illustração Brasileira*, 15 August 1922; and "Foi inaugurado hontem, em S. Paulo, o monumento a Carlos Gomes," *Correio da Manhã*, 13 October 1922.

111. "Cronaca cittadina: La Colonia Italiana pel Centenario dell'Indipendenza" and "Cronaca Cittadina: Per l'apoteosi del Centenario brasiliano," *Fanfulla*, 1 February and 29 August 1922.

112. "O Centenario da Independencia: O Monumento a Carlos Gomes," *O Estado de São Paulo*, 12 October 1922.

113. For example, "L'Uomo e l'Artista," *Fanfulla*, 12 October 1922.

114. "Cronaca cittadina: La Colonia Italiana pel Centenario dell'Indipendenza."

115. "Monumento a Carlos Gomes em São Paulo," *Illustração Brasileira*, 15 August 1922.

116. "Fu anche nostro!" *Fanfulla*, 12 October 1922.

117. Bruno Zucculin, quoted in "O Centenario da Independencia: O Monumento a Carlos Gomes—Homenagem da colonia italiana de S. Paulo ao Brasil," *O Estado de São Paulo*, 13 October 1922.

118. Among them were members of the Dante Alighieri literary society, the Trinacria Humanitaria de São Paulo, the Liga Oberdan, the Sociedade Italiana da Moóca, the Galileo Galilei, the Porta Pia, the Vittorio Emmanuele, the União Catholica Italiana, the Sociedade Operaria da Barra Funda, the Liga Patriotica Italiana, the Sociedade Operaria Fieramosca, the Circulo Italiano, the Liga Lombarda, the Istituto Médio, and the Circulo Garibaldino.

119. Bruno Zucculin, quoted in "O Centenario da Independencia: O Monumento a Carlos Gomes—Homenagem da colonia italiana de S. Paulo ao Brasil," *O Estado de São Paulo*, 13 October 1922.

120. See, for example, *A Exposição de 1922*, nos. 14–15 (no month), 1923, which focuses on the British presence in Brazil and British participation in the fair. Cochrane is discussed throughout.

121. Mota Assunção, "A Colaboração dos Portugueses na Independência do Brasil," *Boletim Mensal*, August–September 1922.

122. For other examples, see Arthur Alves Barbosa, "Hosanna ao Brasil," *Jornal do Recife*, 7 September 1922; and Dr. Marques da Cruz, "O 1º Centenario da Independencia do Brasil," *Boletim Mensal*, August–September 1922. In her survey of Portuguese historiography of Brazilian independence, Zília Osório de Castro shows that this has also been the dominant strain of academic work on the subject, including during the centenary era. She points especially to important works by Rocha Martins and António Vianna, both published to mark the centenary, in which the authors depicted independence as "essentially political," rather than as a cultural or economic phenomenon. Zília Osório de Castro, "A Independência do Brasil na historiografia portuguesa," in Jancsó, *Independência*, 179–204.

123. Carlos Malheiro Dias, quoted in Mota Assunção, "História da Colonização Portuguesa do Brasil," *Boletim Mensal*, November–December 1921.

124. Assunção, "História da Colonização Portuguesa do Brasil."

125. Dias, "O Pantheon Nacional."

126. Ricardo Severo, quoted in "Uma sympathica inciativa."

127. The *Correio Paulistano* called it an "appealing initiative" in June 1920 in an article that also cited the governor's positive response to the project. "Uma sympathica inciativa."

128. Helios [Menotti Del Picchia], "Um monumento," *Correio Paulistano*, 29 June 1920.

129. "Monumento á raça," *Correio Paulistano*, 23 May 1922.

130. "Monumento á raça," *Correio Paulistano*, 28 May 1922.

131. Marcondes, "O monumento á 'raça' e o Trabalho de sapa da 'colonia.'"

132. Strengthening Del Picchia's campaign, the paper reprinted A. Duarte Silva's critique of his compatriots' plans to erect monuments to celebrate the centenary. He called the idea of a Portuguese-sponsored monument to the bandeiras "strange" and argued that the Portuguese in Brazil should maintain a respectful distance from the centenary so as not to offend Brazilian patriots. Silva, "O Centenario da Independencia e a Colonia Portugueza de S. Paulo." The piece was originally printed in *A Noite* on 22 July 1920.

133. Helios, "Monumento das Bandeiras" and "Um monumento," *Correio Paulistano*, 27 July and 29 June 1920.

134. Helios, "Um monumento," *Correio Paulistano*, 29 June 1920.

135. Helios, "Monumento das Bandeiras."

136. Helios, "A victória de um patrício," *Correio Paulistano*, 10 November 1921.

137. The model was displayed at the Casa Byington, its inauguration attended by Governor Washington Luís. Del Picchia gushed, "With this monument, the S. Paulo of the Centenary will certainly possess one of the most beautiful works of art in America. And, when one thinks that it was imagined, created, molded by a Paulista native, when you think the great epic will be evoked by the chisel of one of its children, our faith in the destiny of our land revives, exults." Helios, "Monumento das Bandeiras."

138. "A Colonia Italiana e o Centenario."

139. Helios, "Um monumento," *Correio Paulistano*, 13 October 1922.

140. "O Momento," *Revista do Brasil*, November 1922.

141. "Carlos Gomes," *O Estado de São Paulo*, 12 October 1922.

Epilogue

1. Williams, *Culture Wars in Brazil.*

2. The celebrations of the centenary of the Farroupilha rebellion invite further study. Among the works that historians have undertaken, see, for example, Giovanaz, "As Exposições Universais" and Ceroni, "A Exposição do Centenário da Revolução Farroupilha."

3. Albuquerque Júnior, *Invention of the Brazilian Northeast*, esp. 44–74.

4. See Weinstein, *Color of Modernity*, esp. chapter 5, "Provincializing São Paulo: The 'Other' Regions Strike Back," 192–220.

5. Ribeiro, *O Rio de Janeiro*, 134.

6. On these issues, see Ribeiro, *O Rio de Janeiro*, as well as Trento, "Le associazoni italiane a Sao Paulo" and Bertonha, *O fascismo*.

7. Ribeiro, *O Rio de Janeiro*, 241.

8. Williams, *Culture Wars in Brazil*; Davis, *Avoiding the Dark*; and Nava, "Forging Future Citizens."

9. As Eduardo Silva points out in his discussion of the celebrations of the centenary of the birth of Pedro II in 1925, those who idolized the emperor "dreamed of a strong Republic, guided by a leader with broad powers," and they found that leader in Vargas. E. Silva, "A República comemora o Império," 69.

10. Brenno Ferraz do Amaral, "O Momento: A Geração do Centenario," *Revista do Brasil*, September 1922.

11. José Pereira Coelho de Souza, quoted in "As commemorações do Centenario," *Correio do Povo*, 14 September 1922.

12. Gastão Dias, quoted in "As commemorações do Centenario," *Correio do Povo*, 20 September 1922.

13. Clodomir Silva, "Independencia," *Jornal do Recife*, 8 March 1922; and José Euclides, "Civilisação de fachada," *Jornal do Recife*, 14 September 1922.

14. Cussy Júnior, quoted in "As festas do Centenario," *Jornal do Recife*, 9 September 1922.

15. Souza, quoted in “As commemorações do Centenario.”
16. Dias, quoted in “As commemorações do Centenario.”
17. Cussy Júnior, quoted in “As festas do Centenario.”

Bibliography

Periodicals

Porto Alegre and Rio Grande do Sul

Correio do Povo
A Federação
Imprensa
A Manhã
O Nacionalista
O Separatista

Recife

O Academico
Diario de Pernambuco
Jornal do Recife
Maria
Mês do Clero
Revista Academica da Faculdade de Direito do Recife
Revista do Instituto Archeologico e Geographico Pernambucano
Revista do Instituto de Sciencias e Letras de Pernambuco

Rio de Janeiro

America Brasileira
Boletim da Câmara Portuguesa de Comércio e Indústria do Rio de Janeiro
O Brasil
Careta
Correio da Manhã
A Cruz
A Defeza Nacional
Gil Blas
Diário do Congresso Nacional
Diário Oficial da União
A Exposição de 1922
Fon Fon
Illustração Brasileira
O Imparcial
O Jornal
Jornal do Brasil
Jornal do Commercio
O Malho
A Noite
Revista do Instituto Historico e Geographico Brasileiro
Revista Maritima Brazileira
Revista da Semana
A Voz do Mar

São Paulo

Boletim Mensal—Centro Republicano Português
O Combate
Correio Paulistano
O Estado de São Paulo
Fanfulla
Il Pasquino Coloniale
Revista do Brasil

Other

O Estado (Florianópolis, Santa Catarina)
A República (Natal, Rio Grande do Norte)
O Progresso (Penedo, Alagoas)
Revista do Instituto Historico e Geographico do Rio Grande do Norte (Natal, Rio Grande do Norte)

Primary Sources

Bettencourt-Rodrigues, António Maria de. *Uma confederação luso-brasileira.* Lisbon: Clássica, 1923.

Brazil. Ministerio da Justiça e Negócios Interiores. *Centenario da Independencia, 1822–1922: Programma da Comemoração e Regulamento Geral da Exposição.* Rio de Janeiro: Imprensa Nacional, 1922.

Brazil. Ministerio da Justiça e Negócios Interiores. *Exposição Internacional do Centenario—Rio de Janeiro, 1922–1923: Relatório dos Trabalhos.* 2 vols. Rio de Janeiro: Imprensa Nacional, 1926.

Coutinho, Gago, and Sacadura Cabral. *Relatorio da viagem aérea Lisboa: Rio de Janeiro.* Lisbon: N.p., 1922.

Cunha, Euclides da. *Rebellion in the Backlands.* Translated by Samuel Putnam. Chicago: University of Chicago Press, 1944.

Dias, Carlos Malheiro, ed. *Historia da colonização portuguesa do Brasil: edição monumental comemorativa do primeiro centenario da independencia do Brasil,* 3 vols. Porto: Litografia Nacional, 1921–1924.

Figueiredo, Jackson de. *Do nacionalismo da hora presente. Carta de um catholico sobre as razões do movimento nacionalista no Brazil e o que, em tal momento, é possível determinar.* Rio de Janeiro: Livraria Catholica, 1921.

Guia Official. Exposição Internacional do Rio de Janeiro em 1922. Official Guide of the Exposition—Guide Officiel de l'Exposition. Editado pelo Bureau Official de Informações. Rio de Janeiro: Palacio Monroe. Typ. do Annuario do Brasil, 1922.

Instituto Historico e Geographico Brasileiro. *Annaes do Congresso Internacional de Historia da America,* 9 vols. Rio de Janeiro: Imprensa Nacional, 1925–1930.

Instituto Historico e Geographico Brasileiro. *Diccionario Historico, Geographico e Ethnographico do Brasil (Commemorativo do Primeiro Centenario da Independencia),* 2 vols. Rio de Janeiro: Imprensa Nacional, 1922.

Leopoldo, Duarte. *O Clero e a Independencia: Conferencias Patrióticas.* Rio de Janeiro: Centro D. Vital e Alvaro Pinto, 1923.

Lima, Manuel Oliveira. *O Movimento da Independência, 1821–1822.* São Paulo: Companhia Melhoramentos de S. Paulo, 1922.

Mendonça, Carlos Sussekind de. *O Sport está deseducando a mocidade brasileira: Carta aberta a Lima Barreto.* Rio de Janeiro: Empreza Brasil Editora, 1921.

Menezes, Rodrigo Otávio Langgard de. *Festas Nacionaes.* Rio de Janeiro: F. Briguiet & C. Editores, 1893.

Varnhagen, Francisco Adolpho de. *História da Independência do Brasil.* Brasília: Fundação Alexandre de Gusmão, 2019.

Secondary Sources

Abreu, Berenice. *Jangadeiros: uma corajosa jornada em busca de direitos no Estado Novo*. Rio de Janeiro: Civilização Brasileira, 2012.

Abreu, Regina. *A fabricação do imortal: Memória, história e estratégias de consagração no Brasil*. Rio de Janeiro: Rocco: Lapa, 1996.

Albuquerque Júnior, Durval Muniz de. *The Invention of the Brazilian Northeast*. Durham, NC: Duke University Press, 2014.

Albuquerque Júnior, Durval Muniz de. "Weaving Tradition: The Invention of the Brazilian Northeast." *Latin American Perspectives* 31, no. 2 (2004): 42–61.

Albuquerque, Wlamyra Ribeiro. *Algazarra nas ruas: comemorações da independência na Bahia (1889–1923)*. Campinas: Editora da Unicamp, 1999.

Alvim, Zuleika M. F. *Brava gente! Os italianos em São Paulo, 1870–1920*. São Paulo: Editora Brasilense, 1986.

Andermann, Jens. "Espetáculos da diferença: a Exposição Antropológica Brasileira de 1882." *Topoi* 5, no. 9 (2004): 128–70.

Andermann, Jens. "Tournaments of Value: Argentina and Brazil in the Age of Exhibitions." *Journal of Material Culture* 14, no. 3 (2009): 333–63.

Antonacci, Maria Antonieta. *RS: as oposições & a revolução de 1923*. Porto Alegre: Mercado Aberto, 1981.

Beezley, William H., and David E. Lorey, eds. *Viva Mexico! Viva la Independencia!: Celebrations of September 16*. Wilmington, DE: SR Books, 2001.

Beezley, William H., Cheryl English Martin, and William E. French, eds. *Rituals of Rule, Rituals of Resistance: Public Celebrations and Popular Culture in Mexico*. Wilmington, DE: SR Books, 1994.

Benchimol, Jaime Larry. *Pereira Passos: Um Haussmann Tropical; A renovação urbana da cidade do Rio de Janeiro no início do século XX*. Rio de Janeiro: Biblioteca Carioca, 1990.

Bentes Filho, Giovanni Roberto Protásio. "Do Norte ao Sul: A Missão do Cruzador '*José Bonifácio*' e a incorporação do pescador a um projeto de nação (1900–1930)." MA thesis, Universidade Federal do Rio Grande do Norte, 2018.

Bertonha, João Fábio. *O fascismo e os imigrantes italianos no Brasil*. Porto Alegre: EDIPUCRS, 2001.

Besse, Susan K. *Restructuring Patriarchy: The Modernization of Gender Inequality in Brazil, 1914–1940*. Chapel Hill: University of North Carolina Press, 1996.

Bloch, Marc. *The Historian's Craft*. New York: Vintage Books, 1953.

Bocketti, Gregg. *The Invention of the Beautiful Game: Football and the Making of Modern Brazil*. Gainesville: University Press of Florida, 2016.

Brefe, Ana Cláudia Fonseca. *O Museu Paulista: Affonso de Taunay e a Memória Nacional*. São Paulo: Ed. Unesp / Museu Paulista, 2005.

Brito, Mário da Silva. *História do Modernismo Brasileiro: Vol. I. Antecedentes da Semana de Arte Moderna*, second ed. Rio de Janeiro: Civilização Brasileira, 1964.

Bueno, Clodoaldo. *Política Externa da Primeira República: Os anos de apogeu (de 1902 a 1918)*. São Paulo: Paz e Terra, 2003.

Burns, Benjamin J. *The Flying Firsts of Walter Hinton: From the 1919 Transatlantic Flight to the Arctic and the Amazon*. Jefferson, NC: McFarland & Company, 2012.

Burns, E. Bradford. *Nationalism in Brazil: A Historical Survey*. New York: Frederick A. Praeger, 1968.

Campbell, Courtney J. "Four Fishermen, Orson Welles, and the Making of the Brazilian Northeast." *Past and Present*, no. 234 (2017): 173–212.

Campbell, Courtney J. *Region Out of Place: The Brazilian Northeast and the World, 1924–1968*. Pittsburgh, PA: University of Pittsburgh Press, 2022.

Cancella, Karina Barbosa. "O esporte e as Forças Armadas na Primeira República: das atividades gymnasticas às participações em eventos esportivos internacionais (1890–1922)." MA thesis, Universidade Federal do Rio de Janeiro, 2013.

Carelli, Mario. *Carcamanos e Comendadores: Os italianos de São Paulo: da realidade à ficção (1919–1930)*. São Paulo: Editora Ática, 1985.

Carvalho, José Murilo de. "Brazil 1870–1914: The Force of Tradition." *Journal of Latin American Studies* 24, no. S1 (1992): 145–62.

Carvalho, José Murilo de. *The Formation of Souls: Imagery of the Republic in Brazil*, translated by Clifford E. Landers. Notre Dame, IN: University of Notre Dame Press, 2012.

Carvalho, José Murilo de. *Os Bestializados: O Rio de Janeiro e a República Que Não Foi*, third ed. São Paulo: Companhia das Letras, 1998.

Cascudo, Luís da Câmara. *No caminho do avião: notas de reportagem aérea: (1922–1933)*. Natal: EDUFRN, 2007.

Ceroni, Giovani Costa. "A Exposição do Centenário da Revolução Farroupilha nas Páginas dos Jornais *Correio do Povo* e *A Federação*." MA thesis, Pontifícia Universidade Católica do Rio Grande do Sul, 2009.

Chernavsky, Analía. *A construção dos mitos e heróis do Brasil nos hinos esquecidos da Biblioteca Nacional*. Rio de Janeiro: Programa Nacional de Apoio à Pesquisa, 2009.

Cooper, Frederick. *Citizenship, Inequality, and Difference: Historical Perspectives*. Princeton, NJ: Princeton University Press, 2018.

Corsi, Francisco Luiz. *Estado Novo: Política Externa e Projeto Nacional*. São Paulo: Editora UNESP, 1999.

Costa, Bruno Balbino Aires da. "'A casa da memória Norte-Rio-Grandense': O Instituto Histórico e Geográfico do Rio Grande do Norte e a construção do lugar do Rio Grande do Norte na memória nacional (1902–1927)." PhD diss., Universidade Federal do Rio Grande do Sul, 2017.

Costa, Emilia Viotti da. *The Brazilian Empire: Myths and Histories*, revised ed. Chapel Hill: The University of North Carolina Press, 2000.

Costa, Júlia Furia. "O Culto da Saudade nas Comemorações do Centenário da Independência do Brasil: A Criação do Museu Histórico Nacional, 1922." *Em Tempo de Histórias* 18 (2011): 49–64.

Cruz, Eduardo da. "Paulina Campelo Macedo: Uma Portuguesa na Imprensa Brasileira da Primeira República." *Revista de Escritoras Ibéricas* 4 (2016): 97–120.

Cunha, Paulo Rikardo Pereira Fonseca da. "'Ombro a ombro com os mais fracos': A Inserção de João Café Filho nos espaços do trabalhador na cidade do Natal (1922–1937)." MA thesis, Universidade Federal do Rio Grande do Norte, 2015.

Cunha, Paulo Rikardo Pereira Fonseca da. "Pátria e dever": a Colônia José Bonifácio como espaço da contravenção da ordem (1922)." *Revista Porto* 3, no. 4 (2016): 45–59.

Davis, Darién J. *Avoiding the Dark: Race and the Forging of National Culture in Brazil*. Aldershot: Ashgate, 1999.

Diacon, Todd A. *Stringing Together a Nation: Cândido Mariano da Silva Rondon and the Construction of a Modern Brazil, 1906–1930*. Durham, NC: Duke University Press, 2004.

Dutra, Eliana de Freitas. "The Mirror of History and Images of the Nation: The Invention of a National Identity in Brazil and Its Contrasts with Similar Enterprises in Mexico and Argentina." In *Writing the Nation: A Global Perspective*, edited by Stefan Berger, 84–102. Basingstoke: Palgrave Macmillan, 2007.

Earle, Rebecca. "'Padres de la Patria' and the Ancestral Past: Commemorations of Independence in Nineteenth-Century Spanish America." *Journal of Latin American Studies* 34, no. 4 (2002): 775–805.

Earle, Rebecca. "Sobre Héroes y Tumbas: National Symbols in Nineteenth-Century Spanish America." *Hispanic American Historical Review* 85, no. 3 (2005): 375–416.

Elkin, Noah C. "1922, O encontro do efêmero com a permanência: As exposições (inter)nacionais, os museus e a origem do Museu Histórico Nacional." *Anais do Museu Histórico Nacional* 29 (1997): 121–40.

Elkin, Noah C. "Promoting a New Brazil: National Expositions and Images of Modernity, 1861–1922." PhD diss., Rutgers, The State University of New Jersey, 1999.

Fernández Bravo, Álvaro. "Celebraciones centenarias: nacionalismo y cosmopolitanismo en las commemoraciones de la Independencia (Buenos Aires 1910—Río de Janeiro, 1922)." In *Galerías del progreso: Museos, exposiciones y cultura visual en América Latina*, edited by Beatriz González Stephan and Jens Andermann, 331–72. Rosario: Beatriz Viterbo Editora, 2006.

Fernández Bravo, Álvaro. *El museo vacío: acumulación primitiva, patrimonio cultural e identidades colectivas, Argentina y Brasil, 1880–1945*. Buenos Aires: Eudeba, 2016.

Ferreira, A. Buarque de Holanda. *Dicionario da língua portuguesa*. Rio de Janeiro: Editora Nova Fronteira, 1980.

Ferreira, Antonio Celso. *A epopéia bandeirante: letrados, instituições, invenção histórica (1870–1940)*. São Paulo: Editora UNESP, 2001.

Ferreira, Marie-Jo. "As comemorações do primeiro centenário da independência brasileira ou a exaltação de uma modernidade luso-brasileira." In *Modernidades alternativas*, edited by Daniel Aarão Reis and Dennis Rolland, 119–40. Rio de Janeiro: Editora da Fundação Getúlio Vargas, 2008.

Garcia, Eugenio Vargas. *Entre América e Europa: A política externa brasileira na década de 1920*. Brasília: Editora Universidade de Brasília, 2006.

Geppert, Alexander C. T. *Fleeting Cities: Imperial Expositions in* Fin-de-Siècle *Europe*. New York: Palgrave Macmillan, 2010.

Giovanaz, Marlise Maria. "As Exposições Universais e seu impacto museológico: o caso da Exposição do Centenário Farroupilha, Brasil." *Revista Vox Musei* 1, no. 1 (2013): 318–29.

Gomes, Eduardo de Souza. "O VI Sul-Americano de futebol no âmbito dos Jogos do Centenário de 1922 no Rio de Janeiro: entre os discursos da 'nação brasileira' e a diplomacia internacional." *Arquibancada—Ludopédio* 103 (2018): 1–8.

Greenhalgh, Paul. *Ephemeral Vistas: A History of the Expositions Universelles, Great Exhibitions and World's Fairs, 1851–1939*. Manchester: Manchester University Press, 1988.

Greiner, Christine. "The 1922 Rio de Janeiro International Centennial Exhibition: From Colonialism to 'Anthropophagy." In *International Research Symposium Proceedings: "Expo and Human History,"* edited by Sano Mayuko, 127–35. Kyoto: International Research Center for Japanese Studies, 2017.

Gonzales, Michael J. "Imagining Mexico in 1910: Visions of the Patria in the Centennial Celebration in Mexico City." *Journal of Latin American Studies* 39, no. 3 (2007): 495–533.

Gonzales, Michael J. "Imagining Mexico in 1921: Visions of the Revolutionary State and Society in the Centennial Celebration in Mexico City." *Mexican Studies* 25, no. 2 (2009): 247–70.

Guimarães, Lucia Maria Paschoal. *Da Escola Palatina ao Silogeu: Instituto Histórico e Geográfico Brasileiro (1889–1938)*. Rio de Janeiro: Museu da República, 2006.

Hahner, June. *Emancipating the Female Sex: The Struggle for Women's Rights in Brazil, 1850–1940*. Durham, NC: Duke University Press, 1990.

Hahner, June. "Jacobinos *versus* galegos: Urban radicals *versus* Portuguese Immigrants in Rio de Janeiro in the 1890s." *Journal of Interamerican Studies and World Affairs* 18, no. 2 (1976): 125–54.

Hardman, Francisco Foot. *Trem Fantasma: A Modernidade na Selva*. São Paulo: Companhia das Letras, 1988.

Hobsbawm, Eric. *Nations and Nationalism since 1780: Programme, Myth, Reality*. Cambridge: Cambridge University Press, 1992.

Hobsbawm, Eric, and Terence Ranger, eds. *The Invention of Tradition*. New York: Cambridge University Press, 1983.

Hochman, Gilberto. *The Sanitation of Brazil: Nation, State, and Public Health, 1889–1930*, translated by Diane Grosklaus Whitty. Urbana: University of Illinois Press, 2016.

Jaguaribe, Beatriz. "Imaginando a 'cidade maravilhosa': modernidade, espetáculo e espaços urbanos." *Revista Famecos: Mídia, Cultura e Tecnologia* 18, no. 2 (2011): 327–47.

Jancsó István, ed. *Independência: História e Historiografia*. São Paulo: Editora Hucitec / Fapesp, 2005.

Käfer, Eduardo Luis Flach. "Entre a memória e a história: A historiografia da Independência nos cem anos da emancipação." MA thesis, Pontíficia Universidade Católica do Rio Grande do Sul, 2016.

Kessel, Carlos. *Arquitetura Neocolonial no Brasil: Entre o pastiche e a modernidade*. Rio de Janeiro: Jauá Editora, 2008.

Kessel, Carlos. *A vitrine e o espelho: o Rio de Janeiro de Carlos Sampaio*. Rio de Janeiro: Secretaria das Culturas, Departamento Geral de Documentação e Informação Cultural, Arquivo Geral da Cidade do Rio de Janeiro, 2001.

Klein, Herbert S. "The Social and Economic Integration of Portuguese Immigrants in Brazil in the Late Nineteenth and Twentieth Centuries." *Journal of Latin American Studies* 23, no. 2 (1991): 309–37.

Kraay, Hendrik. *Bahia's Independence: Popular Politics and Patriotic Festival in Salvador, Brazil, 1824–1900*. Montreal: McGill-Queen's University Press, 2019.

Kraay, Hendrik. "Between Brazil and Bahia: Celebrating Dois de Julho in Nineteenth-Century Salvador." *Journal of Latin American Studies* 31, no. 2, (1999): 255–86.

Kraay, Hendrik. *Days of National Festivity in Rio de Janeiro, Brazil, 1823–1889*. Stanford, CA: Stanford University Press, 2014.

Kuhlmann Júnior, Moysés. *As Grandes Festas Didáticas: A Educação Brasileira e as Exposições Internacionais, 1862–1922*. Bragança Paulista: Editora da Universidade São Francisco, 2001.

Lesser, Jeffrey. *Negotiating National Identity: Immigrants, Minorities, and the Struggle for Ethnicity in Brazil*. Durham, NC: Duke University Press, 1999.

Levine, Robert M. *Pernambuco in the Brazilian Federation, 1889–1937.* Stanford, CA: Stanford University Press, 1978.

Levy, Ruth. *A Exposição do Centenário e o meio arquitetônico carioca no início dos anos 1920.* Rio de Janeiro: EBA Publicações, 2010.

Levy, Ruth. *Entre Palácios e Pavilhões: A Arquitetura Efêmera da Exposição Nacional de 1908.* Rio de Janeiro: EBA/UFRJ, 2008.

Love, Joseph L. *Rio Grande do Sul and Brazilian Regionalism, 1882–1930.* Stanford, CA: Stanford University Press, 1971.

Love, Joseph L. *São Paulo in the Brazilian Federation, 1889–1937.* Stanford, CA: Stanford University Press, 1980.

Luebke, Frederick C. *Germans in Brazil: A Comparative History of Cultural Conflict During World War I.* Baton Rouge: Louisiana State University Press, 1987.

Lyra, Maria de Lourdes Viana. "Memória da Independência: marcos e representações simbólicas." *Revista Brasileira de História*, no. 29 (1995): 173–206.

Makino, Miyoko. "Ornamentação do Museu Paulista para o Primeiro Centenário: construção de identidade nacional na década de 1920." *Anais do Museu Paulista* 10/11 (2002–2003): 167–95.

Marques, Rosália Augusta da Cunha. "A viagem do presidente António José de Almeida no âmbito das relações com Brasil no final da Primeira República." MA thesis, Universidade de Porto, 1998.

Martins, Angela Maria Moreira. "A Exposição Internacional de 1922 no Rio de Janeiro: um espaço urbano turístico na jovem república brasileira." In *Arquitetura: pesquisa & projeto*, edited by Vicente del Rio, 121–46. Rio de Janeiro: FAU UFRJ, 1998.

Meade, Teresa A. *"Civilizing" Rio: Reform and Resistance in a Brazilian City, 1889–1930.* University Park: Pennsylvania State University Press, 1997.

Miranda, Luciana Lilian de. "Um 'voo' entre Portugal e Brasil: leituras das relações luso-brasileiras na revista *Seara Nova* no início dos anos de 1920." *História* 28, no. 1 (2009): 483–508.

Morettin, Eduardo. "Cinema e estado no Brasil: A Exposição Internacional do Centenário da Independência em 1922 e 1923." *Novos Estudos* 89 (2011): 137–48.

Motta, Marly Silva da. *A nação faz 100 anos: A questão nacional no centenário da independência.* Rio de Janeiro: Editora da Fundação Getúlio Vargas: CPDOC, 1992.

Nava, Carmen. "Forging Future Citizens in Brazilian Public Schools, 1937–1945." In *Brazil in the Making: Facets of National Identity*, edited by Carmen Nava and Ludwig Lauerhass Jr., 95–117. Lanham, MD: Rowman and Littlefield, 2006.

Needell, Jeffrey. *A Tropical* Belle Epoque: *Elite Culture and Society in Turn-of-the-Century Rio de Janeiro.* Cambridge: Cambridge University Press, 1987.

Nunes, João Paulo Alevãs, and Américo Freire, eds. *Historiografias Portuguesa e Brasileira no Século XX: Olhares Cruzados*. Coimbra: Imprensa da Universidade de Coimbra / Editora FGV, 2013.

Oliveira, Lúcia Lippi. *A Questão Nacional na Primeira República*. São Paulo: Editora Brasiliense, 1990.

Oliveira, Lúcia Lippi. "As festas que a República manda guardar." *Estudos Históricos* 2, no. 4 (1989): 172–89.

Oliven, Ruben George. *A parte e o todo: a diversidade cultural no Brasil-nação*. Petrópolis: Editora Vozes 1992.

Pandolfi, Dulce Chaves. *Repensando o Estado Novo*. Rio de Janeiro: Editora da Fundação Getúlio Vargas, 1999.

Peard, Julyan G. *Race, Place, and Medicine: The Idea of the Tropics in Nineteenth-Century Brazilian Medicine*. Durham, NC: Duke University Press, 1999.

Pereira, Leonardo Affonso de Miranda. *Footballmania: Uma História Social do Futebol no Rio de Janeiro, 1902–1938*. Rio de Janeiro: Editora Nova Fronteira, 2000.

Pereira, Margareth da Silva, ed. *1908, um Brasil em exposição*. Rio de Janeiro: Casa Doze, 2010.

Pesavento, Sandra Jatahy. *Exposições Universais: Espetáculos da Modernidade do Século XIX*. São Paulo: Editora Hucitec, 1997.

Pike, Frederick B. *Hispanismo, 1898–1936: Spanish Conservatives and Liberals and Their Relations with Spanish America*. Notre Dame, IN: University of Notre Dame Press, 1971.

Plum, Werner. *World Exhibitions in the Nineteenth Century: Pageants of Social and Cultural Change*. Bonn-Bad Godesberg: Friedrich-Ebert-Stiftung, 1977.

Rappaport, Roy A. *Ecology, Meaning, and Religion*. Berkeley, CA: North Atlantic Books, 1979.

Rappaport, Roy A. *Ritual and Religion in the Making of Humanity*. Cambridge: Cambridge University Press, 1999.

Rezende, Livia. "Nature and the Brazilian State at the Independence Centennial International Exhibition in Rio de Janeiro 1922." In *Cultures of International Exhibitions 1840–1940: Great Exhibitions in the Margins*, edited by Marta Filipova, 163–82. Burlington, VT: Ashgate, 2015.

Rezende, Livia. "Of Coffee, Nature and Exclusion: Designing the State at Brazil's Independence Centennial International Exhibitions (1867 and 1904)." In *Designing Worlds: National Design Histories in an Age of Globalization*, edited by Kjetil Fallan and Grace Lees-Maffei, 259–73. N.p.: Berghahn Books, 2016.

Rezende, Livia. "The Raw and the Manufactured: Brazilian Modernity and National Identity as Projected in International Exhibitions (1862–1922)." PhD diss., Royal College of Art, 2010.

Ribeiro, Gladys Sabina. *Mata Galegos: Os portugueses e os conflitos de trabalho na República Velha*. São Paulo: Editora Brasiliense, 1990.

Ribeiro, Gladys Sabina. *O Rio de Janeiro dos Fados, Minhotos e Alfacinhas: O Antilusitanismo na Primeira República*. Niterói: Eduff, 2017.

Rydell, Robert W. *All the World's a Fair: Visions of Empire at American International Expositions, 1876–1916*. Chicago: University of Chicago Press, 1999.

Sandes, Noé Freire. *A Invenção da Nação: Entre a Monarquia e a República*. Goiânia: Editora UFG and Agência Goiana de Cultura Pedro Ludovico Teixeira, Instituto Goiano do Livro, 2000.

Sant'ana, Thais Rezende da Silva de. "A Exposição Internacional do Centenário da Independência: Modernidade e Política no Rio de Janeiro do início dos anos 1920." MA thesis, Universidade Estadual de Campinas, 2008.

Santos, João Manuel C. Malaia. "A história econômica entra em campo: o Rio de Janeiro e as competições esportivas internacionais de 1919 e 1922." *Revista de Economia Política e História Econômica* 9, no. 27 (2011): 154–99.

Santos, João Manuel C. Malaia. "A imprensa e o sul-americano de futebol de 1922: a 'defesa das cores nacionais' ou o 'campeonato internacional das futilidades'?" *Revista Estudos Políticos* 5, no. 2 (2012): 60–76.

Santos, João Manuel C. Malaia. "Diplomacia do Pé: o Brasil e as competições esportivas sul-americanas de 1919 e 1922." *Tempo e Argumento* 3, no. 2 (2011): 43–76.

Santos, João Manuel C. Malaia, and Victor Andrade de Melo, eds. *1922: Celebrações esportivas do centenário*. Rio de Janeiro: 7Letras and Faberj, 2012.

Santos, Paula Marques dos, and Paulo Amorim. "As relações Portugal-Brasil na primeira metade do século XX (1910–1945)." In *As Relações Portugal-Brasil no Século XX*, edited by Fernando Sousa, Paula Marques dos Santos, and Paulo Amorim, 121–40. Porto: CEPESE, 2010.

Schwarcz, Lilia Moritz. *The Spectacle of the Races: Scientists, Institutions, and the Race Question in Brazil, 1870–1930*. New York: Hill and Wang, 1999.

Skidmore, Thomas. *Black into White: Race and Nationalism in Brazilian Thought*. Durham, NC: Duke University Press, 1993.

Semenovitch, Jorge Scévola de. *Corcovado: The Conquest of God's Mountain: The History of the Railway and Monument to Christ the Redeemer*, 2nd ed. Rio de Janeiro: Lutécia, 2008.

Silva, Eduardo. "A República comemora o Império. Um aspecto político-ideológico da crise dos anos 20." *Revista do Rio de Janeiro* 1, no. 2 (1986): 59–70.

Silva, Joana Mello de Carvalho e. "A construção do nacional: Ricardo Severo e a Campanha de Arte Tradicional no Brasil (1910–1930)." *Varia Historia* 35, no. 68 (2019): 597–629.

Silva, Marcos da, ed. *República em migalhas: História regional e local*. São Paulo: Marco Zero, 1990.

Sodré, Nelson Werneck. *O tenentismo*. Porto Alegre: Mercado Aberto, 1985.

Stepan, Nancy Leys. *Beginnings of Brazilian Science: Oswaldo Cruz, Medical Research, and Policy, 1890–1920*. New York: Science History Publications, 1976.

Stepan, Nancy Leys. *"The Hour of Eugenics": Race, Gender, and Nation in Latin America*. Ithaca, NY: Cornell University Press, 1991.

Tenorio-Trillo, Mauricio. *I Speak of the City: Mexico City at the Turn of the Twentieth Century*. Chicago: University of Chicago Press, 2015.

Tenorio-Trillo, Mauricio. "A Tropical Cuauhtémoc: Celebrating the Cosmic Race at the Guanabara Bay." *Anales del Instituto de Investigaciones Estéticas* 65 (1994): 93–137.

Topik, Steven. "Middle-Class Brazilian Nationalism: From Radicalism to Reaction." *Social Science Quarterly* 59, no. 1 (1978): 93–104.

Torres, César R. *Jogos Olímpicos Latino-Americanos: Rio de Janeiro 1922*. Translated by Martim S. Silveira. Manaus: Confederação Brasileira de Atletismo, 2012.

Torres, Cesar R. "The Latin American 'Olympic Explosion' of the 1920s: Causes and Consequences." *International Journal of the History of Sport* 23, no. 7 (2006): 1088–111.

Trento, Angelo. "Le associazoni italiane a Sao Paulo, 1878–1960." In *Asociacionismo, Trabajo e Identidad Etnica: Los Italianos en América Latina en una perspectiva comparada*, edited by Fernando J. Devoto and Eduardo J. Miguez, 31–57. Buenos Aires: CEMLA—CSER—IEHS, 1992.

Velloso, Mônica Pimenta. *A brasilidade verde-amarela: nacionalismo e regionalismo paulista*, second ed. Rio de Janeiro: Centro de Pesquisa e Documentação de História Contemporânea do Brasil, 1990.

Vicari, Paulo Renato, and Janice Zarpellon Mazo. "Commemorações do Centenário da Independência do Brasil (1922): Jogos Latino-Americanos no Rio de Janeiro e jogos olímpicos no Rio Grande do Sul." *Anais do XVII Congresso Brasileiro de Ciência do Esporte* (2011): 1–11.

Wadsworth, James E. "Brasil en 1922, la niñez en primer plano: Nacionalismo, infancia, y la ideologia del Estado Benefactor." *Infancia: Bulletin del Instituto Interamericano del Niño-OEA* 68, no. 235 (1999): 11–32.

Wadsworth, James E., and Tamera L. Marko. "Children of the Pátria: Representations of Childhood and Welfare State Ideologies at the 1922 Rio de Janeiro International Centennial Exposition." *The Americas* 58, no. 1 (2001): 65–90.

Weinstein, Barbara. *The Color of Modernity: São Paulo and the Making of Race and Nation in Brazil*. Durham, NC: Duke University Press, 2015.

Williams, Daryle. *Culture Wars in Brazil: The First Vargas Regime, 1930–1945*. Durham, NC: Duke University Press, 2001.

Wirth, John D. *Minas Gerais in the Brazilian Federation, 1889–1937*. Stanford, CA: Stanford University Press, 1977.

Wolfe, Joel. *Autos and Progress: The Brazilian Search for Modernity*. New York: Oxford University Press, 2010.

Wolfe, Joel. *Working Women, Working Men: São Paulo and the Rise of Brazil's Industrial Working Class, 1900–1955*. Durham, NC: Duke University Press, 1993.

Woodard, James P. *A Place in Politics: São Paulo, Brazil, from Seigneurial Republicanism to Regionalist Revolt*. Durham, NC: Duke University Press, 2009.

Index